THE NEW MIDDLE AGES

BONNIE WHEELER, *Series Editor*

The New Middle Ages is a series dedicated to transdisciplinary studies of medieval cultures, with particular emphasis on recuperating women's history and on feminist and gender analyses. This peer-reviewed series includes both scholarly monographs and essay collections.

PUBLISHED BY PALGRAVE:

Women in the Medieval Islamic World: Power, Patronage, and Piety
  edited by Gavin R. G. Hambly

The Ethics of Nature in the Middle Ages: On Boccaccio's Poetaphysics
  by Gregory B. Stone

Presence and Presentation: Women in the Chinese Literati Tradition
  edited by Sherry J. Mou

The Lost Love Letters of Heloise and Abelard: Perceptions of Dialogue in Twelfth-Century France
  by Constant J. Mews

Understanding Scholastic Thought with Foucault
  by Philipp W. Rosemann

For Her Good Estate: The Life of Elizabeth de Burgh
  by Frances A. Underhill

Constructions of Widowhood and Virginity in the Middle Ages
  edited by Cindy L. Carlson and Angela Jane Weisl

Motherhood and Mothering in Anglo-Saxon England
  by Mary Dockray-Miller

Listening to Heloise: The Voice of a Twelfth-Century Woman
  edited by Bonnie Wheeler

The Postcolonial Middle Ages
  edited by Jeffrey Jerome Cohen

Chaucer's Pardoner and Gender Theory: Bodies of Discourse
  by Robert S. Sturges

Crossing the Bridge: Comparative Essays on Medieval European and Heian Japanese Women Writers
  edited by Barbara Stevenson and Cynthia Ho

Engaging Words: The Culture of Reading in the Later Middle Ages
  by Laurel Amtower

Robes and Honor: The Medieval World of Investiture
  edited by Stewart Gordon

Representing Rape in Medieval and Early Modern Literature
  edited by Elizabeth Robertson and Christine M. Rose

Same Sex Love and Desire among Women in the Middle Ages
  edited by Francesca Canadé Sautman and Pamela Sheingorn

Sight and Embodiment in the Middle Ages: Ocular Desires
  by Suzannah Biernoff

Listen, Daughter: The Speculum Virginum *and the Formation of Religious Women in the Middle Ages*
  edited by Constant J. Mews

Science, the Singular, and the Question of Theology
  by Richard A. Lee, Jr.

Gender in Debate from the Early Middle Ages to the Renaissance
  edited by Thelma S. Fenster and Clare A. Lees

Malory's Morte D'Arthur: *Remaking Arthurian Tradition*
  by Catherine Batt

The Vernacular Spirit: Essays on Medieval Religious Literature
  edited by Renate Blumenfeld-Kosinski, Duncan Robertson, and Nancy Warren

Popular Piety and Art in the Late Middle Ages: Image Worship and Idolatry in England 1350–1500
  by Kathleen Kamerick

Absent Narratives, Manuscript Textuality, and Literary Structure in Late Medieval England
  by Elizabeth Scala

Creating Community with Food and Drink in Merovingian Gaul
  by Bonnie Effros

Representations of Early Byzantine Empresses: Image and Empire
  by Anne McClanan

Encountering Medieval Textiles and Dress: Objects, Texts, Images
  edited by Désirée G. Koslin and Janet Snyder

Eleanor of Aquitaine: Lord and Lady
  edited by Bonnie Wheeler and John Carmi Parsons

Isabel La Católica, Queen of Castile: Critical Essays
  edited by David A. Boruchoff

Homoeroticism and Chivalry: Discourses of Male Same-Sex Desire in the Fourteenth Century
  by Richard E. Zeikowitz

Portraits of Medieval Women: Family, Marriage, and Politics in England 1225–1350
  by Linda E. Mitchell

Eloquent Virgins: From Thecla to Joan of Arc
  by Maud Burnett McInerney

The Persistence of Medievalism: Narrative Adventures in Contemporary Culture
  by Angela Jane Weisl

Capetian Women
  edited by Kathleen D. Nolan

Joan of Arc and Spirituality
  edited by Ann W. Astell and Bonnie Wheeler

The Texture of Society: Medieval Women in the Southern Low Countries
  edited by Ellen E. Kittell and Mary A. Suydam

Charlemagne's Mustache: And Other Cultural Clusters of a Dark Age
  by Paul Edward Dutton

Troubled Vision: Gender, Sexuality, and Sight in Medieval Text and Image
  edited by Emma Campbell and Robert Mills

Queering Medieval Genres
  by Tison Pugh

Sacred Place in Early Medieval Neoplatonism
  by L. Michael Harrington

The Middle Ages at Work
  edited by Kellie Robertson and Michael Uebel

Chaucer's Jobs
  by David R. Carlson

Medievalism and Orientalism: Three Essays on Literature, Architecture and Cultural Identity
  by John M. Ganim

Queer Love in the Middle Ages
  by Anna Klosowska

Performing Women in the Middle Ages: Sex, Gender, and the Iberian Lyric
  by Denise K. Filios

Necessary Conjunctions: The Social Self in Medieval England
  by David Gary Shaw

Visual Culture and the German Middle Ages
  edited by Kathryn Starkey and Horst Wenzel

Medieval Paradigms: Essays in Honor of Jeremy duQuesnay Adams, Volumes 1 and 2
  edited by Stephanie Hayes-Healy

False Fables and Exemplary Truth in Later Middle English Literature
  by Elizabeth Allen

Ecstatic Transformation: On the Uses of Alterity in the Middle Ages
  by Michael Uebel

Sacred and Secular in Medieval and Early Modern Cultures: New Essays
edited by Lawrence Besserman

Tolkien's Modern Middle Ages
edited by Jane Chance and Alfred K. Siewers

Representing Righteous Heathens in Late Medieval England
by Frank Grady

Byzantine Dress: Representations of Secular Dress in Eighth-to-Twelfth Century Painting
by Jennifer L. Ball

The Laborer's Two Bodies: Labor and the "Work" of the Text in Medieval Britain, 1350–1500
by Kellie Robertson

The Dogaressa of Venice, 1250–1500: Wife and Icon
by Holly S. Hurlburt

Logic, Theology, and Poetry in Boethius, Abelard, and Alan of Lille: Words in the Absence of Things
by Eileen C. Sweeney

The Theology of Work: Peter Damian and the Medieval Religious Renewal Movement
by Patricia Ranft

On the Purification of Women: Churching in Northern France, 1100–1500
by Paula M. Rieder

Writers of the Reign of Henry II: Twelve Essays
edited by Ruth Kennedy and Simon Meecham-Jones

Lonesome Words: The Vocal Poetics of the Old English Lament and the African-American Blues Song
by M.G. McGeachy

Performing Piety: Musical Culture in Medieval English Nunneries
by Anne Bagnell Yardley

The Flight from Desire: Augustine and Ovid to Chaucer
by Robert R. Edwards

Mindful Spirit in Late Medieval Literature: Essays in Honor of Elizabeth D. Kirk
edited by Bonnie Wheeler

Medieval Fabrications: Dress, Textiles, Clothwork, and Other Cultural Imaginings
edited by E. Jane Burns

Was the Bayeux Tapestry Made in France?: The Case for St. Florent of Saumur
by George Beech

Women, Power, and Religious Patronage in the Middle Ages
by Erin L. Jordan

Hybridity, Identity, and Monstrosity in Medieval Britain: On Difficult Middles
by Jeremy Jerome Cohen

Medieval Go-betweens and Chaucer's Pandarus
by Gretchen Mieszkowski

The Surgeon in Medieval English Literature
by Jeremy J. Citrome

Temporal Circumstances: Form and History in the Canterbury Tales
by Lee Patterson

Erotic Discourse and Early English Religious Writing
by Lara Farina

Odd Bodies and Visible Ends in Medieval Literature
by Sachi Shimomura

On Farting: Language and Laughter in the Middle Ages
by Valerie Allen

Women and Medieval Epic: Gender, Genre, and the Limits of Epic Masculinity
edited by Sara S. Poor and Jana K. Schulman

Race, Class, and Gender in "Medieval" Cinema
edited by Lynn T. Ramey and Tison Pugh

Allegory and Sexual Ethics in the High Middle Ages
by Noah D. Guynn

England and Iberia in the Middle Ages, 12th–15th Century: Cultural, Literary, and Political Exchanges
    edited by María Bullón-Fernández

The Medieval Chastity Belt: A Myth-Making Process
    by Albrecht Classen

Claustrophilia: The Erotics of Enclosure in Medieval Literature
    by Cary Howie

Cannibalism in High Medieval English Literature
    by Heather Blurton

The Drama of Masculinity and Medieval English Guild Culture
    by Christina M. Fitzgerald

Chaucer's Visions of Manhood
    by Holly A. Crocker

The Literary Subversions of Medieval Women
    by Jane Chance

Manmade Marvels in Medieval Culture and Literature
    by Scott Lightsey

American Chaucers
    by Candace Barrington

Representing Others in Medieval Iberian Literature
    by Michelle M. Hamilton

Paradigms and Methods in Early Medieval Studies
    edited by Celia Chazelle and Felice Lifshitz

The King and the Whore: King Roderick and La Cava
    by Elizabeth Drayson

Langland's Early Modern Identities
    by Sarah A. Kelen

Cultural Studies of the Modern Middle Ages
    edited by Eileen A. Joy, Myra J. Seaman, Kimberly K. Bell, and Mary K. Ramsey

Hildegard of Bingen's Unknown Language: An Edition, Translation, and Discussion
    by Sarah L. Higley

Medieval Romance and the Construction of Heterosexuality
    by Louise M. Sylvester

Communal Discord, Child Abduction, and Rape in the Later Middle Ages
    by Jeremy Goldberg

Lydgate Matters: Poetry and Material Culture in the Fifteenth Century
    edited by Lisa H. Cooper and Andrea Denny-Brown

Sexuality and Its Queer Discontents in Middle English Literature
    by Tison Pugh

Sex, Scandal, and Sermon in Fourteenth-Century Spain: Juan Ruiz's Libro de Buen Amor
    by Louise M. Haywood

The Erotics of Consolation: Desire and Distance in the Late Middle Ages
    edited by Catherine E. Léglu and Stephen J. Milner

Battlefronts Real and Imagined: War, Border, and Identity in the Chinese Middle Period
    edited by Don J. Wyatt

BATTLEFRONTS REAL AND IMAGINED

WAR, BORDER, AND IDENTITY IN THE CHINESE MIDDLE PERIOD

Edited by
Don J. Wyatt

BATTLEFRONTS REAL AND IMAGINED
Copyright © Don J. Wyatt, 2008.

Softcover reprint of the hardcover 1st edition 2008 978-1-4039-6084-9

All rights reserved. No part of this book may be used or reproduced in any manner whatsoever without written permission except in the case of brief quotations embodied in critical articles or reviews.

First published in 2008 by
PALGRAVE MACMILLAN™
175 Fifth Avenue, New York, N.Y. 10010 and
Houndmills, Basingstoke, Hampshire, England RG21 6XS
Companies and representatives throughout the world.

PALGRAVE MACMILLAN is the global academic imprint of the Palgrave Macmillan division of St. Martin's Press, LLC and of Palgrave Macmillan Ltd. Macmillan® is a registered trademark in the United States, United Kingdom and other countries. Palgrave is a registered trademark in the European Union and other countries.

ISBN 978-1-349-52631-4   ISBN 978-0-230-61171-9 (eBook)
DOI 10.1057/9780230611719

Library of Congress Cataloging-in-Publication Data

Battlefronts real and imagined : war, border, and identity in the Chinese middle period / edited by Don J. Wyatt.
    p. cm.—(New Middle Ages (Palgrave (Firm)))
Includes bibliographical references and index.
    1. China—History, Military—221 B.C.–960 A.D. 2. China—History, Military—960–1644. I. Title: War, border, and Identity in the Chinese middle period. II Wyatt, Don J.

DS747.43.B38 2008
355.00951—dc22   2007035811

A catalogue record for this book is available from the British Library.

Design by Newgen Imaging Systems (P) Ltd., Chennai, India.

First edition: May 2008
10 9 8 7 6 5 4 3 2 1

For all the past, present, and future generations of students of China's traditional history

CONTENTS

List of Illustrations   xi

Acknowledgments   xii

Dynasties of the Chinese Middle Period   xiv

Introduction   1
Don J. Wyatt

1. Fathoming Consort Xian: Negotiated Power in the Liang, Chen, and Sui Dynasties   11
   Sherry J. Mou

2. Provincial Autonomy and Frontier Defense in Late Tang: The Case of the Lulong Army   43
   David A. Graff

3. The Great Ditch of China and the Song–Liao Border   59
   Peter Lorge

4. In Pursuit of the Great Peace: Wang Dan and the Early Song Evasion of the "Just War" Doctrine   75
   Don J. Wyatt

5. Hidden Time, Hidden Space: Crossing Borders with Occult Ritual in the Song Military   111
   M. A. Butler

6. Frustrated Empires: The Song–Tangut Xia War of 1038–44   151
   Michael C. McGrath

7. "Treacherous Factions": Shifting Frontier Alliances in the Breakdown of Sino-Vietnamese Relations on the Eve of the 1075 Border War   191
   James A. Anderson

CONTENTS

8 From Battlefields to Counties: War, Border, and State
   Power in Southern Song Huainan   227
   Ruth Mostern

9 People in the Middle: Uyghurs in the Northwest Frontier Zone 253
   Michael C. Brose

Notes on Contributors   291

Index   293

ILLUSTRATIONS

1.1	Consort Xian accompanying the imperial emissary	20
1.2	Illustration of Consort Xian in Jin Guliang's Catalogue of the Unparalleled	31
1.3	A poetic sword-handle inscription in Jin Guliang's Catalogue of the Unparalleled	32
1.4	Commemorative poem for Consort Xian by Su Shi, 1036–1101	33
5.1	Six Water Cycles cosmograph (ca. late sixth century CE)	112
5.2	Showing elements of the sexagenary cycle	122
7.1	Map of 1075 Song-Lý frontier war (including contested territories)	213
7.2	An Illustration of Prefectures and Commanderies Beyond the Influence of Our Dynasty (*Benchao huawai zhoujun tu*) from a Song-period edition historical atlas	214

ACKNOWLEDGMENTS

Any edited work, even when under the name of a single author, is necessarily the product of many minds and hands. Consequently, for me to properly recognize the indebtedness that I bear demands a fairly long list. My thanks go first to all those individuals who—largely through their examples in pioneering scholarship—have inspired the present work. Foremost among these individuals are teachers, mentors, and colleagues either long or recently deceased. In particular, I thank the late Yang Lien-sheng, Joseph F. Fletcher, Owen Lattimore, John King Fairbank, James T. C. Liu, Francis Woodman Cleaves, Robert M. Hartwell, Benjamin I. Schwartz, Frederick W. Mote, and Denis C. Twitchett, respectively, for their scholarly inspiration.

Next I thank those who through their forthright, frank, and, in at least one instance, entirely anonymous exchanges have contributed to making this book substantively better than it would otherwise be. These individuals are numerous, and I doubtless fail to acknowledge even all of those who are known to me. Nonetheless, the list most assuredly includes the following individuals, who have all contributed varying degrees of input and insight: David Anthony Bello, Bettine Birge, Renate Blumenfeld-Kosinski, Caroline Walker Bynum, Carolyn Cartier, John Chaffee, Theodore Evergates, Roger Des Forges, Nicola Di Cosmo, Charlotte Furth, Richard Gunde, R. Kent Guy, Robert Hymes, Axel Kassing, Dieter Kuhn, Johannes Kurz, Robert LaFleur, Diana Lary, James Z. Lee, Philippa Levine, Mark Edward Lewis, Laurence J. C. Ma, Steven B. Miles, Timothy Oakes, Peter Perdue, Paul Ropp, Ralph Sawyer, Paul Jakov Smith, David Sneath, Ria Stein, Keith Weller Taylor, Hans van de Ven, Joanna Waley-Cohen, and Jack Wills. My deep gratitude in this connection is reserved for Naomi Standen and Jonathan Skaff.

Finally, I thank those institutions that have generously provided me with resource support for either all or part of the period during which this book was written and those individuals who have contributed directly and technically to producing it. Aside from Middlebury College, where I am based and through the Faculty Professional Development Fund of which I have benefited, especially deserving of inclusion under this rubric of institutional gratitude is the Institute for Advanced Study, where I resided as member in the School of Historical Studies in 2004. The introduction of this book was conceived and largely written during my time spent in the ever-intellectually stimulating environment of the Institute. Marian Zelazny, Terrie Bramley, and Marcia Tucker are among the many individuals there who deserve my thanks for their direct assistance in facilitating that aspect of the production enterprise. At Palgrave Macmillan, I greatly thank Michael Flamini, who was able to envision the publication potential of what originally constituted not much more than a set of sketchy ideas. I thank Farideh Koohi-Kamali, Julia Cohen, Brigitte Shull, Kristy Lilas, and Maran Elancheran for shepherding the project expeditiously through production. Surely most of all, I thank Bonnie Wheeler, who was, by turns, dunning enough to spur and yet also patient enough to permit the fullest articulation and realization of this book.

DYNASTIES OF THE CHINESE MIDDLE PERIOD

(referred in this book; major dynasties and dynastic divisions in bold)

Northern and Southern Dynasties 南北朝	**420–589**
Song 宋 (or Liu Song 劉宋) (southern)	420–79
Liang 梁 (southern)	502–57
Chen 陳 (southern)	557–89
Sui 隋	**589–618**
Tang 唐	**618–907**
Zhou 周	690–705
Five Dynasties 五代	**907–79**
Later Tang 後唐 (northern)	923–36
Later Jin 後晉 (northern)	936–47
Later Zhou 後周 (northern)	951–60
Ten Kingdoms 十國	**907–79**
Southern Han 南漢 (southern)	907–71
Chu 楚 (southern)	927–56
Later Shu 後蜀 (northern)	934–65
Southern Tang 南唐 or Qi 齊 (southern)	937–75
Northern Han 北漢 (northern)	951–79
Liao 遼 (non-Chinese)	**907–1125**
Northern Song 北宋	**960–1126**
Southern Song 南宋	**1127–1279**
Western or Xi Xia 西夏 (non-Chinese)	**1038–1227**
Jin 金 (non-Chinese)	**1115–1234**
Yuan 元 (non-Chinese)	**1279–1368**

INTRODUCTION

Don J. Wyatt

Customary scholarship on Chinese relations with foreigners during the "middle period"—the great swath of time spanning roughly from the sixth to the fourteenth century of the Common Era—has rightly emphasized the role of diplomacy. Whenever possible, diplomacy, then the default mode for conflict resolution for Chinese, was advanced as the most desirable means of settling disputes because, even in the event of failure, it was minimally destructive. The majority ethnic Han Chinese, ever the realists, viewed it as the most efficient, sustainable, and tolerable arrangement to assure coexistence with the succession of non-Han peoples arrayed along their borders. The year 2005 in fact marked the millennial anniversary of the zenith of Chinese middle-period diplomacy—the Treaty of Chanyuan. At the very beginning of 1005, the Chinese of the Song dynasty (960–1279) struck a momentous accord with the Qidan tribes of the Liao dynasty (907–1125). That particular truce remains the most celebrated event in middle-period diplomacy, resulting in more than a century of guardedly peaceful Song-Liao relations.[1] Three of the six authors in this volume who treat the Song period attest to the singularity of Chanyuan as a diplomatic milestone and deliberate on its significance.

But, by Song times or even slightly earlier, if for no other reason than that the most consistent strategies of the various outlying groups in dealing with China were encirclement, constriction, and penetration, diplomatic solutions to conflict failed more frequently than they succeeded. War oftentimes seemed to be the only credible response. As the scholarship of Jing-shen Tao and others has stressed, precisely because they, more than ever before, came to regard their state as merely one among many, Chinese of the middle period correspondingly became intent on maintaining the territorial integrity of China by any means necessary.[2] Nevertheless, this development notwithstanding, most prior scholarship has not adequately observed the fact that middle-period Chinese, when seeing confrontation as advantageous to their ends, had just as much recourse to the prosecution of war as they did to the pursuit of negotiation. War as well as diplomacy was a vital and consequential part of the Chinese middle-period arsenal.

Gradually, however, this condition of scholarly inattentiveness to the Chinese middle-period investment in war has begun to change, as works emerging especially during the present decade have contributed to the development of a more balanced perspective.[3] The chapters collected herein also contribute to the advancement of this new trend. These chapters are also intended as resources for guiding us still further toward a better understanding of the factors that impinged on the thinking and influenced the decision-making processes of the middle-period Chinese civil and military leaders as well as their non-Chinese counterparts with respect to war and diplomacy. In their individual ways, the authors of these studies all raise questions and provide answers about when and under what conditions war was preferable to negotiation and negotiation preferable to war in the Chinese middle-period context. But, in addition, the contributors all demonstrate that, of all the causal factors for conflict, none surpassed the differing and often clashing conceptions of border and identity as determinants of when and why middle-period Chinese and non-Chinese ruling elites decided in favor of war or peace.

The nine contributors to this volume have collectively committed themselves to the task of revealing the singularity of China's middle period with respect to the crucial baselines of war, border, and identity. Each author deliberates on some individuated historical confluence of event and personality that stands at or very near the nexus of war, border, and identity. Each reflects on the battle as risky proposition and the truce as unsatisfying and uneasy stalemate. Each addresses the compelling extent to which contested space—variously defined and delineated—functioned as an undeniable and inescapable motive force in determining the cooperative or hostile tenor of interstate relations. Each focuses on the unique tensions provoked by attachment to and departure from conventional understandings of identity. Yet, no two authors attend to the three intersecting themes of war, border, and identity in equal combination. Nor do they emphasize them in equal proportion. Thus, even as it contributes coherently and rationally to the formulation of an aggregated whole, each study nonetheless constitutes a freestanding exploration. The proof of these robust claims surfaces in an introductory way through the brief synopses of the chapters that follow.

Sherry Mou, a scholar of traditional Chinese literature, investigates the singular life of the obscure Grand Mistress Xian, whose activities, while heretofore little known, provide us with a near-perfect locus at the intersection of gender, ethnicity, and power. Coming from an elite ethnically non-Han family in the Baiyue region of South China and marrying a local official, Xian became increasingly influential in political and military affairs prevailing among the southern ethnic peoples in China during the second half of the sixth century. Even before but especially upon the death of her husband Feng Bao in 558, Xian had situated herself as the prime mediator between the central government of the south-based Chen dynasty (557–89) and the diverse local ethnic tribes. For the next half-century, she dictated the policies that maintained peace between these peoples and the changing central courts in China over the course of three dynasties.

Grand Mistress Xian's mediating role took on enhanced prominence when the unifying Sui dynasty (581–618) replaced the Chen. While retaining her independence, she continued to maintain cordial relations with the new government, even commanding her son and grandsons to undertake various military campaigns in the Sui's behalf. After her death at the age of about eighty in the early 600s, the Sui court sent elaborate funeral offerings and awarded her a posthumous title. As an ethnic woman ruler, Xian was in a unique position to negotiate peace between her region's unassimilated peoples and a succession of predominantly ethnic Han central courts. As a shrewd strategist, she successfully governed over an array of dissimilar groups, quelled local revolts, and allied herself with the winners in nearly every political transition. Her rule thus raises fascinating interpretive issues pertaining to the access that aristocratic ethnic women had to power during divisive periods in China's mid-imperial history.

Moving to the Tang dynasty, historian David Graff presents us with a study of the Youzhou military province from the time of the An Lushan Rebellion (755–63) to the early tenth century, focusing on its frontier position as a key factor contributing to its uniquely loyalist orientation and identity. The failure of Tang empire to return fully to a state of centralized polity in the wake of its mid-eighth-century experience of civil war is a well-known fact. Also well known is that the approximately forty military provinces that comprised the post-rebellion situation exhibited great variation in their degrees of deference to Tang central authority. In conventional typologies, Youzhou, which was also known as Lulong, was one of the most refractory of these autonomous military provinces.

However, through analyses that are as much ironical as revisionist, Graff reveals that, purely from the standpoint of its military functions, Youzhou Lulong shared more in common with the loyalist provinces that surrounded the capital at Chang'an than with its fellow wayward provinces of the northeast. Thus the stance of Youzhou Lulong toward residual Tang authority was hardly unique, and there were even other similarly disposed, if smaller, outer military provinces. But Graff does find Youzhou Lulong to have been unique in at least one crucial way, and the source of this uniqueness was the strategic location of this particular frontier province as the sole defensive bulwark against contiguous populations of Qidan, Xi, and Uyghur peoples. Moreover, he also finds that perhaps even more important than the happenstance of location and its internal politics in defining the identity of Youzhou Lulong in relation to centralized imperial authority was a host of "external" factors—including its relations with bordering nomadic peoples, with other military provinces, and even with the Tang court itself.

The extensive slate of six Chinese Song-period studies that forms the centerpiece of this book is initiated by Peter Lorge, who uses the archetypal symbol of the Chinese geopolitical boundary as a kind of foil for apprising us of another boundary of which few today are probably already aware. Lorge regards China's Great Wall of the late tenth and early eleventh centuries as chiefly symbolic of the wholly futile attempt on the part of the Chinese to erect a physical barrier *as* border of cultural safety, between their own empire and that of the northern Qidan "barbarians." Yet, whereas the Great Wall failed miserably, the Song dynasty's conterminous construction of an enormous ditch that connected existing natural barriers on the northeastern border of the empire, by and large, succeeded. This Great Ditch was more instrumental than is realized in creating a stable, peaceful border between the Song dynasty and its Liao counterpart for over a century.

The Great Ditch was not originally conceived as a permanent solution to the unresolved conflict with the Liao empire, and it is unclear whether the Song saw it as a temporary expedient to relieve pressure, a long-term defensive system, or a forward position from which to launch an eventual decisive offensive. But the effectiveness of the ditch most assuredly alarmed the Liao court by diminishing the destructiveness of its raids and invasions that were launched to pressure the Song into a favorable resolution of the border conflict. Liao raids thus became increasingly desperate as the Song ditch neared completion.

But the resultant "border" of the Great Ditch was not only a product of the military outcomes of the Song-Liao battles. It was also a consequence of the mindsets of the opposing emperors and their courts. Whereas the Song saw itself facing a growing threat to its existence in the form of the escalating Liao incursions, the Liao saw an increasingly strong opponent, as symbolized by the construction of the Great Ditch. Both sides were thus much relieved when peace was achieved.

Among all of China's imperial epochs, the Song dynasty is assuredly distinctive for the conspicuousness with which the deployment of human agents in the interest of preserving or securing peace exceeded their deployment in the interest of prosecuting war. My own contribution herein closely examines the career and motives of one such agent of peace because just as surely as the Song had its Yue Fei (1103–41)—the arch advocate of war, it also had its Qin Gui (1090–1155)—the arch advocate of peace. Moreover, turning to examine the historical record objectively and scrutinizing the short-term unfolding of events, we can even deem the influence of the latter man to have surpassed the former.

However, preceding both these individuals in the history of the Song debate over war versus peace was Wang Dan (957–1017), who was at the helm of the bureaucracy during the critical period of the earliest effectuation of a policy of concession. Wang served as grand councilor for an uninterrupted span of twelve years under the militarily inept and diplomatically challenged third emperor Zhenzong (r. 997–1022). Before his death, Wang Dan presided over the full installation of a policy whereby the Song state—in a stunning reversal of past precedent—sent tribute-bearing missions to the Liao state in exchange for peace. This chapter examines the internal and external constraints that likely led Wang Dan to direct the Song in such a passive strategy and his concomitant abandonment of the longstanding principle that at least some wars are justifiably waged.

M. A. Butler returns us to a concern with the implications of boundaries in conflict. However, through a study of a very different stripe than that provided by Peter Lorge, Butler makes us mindful that the battlefronts confronted by middle-period Chinese were oftentimes, in our modern terms and by the standards of our conventional science, imaginary. Through her study, Butler communicates how fully the divination rituals recorded in military manuals of the Chinese middle period—*Secret Classic of Venus, Planet of War* (ca. 756); *Tiger Seal Classic* (1005), and *Comprehensive Military Essentials* (1044)—were latter-day representative expressions on the primarily military plane of the age-old genre that Mark Edward Lewis has called "discourses dealing with the historical construction of ordered human space."[4]

Within the framework of the sexagenary calendrical cycle, coincidences and ruptures of the cycle and their convergence with alternate space were more meaningful than the cycle itself, and the Hidden Period (*dunjia*) and Irregular Opening (*qimen*) methods of divination were deployed to contour this space/time metaphysic. By using combinations of the Heavenly stem and Earthly branch calendar that were cyclically impossible at certain systemic intersections, and with the right human "key" (commander-as-record) in place, the Hidden Period and Irregular Opening purportedly allowed humans to vanish by jumping through and across time and space. At certain "time" locations, in conjunction with ritual performance, doors opened up between a series of nested spatiotemporal universes—thus, abetting success on the battlefield.

But Butler also finds the success of the Hidden Period and Irregular Opening systems to have been dependent on its spatial context. Through the proper use of battle arrays and alignments in an auspicious setting, Chinese middle-period warriors in the field were convinced that time/space alignments themselves could foil the enemy. To this end, these warrior-practitioners also indulged in five-phase theory and other rituals that they attributed with assuring the proper functioning of these seemingly imaginary doors in the spatiotemporal universe and thereby securing very real victories.

Next and overtly reemphasizing the problematique of internecine interstate conflict is an essay by Michael McGrath involving relations and nonrelations between the Song and another of its enemies—the Tangut Xia dynasty (1038–1227). During the 1030s and 1040s, the Xia state was led by an extraordinary figure, Li Yuanhao (ca. 1000–1048), whose chief claim to fame was as an ever-resistant opponent of the Song hegemonic agenda. As a mature leader, Yuanhao, as he is best remembered in history, continually challenged the Song court by means of his military provocations, his emulation of Chinese imperial prerogatives, and his simple refusal to heel or pay homage to the Chinese emperor or the great hierarchical "ladder of being" of which he was supposedly situated at the apex. McGrath accounts for and assesses the various responses of the Song court to the resistance tactics of this Tangut leader. But equally important is the story that he tells from the side and the perspective of the Xia.

The event on which McGrath relies for conveying this story—the war fought between the two powers from 1038 to 1044—is well known, and it is an episode that has forever fused the Song and the Xia together in historical consciousness. However, McGrath concentrates on certain elements of that war that have heretofore been little studied. Among these elements are the many failed efforts made by both sides at achieving a lasting truce via negotiation and the role of economic machinations, under the ostensible guise of tribute exchanges, in those efforts. The resulting description of an unsatisfying interstate stalemate is a nuanced one in which two clashing powers are eager to forestall total war and yet seemingly unable to avoid it. We are also presented with a sublimated history that is laced with issues of ethnic identity as well as the undercurrent struggle for cultural and historiographical advantage. More fleetingly, but whenever it is relevant, McGrath also directs his attention to a consideration of the diplomatic aspects of Han-Tangut interethnic relations, in order to frame the responses in the heat of war between the Song court and the enlarged and partially sinicized Xia court of the 1030s and 1040s in the expanded context of Chinese imperial history.

In the succeeding chapter James Anderson directs us again toward war but also toward its threatened prosecution in a much different and far-flung corner of the Song empire. Anderson's essay describes the salient aspects of the rebellion of the frontier chieftain Nong Zhigao (1025–53) and it concentrates in particular on the escalation of Sino-Vietnamese border tensions in the years following the Chinese suppression of Nong's revolt. Anderson argues that the pacification campaign launched against Nong Zhigao's followers in the 1050s and the subsequent submissions of strategic frontier communities to direct Song control were occurrences that contributed directly to the outbreak of the Sino-Viet border war of 1075–77.

Anderson determines that shifting alliances between the Chinese Song and Vietnamese Ly (1010–1225) courts and their respective frontier communities were key factors leading to this 1070s border conflict. However, even while they were important, these volatile alliances were not all-determinative factors. Other factors were influential in giving rise to the conflict that brought about the breakdown in relations between the Chinese and Vietnamese courts. Among those that Anderson discusses in passing were the Chinese court's efforts to increase frontier economic activity under Wang Anshi's New Policies (1068–85) and the Vietnamese Ly court's consolidation of peripheral fiefdoms during an accelerated period of state building. Nevertheless, after deliberating at length and in detail on the host of factors that led to rebellion, Anderson finds that, in the aftermath of hostilities, the negotiated border established between the Dai Viet kingdom and the Song empire signaled a diplomatic watershed in middle-period Sino-Vietnamese relations. The chapter concludes by discussing the role these frontier Tai-speaking communities played in shaping this firm line of demarcation between Chinese and Vietnamese domains.

In the closest approximation of a longitudinal topographical study in the volume, Ruth Mostern investigates the imprint of the devastating effects of war over the course of several decades of the twelfth century on the chameleon-like political geography of the Huainan region, whereby what had been a stable and populous territory within relatively recent historical memory was converted into a war-torn wasteland. Beginning in the late 1120s and 1130s, Huainan was the site of innumerable offensives and counteroffensives, as Jurchen Jin armies repeatedly tried to gain a strategic foothold in South China and the Song struggled to establish a defensible boundary. Following several major battles and almost incessant skirmishing, an 1142 treaty established the northern boundary at the Huai River. Although the peace was interrupted twice, by a Jin invasion in 1161 and a Song invasion in 1205, the border held until the fall of the Southern Song to the Mongol Yuan dynasty in 1276.

Since ancient times, the Chinese have held the wastefulness of war to be axiomatic, and Mostern's consideration of the fate of Huainan thoroughly confirms that assumption. But whereas chroniclers have traditionally assessed this wastefulness in principally in terms of human casualties and body counts, Mostern graphically substantiates the comparable depreciatory costs that the ravages of war can wreak upon a once completely civilized and sedate terrain. Mostern authenticates how the uncommonly destructive battles that convulsed the twelfth-century landscape of Huainan reduced what had long been a conglomeration of domesticized and prosperous counties and prefectures to the level of a frontier zone. She furthermore describes how this process of the devolution of Huainan forced officials stationed in the fragmenting region to adopt an administrative strategy calling for the provisional abolition of many counties in order to ensure the stability and viability of others and the survival of Huainan as a whole.

Finally, Michael Brose provides us with the only entry in the volume set in the era and amidst the circumstances that prefigured the Yuan dynasty (1279–1368). In this fitting conclusion, which emphasizes the often subliminal but always persistent theme of cooperation, Brose supplies what is perhaps a necessary corrective study in which ethnic Han Chinese, playing no major role, are at the margins. He examines the multiple roles of Uyghur aristocrats in nomadic and sedentary societies before and immediately following their submission to the Mongols in 1209. The Uyghur Kingdom in the Tarim Basin had representatives at a number of courts prior to the Mongols, including the Qidan, the Naiman, and the Qarakhitai. After submitting to the Mongols, the Uyghurs continued to act as advisors to the Mongol Qans and were also employed in China, Persia, and other kingdoms. Examining the roles of the Uyghur aristocrats who filled these offices reveals a great deal about the relative importance of ethnicity and various other forms of cultural capital in border relations among states and peoples on China's northern frontier at the time, including China itself.

The data appears to show that ethnicity itself was a powerful form of social and cultural capital but only one among many of those used by the Uyghurs who were involved in interstate affairs. Just as important were factors such as literacy and experience at administering over ethnically diverse populations. Neither Uyghur literacy of non-Uyghur cultural traditions nor their accumulated administrative experience should surprise us. After all, the Uyghur kingdom itself, situated amidst the major trade routes, was an entity long populated by various groups. Therefore, well before the thirteenth century, it had already inherited and incorporated a great variety of administrative traditions, ranging from those of the Sogdians to those of the Chinese.

In this book, by means of what is essentially a collection of highly illustrative case studies, the case for "middle-period" uniqueness with respect to the interlocking themes of war, border, and identity is most assuredly made. While avoiding becoming doctrinaire, each of the contributors has argued his or her case directly, vigorously, and earnestly. But ours are also cases made with no pretensions either to exhaustiveness or conclusiveness, for we have here endeavored to construct much more of a micro- than a macrohistory. Each of our chapters is dedicated to exposing a salient but focused, expressive but elemental, significant but localized facet of a strife-ridden and therefore pivotal time—a time when the concerns of war, border, and identity became inextricably bound together and when they rose to preeminence in the minds of every consequential historical actor, as they all sought either to shrewdly finesse or crudely press these difference-making factors to their own particular advantage.

Although we can choose to regard them as discrete phenomena for heuristic purposes, whether for the Chinese middle period or for any other intersection of time and place, war, border, and identity were, are, and will continue to be interlinked. Pausing to reflect, we encounter little difficulty in construing the inextricable fusions in their interrelationships, apprehending the entangled condition of their bonds. In an almost matrix-like configuration, war has always implied border, just as border has implied identity, and identity has implied war. They each have had the effect of requiring, summoning forth, and informing one another. In observing how, for example, identity and war are mutually conjoined, in his inquiry expressly on the latter, philosopher Michael Gelven has stated, "*War* must be distinguished from other forms of conflict in that it is fought *because of* the communal sense of being-with-others and not merely fought *by* groups."[5] In other words, to state the case yet again, herein, war implies identity.

In the end, my contributors and I obviously find our central thesis of the hyper-contested nature of the forces of war, border, and identity particularly during the Chinese "middle period" to be a compelling one. But, like all other conjectures, the thesis itself deserves to be contested, and it is our genuine hope that our readers will be quick to join in the task. By any standard and on every level, China's "middle period" was unquestionably rife with contestation. Yet, can one really argue that it either spawned or was the proving ground for contestation on a scale unparalleled by any prior or subsequent era in China's very long *imperial*—that is, *post-unification*—history? Without having been there, no one can ever hope to prove any such claim for the uniqueness of the "middle period" beyond all doubt. But, nonetheless, the occasions in the "middle period" for observing strife and contestation in conformance to the criteria of war, border, and identity are so abundantly legion that we feel we have here tendered the plausible case.

Still, few claims about any past, especially a past as culturally remote as the Chinese "middle period," are unassailable. Perhaps we are one day destined to break through the present limitations and discover incontrovertible proof of a nature that is beyond that which forms the bases for the preliminary arguments proffered here. But, recognizing the limits of what we can demonstrably illustrate, my fellow contributors and I have aspired to stop at nothing short of those limits, and we now leave the traversing beyond them into any new terrain of ironclad certainty to the discretion and the initiative of future researchers.

Notes

1. One recent work that commemorates, emphasizes, and analyzes the dominating and comprehensive importance of the treaty as a turning point in Song-Liao diplomatic relations is David Curtis Wright, *From War to Diplomatic Parity in Eleventh-Century China: Sung's Foreign Relations with Kitan Liao.*
2. Jing-shen Tao, *Two Sons of Heaven: Studies in Sung-Liao Relations*, p. 99.
3. Certainly to be listed among this new scholarship are the works of David A. Graff, especially his *Medieval Chinese Warfare, 300–900*. There is also Peter Lorge, *War, Politics and Society in Early Modern China, 900–1795*.
4. Mark Edward Lewis, *The Construction of Space in Early China*, p. 1.
5. Michael Gelven, *War and Existence: A Philosophical Inquiry*, p. 48.

Bibliography

Gelven, Michael. *War and Existence: A Philosophical Inquiry*. University Park: Pennsylvania State University Press, 1994.
Graff, David A. *Medieval Chinese Warfare, 300–900*. London: Routledge, 2002.
Lewis, Mark Edward. *The Construction of Space in Early China*. Albany, NY: SUNY Press, 2006.
Lorge, Peter. *War, Politics and Society in Early Modern China, 900–1795*. London: Routledge, 2005.
Tao, Jing-shen. *Two Sons of Heaven: Studies in Sung-Liao Relations*. Tucson: University of Arizona Press, 1988.
Wright, David Curtis. *From War to Diplomatic Parity in Eleventh-Century China: Sung's Foreign Relations with Kitan Liao*. History of Warfare, vol. 33. 47 vols. Leiden, Holland: E. J. Brill, 2005.

CHAPTER 1

FATHOMING CONSORT XIAN: NEGOTIATED POWER IN THE LIANG, CHEN, AND SUI DYNASTIES

Sherry J. Mou

Women's biographies constitute a long tradition in China, tracing back to the first century BCE, when the Confucian historian Liu Xiang (77–76 BCE) compiled the first collection of women's biographies.[1] This practice soon entered the official histories.[2] The History of the Later Han Dynasty (*Hou Hanshu*)—the third of the official histories, which was compiled in the fifth century CE—presents the first special chapter of the biographies of ordinary women, one distinct from the standard chapter on the lives of imperial consorts.[3] Thus, a tradition was established, such that, in all, thirteen of the twenty-five official histories include chapters on the lives of ordinary women. In turn, these life-writings often became the proto-texts for vernacular literature in various forms, as the genres of poetry, drama, legend, and fiction evolved to feature characters from them.

Yet in another sense we can hardly call most of these life-writings *biographies* at all, at least as written accounts of people's lives, following any typical dictionary or common understanding. Highlighting only certain events in the women's lives, these accounts in the histories are sketches at best. Nevertheless, as they were appended to the basic core of Confucian texts, these life-writings form an important part of Confucian discourse on womanhood, comprising a foundation upon which later generations of writers would erect new paradigms to inspire Chinese women and to evaluate their lives. But if the "real" women in these historical proto-texts are obscure, their original identities as framed by other genres become even less visible and less relevant in this continual process of rewriting women's lives. Like making a papier-mâché mask over a balloon, each reconstructed text (whatever the genre) obscures the shape and the color of the original woman's identity, while forming a new one. When finally the mask is completed and the balloon is popped, the original subject (the woman) is objectified into a new subject: in much the same fashion, we can see these different versions of women's lives as forming what can be called "the discourse of Confucian woman."

Whether or not they can be traced back to an original historical model, these later texts nonetheless present an interesting context for understanding the formation and development of Confucian ideology toward women. As Michel Foucault suggested, the archaeology of knowledge (of women, in this case) "is a comparative analysis that is not intended to reduce the diversity of discourses, and to outline the unity that must totalize them, but is intended to divide up their diversity into different figures."[4] In keeping with this view, what I attempt in this chapter is not so much an excavation of a "woman" from the layers of discourse, as an examination of the layers of veils "covering" a woman—namely, an analysis of the various reconstructions of one woman's life. More specifically, through a close reading of three texts written in different eras on the Consort Xian (Xian furen),[5] a woman leader of the sixth century of the Common Era in South China, I examine how the various versions of a woman's life, like many a historical subject, are in fact the tools of their authors for engaging the past, present, and future. Thus, despite Foucault's further claim that we can easily imagine a culture of authorless discourse, one in which "discourses, whatever their status, form, or value, and regardless of our manner of handling them, would unfold in a pervasive anonymity,"[6] we find that the texts under scrutiny here reveal as much, if not more, about the authors and their times as they do about their more ancient subject.

But who was the subject in question? Who was Consort Xian? Briefly, *Xian furen*—actually, a title awarded by one of the emperors she served—was a sixth-century woman leader of the Yue area in South China (present-day Guangdong and Guangxi provinces). Unlike legendary woman warriors like Mulan[7] (late-sixth century?) or the women generals (*jia jiang*) of the Yang family[8] (late-tenth to the eleventh centuries), or even historical women commanders like Liang Hongyu (twelfth century) and Qin Liangyu[9] (1574–1648), Consort Xian is hardly a household name, even within Chinese culture. Yet a closer look will reveal that her life and activities provide a little-known but near-perfect locus of gender, ethnicity, and power. The earliest record of Consort Xian is found in the History of the Sui Dynasty (*Suishu*),[10] one of the official histories. Shortly afterward, Li Yanshou (seventh century CE) included the same biography in his History of the Northern Dynasties (*Beishi*) with minimal omissions.[11] Her given name is unknown: she is usually simply referred to as "Consort Xian" or "Consort of State Qiao" (*Qiao guo furen*), another title awarded her by the Sui emperor. Consort Xian's natal family most likely belonged to the minority people of South China called the Li.[12] Despite or perhaps because of her having come from an elite non-Han family in the Baiyue region of southern China, Consort Xian married a local official appointed by the Han-dominated central government and became increasingly influential in political and military affairs among the southern tribal peoples[13] during the second half of the sixth century. Even before but especially upon the death of her husband Feng Bao in 558, Consort Xian situated herself as the prime mediator between the central government of the southern-based Chen dynasty (557–89) and the diverse local ethnic tribes. For the next half-century, she dictated the policies that maintained peace between these peoples and the changing central courts in China over the course of three dynasties.

The three versions of biographies I use for my study of Consort Xian are her biography in the *Suishu*; a vernacular version in a Ming-dynasty (1368–1644) collection of women's biographies; and a twentieth-century version written by Wu Han (1909–69), a Marxist historian. Her biography in the official history presents a set of values different from those commonly found in Confucian biographies of women, especially those included in the *Suishu*. In comparison, the Ming-dynasty vernacular version shows how a woman's life was tailored to suit the purpose of Confucian discourse and how, at the same time, her life is both valorized and assimilated into that very discourse. Finally, through Wu Han's Marxist view, we see how Consort Xian is offered as an exceptional historical personage who united the "minorities" to the Han center, a historical hindsight from the perspective of a modern political entity nearly thirteen centuries after Consort Xian died. What do all these transformations of a woman's life mean, and how do we assess women's position or even define an individual woman's identity amid the myriad versions of her life stories? Perhaps what Carolyn G. Heilbrun sums up as "history" in her introduction to *Writing a Woman's Life* may shed some light on these questions: "much of what passes as history is in fact evidence from the prevailing or established opinion of the age under consideration or, as likely, of the age in which the author of the history lives."[14] Let us now turn to Consort Xian's biography in the official history and see how well she fits into this Confucian frame.

Consort Xian in the *Suishu*

Consort Xian's biography is the second longest of all the biographies of women in the official histories, shorter only than that of the historian Ban Zhao (ca. 49–ca. 120 CE), the "foremost woman scholar of China," as Nancy Swann calls her.[15] Yet removing the extensive quotes of Ban Zhao's works from her biography,[16] we find that what remains, amounts to only about a third of Consort Xian's biography. Consort Xian's biography contains by far more details than any other woman's biography in the official history. Following a roughly chronological order from when she was a young girl at her parents' home to her death in around 601, it can be divided into three sections: the first relates her origins, including her parentage and the ancestors of her husband Feng Bao; the second includes a long account of her military achievements, spreading over sixty-something years and three dynasties; and the third is a formulaic ending of official posthumous recognition, similar to those in many official biographies of male bureaucrats. As this is the earliest and most detailed version of Consort Xian's biography, my discussion of its form, content, and chronology is also lengthier and more detailed than those the other two.

The Xians and the Fengs

Consort Xian's biography conforms to the conventional formula and begins with the traditional identification of her ancestral hometown and parentage. For generations, Consort Xian's family was the leader of Nanyue,[17] commanding over a hundred thousand households.[18] The biography asserts her virtue and ability in strategy and pacification even from youth; as she urged beneficence, local people were united.[19]

More specifically, she tempered her brother's rough rule with frequent admonitions and thus mollified many.[20] As a result, "Over a thousand households from Hainan and Dan'er pledged their allegiance to him."[21] The biography is obviously intended to emphasize Consort Xian's leadership over her own people and love of peace in general, both important assets for an ethnic leader from the perspective of the Han-dominated central government. Interestingly, in Consort Xian's family history, there is no mention of any feminine characteristics—nothing about her appearance or womanly deportment—instead, it is her skills in commanding troops and in curtailing her brother's aggression that are highlighted. We will return to this point later when we compare Consort Xian's biography with the other fourteen biographies of women in the *Suishu*.

Next, the biography turns to her marriage, which was very much a political ploy on part of her father-in-law Feng Rong, the regional inspector of Luozhou. According to the biography, "Feng Rong heard that The Consort was principled and purposeful. He offered to marry her to his son Feng Bao, who was the grand protector (*taishou*) of Gaoliang."[22] The Fengs also had a distinguished line, tracing back to the royal line of the Northern Yan (Bei Yan) dynasty (409–36), and the family had long been appointed regional officials by the Liang government (502–57). But because the Fengs were outsiders, the locals often ignored them.[23] Feng Rong's move to make a marriage alliance with the local ruling family served him well, because the Consort got the Xian and Feng clans to respect local customs and procedures, thus gaining the good will and cooperation of the residents.[24] Once again, from her marriage, the narration shifts its emphasis first to the family genealogy of the Fengs and then to her role in the public arena and focuses on her helping the Fengs govern the region.

Military Achievements

The second section of the *Suishu* biography covers Consort Xian's life from her marriage to her death. In it, her military achievements are laid out chronologically to correspond with the three dynasties that she served. Interestingly, the end of each period is punctuated with the death of a person of importance: her husband, her son, and herself, respectively.

The first period under the Liang dynasty (502–57) covers approximately from 535, when Consort Xian and Feng Bao married, to the 550s, when Feng Bao died.

It is marked by a single important event: the rebellion of Li Qianshi. The event was in fact an offshoot of a larger rebellion that shook the Liang capital. In 548, Hou Jing (d. 552), a Liang general, rebelled, captured the capital, and took the emperor hostage.[25] The commander-in-chief (*dudu*) of Guang[1]zhou Xiao Bo conscribed troops from the region to rescue the emperor. Under pretext of illness, Li Qianshi, a regional inspector under Xiao Bo, declined to send his troops; later, in 550, Li summoned Feng Bao. Consort Xian suspected that Li Qianshi was motivated by Hou Jing's rebellion and wanted to provide Hou Jing with support from the south. She analyzed the situation for Feng Bao: Li wanted Feng Bao's allegiance and would imprison him without it, so Feng Bao should just sit tight for a while and watch.[26] As Consort Xian predicted, a few days later, Li indeed rebelled, and sent his best commander to attack the government troops at Ganshi. Consort Xian then devised a scheme that would both relieve Li Qianshi's suspicions about Feng Bao's intentions and, at the same time, possibly defeat him. She led over a thousand people to pay tribute to Li, carrying miscellaneous presents and supplies for his army. Li's inspectors confirmed that Consort Xian and her entourage were indeed carrying gifts, so Li accepted the story and took no further precautions. As soon as Consort Xian and her people entered the barricade, they attacked and won gloriously. Li retreated, and Consort Xian led her troops to meet the Liang commanding officer Chen Baxian (503–59), the duke of Changcheng (*Changcheng hou*), at Ganshi. After Consort Xian returned, she told Feng Bao, "Grand Protector Chen [Baxian] is very popular with the people. He will be able to eliminate the bandits in the end. You should support him generously."[27] The advice underscores Consort Xian's prescience because, merely seven years later, Chen Baxian founded the Chen dynasty (557–89).

Sometime during the 550s, Feng Bao died, and the coastal area slipped into turmoil. Consort Xian took command and made peace among leaders of the Baiyue area; the peace she brought lasted for over a decade. It is also during this decade that Consort Xian groomed her son Feng Pu to succeed his father as a military commander. Father and son seem closely related in the biographer's mind, for in the same line where Consort Xian is reported to have become a widow she is also described as assuming the role of a mentor-like mother. In 558, the second year of the newly founded Chen dynasty, Consort Xian took her nine-year-old son Feng Pu and other commanders to pay their allegiance to the emperor, Chen Baxian. Chen was pleased and awarded Feng Pu the position of grand protector of Yangchun (*Yangchun junshou*).[28]

As Consort Xian had fought for him, Chen Baixian was cordial and their allegiance strong. Later, Guangzhou regional inspector Ouyang He rebelled against the Chen dynasty (557–89), which, according to the *Suishu* account, constitutes the major event in the second period of Consort Xian's activities. Ouyang sent for Feng Pu to meet him in Gaoan and kept him there. Feng Pu sent a messenger to notify his mother of the situation, and she replied: "I have been loyal and steadfast [to the imperial court] for two generations. I can't betray the state because of you."²⁹ So she sent troops to guard her border and led other chieftains from Baiyue to meet Zhang Zhaoda, the Chen general sent by the emperor to quell the rebellion. Thus, forces from both within and without finally defeated Ouyang He.

The victory brought her much recognition from the Chen court. Owing to Consort Xian's achievement, her son Feng Pu was given the title "Duke of Xindu" (*Xindu hou*), in addition to "Leader of Court Gentleman Who Quelled the Yue" (*ping Yue zhonglang jiang*), and then converted to governor of Shilong (*Shilong taishou*). The emperor also sent an emissary with an emblem to give Consort Xian the title "Grand Consort of Shilong" (*Shilong tai furen*), a four-horse carriage with embroidered curtains and colorful braids, a military band, an official banner, and a staff and honor guard appropriate in size for a regional inspector. However, in the middle of the Zhide years (583–86) Feng Pu died.³⁰

In 589, the Chen dynasty finally was replaced by the Sui dynasty (581–618), which had been declared in 581. Lingnan was again in turmoil except for the few prefectures under Consort Xian. The local people worshiped her as their "holy mother,"³¹ who protects their territory and pacifies all under her. Acting pragmatically and being intent on retaining her position as a regional leader, Consort Xian now had to make another decision with regard to her loyalty. Changing her allegiance to the Sui, however, took much more effort than allying herself with the Chen had.

At first, the Sui emperor Gaozu (r. 581–604) dispatched the area commander-in-chief (*zongguan*) Wei Guang (d. 590) to pacify regions beyond the Ling Mountain Range. The Chen-dynasty general Xu Deng continued to resist in Nankang, and Wei Guang dared not advance. Realizing that having Consort Xian as an ally would be essential to the peaceful transition of this area, Prince Jin (later Emperor Yangdi) asked the hostage Chen emperor to send Consort Xian a letter accompanied by a military tally and a rhinoceros-horn cane from Funan as tokens of recognition. When Consort Xian received the letter and other items, she recognized the cane as the gift that she herself had sent earlier to the throne as tribute. She was thus finally convinced that the Chen dynasty was over, so she summoned several thousand local chieftains, wept for an entire day, and sent her grandson Feng Hun to welcome Wei Guang to Guangzhou. Peace was restored in Lingnan, and, at Wei Guang's request, the Sui emperor conferred upon Feng Hun the title of "Unequaled in Honor" (*yitong sansi*) and upon Consort Xian that of "Commandery Consort of Songkang" (*Songkang jun furen*).³²

According to the *Suishu* account, the third and final period of Consort Xian's military activity occurred under the Sui dynasty, terminating in about the year 601. Soon after Consort Xian converted her allegiance, Wang Zhongxuan, a local chieftain rebelled and, with the aid of many other leaders, besieged the area commander-in-chief Wei Guang, who was in Wang's prefecture. Consort Xian sent one grandson—Feng Xuan—to rescue the emissary, but Feng Xuan delayed because he was a good friend of one of the rebel chieftains. When Consort Xian learned of his hesitation, she arrested and imprisoned him and sent another grandson—Feng Ang—to fight the rebels; they eventually defeated Wang Zhongxuan and put down the rebellion.[33]

Afterward, Consort Xian paraded in style and accompanied "Pei Ju, Sui emperor's emissary, in inspecting and pacifying the nearby prefectures."[34] The local authorities came forth to pay him tribute. Not until then could the Sui claim control of this area. Marveling at what Consort Xian had accomplished, Emperor Gaozu lavished on the Fengs official titles and positions: he raised Feng Ang's rank to regional inspector of Gaozhou (*Gaozhou cishi*), pardoned Feng Xuan and promoted him to regional inspector of Luozhou (*Luozhou cishi*), bestowed upon Feng Bao the posthumous title of "Area Commander-in-chief of Guang[1]zhou" (*Guangzhou zongguan*) and "Duke of the State of Qiao" (*Qiao guo gong*), conferred upon Consort Xian the title "Consort of State Qiao," and transferred the enfeoffment of the district of Songkang (*Songkang yi*) from the Consort to Ms. Xian (the concubine of Feng Pu, Consort Xian's late son).[35] In addition, the emperor also established a Consort of State Qiao's private secretariat (*mufu*) for Consort Xian, complete with aides and other subordinate officials. She was given a seal and, with it, the power to dispatch the troops of six prefectures in any emergency.[36]

The emperor also sent a decree commending Consort Xian for her loyal sentiment, deep conviction to justice, and great achievement in defeating bandits. For these reasons, she was awarded 5,000 bolts of cloth and the life of her grandson Feng Xuan was spared, despite his inaction. The decree ended with a further call to duty: "The Consort should teach her descendants to venerate and revere rites and morality, and to abide by the teaching of the court in order to concur with my wishes."[37] The empress also lavished much jewelry and many fine articles of clothing upon Consort Xian. The rich material rewards the Sui imperial house conferred to her and her family imply that the Lingnan area was important to the dynasty's stability and that Consort Xian's leadership role in this area was keenly recognized.

The last major event recorded in the biography shows that Consort Xian would not tolerate a corrupt official, even one appointed by the imperial court. The incident happened when Consort Xian was in her seventies. The area commander-in-chief Zhao Na was greedy and atrocious; as a result, many Li and Liao[38] people ran away or rebelled. Consort Xian dispatched her aide to the capital with suggestions for how to pacify local peoples and with details of Zhao Na's crimes. After further investigation, the emperor executed Zhao Na, bestowed upon Consort Xian a new fiefdom with its 1,500 families, and directed her to mollify those offended, which she easily accomplished.[39] To the end of her life, Consort Xian was very active in commanding the Yue area and mediating between the Sui court and the local ethnic peoples.

Official Honors

The final section of Consort Xian's *Suishu* biography echoes the formulaic ending that we read in most biographies of court officials in official histories: "At the beginning of the Renshou years [601–4], she died. The Sui court sent a thousand pieces of brocade as a funeral offering, and she received the posthumous title of 'Consort of Sincerity and Respect (*Chengjing furen*).' "[40] The posthumous title shows both the court's recognition of an ethnic leader's loyalty and its suspicion of the peripheral peoples' sincerity.

To sum up, although Consort Xian was clearly the military leader and governing agent for over half a century, the biography never loses sight of her role as a wise wife, a capable mother, and an efficient grandmother, whose prescience and loyalty enabled her to guide the Fengs to safe ground every time a dynasty changed or a male relative's death created uncertainty. Her womanly role as wife, mother, and grandmother is embedded in the narration of her military achievements to ensure that she was not acting in her own interest but always in the interests of the Feng clan. With every achievement, she brought not just honor to herself but titles, ranks, and material rewards to her male relatives. In fact, the narrative often lists the titles and ranks conferred upon her dead husband (posthumously) and sons before it lists those awarded to her. We can interpret this in two ways. First, Consort Xian is cast as a typical Confucian mother, who tried the best she could to bring glory to her husband's clan. She was a capable and helpful spouse; after becoming a widow, she educated her sons and grandsons to become loyal officials of the court while continuing to bring honor, fame, and political power to her husband's clan family. Second, Consort Xian is framed as a model non-Han regional leader. Her biography shows what honor, glory, prosperity, and political power the Han central government is willing to shower on an ethnic leader who faithfully follows its dictates. In our discussion of the other two biographies, we will see how this Han-centric perspective is carried through the dynasties and all the way into our own time.

Alongside the Biographies of Han Women

When we contextualize Consort Xian's biography with the other fourteen biographies of women in the *Suishu*, we see that Consort Xian's behavior both confirms and deviates from the traditional images of women described in them. As mentioned above, Consort Xian is framed as a Confucian mother, whose prescience, capability, determination, and farsightedness not only save men of the family from the impediments of the day but also pave the way for a prosperous future of the patrilineal family, namely the Fengs. Apart from this Confucian motherly trait, Consort Xian's actions by and large defy the image of women described in most biographies. In other words, her biography does not fall in line with the Confucian discourse of virtuous women. As the preface to the "Biographies of Women" section in the *Suishu* implies, the purpose of recording the lives of these women is to define "womanly virtue" (*nüde*). The attributes of women given in these biographies can serve to define the expected Confucian womanly virtues of that time. Traditional as well as modern scholars have developed whole taxonomies of virtuous Chinese womanhood based on the virtues, appearance, personality, and primary roles depicted in each biography.

Women in most biographies are noted for their feminine appearance or personality traits, such as beauty, poise, amicability, principle and integrity (*zhijie*), and abiding by appropriate behavior (*li*). In contrast, although Consort Xian is said to be a capable daughter, sister, wife, mother, grandmother, and a judiciously loyal commander, no common female virtues are found in her biography. There is virtually no description of her physical appearance, except when she is in full military gear. The only time Consort Xian is said to cry is when she learned about the end of the Chen dynasty. The loyalty motif underlying her crying makes the otherwise feminine gesture gender-neutral, if not masculine.

As for female virtues in general, the three most common are chastity, filiality, and loyalty. Although Consort Xian was widowed very young, chastity is not singled out as one of her distinctive virtues. Similarly, although we learn about her advice and help to her brother and husband, there is no hint of her being filial. She lived a long life with the Fengs, but there is no mention of her relationship with her in-laws, whereas in many other biographies women are praised for their filiality toward their in-laws or their obedience and faithfulness to husbands.

Instead, loyalty is highlighted throughout her biography, but this is not the loyalty commonly depicted as a female virtue. A closer look at loyal women in other biographies indicates that their loyalty is defined narrowly as faithfulness to their husbands and families. Those who express loyalty to the state usually convey it through their relations to fathers, husbands, or sons.[41] This appropriation of women's indirect homage to the state implies that women's position should stay at home, and sentiments reaching outside the familial sphere need to go through the mediation of their men. Not surprisingly, the primary roles these women assumed in the biographies are mostly familial ones, namely mothers, wives, sisters, daughters, mothers-in-law, and daughters-in-law.[42] Although Consort Xian's biography gives token acknowledgment of her familial roles as a daughter, sister, daughter-in-law, wife, mother, and grandmother, her central role is that of a military and political leader. It is through her leadership as a commander and peacemaker that she is given a spotlight in the history.

The Ming Version

The Ming version of Consort Xian's biography is collected in a sixteen-*juan* illustrated version of Biographies of Women (*Lienü zhuan*), illustrated by the famous Ming illustrator Qiu Ying (ca. 1495–1552) and attributed to the Ming playwright Wang Daokun (1525–93) in the 1779 preface by Wang Yu.[43] The selection includes nearly all the "good" women in Liu Xiang's early-Han collection and additional ones from the late-Han through the early-Ming dynasty. Consort Xian's biography is collected in the seventh *juan*, and it is, as in the case of every other biography in the collection, preceded by an illustration of its subject. In Consort Xian's case, she appears fully armed, riding upon an armored horse, and she is shielded by an embroidered umbrella, while escorting the imperial emissary on his way to receive respects from local chieftains (see figure 1.1).[44] The biography's

Figure 1.1 Consort Xian accompanying the imperial emissary.
Source: Biographies of Women or *Lienü zhuan*, as compiled by Wang Daokun, 1525–93.

organization is similar to that in the *Suishu*: it starts with an introduction of her parental and marital lineages, follows with an account of her military career, and ends with a eulogy. However, within each section information is presented differently, with significant omissions and additions.

A Brief Genealogy

The introduction of Consort Xian's parental and marital families is terse, and her natal family is subordinated to the Feng's genealogy. Although the Fengs and the Xians were introduced with almost equal length in the *Suishu*, the choices of both words and details in this introduction show that the Xian clan is secondary to the Fengs:

> Consort Xian was the wife of Feng Bao, a grand protector of the Six Dynasties. At the beginning, as a result of Northern Yan's Emperor Zhaocheng's expedition to Korea, the Fengs' ancestor Feng Ye was sent across the sea to Song [in the south] with three hundred people. They stayed on at Xinhui. From Feng Ye to Feng Rong, the Fengs were hereditary regional inspectors of Luozhou. Rong's son Bao became the grand protector of Gaoliang.
>
> The Xians of Gaoliang had been the barbaric chieftains for generations and commanded over a hundred thousand families. They had a daughter who was very strategic and good at military deployment. Bao's father Rong betrothed her to be Bao's wife.[45]

Comparing this introduction to that in the *Suishu*, we can see a clear bias toward the Xians in terms of gender and ethnicity. Not only is Consort Xian framed more as a woman (daughter-in-law) of the Fengs than as a daughter of the Xians, but also the two families' social statuses are presented in very different spirits. While the Fengs' genealogy is carefully crafted to be traceable back to the royal connection of the family to the north generations ago, the lineage of the Xians is lumped into a sentence highlighting its "barbaric origin."

To be fair, we can trace the gender bias to a broader development of women's position in Chinese history since the Former Han dynasty, when women's influence over men was recognized as something potentially destructive and therefore warranting regulation.[46] Wang Daokun's treatment of Consort Xian as the wife of Feng Bao instead of the daughter of the Xian clan is merely a reflection of this change. Thus, the introduction of Consort Xian's biography in the *Suishu* ("Consort of State Qiao was the daughter of the Xian clan of Gaoliang")[47] simply follows the common practice of early Chinese historiography in identifying a person's title, place of origin, and clan name, before giving details of actions or events. After the Tang dynasty (618–907), but especially after the popularization of the neo-Confucian view of women during the Song dynasty (960–1279), women's lives centered on those of their husbands and they were identified as "wives" instead of "daughters." Wang Daokun's introducing Consort Xian as "the wife of Feng Bao, a regional inspector during the Six Dynasties" is therefore a reflection of this reappropriation of women's identity to their husband's clan instead of their natal families.

But the shifted gender position also overlaps with an important ethnicity issue: the Fengs are presented with a more illustrious family history while the Xians are depicted as a barbarian clan. The fact is that Fengs were recent immigrants to this region, and the Xians were indigenous to southern China. But the Fengs' Han ethnicity gave the clan a higher social position in the eyes of the Confucian historians, and the Xians' non-Han status always cast a shade of doubt in the minds of the same historians, even when the Xians pledged their loyalty wholeheartedly. From the beginning of the introduction, the Fengs' family history is exaggerated, for the "expedition to Korea" by Emperor Zhaocheng, the ancestor of the Fengs, was in fact a retreat from the Northern Wei Dynasty (Bei Wei) (386–534), which captured the Northern Yan Dynasty capital Longcheng in 436.[48] Furthermore, Feng Rong's idea of forming a marriage alliance with the local power to help control of local affairs is omitted, thus undermining the fact that, when the marriage alliance was formed, the Xians were socially and politically much more powerful than the Fengs. Wang Daokun's use of the term "barbaric chieftain" in describing the Xians further underlines his Han-centric bias against the indigenous peoples. Wang Daokun also omitted intimate details about Consort Xian—how she admonished her brother not to be so aggressive and how she helped Feng Bao with court cases, making certain that the local peoples followed the law. The shortened account of her parental family and the omission of intimate details about her actions as a sister and as a wife kept Consort Xian further apart from her Han counterparts. She is less a real person and more a historical function.

Reexamining the Military Career

Consort Xian's military exploits are covered in the same chronological sequence as those in the *Suishu*. However, details that highlight Consort Xian's loyalty to the central governments are either shortened or omitted. Most of these omitted details portray the personal side of Consort Xian, making her a much more humane subject and someone who is easier to identify with.

Li Qianshi's rebellion during the Liang period is a good example of how Wang Daokun tailors materials from earlier times. Whereas in the *Suishu* Consort Xian's advice to Feng Bao is offered in exchanges between husband and wife, not given unsolicited, in the Ming biography it is condensed into the longish advice Consort Xian gave Feng Bao and the short description of the successful result of her strategy. Furthermore, Consort Xian's meeting with Chen Baxian, the Liang commanding officer fighting the rebels, is left out. As a result, her final advice to Feng Bao that Chen Baxian is "very popular with the people," that "he will be able to eliminate the bandits in the end," and that Feng Bao "should support him generously"[49] is also left out. The omission of this personal and personable encounter between Consort Xian and Chen Baxian is closely related to the most emotional scene in Consort Xian's biography in the *Suishu*. Given her close ties to Chen Baxian, her relationship with the Chen dynasty was more than cordial. Thus, even after the Chen dynasty ended, she refused to acknowledge that fact, until the hostaged Chen emperor produced evidence to confirm what she was told by the new Sui court. Consequently, the account left out the striking scenes of Consort Xian's mustering several thousand local chieftains and crying in front of them for an entire day to lament the demise of the Chen dynasty.

There are a few other changes. Both the royal decree commending Consort Xian's role in quelling the rebellion of Wang Zhongxuan and the resulting lavish royal awards are reduced to simply a list of ranks and titles. As a result, Consort Xian's careful handling of imperial gifts from three dynasties and her admonitions to her sons and grandsons to be loyal to the central governments are also absent from this version. All these omissions have to do with Consort Xian's loyalty. If we look closely, although alongside biographies of other women, Consort Xian's life is depicted primarily as that of an indigenous tribal chieftain. Although she was a widow, chastity was never mentioned as a "virtue"; instead, loyalty for her means obeying the central government, whichever dynasty it was. Thus, the point of view is mainly from the center to the peripheral ethnic minority. This is why, even though Consort Xian changed her allegiance three times, she is never depicted as disloyal or unfaithful—a stance not usually tolerated among the Han officials, for during this period of fleeting dynasties, the sentiment of loyalty was crucially important to Han officials. Just as a woman was not expected to marry a second time, a loyal subordinate was not to serve a second master. Were the dynasty ever to be replaced by a new imperial family, a truly loyal subordinate could not serve a new court; many even committed suicide to express their loyalty. Even the rebel Hou Jing was said to be so uncomfortable that, when he finally confronted the Liang emperor whom he took hostage, his face was covered with sweat.[50]

However, none of this was demanded of Consort Xian. To the Han center, Consort Xian represented the threat of the powerful ethnic periphery whose steadfast loyalty to one regime could become a major problem for the next. That is why at the beginning of the Sui dynasty, the emperor was so keen on having her accept the demise of Chen dynasty and transfer her loyalty to the new dynasty. That is also why Consort Xian's changes in allegiance to three new governments were lauded rather than denounced. As an ethnic leader, her flexibility allowed the central government to continue its change of dynasty without having to deal with peripheral forces. Rather than holding her to the same kind of moral standard, the Ming biographer chose to emphasize her loyalty in terms of a much more general phrase: the peripheral to the center.

A Eulogy

Perhaps the most noticeable differences between Wang Daokun's biography and the one in the *Suishu* are the omission of Consort Xian's death, the additions of her grandson Feng Ang's career, and Wang Daokun's eulogy in the final section of the Ming biography. In all three changes, what is showcased is the Fengs. As for Consort Xian, however ethereal her image is in the official history, it is further diluted in the Ming case by overzealous dwelling on the Fengs. First of all, instead of a formulaic mention of Consort Xian's death, the final paragraph of the text focuses on the career of Consort Xian's grandson Feng Ang and returns to Consort Xian only as an afterthought:

> In the first year of Renshou [601], the Liao people in five nearby prefectures, including Chao and Cheng, rebelled. [Feng] Ang rode a fast horse to the capital to request troops to help quell the rebellion. The emperor ordered Yang Su to discuss the situation of the rebels. [Afterward] Su sighed [in admiration]: "[I] didn't expect to have such talent among the barbarians." Ang was then dispatched to lead troops in the Jiang[nan] and Ling[nan] areas to fight the bandits. After the matter was settled, Ang was granted the title of "Grand Protector of Hanyang" (*Hanyang taishou*). Ang's bravery in carrying out righteousness came from his grandmother Consort Xian's instruction.[51]

The rebellion of the Liao and the meeting between Feng Ang and Yang Su happened after Consort Xian's death and had little bearing with her life.[52] Reading this passage today, we can hardly overlook the Han-centric tone of Yang Su's comments about "such talent among the barbarians," which were meant as praise. As this is, after all, Consort Xian's biography, Feng Ang's good sense is attributed to her instruction. Ironically, the attribution relegates her to the position of a prescient grandmother whose primary function in life is to ensure the prosperity of the patriarchal line; thus, her importance as a sociopolitical leader of the region is short-changed by her familial role as a female patriarchal head.

Wang's eulogy further supports the view that Consort Xian is worth noticing less as an individual and more as a brilliant member of the Feng clan, for it first comments on the Fengs as being a complacent subordinate family for a period of five dynasties before it turns to sing his praise of Consort Xian:

> Although a woman, Xian does man's business, quelling rebellions many times over and receiving official titles and ranks from the emperors. It was not owing to luck but because of propriety. As for her instructing her sons and grandsons not to slack but to devote themselves to loyalty and righteousness, it is indeed a very admirable thing![53]

Thus, Wang Daokun's rendition of Consort Xian's life further reduces her from an individual to a minority type. She is the model ethnic leader who maintains peace of the region through her steadfast loyalty to the Han government. This tension between the center and the peripheral becomes even clearer in a modern version of Consort Xian's story.

A Modern Version

In 1961, Wu Han, a historian of the Ming dynasty, published "Consort Xian" ("Xian furen") in China's main newspaper, the *People's Daily*.[54] The article is "mostly a recount based on the original biographies," as Lin Tianwei, a modern scholar from Taiwan, comments in his study of Consort Xian.[55] Indeed, "Consort Xian" includes all the incidents recorded in the other two biographies, and more. Structurally, we can divide the article into three portions: Consort Xian's life (about four-fifths of the text), a brief mention of some well-known Fengs during the Tang dynasty, and a conclusion that assesses Consort Xian's career and her historical position. Wu Han's piece displays an interesting Han-centric overtone at several places, but especially in his conclusion. I will focus on Wu Han's conclusion here and leave the minor incidents in the text to the last section, where I contextualize all three biographies.

With its historical hindsight, Wu Han's version elaborates on the Ming biography's final eulogy that praises Consort Xian as a sage instructress, whose fine teaching directly affected her descendants' decision to be loyal and righteous in their behavior. Although Wu Han did not record Feng Ang's analyzing military deployment to Yang Su in court, he cited a similar event that echoes the loyalty Feng Ang's grandmother displayed in earlier times.

> At the time when the Sui dynasty ended, Feng Ang controlled a region spanning around two thousand square miles in the areas of Guangzhou, Wuzhou, and Hainan Island. With such a sizable area in control, some people encouraged him to establish himself as the king of Nanyue, but he outright refused to comply. A few years later, in the fifth year of Wude reign (622), he pledged his loyalty to the Tang court with the twenty prefectures he governed. Emperor Gaozu appointed him supreme pillar of state (*shang zhu guo*), area commander-in-chief of Gaozhou, and conferred upon him the title of "Duke of the State of Yue" (*Yue guo gong*). Among his sons, Zhidai was appointed inspector of Chunzhou and Zhiyu was appointed inspector of Donghezhou. Zhidai, who was brave and strategic, also became famous during his time and rose to the rank of general of militant guard of the left (*zuo wuwei jiangjun*).[56]

Wu Han continues to introduce another well-known descendant of the Fengs during the Tang dynasty: Emperor Xuanzong's (r. 712–55) favorite eunuch Gao Lishi, the great-grandson of Feng Ang and the great-great-great-grandson of Consort Xian. He then provides two paragraphs of praise, commending Consort Xian's contributions to history and to China as a nation.

> Consort Xian was a famous leader of the Yue minority people of our nation in the ancient time. Throughout her life, she was a hero in her youth and became even more courageous as she grew older. She was brave and good at war; she was composed and strategic. She strove to cooperate with the Han people and the enterprise of unifying the country: in her own circles, she advocated peace and

stability and forestalled peoples' fighting with each other; to rebels and corrupt officers, she was relentless in sending out punitive expeditions and in uncovering them. In the seventy years of her life from when she started commanding troops to her death, she was the stalwart who presided with peace and stability in southern Guangdong. Because of her teaching and example, her sons and grandsons were also brave and good at war, and who became famous military commanders who strove for ethnic cooperation and national unity. For the hundred and ten or so years between her and Feng Zhidai [her great-grandson], the history of the Fengs is inseparable from that of the peaceful and steady lives of the many southern peoples of Guangdong. Because of her and her sons' and grandsons' efforts, the local area was stable and productive. They provided extraordinary contributions to the ethnic harmony and development of our nation.

Consort Xian was an outstanding personage of the Yue people of our country and one of the most outstanding women in the history of our country. She contributed to the stability of people's lives and the development of products of the local area during her time, and she contributed to the unity and unification of many ethnic peoples of our homeland. Such people should be affirmed and praised.[57]

The central focus of these two paragraphs is national unity, but since nationhood is such a modern notion, it is difficulty to fathom what exactly would be the definition of "national unity" for Consort Xian's time. Did it mean the point of view of the Han people or a central government (namely, a political entity presiding over the central plain, of whichever ethnic people)? The first would not make sense for dynasties not founded by the Han people; this means not only the many transient dynasties during Consort Xian's own time but also the Yuan (1279–1368) and the Qing (1644–1912) dynasties of strong Mongolian and Manchurian rulers. The second definition of a central government is even more vague. How should the central plain be defined, when each dynasty had a different capital and territory? To credit Consort Xian's contribution to the "national unity" is to apply a historical event to a modern notion formed long after the event. There is something ahistorical about such an application, the frequent use of "nation" (*minzu*, literally "people of the clan"), and the call for other "minority peoples" to cooperate with the Han people. The ethnocentric position is clear: this mentality comes from the Han point of view.

But Wu Han is not alone in this Han-centric interpretation. Lin Tianwei's comments on Consort Xian's activities and their influence are similar in spirit. Although all three biographies focus on the Fengs and practically ignore the Xians after the initial introduction of Consort Xian's family background, it is Lin Tianwei who drives home the point that the later development of the two families is closely related to Consort Xian. According to Lin, influenced by Consort Xian's attitude in embracing "the culture of the Central Plain," the Fengs prospered, especially during the Sui and Tang dynasties; on the other hand, the Xians opposed Consort Xian's policy and maintained their local cultural color, and therefore produced fewer famous people.[58] The fact is that both the Fengs and the Xians remained prominent clans of South China well into our own time.[59] Somehow, it is hard to assume that any family is not flourishing when it survives well over fourteen centuries and maintains a sound line of descendants.

The last part of Wu Han's conclusion calls for dramatists to write historical plays based on her life. Wu Han's suggestion actually reflects an age-old Chinese saying: "history and literature are inseparable" (*wen shi bufen*). If there is any doubt about an incident in the biographies, a dramatization of Consort Xian's story will legitimize it in the collective mind of the people. Vague references will come to life through lively embellishments by a mighty pen. Regardless of how the historical Consort Xian actually lived, a new fictional Consort Xian will replace her in much more vivid details, as with the women generals of the Yang family and many other legendary women warriors in Chinese opera.

Conclusion

To be sure, the three biographies tell us very few intimate details about the historical person of Consort Xian; nevertheless, they provide us with remarkable information about the biographers' own times and about themselves. In general, the biography in the *Suishu* is most personal; there are details describing her as a young woman before marriage, as a capable wife helping Feng Bao govern, and as a capable mother and grandmother admonishing her children. She is no doubt the subject of the biography, and the direct dialogue gives her own voice, whether it is truly hers. The Ming biography presents Consort Xian mainly as a sage ancestor of the Feng clan, reflecting the stringent development of Confucian discourse on women of the late-imperial times. The modern version by Wu Han recognizes Xian as a remarkable minority woman, who contributed tremendously to the unity of the Han people, displaying his own inclination of a pan-Han China.

More specifically, through the examination of how the three biographies treat one single incident, we can see the different foci and preoccupations of each era. Toward the end of her life during the Sui dynasty, the court awarded posthumous ranks and titles to her dead husband and son and new ranks and higher positions to her grandsons, her late son's concubine, and herself. The biography in the *Suishu* gives a detailed account of how Consort Xian carefully placed the gifts from the Sui emperor and empress in gold chests (along with previous imperial gifts from the Liang and the Chen dynasties), and displayed them every year on important occasions. At such times, she would also instruct her children and grandchildren:

> You should all pay loyalty to the throne. I have served masters of three dynasties, and always with the same good intention. Now all the rewards from them are here as evidence. They are the *reward* [my emphasis] of loyalty and filial piety; you should all ponder this.[60]

The direct quotation of Consort Xian's instruction to her posterity is a curious convention of Chinese historiography, in which direct quotations are often only the historian's interpretations of conjectured historical events. More likely, such direct quotes become a means for the historian to give life to his subject, a practice applied by the Grand Historian Sima Qian (ca. 145–ca. 85 BCE) when he wrote the first official history some 2,000 ago. However unreal, the voice is identified with a woman subject; however questionable, the voice becomes Consort Xian. In contrast, Wang Daokun's Ming biography simply lists the ranks, titles, private secretariat, and seal granted to Feng Ang (one of the grandsons), Feng Bao, and Consort Xian. None of the material awards given to Consort Xian personally is mentioned, and the whole incident of her admonishing her sons and grandsons is omitted. Thus, not only is her voice gone, but also the focus shifts to how her actions benefited the Fengs, changing the subject matter at the end of the biography from Consort Xian to her grandson Feng Ang.

Wu Han's "Consort Xian" tends to be the most inclusive, and this incident is no exception. However, where the *Suishu* gives Consort Xian an active voice and employs an idea of karmic retribution to emphasize the gravity of loyalty and filiality, Wu Han's text drops the phrase "reward of loyalty and filiality" (*zhongxiao zhi bao*), which simply contains too many contradictions. First, the embedded connotation of karmic retribution embedded in the character *bao* would not go well with a Marxist view of social evolution. Second, applying the notions of loyalty and filiality to Consort Xian's shifting allegiance is simply problematic. If to be loyal means to be faithful to the state, which one—the Liang, the Chen, or the Sui—is Consort Xian loyal to? Wu Han resorts to a third-person narrative and avoids the phrase altogether: she "admonished her sons and grandsons to be loyal to the country. She also said that she herself lived through three dynasties with none but good intentions. That was how she was able to accumulate all these items, and all future generations should do as she did."[61] Only when we see a Han government as representing the center does Consort Xian's unfailing loyalty make sense.

The three biographies reflect how the Confucian tradition produced a specific discourse to assimilate the history of a peripheral woman. As Michel Foucault opined, "in every society the production of discourse is at once controlled, selected, organized and redistributed according to a certain number of procedures, whose role is to avert its powers and its dangers, to cope with chance events, to evade its ponderous, awesome materiality."[62] Here, Consort Xian's biography is tailored to fit within the Confucian moral framework. With military prowess, love of peace, and loyalty as her underlying virtues, Consort Xian's life was written to epitomize that of an obedient ethnic subject. Although the dynasties changed, her faithfulness to the central regime—the one in power at the moment—remained constant. Hence, in stark contrast to the later non-Han challengers to Chinese dominion, such as those discussed in this volume by Michael McGrath and James Anderson, while remaining autonomous, Consort Xian negotiated a relationship with the Han state that was felicitous and characterized most of all by a spirit of cooperation. Her sixth- and early-seventh-century interactions with Han central authority were more keeping with what Michael Brose describes of the dealings of the various Uyghur leaders with their Mongol patrons in the thirteenth and early-fourteenth centuries. Her exemplary life and approach to governance therefore became lauded as typifying those of a model ethnic leader, with her absolute loyalty to the central government taken as surpassing even that of many Han military officials.

Thus, rather than being merely a paradigm for women to emulate, Consort Xian's biography is intended to reach even further to influence and inspire scholars and officers who either were or one day would be ruling the people and serving the throne. She was a reminder to Han officials that peripheral ethnic loyalty could and should be achieved by the center; thus her shifts of loyalty were overlooked. It is with such sentiments that the famed poet-politician Su Shi (1036–1101) wrote a commemorative poem on Consort Xian, when he was exiled to Dan'er and visited her temple (see figure 1.4).[63] The first part of the poem reviews her life contribution, and the second part Su Shi's sentiments toward this extraordinary woman. What unites the past and the future is the present, the dilapidated temple of a bygone paragon: "Her temple—though bare—survived;/The tablets, their inscriptions gone, lie scattered around." This poetic structure reflects what Consort Xian does to those who wrote about her: her life provides them with a means to breach the past and the future and, more importantly, to reconcile with their own unfulfilled present. Recognizing her steadfast loyalty to the central governments gives meaning and value to the poet's own suffering.

Similarly, the late-Ming and early-Qing painter-poet Jin Guliang collected Consort Xian along with thirty-nine other unusual personages throughout history in an illustrated volume.[64] Each illustration is accompanied by a brief introduction on the side and a "music-bureau" (*yuefu*) poem within a stylish traditional design on the following leaf. The poem that Jin Guliang sang for Consort Xian is appropriately enclosed in a circle clasped in the mouth of a lion on the handle of a highly decorated sword (see figures 1.2 and 1.3). Both the short introduction next to the illustration and the poem Jin composed describe the fulfilling life of a "minority" woman recognized by the Han court for her military valor. Yet, according to one of Jin's friends, Jin compiled this volume to "vent the frustrations of those who were treated unfairly through hundreds and thousands of years."[65] It is not clear if this indeed is Jin Guliang's intention, especially when the courts that Consort Xian served clearly acknowledged and respected her achievements. Thus, the inclusion of Consort Xian in Jin Guliang's collection may well reflect more his own sentiments and those of fellow literati scholars whose allegiances toward the court were, for one reason or another, either neglected, unfulfilled, or unrecognized.

I here offer a final speculation on how we should distinguish Consort Xian from most male commanders in traditional Chinese history, and certainly from all those who appear in her biographies. The goal of her rule and her strategies was never to surpass others. She fought her battles to maintain peace in the region, exemplifying the ancient wisdom of "fighting for the sake of peacekeeping." As a shrewd strategist, she successfully governed over an array of dissimilar groups, quelled local revolts, and allied herself with the winners in nearly every political transition. Her leadership raises fascinating interpretive issues pertaining to the essence of warfare and fighting. Might she have done more? This is a legitimate question to ask. But given the fates of all those rebels she helped to quell, she might have been intentionally measured in what she wanted to accomplish. In the end, perhaps we are left

The Consort Surnamed Xian of the State of Qiao

Translated by Sherry J. Mou

Consort Xian was from Gaoliang, and she was married to Feng Bao, the grand protector of Gaoliang. She assisted Feng Bao in military affairs. When Li Qianshi rebelled, she came up with a stratagem to defeat him. After Feng Bao died, the Consort called together tribes all over Baiyue to be under her command. Her son Feng Pu was awarded the title Duke of Xindu because of her military merits. After Feng Pu died, the Consort led her grandsons to inspect all regions, thus, bringing peace to the entire Lingnan area. Later Li and Liao peoples rebelled, and the Consort brought with her an edict from the emperor and conveyed the emperor's words to people. Wherever she went, people surrendered. She lived from the beginning years of the Datong reign of the Liang dynasty to the Renshou years of the Sui dynasty. She was bestowed the title of Consort of Sincerity and Respect posthumously.

Figure 1.2 Illustration of Consort Xian in Jin Guliang's Catalogue of the Unparalleled.

Source: *Wushuang pu*, seventeenth century CE.

Consort Xian

Translated by Sherry J. Mou

As the wife of the grand protector of Gaoliang
    She led steely revelry and defeated all those to the west of Gan;
As the mother of the grand protector of Gaoliang
    She snatched a gold seal to decorate her son's arm;
As the emissary of Gaoliang
    She recruited even rebels and ensured their unwavering loyalty.
Thus, all tribes in Baiyue enjoyed sustained peace,
    As the Consort took the helm for seventy years.
The men in the Middle Country changed dynasties three times all the while
    When a mere woman was able to hold on to the scepter.

Shetang

Figure 1.3 A poetic sword-handle inscription in Jin Guliang's Catalogue of the Unparalleled.

Source: *Wushuang pu*, seventeenth century CE.

with nothing more than one woman's practical and calculating strategies for meeting life's countless challenges of fighting off the enemies of one's family, territory, and autonomy. Consort Xian did no less, and she did so with resolve and finesse that were as winning as they were peaceful. But this, too, is only another version of a life most likely well spent.

蘇軾 〈和陶擬古九首〉之五

馮冼古烈婦，翁媼國於茲。
策勳梁武後，開府隋文時。
三世更險易，一心無磷緇。
錦繖平積亂，犀渠破餘疑。
廟貌空復存，碑版漫無辭。
我欲作銘誌，慰此父老思。
遺民不可問，僂句莫予欺。
犧牲菌雞卜，我當一訪之。
銅鼓壺盧笙，歌此送迎詩。

Su Shi, Fifth of "Nine Responses to Tao Qian's 'Imitations of the Ancient'"

Translated by Sherry J. Mou

An ancient staunch woman was this Mrs. Feng of the Xian family,
An old woman of state.

Her deeds awarded her honorable ranks shortly after the reign of Emperor Wu of the Liang dynasty, and
She established her own private secretariat during Emperor Wen of the Sui dynasty.

Over three dynasties she passed through dangers and changes,
Yet her devotion was not shaken at all.

Under an embroidered umbrella, she quelled chronic turmoil, and
Her lingering doubt (about her loyalty to the demised Chen dynasty) was removed through the bringing of the rhinoceros horn (cane).

Her temple—though bare—survived;
The tablets, their inscriptions gone, lie scattered around.

I would like to write some eulogy
To ease the concern of the local elders.

But forgotten people cannot be consulted,
Nor do I understand the Lo dialect.

It is said that they offer sacrifices and read fortunes from chicken marks;
I should like to go and visit them

To hear the bronze drums and gourd pipes
and to sing this poem as my eulogy.

Figure 1.4 Commemorative poem for Consort Xian by Su Shi, 1036–1101.

Notes

I extend my thanks to the following DePauw University colleagues for their comments: Meryl Altman, Scott Sanborn, Andrea Sununu, Melanie Finney, Harry Brown, Kerry Pannell, Kevin Howley, and Scott Spiegelberg. My thanks also go to the DePauw Asian Studies Committee for awarding me the Freeman Faculty Summer Scholarship through the Freeman Foundation that enabled me to travel to Hainan Island and secure material that has substantially augmented this chapter. Finally, I give my sincerest thanks to Juris Lidaka and Don Wyatt for their unlimited patience and support. All translations are mine unless otherwise noted.

1. See Liu Xiang, *Lienü zhuan*, *SBBY* edn. (rpr. Taibei, 1983).
2. The official histories are government-sponsored official dynastic histories. There are twenty-five such histories all together, covering events over four millennia. For an account of the development of the tradition of women's biographies in Chinese official history, see Chapter 1, "From Biographies of Women to Biographies of Chaste Women," in Sherry J. Mou, *Gentlemen's Prescriptions for Women's Lives: A Thousand Years of Biographies of Chinese Women* (Armonk, NY, 2004).
3. The term *ordinary women* is here intended as relative, in comparison to *imperial women*, for many of the women recorded in these histories acted most extraordinarily compared to common people. As far as official historiography is concerned, *Hou Hanshu* was the first work with a special chapter on the empresses. See "Chronicles of the Empresses" ("Huanghou ji") section in the History of the Later Han Dynasty ("Hou Hanshu") of Fan Ye (398–446) (Beijing, 1965), *juan* 10. "Biographies of Women" ("Lienü") is found in *juan* 84 of the same work.
4. Michel Foucault, *The Archaeology of Knowledge*, tr. A. M. Sheridan Smith (New York, 1972), pp. 159–60.
5. All official titles follow Charles O. Hucker, *A Dictionary of Official Titles in Imperial China* (Stanford, 1985).
6. Michel Foucault, "What Is an Author?" In *Language, Counter-Memory, Practice: Selected Essays and Interviews by Michel Foucault*, tr. Donald F. Bouchard and Sherry Simon (Ithaca, NY, 1977), p. 138.
7. The earliest reference to Mulan derives from "The Ballad of Mulan" ("Mulan ci"). See Guo Maoqian, comp. and ed., *Yuefu shiji* (Shanghai, 1998), 25.307–8. Maxine Hong Kingston's *Woman Warrior* introduced Mulan to feminist scholars in 1980s and 1990s, and the Disney animated film feature has made her a household name. Mulan's historical existence is, however, still much debated.
8. The women generals of the Yang family remain a favorite Peking opera topic.
9. Qin Liangyu (1574–1648) is the only woman in all the official histories whose biography is not among the "biographies of women" (*lienü zhuan*) or the "empresses and imperial concubines" (*houfei zhuan*) sections. The implication is that Qin is included instead in the sections of the *Mingshi* (History of the Ming Dynasty) usually reserved for men because of what she did, not just for being a woman. See Zhang Tingyu, *Mingshi* (Beijing, 1974), 270.6944–48. Liang Hongyu's twelfth-century life is described within the official biography of her husband Han Shizhong (1089–1151) in the *Songshi* (History of the Song Dynasty). See Tuotuo, *Songshi* (Beijing, 1977) 364.11355–72.
10. See Wei Zheng, *Suishu* (Beijing, 1973), 80.1800–1803.
11. See Li Yanshou, *Beishi* (Beijing, 1974), 91.3005–7.

12. See Ruan Yuan, [*Daoguang*] *Guangdong tongzhi* (*1821–50*), *juan* 28. For a detailed discussion of the history and development of Li people, see Bai Cuiqin, *Wei-Jin Nanbei chao minzu shi* (Zigong, Sichuan, 1996), pp. 440–45; and Lu Xun, Xiao Zhixing, and Liang Qiyuan, *Sui-Tang minzu shi* (Zigong, Sichuan, 1996), pp. 216–48.
13. My use of "tribal peoples" refers to the non-Han inhabitants who lived semi-autonomous of the jurisdiction of Han central governments. Although many received titles and ranks from the central governments, they generally lived by their own customs, social organization, and norms.
14. Carolyn G. Heilbrun, *Writing a Woman's Life* (New York, 1988), p. 28.
15. Nancy Swann, *Pan Chao: Foremost Woman Scholar of China* (New York, 1932). For Ban Zhao's biography, see *Hou Hanshu*, 84.2784–92.
16. Ban Zhao's biography contains about 2,218 characters, of which her "Admonitions for Women" takes about 1,512 characters and a memorial to the empress dowager takes another 207, leaving the actual biography at some 499 characters. Consort Xian's biography contains about 1,425 characters.
17. Nanyue ranges generally from modern Guangzhou to the Hainan Island area.
18. Some sources trace the Xians' genealogy back to the end of the First Emperor's reign in the late-third century BCE. But Lin Tianwei expresses reservations because supporting historical evidence is absent. See Lin Tianwei, "Sui Qiaoguo furen shiji zhiyi ji qi xianghua yu yingxiang," in *Zhongguo funü shi lunwen ji*, ed. Li Youning and Zhang Yufa (Taibei, 1988), 2:146–47.
19. *Suishu*, 80.1800–1801.
20. *Suishu*, 80.1801.
21. *Suishu*, 80.1801.
22. *Suishu*, 80.1801.
23. *Suishu*, 80.1801.
24. *Suishu*, 80.1801.
25. For Hou Jing's rebellion, see Sima Guang, *Zizhi tongjian* (Beijing, 1995), *juan* 161–64.
26. *Suishu*, 80.1801.
27. *Suishu*, 80.1801.
28. *Suishu*, 80.1802.
29. *Suishu*, 80.1802.
30. *Suishu*, 80.1802.
31. *Suishu*, 80.1802.
32. *Suishu*, 80.1802.
33. *Suishu*, 80.1802.
34. *Suishu*, 80.1803.
35. That the concubine of Consort Xian's late son shared the same surname may indicate a close relationship between the two women. Perhaps the concubine was chosen from her own kinspeople. The transferred title of *Songkang*, a commandery that was conferred to the Consort earlier, also suggests a close tie between the two women because such transfers were usually made at the request of the individuals holding the titles.
36. *Suishu*, 80.1803.
37. *Suishu*, 80.1803.
38. Starting with the *Songshu* (History of the Song [of the Southern Dynasties]), Li and Liao peoples are often mentioned together in most of the later official histories. See Shen Yue, *Songshu* (Beijing, 1973) 97.2379. Some sources cite the

two as different peoples, while others consider the two to be the same. See Lu Xun, Xiao Zhixing, and Liang Qiyuan, *Sui-Tang minzu shi*, pp. 216–20.
39. *Suishu*, 80.1803.
40. *Suishu*, 80.1803.
41. For example, in the eleventh biography, Zhong Shixiong's mother instructed him not to forget the favor from the current emperor, enabling them to be reunited, and warned that she would commit suicide in front of him if he joined the rebels. See *Suishu*, 80.1809.
42. As most women assume more than one of these roles, the primary roles assumed by these women were often distinguished in their biographies.
43. Wang Daokun, comp. and ed., *Lienü zhuan* (rpr. Beijing, 1991). The preface by Wang Yu indicates this work is a reproduction of the Ming edition, which was possibly compiled in the early sixteenth century and published during the Wanli reign years (1573–1620).
44. Wang Daokun, *Lienü zhuan*, 7.21a–22b.
45. Wang Daokun, *Lienü zhuan*, 7.22.
46. The most visible and effective result is Liu Xiang's compilation of the first collection of women's biographies.
47. *Suishu*, 80.1800.
48. *Beishi*, 93.3079–80.
49. *Suishu*, 80.1801.
50. *Zizhi tongjian*, 162.3361.
51. Wang Daokun, *Lienü zhuan*, 7.24b.
52. This incident, in which Feng Ang met with Yang Su and Yang offered his subsequent comment about Feng, has its origin first in the *Xin Tangshu* (New History of the Tang Dynasty) and later in Sima Guang's *Zizhi tongjian*. See Ouyang Xiu and Song Qi, *Xin Tangshu* (Beijing, 1975), 110.4112 and *Zizhi tongjian*, 179.3747.
53. Wang Daokun, *Lienü zhuan*, 7.24b.
54. Wu Han's "Xian furen" is collected in his *Chuntian ji* (Collection of the Spring) (Beijing, 1961), pp. 179–84.
55. See Lin Tianwei, "Sui Qiaoguo furen," 2:159, n. 4.
56. Wu Han, "Xian furen," p. 183.
57. Wu Han, "Xian furen," pp. 183–84.
58. Lin Tianwei, "Sui Qiaoguo furen," 2:157–59.
59. Although the Xians are not as prominent as the Fengs in the official histories, the Xian clan has undoubtedly thrived well into the modern times. The Xians remain one of the established families in many quarters of the Guangdong area, as Lin Tianwei himself has quoted many times from various sources about the Xians. See Lin Tianwei, "Sui Qiaoguo furen," 2:159 and n. 2, 5–8, and 47.
60. *Suishu*, 80.1803.
61. Wu Han, "Xian furen," p. 182.
62. Foucault, *Archaeology of Knowledge*, p. 216.
63. Su Shi's poem as well as a translation are provided in figure 1.4. The poem, the fifth of nine in a series in response to those of Tao Qian (365–427) ("He Tao nigu jiushou"), is taken from Su Shi, *Su Wenzhong gong shi bian zhu jicheng* (1819; rpr. Taibei, 1967), 6:3506–8.
64. Jin Guliang, *Wushuang pu*, with the portions of the version reproduced here being from a reprint of an edition printed during the Kangxi reign (1662–1722) (Shanghai,

1961). *Wushuang pu* [Catalogue of the Unparalleled] is a collection covering forty famous people from the former Han dynasty (206 BCE–CE 25) to the Southern Song dynasty (1127–1279), including military commanders, historians, writer-poets, and other prominent men and women, such as Zhang Liang, Zhuge Liang, Yue Fei, Sima Qian, Ban Zhao, Tao Qian, Li Bo, Zhao E, Lü Zhu, and the legendary Mulan.

65. See Tao Shiyu, "Preface to Catalogue of the Unparalleled" ("*Wushuang pu* xu") in Jin Guliang, *Wushuang pu*.

Glossary

Bei Wei 北魏
Bei Yan 北燕
Baiyue 百越
Ban Zhao 班昭
Beishi 北史
Changcheng hou 長城侯
Chao 潮
Chen Baxian 陳霸先
Cheng 成
Chengjing furen 誠敬夫人
Chuntian ji 春天集
Chunzhou 春州
Dan'er 儋耳
Donghezhou 東合州
dudu 都督
Fan Ye 范曄
Feng Ang 馮盎
Feng Bao 馮寶
Feng Hun 馮魂
Feng Pu 馮僕
Feng Rong 馮融
Feng Xuan 馮暄
Feng Ye 馮業
Funan 扶南
Ganshi 灨石
Gao Lishi 高力士
Gaoan 高安
Gaoliang 高涼
Gaozhou cishi 高州刺史
Gaozu 高祖
Guangdong 廣東
Guangxi 廣西
Guangzhou 廣州
Guangzhou zongguan 廣州總管
Guo Maoqian 郭茂倩
Hainan 海南
Han 漢
Han Shizhong 韓世忠
Hanyang taishou 漢陽太守

"He Tao nigu jiushou" 和陶擬古九首
Hou Hanshu 後漢書
Hou Jing 侯景
houfei zhuan 后妃傳
"Huanghou ji" 皇后紀
Jin 晉
Jin Guliang 金古良
juan 卷
Kangxi 康熙
Li 俚
li 禮
Li Bo 李白
Li Qianshi 李遷仕
Li Yanshou 李延壽
Liang Hongyu 梁紅玉
Liao 獠
"Lienü" 列女
lienü zhuan 列女傳
Lin Tianwei 林天蔚
Lingnan 嶺南
Liu Xiang 劉向
Longcheng 龍城
Lü Zhu 綠珠
Luozhou 羅州
Luozhou cishi 羅州刺史
minzu 民族
Ming 明
mufu 幕府
Mulan 木蘭
"Mulan ci" 木蘭辭
Nankang 南康
Nanyue 南越
nüde 女德
Ouyang He 歐陽紇
Ouyang Xiu 歐陽修
Pei Ju 裴矩
ping Yue zhonglang jiang 平越中郎將
Qiao guo furen 譙國夫人
Qiao guo gong 譙國公
Qin Liangyu 秦良玉
Qing 清
Qiu Ying 仇英
Renshou 仁壽
Shilong taishou 石龍太守
Shilong tai furen 石龍太夫人
Sima Guang 司馬光
Sima Qian 司馬遷
Songkang jun furen 宋康郡夫人
Songkang yi 宋康邑

Su Shi 蘇軾
Suishu 隋書
taishou 太守
Tao Qian 陶潛
Tao Shiyu 陶式玉
Wanli 萬歷
Wang Daokun 汪道昆
Wang Yu 汪庾
Wang Zhongxuan 王仲宣
Wei Guang 韋洸
wen shi bufen 文史不分
Wu Han 吳晗
Wude 武德
Wushuang pu 無雙譜
"*Wushuang pu* xu" 無雙譜序
Xian furen 冼夫人
Xiao Bo 蕭勃
Xindu hou 信都侯
Xinhui 新會
Xu Deng 徐璒
Xuanzong 玄宗
Yang *jia jiang* 楊家將
Yang Su 楊素
Yangchun junshou 陽春郡守
Yangdi 煬帝
yitong sansi 儀同三司
Yue 越
Yue Fei 岳飛
Yue guo gong 越國公
yuefu 樂府
Zhang Liang 張良
Zhang Zhaoda 章昭達
Zhaocheng 昭成
Zhao E 趙娥
Zhao Na 趙訥
Zhidai 智戴
Zhide 至德
zhijie 志節
Zhiyu 智彧
Zhong Shixiong 鍾士雄
zhongxiao zhi bao 忠孝之報
Zhuge Liang 諸葛亮
zongguan 總管

Bibliography

Bai Cuiqin 白翠琴. *Wei-Jin Nanbei chao minzu shi* 魏晉南北朝民族史 [Ethnic History of the Wei-Jin and Northern and Southern Dynasties]. Zigong, Sichuan: Xinhua shudian, 1996.

Fan Ye 范曄. *Hou Hanshu* 後漢書 [History of the Later Han Dynasty]. Beijing: Zhonghua shuju, 1965.

Foucault, Michel. *The Archaeology of Knowledge*, tr. A. M. Sheridan Smith. New York: Pantheon Books, 1972.

———. *Language, Counter-Memory, Practice: Selected Essays and Interviews by Michel Foucault*, tr. Donald F. Bouchard and Sherry Simon. Ithaca, NY: Cornell University Press, 1977.

Guo Maoqian 郭茂倩, comp. and ed. *Yuefu shiji* 樂府詩集 [Collection of Music-Bureau Poems]. Shanghai: Shanghai guji chubanshe, 1998.

Heilbrun, Carolyn G. *Writing a Woman's Life*. New York: Ballantine Books, 1988.

Hucker, Charles O. *A Dictionary of Official Titles in Imperial China*. Stanford: Stanford University Press, 1985.

Jin Guliang 金古良. *Wushuang pu* 無雙譜 [Catalogue of the Unparalleled]. rpr. Shanghai: Zhonghua shuju, 1961.

Li Yanshou 李延壽. *Beishi* 北史 [History of the Northern Dynasties]. Beijing: Zhonghua shuju, 1974.

Lin Tianwei 林天蔚. "Sui Qiaoguo furen shiji zhiyi ji qi xianghua yu yingxiang" 隋譙國夫人事蹟質疑及其嚮化與影響 [Inquiring into Certain Doubts about the Life of as well as the Sinicization and Its Influence on the Consort of the Qiao State of the Sui Dynasty]. In *Zhongguo funü shi lunwen ji* 中國婦女史論文集 [Collections of Essays on Chinese Women's History], vol. 2, ed. Li Youning 李又寧 and Zhang Yufa 張玉法, 2 vols. Taibei: Shangwu yinshuguan, 1988:145–62.

Liu Xiang 劉向. *Lienü zhuan* 列女傳 [Biographies of Women]. *Sibu beiyao* (*SBBY*) 四部備要 [Essentials of the Four Literary Divisions] edn. Taibei: Zhonghua shuju, 1983.

Lu Xun 盧勛, Xiao Zhixing 蕭之興, and Liang Qiyuan 梁啟源. *Sui-Tang minzu shi* 隋唐民族史 [Ethnic History of the Sui and Tang Dynasties]. Zigong, Sichuan: Xinhua shudian, 1996.

Mou, Sherry J. *Gentlemen's Prescriptions for Women's Lives: A Thousand Years of Biographies of Chinese Women*. Armonk, NY: M.E. Sharpe, 2004.

Ouyang Xiu 歐陽修 and Song Qi 宋祁. *Xin Tangshu* 新唐書 [New History of the Tang dynasty]. Beijing: Zhonghua shuju, 1975.

Ruan Yuan 阮元. *[Daoguang] Guangdong tongzhi* 道光廣東通志 [General History of Guangdong (for the Daoguang Years, 1821–50)]. 7 vols. Shanghai: Shanghai guji chubanshe, 1995–99.

Shen Yue 沈約. *Songshu* 宋書 [History of the Song Dynasty]. Beijing: Zhonghua shuju, 1973.

Sima Guang 司馬光. *Zizhi tongjian* 資治通鑒 [Comprehensive Mirror Aiding Government]. 6 vols. Beijing: Gaige chubanshe, 1995.

Su Shi 蘇軾. "He Tao nigu jiushou" 和陶擬古九首 [Responding to Tao Qian's "Nine Poems Imitating the Ancient Style"]. In *Su Wenzhong gong shi bian zhu jicheng* 蘇文忠公詩編註集成 [Collectania of Su Shi's Poetry with Annotations], ed. Wang Wengao 王文誥 (1819). 6 vols. rpr. Taibei: Xuehsheng shuju, 1967.

Swann, Nancy. *Pan Chao: Foremost Woman Scholar of China*. New York: Century, 1932.

Tuotuo 脫脫. *Songshi* 宋史 [History of the Song Dynasty]. Beijing: Zhonghua shuju, 1977.

Wang Daokun 汪道昆, comp. and ed. *Lienü zhuan* 列女傳 [Biographies of Women]. 16 *juan*. With a Preface by Wang Yu 汪庚 (1779). rpr. Beijing: Zhongguo shudian, 1991.

Wei Zheng 魏徵. *Suishu* 隋書 [History of the Sui Dynasty]. Beijing: Zhonghua shuju, 1973.

Wu Han 吳晗. *Chuntian ji* 春天集 [Collection of the Spring]. Beijing: Zuojia chubanshe, 1961.

Zhang Tingyu 張廷玉. *Mingshi* 明史 [History of the Ming Dynasty]. Beijing: Zhonghua shuju, 1974.

CHAPTER 2

PROVINCIAL AUTONOMY AND FRONTIER DEFENSE IN LATE TANG: THE CASE OF THE LULONG ARMY

David A. Graff

We can group the forty or so military provinces into which Tang China was divided in the aftermath of the An Lushan Rebellion (755–63) in several broad categories on the basis of their region, function, and attitude toward the Tang court in Chang'an. Representing one extreme were several highly militarized provinces that enjoyed a very high degree of autonomy, paid no taxes to the center, and insisted on the right of hereditary succession to the office of military governor (*jiedushi*). The longest lasting of these autonomous provinces were the so-called "three garrisons of Hebei" (*Hebei san zhen*: Youzhou, Chengde, and Wei-Bo), whose military leaders traced their origins to the rebel armies of An Lushan (d. 757). Facing these recalcitrant provinces across a confrontation line that ran along the Taihang Mountains (Taihang shan) and over the Henan Plain was a string of loyalist provinces that also maintained powerful military forces. Those in Henan were especially sensitive because they guarded the Bian Canal (Bian he), the principal route for tax and tribute revenues from the rich Lower Yangzi region and therefore the logistical lifeline of the Tang court. The southern provinces that provided the economic underpinning for imperial power were only lightly garrisoned, and their governors tended to be civil officials rather than military men. Revenues from the south made it possible to sustain another group of heavily armed loyalist provinces, located in relatively poor areas north and west of Chang'an, whose primary responsibility was to protect the capital from the Tibetans. The functional differentiation and interdependence of the late Tang military provinces was noted as early as the middle of the ninth century, and the picture has since been elaborated by modern scholars such as Chen Yinque (1889–1969), Denis Twitchett, and Zhang Guogang.[1]

The differing regional characteristics of the provinces provide an important key to understanding late Tang politics. At the same time, however, the regional classification tends to obscure the fact that each of the Tang provinces was different and unique, with its own distinct history and problems. Not all of them fit comfortably in the categories to which they have been assigned. A particularly anomalous case is that of Youzhou (also known as Lulong, as one of its governor's concurrent titles was military commissioner of the Lulong army), which occupied the northernmost part of Hebei and had its headquarters at Jixian, roughly the site of today's Beijing. Youzhou Lulong is almost always classified as one of the troublesome autonomous provinces. It was the original base of An Lushan, and its early post-rebellion leaders were men who had served An and his successors in their war against the Tang court. Nominally pacified by the beginning of 763, the military men of Lulong chose their own leaders and sent no taxes to the capital, and their autonomous regime managed to outlive the Tang dynasty by several years. Alone among the autonomous provinces, however, Youzhou faced one of the empire's sensitive external frontiers; to the north and northeast of its garrisons and border forts were the pastures of the nomadic Qidan [Khitan] and Xi peoples. In this respect, it had much in common with loyalist provinces that guarded the frontiers north and west of Chang'an. In effect, Youzhou inherited the frontier defense role of the pre-rebellion Fanyang and Pinglu armies. And it proved to be more successful in this role than the forces that guarded this frontier zone both before and after—forces that were fielded by imperial regimes with access to far greater resources than the single province of Youzhou could ever hope to mobilize. How was the Lulong army of Youzhou able to accomplish this feat, and in what ways (if any) did the province's exposed frontier position influence the behavior and policies of its military leaders?

Perhaps the earliest answer to these questions was offered by the authors of the chapter on the Qidan and Xi in the Old Tang History (*Jiu Tangshu*), who pointed out that the provincial military leaders were concerned primarily with ensuring their own security and had no interest in picking fights on the border, with the result that the Qidan and the Xi were not provoked and seldom came to raid.[2] This wise policy is implicitly contrasted with the aggressive behavior of the frontier generals during the reign of Xuanzong (685–762; r. 712–56), who were criticized for starting unnecessary fights (which did not always end in Tang victories) in order to win merit by pandering to the emperor's taste for military glory.[3]

Rather different answers were offered by Matsui Shūichi in his detailed modern study of the political and economic characteristics of the Lulong province, published in *Shigaku zasshi* in 1959.[4] Matsui attributed the defensive strength of Youzhou to intense local loyalties, firm leadership by local elites, and a decentralized military structure placing heavy reliance on local militia forces. Though this structure was an expedient adopted on account of the province's poverty, it yielded impressive results for frontier defense; it was not until after Youzhou had been defeated and absorbed by the Later Tang regime based in Hedong (Shanxi) that the

Qidan were able to make deep inroads into Hebei. While he was concerned primarily with the political, military, and economic peculiarities of Youzhou and did not seek to explore all of the implications of its frontier position, Matsui did offer an ingenious frontier-based explanation for the province's particularly vicious brand of military politics. In contrast to the other autonomous provinces in Hebei and Henan which enjoyed fairly long periods of stable rule by local dynasts, Youzhou was torn by frequent mutinies and coups; of the twenty-seven men who served as military governor between 763 and 913, sixteen came to power through acts of violence directed against their predecessors.[5] The other provinces were not entirely free of coups, but the pattern in Youzhou was unique; not only were there more leadership crises but many of these were also brought on by revolts of outlying garrison commanders—very different from the headquarters coups that were the rule in the other provinces. This situation, Matsui suggested, was because of the need for greater dispersal of military power in order to defend against a greater variety of potential threats: Not only did the Youzhou military governors have to worry about the other provinces to the south and west, but they also had to protect themselves from the Qidan, Xi, and other peoples to the north. Stronger outlying garrisons secured the borders of the province, but they also provided the garrison commanders with bases from which to challenge the authority of the military governor. At the same time, however, Youzhou's exposed frontier position also worked to prevent the province from flying apart entirely; the external threat was so great that the local military leaders had no choice but to hang together for survival, in spite of their occasional bloody disagreements.

This chapter supplements Matsui's work by examining other aspects of Youzhou's frontier situation and other ways in which the frontier defense burden shaped the behavior of the province's leaders. Rather than focusing, as Matsui did, on the internal structures and politics of the Lulong army, it will deal primarily with Youzhou's "foreign relations"—its dealings with the Tang court, with the other military provinces, and with the Qidan, Xi, and Uyghurs (Huihe). Although Matsui saw Youzhou as the most strongly anti-Tang of all the provinces in its attitude and orientation, this view is not borne out by a study of its external relations. On the contrary, the special problems of frontier defense created special bonds between court and province, and Youzhou's frontier location seems to have confirmed rather than weakened its identity as a part of the Tang Empire.

Resources

The Youzhou military province enjoyed far greater administrative stability than the twelfth-century Huainan frontier zone studied by Ruth Mostern. For most of its 150-year history, the province consisted of nine prefectures: You, Zhuo, Mo, Ying[1], Gui, Tan, Ji, Ping, and Ying[2]. These belonged to two very different zones. The prefectures of You, Zhuo, Mo, and Ying[1], stretching southward from today's Beijing to the Zhang River (Zhang shui) in central Hebei, were the economic and demographic heartland of the province. Watered by a number of rivers flowing east and southeast into the Gulf of Bohai (Bohai wan), they had benefited from the construction of irrigation canals and other land reclamation efforts in earlier times. And they were quite densely populated: figures for registered population dating from before the An Lushan Rebellion show several hundred thousand people in each of these four prefectures.[6] If we assume that the population and its distribution were basically the same in the post-rebellion period, they would have accounted for well over 90 percent of the province's total population of approximately 1.5 million. The other five prefectures—Gui and Tan north of the Youzhou Mountains, and Ji, Ping, and Ying[2] reaching eastward along the northern shore of the Bohai—were all sparsely populated areas that were for the most part mountains and grasslands rather than cultivated fields. It was in this marginal zone that the lands dominated by the Lulong garrisons gave way to territories roamed by the Qidan and Xi.

On the basis of this rather limited territory and population, the Lulong leaders seem to have been able to support a regular military establishment of perhaps 40,000 or 50,000 men, not counting militia forces and temporary conscripts.[7] The sources report Youzhou field armies ranging in size from 20,000 up to 100,000 men. The army that Zhu Tao (d. 785) led to rescue Tian Yue (d. 784) of Wei-Bo in 782 was 25,000 strong, and two years later he managed to field 50,000 men (plus 10,000 private retainers and three thousand Uyghur cavalry). In 810, the Lulong military governor Liu Ji (757–810) campaigned against Chengde with 70,000 men and, in 906, Liu Rengong (d. 914), the penultimate military governor of autonomous Youzhou, raised 100,000 reinforcements by scouring the villages and conscripting all males between the ages of fifteen and seventy.[8] Youzhou leaders sometimes claimed to have 300,000 or even 400,000 men at their disposal. Such claims were clearly made to impress and may be safely discounted, but the other figures given in the histories may not be grossly exaggerated.[9]

The frontier location of their province conferred one special advantage upon the Lulong forces in that it gave them relatively easy access to large numbers of horses in an age when cavalry enjoyed both superior mobility and superior striking power on the battlefield (As Michael McGrath points out, this advantage was also enjoyed by another northern frontier power, the Xia State, in its conflict with Northern Song.). The Lulong authorities maintained their own stud farms in their border prefectures and also acquired horses through trade with the steppe peoples (and occasionally as spoils of war).[10] Their access to the resources of the grasslands is evident in the tribute that some of the Youzhou military governors sent to the Tang court. In 821, Liu Zong (d. 821) presented 15,000 horses, and in the following year Zhu Kerong (d. 826) offered to send 10,000 horses and 100,000 sheep.[11] There is some evidence that this abundance of horseflesh enabled Lulong to outfit a very high proportion of its forces as cavalry.[12]

As Matsui has pointed out, Youzhou was surely a poorer province than its more heavily populated southern neighbors, Chengde and Wei-Bo, which occupied rich agricultural regions in central and southern Hebei.[13] Noteworthy, however, is the fact that Youzhou was still able to maintain large military forces on the basis of its own resources. In 742, before the An Lushan Rebellion, there were approximately 90,000 Tang soldiers defending the Youzhou frontier region. These forces had required the annual shipment of 800,000 lengths of fabric and 500,000 *shi* (1 *shi* is a capacity measure equivalent to approximately 60 liters) of grain into Hebei, in addition to whatever could be raised locally.[14] After 763, Youzhou was able to maintain forces of comparable size with no such assistance or subsidy from the outside.[15] And on this basis it was apparently able to do a better job of frontier defense than had been the case before the rebellion: There is no record that the Lulong forces ever suffered a defeat at the hands of the steppe peoples as severe as that which the Qidan inflicted on An Lushan in 751.[16] Youzhou's ability to defend the northeastern frontier on the basis of its own resources may also be contrasted with the situation in much the same region in the years around 1000, when the Song government made substantial commitments of troops and supplies to defend "the great ditch of China."

The Threat from the North

To understand the success of the Lulong military governors in defending their northern border, it is necessary to look not only at the strengths of Youzhou but also at the nature and magnitude of the threat that the province faced. Any meaningful assessment of military power must be couched in relative terms, taking the capabilities and intentions of both sides into account.

The principal threat to Youzhou's northern borders came from the nomadic Qidan and Xi peoples. The Xi roamed the mountains and plains directly to the north of the prefectures of Gui, Tan, and Ping, with their ruler's camp normally located on the upper course of the Tuhuzhen River (Tuhuzhen he). The somewhat stronger Qidan, who, according to Chinese accounts, often feuded with the Xi, were more remote from You. Their territory lay north and east of that of the Xi, and came close to the Lulong territories in only one area—north of the remote northeastern outpost of Yingzhou. Beyond the Qidan were even more remote peoples, the Malgal (Mohe) and the Shiwei, who seldom disturbed the province's borders and on some occasions might even ally with Lulong against the "two barbarians" (as the Qidan and Xi are sometimes labeled in Tang sources). For most of the century and a half of Youzhou's autonomous existence, these peoples were not especially numerous. According to the Old Tang History, the Qidan had 43,000 men capable of bearing arms (*sheng bing*), and the Xi only 30,000.[17] Despite these rather unimpressive numbers, they were capable of doing considerable damage, especially on the rare occasions when they were able to combine their forces. In 696–97, the Qidan captured Yingzhou and Youzhou and overran much of northern and central Hebei before their Xi allies turned against them.[18]

For most of the first century of Youzhou's autonomy, the Qidan and Xi were restrained by Uyghur domination of the steppe. The Uyghurs, with their base on the Orkhon River, were interested primarily in extorting silk from the Tang government in exchange for horses. Their relationship with Tang China was usually not adversarial (at least not in a military sense), and the Qidan and Xi were vassals of the Uyghurs who were watched over by Uyghur supervisors.[19] Even after they regained their freedom of action in 842 following the collapse of the Uyghur Qaghanate, the Qidan at first had little interest in conquering Chinese territory. The unusually long tenure of the Lulong military governor Zhang Yunshen (785–872), twenty-two years beginning in 850, was said to have been a time when the northern border was without alarms.[20] It was only after Abaoji (872–926) emerged as military leader of the Qidan at the beginning of the tenth century that they turned to territorial conquest and began to launch repeated, large-scale offensives against Youzhou.[21] Even then, when Qidan numbers had been greatly augmented through the subjugation of other steppe peoples, Youzhou still managed to retain the upper hand at least until 911 when Ping prefecture was taken by the Qidan.[22] At this time Youzhou had also been weakened by incessant conflicts with powerful Chinese (and Shatuo Türk) warlords to the south and west, and it lost its independence in 913 not to the Qidan but to the Shatuo ruler of Hedong, Li Cunxu (d. 926).

In contrast to the desperate situation on Youzhou's northern frontier at the beginning of the tenth century, the threat to the province during the period of Uyghur dominance was of relatively low intensity. For most of its history, the Lulong army did not have to deal with any foreign threats as serious as those faced by the defenders of some other frontiers examined in this volume, such as late-tenth-century Hebei (Lorge) or twelfth-century Huainan (Mostern). Still, Youzhou's military leaders could never afford to neglect their northern defenses. The following incursions and clashes are known to have occurred on the Youzhou frontier between 763 and 850, and there are surely many others of which there is now no record.

- Youzhou reported Xi raids in 788.[23]
- The Qidan raided Yuyang in 789.[24]
- In 795, Youzhou reported the defeat of more than 60,000 Xi, including their king, Chuoli (d. 795). After Chuoli plundered "Youbeiping," the military governor Liu Ji pursued and defeated him at Qingdushan.[25]
- In 803, a mixed band of men from several tribes plundered north of Tanzhou and Jizhou. Liu Ji joined forces with the Shiwei to chastise them.[26]
- The Xi raided Youzhou in the fourth lunar month of 830. The Lulong military governor Li Zaiyi (788–837) defeated them and captured their king.[27]
- In the fifth month of 842, Lulong forces defeated a group of Uyghurs pressing against the frontier.[28]
- In the fifth month of 847, the Lulong military governor Zhang Zhongwu (d. 849) inflicted a major defeat on the Xi.[29]

The Frontier Role

It is clear that frontier defense remained an important concern for Lulong's military governors throughout the post-rebellion period. It was also a major concern of the imperial court in Chang'an. This created a basis for cooperation between court and province that served the interests of both parties. The Tang court was able to use Youzhou as an intermediary in its dealings with the Qidan and Xi, and might also bring Youzhou's formidable military forces to bear when it wished to guard against a possible incursion from the steppe or launch a strong counterstroke. The benefits gained by Youzhou are less obvious since the center never sent any troops to help defend the province. But the court's goodwill and tacit acquiescence in the province's de facto autonomy were certainly of considerable value in easing Youzhou's difficult security situation, while the military governors were dependent upon the court-bestowed office of *jiedushi* to consolidate their own authority. A provincial military leader who was unable to secure the court's blessing was unlikely to survive for long.[30]

It is possible that cooperation between the Lulong leaders and the Tang court was facilitated not only by local security needs, but also by traditions inherited from the pre-rebellion period. Both before and after the An Lushan Rebellion, the military governor based at Youzhou carried the concurrent title of "commissioner controlling the Xi and Qidan" (*ya Xi Qidan liangfan shi*).[31] Unlike the ex-rebel armies that settled further south in Hebei, the Lulong troops were never separated from their frontier base and their frontier roots. Many of the subordinate units of the Youzhou command, such as armies (*jun*), defense detachments (*shouzhuo*), garrisons (*zhen*), and posts (*shu*), seem to have had a continuous institutional existence since pre-rebellion days, and the ancestors of many of the later Lulong officers had served on the frontier before 755.[32] In what must surely also have been a survival of pre-rebellion practices, Youzhou served as an intermediary in the court's relations with the Qidan and Xi. Tang envoys to the "two barbarians" traveled by way of Youzhou, as did tribute missions going the other direction. It was the custom for Lulong to send thirty to fifty of the more important chiefs on to Chang'an, while the rest of the party of several hundred remained in official lodgings at Youzhou.[33]

Communications from the court to Youzhou seldom failed to include words of praise for the important and heroic service that its leaders were performing on the frontier, and this was especially true of edicts bestowing rewards and conferring new appointments. The edict appointing the second Youzhou military governor, Zhu Xicai (d. 772), to the concurrent post of civil governor (*guanchashi*) describes him as "our battlement and buttress, protecting You and Yan."[34] In 821, the recently deceased military governor Liu Zong was credited with having defended the same regions and kept the North peaceful.[35] An edict sent to Zhang Zhongwu in 842 urged him to "be our Great Wall," and the same image was later employed again to flatter another Youzhou military governor, Liu Rengong.[36] Though it is easy to dismiss this sort of language as the rhetorical boilerplate of the

Secretariat-Chancellery, it is also possible that the court was making a conscious effort to play up the frontier role of the Lulong commanders in the hope of encouraging latent sentiments of loyalty toward the political center of the Chinese world. By drawing a sharp rhetorical line between Youzhou and the pastoral peoples to its north, the court was also reducing the political and emotional distance between Youzhou and Chang'an.

What effect institutional continuities, residual feelings of loyalty, and the rhetorical blandishments of the Tang court had on the actual behavior of the Lulong military leaders is all but impossible to determine. The argument can also be made that, regardless of the sentiments of the province's leaders, Youzhou's frontier position compelled it to serve at least some of the court's interests. This was the position taken by the chief minister Niu Sengru (d. 847) in 831, when the court was faced with the decision of whether or not to confirm a usurper as the Lulong *jiedushi*: "Fanyang [Youzhou] is what the dynasty relies on to hold off the Türks to its north, not allowing them to come south to pillage. If we now grant Yang Zhicheng (d. 835) the insignia of command and give up the land to him, he will certainly exert himself on his own behalf. He will then serve as our teeth and claws, regardless of whether he is obedient or disobedient."[37] In other words, simply by defending his own territory of Youzhou, Yang would also be protecting an important sector of the empire's frontier.

Ideally, however, the Tang court sought not just the passive defense of a frontier zone but the active cooperation of an ally who might strengthen the empire's overall position vis-à-vis the steppe. As the nomadic peoples who lived nearest the Youzhou frontier were also in a position to menace other sectors of the northern border, the mobilization of Youzhou's forces might serve to neutralize the threat. This effect was demonstrated in 788, when a party of Xi and Shiwei raided the territory of the Zhenwu military province at the northeastern corner of the Ordos; if we are to believe the claim made in his epitaph, a show of force by the Youzhou military governor Liu Ji succeeded in putting an end to the disturbance.[38] The closest and most effective cooperation between Youzhou and the court in a matter of frontier defense occurred in 842, when the sack of their capital, Karabalghasun, by the Kirghiz had set large numbers of Uyghurs in motion toward Chinese territory. The Lulong military governor Zhang Zhongwu sent his brother with 30,000 men to attack and defeat an Uyghur chief who had led 7,000 tents of his people to the edge of Youzhou's territory, and then he sent officers to the Qidan and Xi to persuade them to kill their Uyghur supervisors. His activities were part of a concerted effort to cope with the crisis created by the arrival of the Uyghur refugees that was orchestrated from Chang'an by the chief minister Li Deyu (787–850) and involved close cooperation with the forces of several other military governors.[39]

Behavior

Zhang Zhongwu's cooperation with the Tang court during the crisis of 842 fits into a larger pattern of cooperative "foreign policy" behavior on the part of

Lulong's leaders. Although it paid no taxes to the center and insisted on the right to choose its own leaders from within the province, the Lulong army rarely challenged the court once these privileges had been recognized. In its stance toward the imperial court, Lulong occupied an intermediate position among the various "peripheral forces" considered in this volume. Its leaders never adopted the full trappings of sovereignty (as did the Xia leader Yuanhao in 1037, discussed by Michael McGrath) and yet controlled a more substantial base for autonomous power and potential independence than either the Xian family of the far south in the sixth century (examined by Sherry Mou, chapter 1) or the local elites of eleventh-century Huainan (mentioned by Ruth Mostern, chapter 8).

Before the 880s, when the rebellion of Huang Chao (d. 884) fatally weakened the central authority and turned the political situation in North China into a free-for-all between competing warlords, Lulong was in active revolt against the court on only two occasions. The first was from 782 to 784, when Youzhou, led by the unusually ambitious Zhu Tao, first allied with other autonomous military provinces to resist the attempted reassertion of imperial authority by Dezong (742–805) and then made a brief, unsuccessful bid to dominate the empire. The second revolt came in 821, when the only court-selected civilian governor in the province's history, Zhang Hongjing (760–824), was overthrown by mutinous officers. The leader of the mutineers (Zhu Kerong, a grandson of Zhu Tao) ceased his military operations in support of other rebellious provinces as soon as the court recognized him as military governor and acquiesced to the restoration of Youzhou's traditional autonomy.[40]

In contrast to these two instances of rebellion, there were many other occasions when Lulong aligned itself on the side of the court. In 774, for example, Zhu Tao's elder brother and predecessor as military governor, Zhu Ci (742–84), brought several thousand cavalrymen to help defend the capital region against the Tibetans and became the first of the autonomous military governors to come to the imperial court.[41] When Chengde and Wei-Bo rebelled in 780, Zhu Tao initially fought for the court, switching sides only after he was not granted permanent control of some of the territory that he had conquered. During the various crises of the reign of Xianzong (778–820) in the early ninth century, Youzhou's leaders consistently sided with the court and fielded large forces to attack their rebellious southern neighbor, Chengde. In 829, the Youzhou military governor Li Zaiyi intervened on the court's behalf to put down a revolt in the small neighboring province of Henghai (on the coast south of today's Tianjin).[42] When the military province of Ze-Lu in southeastern Shanxi rebelled in 843, Zhang Zhongwu was ordered to keep an eye on the remnant Uyghurs while troops from other provinces were sent to put down the rising.[43] In 869, the military governor Zhang Yunshen voluntarily contributed 500,000 *shi* of grain and 20,000 *shi* of salt to supply government forces campaigning against the rebel Pang Xun (d. 869), and offered to send troops as well. The last instance of military cooperation comes from 878, when the court ordered the Youzhou *jiedushi* Li Keju (d. 885) to attack the Shatuo leader Li Guochang (fl. ca. 885).[44] At the same time that they jealously guarded their local autonomy and privileges, the leaders of the Lulong army followed a fairly consistent external policy of alliance with the Tang court. This pattern of behavior may well have been influenced by Youzhou's frontier position, which made the court more willing to concede autonomy in exchange for cooperation and also gave provincial leaders a strong incentive to maintain good relations with the center.

Identities and Alignments

The first half of the eighth century saw the settlement of large numbers of surrendered nomads—Türks, Qidans, Xi, and others—in the northern part of Hebei and around Youzhou in particular, and many of these people were incorporated into the Tang frontier armies. This influx of outsiders is of course an important element of Chen Yinque's famous thesis that Hebei was a culturally "barbarianized" (*huhua*) region in the wake of the An Lushan Rebellion.[45] Whatever influence this non-Han settlement may have had on the general cultural level of Hebei, it seems to have had no discernible effect on the external policies and alignments of the Lulong province, nor on its internal structure. On the contrary, the evidence suggests that the leaders of Youzhou tended to draw a clear line between themselves and the various peoples to the north.

In sharp contrast to several of the other autonomous provinces that were ruled by leaders of non-Han origin almost from start to finish, only three of Youzhou's twenty-seven post-rebellion military governors can be identified as foreigners.[46] One of these three was Li Huaixian (d. 768), a *hu* (Sogdian) from Liucheng (Yingzhou) who served as a general under An Lushan and his successors. Li was the first military governor of autonomous Youzhou, and held power from 763 until he perished in a headquarters coup in 768.[47] The other two were the Uyghur Li Maoxun (fl. ca. 875) and his son Li Keju, who ran the province from 875 to 885.[48] There is no evidence that non-Han troops were a distinct or separate component of the Lulong military establishment, or that they exerted any special influence in the province's internal politics. Steppe origin does not seem to have carried any cachet in Youzhou. It is interesting that when the Uyghur frontier commander Li Maoxun launched his rising against his predecessor Zhang Gongsu (fl. ca. 875), he did not do so in his own name but claimed to be acting on behalf of a popular general named Chen Gongyan (d. 875); it was only after Li had already taken control of the provincial headquarters that the subterfuge was revealed.[49]

The submissions and settlements that marked the first half of the eighth century did not continue into the post-rebellion period. The only important exception came in 842–43, after the collapse of the Uyghur Qaghanate, when as many as 30,000 Uyghurs submitted to the Lulong authorities.[50] It is not clear what happened to these people afterward, or how many of them were incorporated into the Lulong army. At least one of the Uyghur leaders, Li Maoxun, became a general in the service of Youzhou, won merit on the frontier, and eventually established himself as military governor, but it is not clear whether he continued to command an ethnically distinct tribal following.[51] There is also little evidence that Youzhou made use of its frontier position to ally with foreign peoples and secure their assistance in order to strengthen its hand against the Tang court and the other military provinces. The only example comes from the period of Zhu Tao's rebellion in the early 780s when Zhu took an Uyghur princess as his concubine and recruited a force of 3,000 Uyghurs and other tribesmen to participate in his great southern expedition at the beginning of 784.[52]

Youzhou's special position as an autonomous province on the external frontier of the Tang Empire would seem to have afforded its leaders a range of options not available to the other garrisons farther south. These included the ability to tap external resources and establish trans-border alliances to buttress their autonomy, and even the possibility of opting out of the empire entirely. The mixed population of the province, which included many people of steppe origin who were especially active in the military, added a further element of ethnic ambiguity and cultural malleability. And yet, except perhaps for importing horses from beyond the frontier, the leaders of Youzhou rarely chose to exercise these options or define themselves as anything other than Tang military governors. The frontier position of the province appears to have strengthened rather than weakened its relationship with the Tang court. Instead of positing the existence of a primordial "Chinese" identity reinforced by constant confrontation with a "barbarian" other, it is more consistent with the available evidence to point to a mutually beneficial alliance of convenience between court and province driven by the logic of Youzhou's strategic position. This position held dangers as well as opportunities, and the behavior of the province's military governors suggests that it was the dangers that were usually uppermost in their thinking. Situated as it was along several battlefronts real or potential, caught between formidable steppe powers on one side and the forces of the Tang court and rival military governors on the other, Youzhou had little choice but to try to minimize at least some of the threats that it faced. In this context, the court's own concern with frontier defense and foreign relations provided the basis for a relatively stable alliance of convenience that lasted almost without interruption from 785 to the end of the Tang dynasty in 907.

Notes

1. Du Mu, "Zhan lun" (Chapter 5) in *Fanchuan wenji* (Shanghai, 1984), pp. 91–93. Also see Chen Yinque, *Tangdai zhengzhi shi shulun gao* (Beijing, 1956), pp. 19–20; Denis Twitchett, "Varied Patterns of Provincial Autonomy in the T'ang Dynasty," in *Essays on T'ang Society*, ed. John Curtis Perry and Bardwell L. Smith (Leiden, 1976), pp. 98–102; and Zhang Guogang, *Tangdai fanzhen yanjiu* (Changsha, 1987), pp. 77–103. All translations are mine unless otherwise noted.
2. Liu Xu, *Jiu Tangshu* (Beijing, 1975) [hereafter cited as *JTS*], 199B.5356. A more elaborate paraphrase of the same point can be found in Ouyang Xiu and Song Qi, *Xin Tangshu* (Beijing, 1975) [hereafter cited as *XTS*], 219.6172.

3. The contrast is fairly explicit in *XTS*, 219. The classic criticism of Xuanzong's frontier policy is in Du You, *Tongdian* (Beijing, 1988), 148.3780.
4. Matsui Shūichi, "Roryō hanchin kō," *Shigaku zasshi* 68 (1959): 1397–1432.
5. Matsui, "Roryō hanchin kō," p. 1398.
6. For the pre-rebellion population figures, see *XTS*, 39.1019–23; *JTS*, 39.1513–27; and Du You, *Tongdian*, 178.4709–4716. Irrigation and land reclamation efforts are mentioned in *XTS*, 39.1020–21.
7. Matsui, "Roryō hanchin kō," p. 1415.
8. Sima Guang, *Zizhi tongjian* (Beijing, 1956) [hereafter cited as *ZZTJ*], 227.7324; 229.7388; 238.7671; 265.8662.
9. *ZZTJ*, 268.8743; *XTS*, 212.5986; Dong Gao, comp. and ed., *Quan Tangwen* (Taipei, 1965) [hereafter cited as *QTW*], 526.14. For a discussion of the reliability of the army sizes reported in Tang sources, see David A. Graff, "Early T'ang Generalship and the Textual Tradition" (Ph.D. diss., Princeton University, 1995), pp. 1.35–64.
10. Matsui, "Roryō hanchin kō," p. 1422.
11. *ZZTJ*, 241.7792; *XTS*, 212.5976 (Liu Zong). *ZZTJ*, 242.7818; *XTS*, 212.5977 (Zhu Kerong). It also seems that Lulong military governors made gifts of unusually fine horses in smaller batches; see Li Fang, comp. and ed., *Taiping guangji* (Beijing, 1959), 435.3533.
12. Zhu Tao's *XTS* biography reports that the army of 50,000 men that he led south at the beginning of 784 included twenty thousand cavalry (*XTS*, 212.5972). The usual proportion of cavalry in Tang armies was much less than 40 percent; see Graff, "Early T'ang Generalship," pp. 1.170–75.
13. Matsui, "Roryō hanchin kō," pp. 1419–21.
14. Zhang Guogang, *Tangdai fanzhen yanjiu*, p. 202. For the support of frontier armies during Xuanzong's reign, see Denis Twitchett, "Lands Under State Cultivation Under the T'ang," *Journal of the Economic and Social History of the Orient* 2 (1959): 162–203.
15. This must be qualified slightly: Provincial forces that moved out of their home provinces to participate in campaigns ordered by the Tang court did receive "expeditionary rations" (*chujie liang*) from the center. Youzhou forces sometimes received such subsidies, as when Liu Ji campaigned against Wang Chengzong (d. 820) of Chengde in 810. But such occasions were rare, brief, and did not involve the whole of Youzhou's military establishment.
16. For the 751 defeat see, Edwin G. Pulleyblank, *The Background of the Rebellion of An Lu-shan* (London, 1955), p. 98.
17. *JTS*, 199B.5349, 5354.
18. *JTS*, 199B.5350–51; *XTS*, 219.6169.
19. Denis Twitchett and Herbert Franke, ed., *The Cambridge History of China*, Vol. 6: *Alien Regimes and Border States* (Cambridge, 1994) [hereafter cited as *CHC* 6], pp. 50–53.
20. *ZZTJ*, 252.8162; *JTS*, 180.4680.
21. *CHC* 6, pp. 54, 57–58, 61.
22. *ZZTJ*, 264.8623; 268.8745. Also see Xue Juzheng, *Jiu Wudaishi* (Beijing, 1976), 137.1827.
23. Wang Pu, comp. and ed., *Tang huiyao* (Beijing, 1955), 96.1718.
24. *QTW*, 505.11; *JTS*, 143.3900.
25. *ZZTJ*, 235.7568; *JTS*, 199B.5356; *XTS*, 212.5974; *QTW*, 484.2a–b; 505.11.

26. *QTW*, 505.11a–b; *XTS*, 212.5974.
27. *ZZTJ*, 244.7871; *JTS*, 180.4674; *XTS*, 219.6175.
28. *ZZTJ*, 246.7962; *QTW*, 788.15.
29. *ZZTJ*, 247.8030; *XTS*, 212.5981; 219.6175; *QTW*, 774.7; Li Shangyin, *Li Yishan wenji*, SBCK edn. (Shanghai, 1919–22), 1.12–14.
30. Zhang Guogang, *Tangdai fanzhen yanjiu*, pp. 110, 120. The fate of two would-be Lulong *jiedushi*, Chen Xingtai (d. 841) and Zhang Jiang (fl. ca. 840), provides a fine illustration of the vital importance of imperial appointment; see *ZZTJ*, 246.7954–56.
31. See, e.g., *QTW*, 413.7 and 698.3.
32. For multi-generational traditions of frontier service, see Matsui, "Roryō hanchin kō," p. 1410. One example of a unit that survived the rebellion is the Jinglue army (*Jinglue jun*), which was based within the walled city of Youzhou. See *Tang huiyao*, 78.1429, and *QTW*, 413.7.
33. *JTS*, 199B.5356; *XTS*, 219.6172. For Tang envoys, see *ZZTJ*, 244.7884.
34. *QTW*, 413.7–8.
35. *QTW*, 666.3.
36. *QTW*, 699.2; 840.13. For additional examples of this sort of language, see *QTW*, 698.3–4, and 788.10.
37. *JTS*, 180.4676; also see *ZZTJ*, 242.7874.
38. *ZZTJ*, 233.7514; *QTW*, 505.11.
39. *ZZTJ*, 246.7962–63, 7966–67; *JTS*, 180.4678; *XTS*, 212.5980; *QTW*, 698.18. The Tang court's management of the Uyghur crisis is examined in detail in Michael R. Drompp, *Tang China and the Collapse of the Uighur Empire: A Documentary History* (Leiden, 2005).
40. *ZZTJ*, 242.7810.
41. *ZZTJ*, 225.7226–27.
42. *JTS*, 180.4674.
43. *ZZTJ*, 247.7981; 248.8012.
44. *ZZTJ*, 253.8209.
45. Chen Yinque, *Tangdai zhengzhi shi shulun gao*, p. 26ff.; see especially pp. 44–48. Some of the many serious weaknesses of the "barbarianization" thesis are pointed out by Zhang Guogang in *Tangdai fanzhen yanjiu*, pp. 84–88.
46. The total of twenty-seven comes from Matsui, "Roryō hanchin kō," p. 1398. See also Wu Tingxie, *Tang fangzhen nianbiao* (Beijing, 1980), pp. 552–75.
47. See his biography in *JTS*, 143.3895.
48. *XTS*, 212.5983. The surname of Shi Yuanzhong (d. 841), who governed Youzhou from 834 to 841, suggests a possible Türk origin, but the dynastic histories (*JTS*, 180.4677; and *XTS*, 212.5979) are silent on this point.
49. *ZZTJ*, 252.8180–81.
50. *ZZTJ*, 247.7976.
51. *XTS*, 212.5983.
52. *ZZTJ*, 228.7365–66; *XTS*, 212.5972. The last Youzhou military governor, Liu Shouguang (d. 914), called for help from the Qidan in 913, when his province was about to fall to the Hedong forces of Li Cunxu (see *ZZTJ*, 268.8777). By this time, however, the political environment had changed completely with the collapse of Tang dynasty, and the Qidan did not answer Liu's call in any case.

Glossary

Abaoji 阿保機
An Lushan 安祿山
Bian he 汴河
Bohai wan 渤海灣
Chang'an 長安
Chen Gongyan 陳貢言
Chen Xingtai 陳行泰
Chen Yinque 陳寅恪
Chengde 成德
chujie liang 出界糧
Chuoli 啜利
Dezong 德宗
Fanyang 范陽
guanchashi 觀察使
Gui 媯
Hebei 河北
Hebei san zhen 河北三鎮
Hedong 河東
Henan 河南
Henghai 橫海
hu 胡
huhua 胡化
Huainan 淮南
Huang Chao 黃巢
Huihe 回紇
Ji 薊
Jixian 薊縣
Jizhou 薊州
jiedushi 節度使
Jinglue jun 經略軍
jun 軍
Li Cunxu 李存勗
Li Deyu 李德裕
Li Guochang 李國昌
Li Huaixian 李懷仙
Li Keju 李可舉
Li Maoxun 李茂勳
Li Zaiyi 李載義
Liu Ji 劉濟
Liu Rengong 劉仁恭
Liu Shouguang 劉守光
Liu Zong 劉總
Liucheng 柳城
Lulong 盧龍
Matsui Shūichi 松井秀一
Mo 莫
Mohe 靺鞨

Niu Sengru 牛僧孺
Pang Xun 龐勛
Ping 平
Pinglu 平盧
Qidan 契丹
Qingdushan 青都山
Shatuo 沙陀
Shanxi 山西
sheng bing 勝兵
Shiwei 室韋
Shi Yuanzhong 史元忠
shouzhuo 守捉
shu 戍
Taihang shan 太行山
Tan 檀
Tanzhou 檀州
Tianjin 天津
Tian Yue 田悅
Tuhuzhen he 土㴲真河
Wang Chengzong 王承宗
Wei-Bo 魏博
Xi 奚
Xianzong 憲宗
Xuanzong 玄宗
ya Xi Qidan liangfan shi 押奚契丹兩蕃使
Yang Zhicheng 楊志誠
Ying[1] 瀛
Ying[2] 營
Yingzhou 營州
Youbeiping 右北平
Youzhou 幽州
Yuyang 漁陽
Ze-Lu 澤潞
Zhang Gongsu 張公素
Zhang Guogang 張國剛
Zhang Hongjing 張弘靖
Zhang Jiang 張降
Zhang shui 漳水
Zhang Yunshen 張允伸
Zhang Zhongwu 張仲武
zhen 鎮
Zhenwu 振武
Zhu Ci 朱泚
Zhu Kerong 朱克融
Zhu Tao 朱滔
Zhu Xicai 朱希彩
Zhuo 涿

Bibliography

Chen Yinque 陳寅恪. *Tangdai zhengzhi shi shulun gao* 唐代政治史述論稿 [Draft Explanatory Essays on Tang Political History]. Beijing: Sanlian, 1956.
Dong Gao 董誥, comp. and ed. *Quan Tangwen* 全唐文 [Complete Tang Prose]. Taipei: Jingwei shuju, 1965.
Drompp, Michael R. *Tang China and the Collapse of the Uighur Empire: A Documentary History.* Brill's Inner Asian Library. Leiden, Holland: E. J. Brill, 2005.
Du Mu 杜牧. "Zhan lun 戰論 [On War]." *Fanchuan wenji* 樊川文集 [Literary Collection of Fanchuan]. Shanghai: Shanghai guji chubanshe, 1984.
Du You 杜佑. *Tongdian* 通典 [Encyclopedic History of Institutions]. Beijing: Zhonghua shuju, 1988.
Graff, David A. "Early T'ang Generalship and the Textual Tradition." 2 vols. Ph.D. diss. Princeton: Princeton University, 1995.
Li Fang 李昉, comp. and ed. *Taiping guangji* 太平廣記 [Wide Gleanings Made in the Taiping Era]. Beijing: Renmin wenxue chubanshe, 1959.
Li Shangyin 李商隱 *Li Yishan wenji* 李義山文集 [Literary Collection of Li Yishan]. *Sibu congkan (SBCK)* 四部叢刊 [Four Branches of Literature] edn. Shanghai: Shangwu yinshuguan, 1919–22.
Liu Xu 劉昫. *Jiu Tangshu* 舊唐書 [Old Tang History]. 16 vols. Beijing: Zhonghua shuju, 1975.
Matsui Shūichi 松井秀一. "Roryō hanchin kō 盧龍藩鎮考 [A Study of the Lulong Military Province]." *Shigaku zasshi* 史學雜誌 [Historical Journal of Japan] 68 (1959):1397–1432.
Ouyang Xiu 歐陽修, Song Qi 宋祁. *Xin Tangshu* 新唐書 [New Tang History]. 20 vols. Beijing: Zhonghua shuju, 1975.
Pulleyblank, Edwin G. *The Background of the Rebellion of An Lu-shan.* London Oriental Series. London: Oxford University Press, 1955.
Sima Guang 司馬光. *Zizhi tongjian* 資治通鑑 [Comprehensive Mirror for Aid in Government]. Beijing: Guji chubanshe, 1956.
Twitchett, Denis. "Lands under State Cultivation under the T'ang." *Journal of the Economic and Social History of the Orient* 2 (1959):162–203, 335–36.
———. "Varied Patterns of Provincial Autonomy in the T'ang Dynasty." In *Essays on T'ang Society,* ed. John Curtis Perry and Bardwell L. Smith. Leiden, Holland: E. J. Brill, 1976.
Twitchett, Denis and Klaus-Peter Tietze. "The Liao." In *The Cambridge History of China, Vol. 6: Alien Regimes and Border States,* ed. Denis Twitchett and Herbert Franke. Cambridge: Cambridge University Press, 1994.
Wang Pu 王溥, comp. and ed. *Tang huiyao* 唐會要 [Important Documents of the Tang]. Beijing: Zhonghua shuju, 1990.
Wu Tingxie 吳廷燮. *Tang fangzhen nianbiao* 唐方鎮年表 [Chronological Tables of the Tang Military provinces]. Beijing: Zhonghua shuju, 1980.
Xue Juzheng 薛居正. *Jiu Wudaishi* 舊五代史 [Old History of the Five Dynasties]. 6 vols. Beijing: Zhonghua shuju, 1976.
Zhang Guogang 張國剛. *Tangdai fanzhen yanjiu* 唐代藩鎮研究 [Researches on the Military Provinces of the Tang Dynasty]. Changsha: Hunan jiaoyu chubanshe, 1987.

CHAPTER 3

THE GREAT DITCH OF CHINA AND
THE SONG-LIAO BORDER

Peter Lorge

In his 1990 book, *The Great Wall of China: From History to Myth*, Arthur Waldron described how the inability of the central government of the Ming dynasty (1368–1644) to make a strategic policy choice, combined with the ad hoc measures taken by local border commanders desperate to contain Mongol raids, brought about the creation of what we now call "The Great Wall of China."[1] The Great Wall has now become an iconic symbol of China in a positive sense, there is a "Great Wall" visa card and a "Great Wall" wine, as well as a negative symbol of conservatism, and defensive-mindedness, which, like the Maginot Line, ultimately proved unable to prevent the incursions of dynamic foreign adversaries. In this latter sense, the Great Wall has become a symbol of a particular mind-set among the Chinese leadership, a large-scale fortification indicative of a paralyzed leadership. By itself, however, such a connection between a defensive military policy and an ossified imperial court is not necessarily valid. This chapter aims to describe a case in which the construction of a large-scale fortification led to a change of mentality at court, and also to a peace that lasted for over a century. In short, it describes the brief history of a fortification that led to a successful military and political policy.

In the late-tenth and very beginning of the eleventh century, the Song dynasty (960–1279) undertook a large-scale defensive project to protect its northeast border. Confronted with a powerful steppe empire of the Qidan people, the Liao (907–1125), the Song government gradually constructed a continuous band of water obstacles, spanning hundreds of miles across northern Hebei province from the Taihang Mountains (Taihang shan) in the west to the Gulf of Bohai in the east. The spine of these obstacles was a dike that connected its surrounding rivers and swamps into a continuous defense line. Unlike the Great Wall, the role of which was miniscule, this Great Ditch[2] played a large part in stabilizing the military situation between the Song and Liao, leading to the Chanyuan Covenant (*Chanyuan zhi meng*) in 1005, and a peace that lasted for more than a century.

Despite this success, or perhaps because of it, the Great Ditch is virtually unknown to the public at large and even most historians of this period are unaware that it existed, oblivious to its crucial effect upon Chinese middle-period interstate relations. In the discussion which follows, I explain how the ditch came to be created, what its military effect was, and, I believe, most importantly, how the Song court's changing mentality, partly as a result of the accession of a new emperor, led to a lasting peace. I argue that concluding a peace became possible not so much because the Great Ditch was any more effective than the Great Wall in forestalling conflict, for it was not. Rather, I contend that peace between the two sworn-enemy states became possible because the security of the political and military positions of the third Song emperor, to which the Great Ditch contributed, allowed him to conclude such a covenant, and because he and his officials were able to change their minds over the course of the conflict. This change in mentality in particular had an enabling capacity, leading all of the parties involved to soften their stances and to recognize and appreciate the value of peace over the continuation of war.

This chapter therefore sits conceptually between the chapters of David Graff, Michael McGrath, Ruth Mostern, and M. A. Butler. The Great Ditch was not on the border, or even in a border region, but it reinforced and created a border at some remove from itself. Its status was anomalous, originating in a rejected national strategy, created locally, then incorporated into the previously rejected strategy, it profoundly shifted both the Liao and Song courts' respective conceptions of space and military activity, before being abandoned after its immediate purpose was served. As Mostern points out so clearly, the inherent tension between local administration and military necessity created dramatic swings in local government organization. The localities affected by the Song-Liao War, and by the creation of the Great Ditch, had a special relationship to the court. Yet the central government only involved itself with local Hebei administration when faced with a military crises; it disengaged itself as soon as that crisis was over. Because of the Great Ditch's success, it had to be abandoned, on the ground, in the mind of the court, and in history.

Building the Great Ditch (993–1004)[3]

After the failure in 986 of the second campaign of the Song's Emperor Taizong (r.976–97) to capture the originally Chinese territory of the Sixteen Prefectures[4] from the Qidan, the Liao state threatened the Song Empire through persistent retaliatory raids and invasions. Taizong had proven that the Song army, at least under his direction, was incapable of capturing the Sixteen Prefectures, but it was not clear at that time whether it was also, particularly after its heavy losses, incapable of defending the empire against a determined Liao invasion. In 987, a general who spent much of his career building canals and other large-scale projects, He Chengju (946–1006), proposed constructing a continuous water obstacle to strengthen

Hebei's defenses, which were expected to bear the brunt of any Liao response. But several officials convinced the emperor to reject the proposal by claiming that constructing such a defense would make the empire appear to be weak. Even the possibility of the empire, and hence the emperor, appearing "weak" was enough to scare Taizong off. The emperor's poor military record contributed to his political weakness, and he could not risk any further diminution of his personal prestige. Yet in trying not to appear weak, he rejected a good policy for improving the empire's defenses. This rejection was not just a matter of pride; Taizong believed that he could not afford the political cost of implementing such a defense policy. It was not good politics to adopt a passive defense, despite the military need for it, and, as such, the explicit rejection of the Great Ditch at that time was indicative of a certain mindset within the court. Taizong and his court were not willing to concede that their immediate goal was no longer to conquer the Sixteen Prefectures, but merely to defend the empire from the Liao.

Despite rejecting the plan as a whole, several years later (in 993) Taizong did begin to allow local officials, among them the architect of the original plan, He Chengju, to construct parts of the hydraulic network in their jurisdictions. The system thus got under way in a piecemeal fashion that avoided undermining the perceived prestige of the empire or the emperor. The benefits of the system were immediately felt, as the dikes made the transportation of troops and supplies easier, increased local food production through irrigation (which diminished the need for outside food), and acted as a barrier to Liao cavalry. Ironically, the Qidan were most worried by the logistical support that the system provided, as they could see that the ability to maintain more troops near the border allowed the Song to project more power offensively. This interpretation of these barriers as part of an offensive strategy seems to have eluded the Song court, which conceived of the system in purely defensive terms. From the Liao perspective, the construction of the Great Ditch was not a sign of weakness, but an ominous sign of offensive intentions on the part of the Song court.

Nevertheless, as Liao raids and invasions increased, and the effectiveness of the hydraulic defenses became more apparent, the system was extended. By 999, the Liao kept almost exclusively to invasion routes that avoided the dikes and paddy fields. With the succession of Taizong's son, posthumously known as Zhenzong (r.998–1023), the political constraints on officially sanctioning the complete network were removed because the new emperor's personal prestige was no longer tied to military conquest. Zhenzong sanctioned the completion of the system, including attempts to connect those areas that were topologically difficult. By the time the Song-Liao contest had reached its climax in late 1004, the system was virtually complete, ironically in much the form that He Chengju had proposed years before. Military exigencies at the local level, much like those that would later stimulate commanders during the Ming dynasty, had provided most of the impetus to build the system. Zhenzong's support shifted the policy from the local to the national level, and recognized the fundamentally passive defensive stance of the empire vis-à-vis the Liao. As I will argue below when I return to this point in the third section of this study, this recognition of the real military posture of the Song by its leader was a critical shift in the emperor and his court's thinking, which allowed the conclusion of a lasting peace.

The Military Effect of the Ditch

The Great Ditch changed the military situation between the Song and Liao by vastly strengthening Song defenses, making it possible for the Song army to successfully defend the empire from Liao incursions, and to maintain that defense regularly over the long term. Its effectiveness was still increasing when the cessation of hostilities rendered it no longer necessary. Had the fighting continued it is even conceivable that the Ditch would have enabled the Song to shift back to offense after repelling the Liao offensives. Indeed, the Liao seem to have had just that concern, not seeing the network as a purely defensive system, and understanding the more general military potential of a broad band of military outposts connected by a supply system capable of maintaining a large number of soldiers. It appeared to them that such a military complex could just as easily serve as a staging area for future Song offensives into their territory. Whether they understood that potential to exist in contrast to the current Song defensive-mindedness, or whether they did not believe that the Song court had become passive defensive-minded is uncertain.

The Great Ditch differed from a fortification like the Great Wall in that it provided logistical, agricultural and economic benefits in addition to its defensive functions. An earlier canal transport system in Hebei predated the Great Ditch, but it had largely broken down by the middle of the tenth century. The immense military value of a water transport system connecting the capital on the Yellow River with the northern border of Hebei, however, prompted Zhou Shizong (r. 954–59) to order the canals renovated as part of his campaign against the Liao in 959. Shizong captured the Guannan region, a piece of territory on the Song-Liao border much at the center of their conflict, but fell ill shortly afterward and died. He and his troops traveled much of the distance to the battlefield on the canals, proving their utility in rapidly, cheaply, and efficiently transporting an expeditionary army to its theatre of operation.[5] As the Song army settled into defensive positions in northern Hebei after 986, it was clear that an improvement in agricultural production would be similarly useful to the garrison armies. I will now deal separately with the Great Ditch's logistical, agricultural, economic, and defensive functions, before discussing the overall effect these interrelated functions had on the Song-Liao military balance.

Northern Hebei province was not a wealthy area of China in the late-tenth century. The added burden of tens of thousands of troops necessitated shipments of food and supplies to maintain the border's defenses. This logistical burden was much more manageable with an effective canal system as water transport was the cheapest and most efficient way then available for moving large quantities of goods or men. Troops transported by water would also arrive better rested and organized, avoiding the need to spread them out over dozens of miles of road, and frequently along multiple routes, during a march. Thus in military terms, the canals were a real multiplier of military force. They also created the possibility of strategic surprise for the Song by making it possible for it to swiftly bring large military forces and supplies up to the border.

Improvements in agriculture, just like improvements in transport, went a long way toward diminishing the Song garrison forces' supply burden on the local community. The new or renovated canals were linked to dikes and other irrigation works, markedly increasing the existing agricultural production and opening up new fields. The army controlled much of the new agricultural work, providing direct support for particular outposts or cities in order to make them more self-sufficient. The border outposts and cities required less support from the south as they became more self-sufficient, and became better able to withstand Liao attacks as a direct result of this logistical independence. A sudden raid might cut off a city or position, and the Liao might even interdict attempts to resupply the outpost, but a well-supplied position could, and frequently did, hold out logistically much longer than the Liao army. This was particularly true as the defense line developed, when the improved local food supply backed up the improved defensive works of the cities.

Beyond just providing food to the cities and outposts, the improved agriculture and transport system improved the local economy. That economy was then, in turn, able to supply more tax revenues for the already overstrained border area. But more than that, the better economy created incentives for locals to remain and farm or work in an area beset by frequent enemy raids. In effect, the construction of the canals and irrigation works for military purposes also functioned as a large-scale government investment in the economic infrastructure of Hebei. As perhaps few other places in Song China, the border zone received sustained government support to maintain and improve its agriculture and economy. When the crisis was over, that support faded, along with much of the economic benefit.

Among my considerations, I have placed the Great Ditch's defensive function, the role it played in blocking, delaying or inconveniencing Liao troops, last, even though it would appear to be my primary concern, in order to emphasize the importance of all of its functions. The purely military benefits of the canals with their adjacent irrigated paddy fields and elm trees, was that they inhibited the ability of the Liao cavalry to move freely over Hebei's otherwise unobstructed terrain. Fundamentally, the Song-Liao conflict was a fight over which side would control the mountainous terrain and strategic passes separating the plains of Hebei from the steppe lands to the north. Both sides controlled part of the Sixteen Prefectures, which under the Tang dynasty had been the Lulong defense area, designated to defend the empire from the steppe threat, but neither had the complete topographic advantage over the other. The Great Ditch filled in the topographic gaps in the Song defense-line, making up for the defensive value of the difficult terrain that the Song did not hold. Without this artificial obstacle, the entire province was open all the way to the Yellow River. A fast-moving all-cavalry army like the Liao's could almost reach the Song capital within weeks of breaching the border defenses. And whereas the Yellow River itself would be a significant barrier protecting the capital from such an army, it could not guarantee it. It was therefore essential that the Song create a strong forward defense, which would either completely block, or at least significantly slow down any possible Liao advance.

Thus, taken as a whole, the military effects of the Ditch were widespread, multifaceted and significant. It changed the balance of power along the active section of the Song-Liao border, bolstering Song power. The Great Ditch both increased the Song's overall military capabilities, and decreased the ability of the Liao to project power into Song territory. On a tactical level it increased the costs to the Liao of military operations and decreased their returns. This in turn blunted the effects of Liao strategic plans, vastly increasing the risks of pursuing a force-based policy. As the Ditch became more complete and stronger, these concerns became increasingly important for the Liao leadership. Even if the Song did not see the possibility of returning to the offense, it must have been apparent to the Liao that such an eventuality was more likely if its own armies repeatedly failed in their incursions, particularly if they were damaged significantly in the process. That is to say, the Ditch contributed to the danger that the Liao could encourage future Song offensives by losing too many times in its own invasions, which thus added a further risk to pursuing a force-based policy.

The Ditch hardened Song defenses, and gave the imperial army time to rebuild after Taizong's disastrous second campaign. The canals, paddy fields, and elm trees evened the odds for the Song's predominantly infantry-based army against the Liao's all-cavalry army, slowing the steppe riders down and diverting their attacks. Time was very important as Liao armies tried to live off the land and brought few supplies with them. The Song army could therefore gain enough time to shut up its cities and keep the Liao from striking quickly over a large area. Infantry forces could also trap cavalry forces against the Ditch and its surrounding paddies, a significant advantage in what would have otherwise been open terrain. There were, in fact, no tactical disadvantages for the Song army. The only danger they faced was that they might become too passive defensive in their tactics and strategy, more content to hide behind the Ditch, and thus completely cede the initiative to the Liao. As much as the court tried to prevent this trend, it could not entirely counteract it. But, as I will argue at greater length below, the defensive-mindedness that the Ditch promoted contributed in a positive way to the willingness of the Song court to seek and accept a peace agreement.

The improvement in Song defenses was primarily a result of the construction of the Ditch. Like the Great Wall, it was not a perfect defense, but because the military balance between the Song and Liao was closely balanced beforehand, its contribution to the Song side was very important in its struggle. The Great Ditch was constructed to defend a much smaller area than the Great Wall would be, and one that was more distant from the capital. The theatre for the Song-Liao War was restricted, and the Ditch was effective in that limited area. Hebei thus became the cockpit of the two empires. The Ditch also transformed the Song army and its attendant defensive mentality. Taizong's campaigns had mostly destroyed the expeditionary army and military machine that had created the empire. With the rebuilding of the army and building of the Ditch, the Song army was changed into an army of defense, a tool of an established empire rather than that of a developing, growing one.

Changing Mentalities and the Road to Peace

I have argued above that the Great Ditch had a significant military effect on the war between the Song and the Liao. I will now argue that its military effect directly contributed to a change in mentality in both the Song and Liao courts regarding their conflict. The changing military situation, and its effect upon the political circumstances in both courts, influenced the thinking of both emperors and their advisers. Battlefield results affected two things: first, the direct understanding of the costs and benefits of waging a war, and, second, the political fortunes of rulers and officials. It is therefore important to connect the Great Ditch's military value to the course of the war, and to what impact that had on the thinking at both courts. Peace was not concluded because of an objectively decisive battle or campaign that allowed one side to dictate terms to the other, but because the respective rulers and their courts concluded that, given the military situation as they understood it, it was better to make peace than to continue fighting. The border that they agreed upon was virtually the same as the antebellum border. What had changed was that, after a protracted struggle, both sides, and it is critical that it *was* both sides, came to understand that military action would not convince their opponent to concede to their demands. In the discussion that follows, I will delineate the original political and territorial goals of the Liao and Song, sketch out the changing Liao strategy, followed by Song Zhenzong's changing position on strategy, and, finally, discuss the attitudes of both sides just before they made peace.

The Liao originally wanted peace with the existing borders, so their position changed very little over the course of the war. They had some interest in retaking the Guannan area captured from them by Zhou Shizong in 959, both because they had recently held it and because it contained several strategic passes controlling the north-south routes to the Hebei plains. But, even though the Song thought otherwise, the Liao really had no interest in actually trying to destroy the Song Empire. This was demonstrated by the Liao court's repeated refusal to aid its longstanding diplomatic partners in southern China during the Song conquest of that area.[6] It was, however, in the Liao court's interest when negotiating to convince the Song court that they were ready, willing and able to destroy them. The great influence of empress and then Dowager Empress Chengtian (Chengtian taihou) at the Liao court during the entire Song-Liao conflict permitted the Liao to pursue a consistent policy over an extended period of war and diplomacy. Although the Liao did not have territorial goals, it did have political ones. In addition to peace and trade, the Liao rulers wanted to deal diplomatically with the Song on some sort of equal terms. This was, of course, directly contrary to Chinese imperial ideology, which did not admit equals to the Son of Heaven, and required the creation of a fictitious family relationship between the Song and Liao emperors in the final peace arrangements. This was a concession on the Liao's part, further proof of the dynasty's desire for peace, as their solution to the problem of inter-court relations was intermarriage between the respective imperial families. The Song absolutely rejected imperial intermarriage, and because it would not accept a nonkin imperial equality formulation, preferred the fiction of imperial kinship. The Liao accepted this solution to achieve their goals of peace and equality.

Song goals, in sharp contrast to those of the Liao, changed greatly over the course of the war, with the greatest change taking place after Zhenzong became emperor. Zhenzong and his court at first maintained the policy goals of his father, Taizong, in part because there was initially almost no change in the personnel advising the new emperor. To understand how much Zhenzong had changed his position by the time he made peace in 1005, then, it is useful to first adumbrate Taizong's policy goals.

Taizong came to the throne under the suspicion that he had either poisoned his older brother, the first emperor, or, at least, stolen the throne from his nephew, or both. He was therefore politically weak, and consequently interested in using military conquest to boost his personal prestige and prove his qualifications to rule. At that time, in 976, there were two obvious military targets: the Northern Han Kingdom, and the Sixteen Prefectures, held by the Liao. The Northern Han was a Liao tributary, so both possibilities entailed a confrontation with the Liao. Song Taizu, the first Song emperor, had earlier worked out some sort of modus vivendi with the Liao that left the issue of the Northern Han ambiguous. Taizu had tried, and failed, to conquer the Northern Han on two occasions.[7] But Taizong determined that he would succeed where his brother had failed, and proceeded with his campaign to conquer the Northern Han in 979. He was initially successful, however, in his moment of triumph he overreached, ordering a continued campaign to capture the Sixteen Prefectures, which ended in disaster several months later.

The failure of the Sixteen Prefectures campaign severely damaged Taizong politically, and undermined any military credibility his initial success had provided. With his authority and grip on the throne weakened, Taizong took two steps to shore up his position. First, to bolster his damaged military and political prestige, he adopted an extremely belligerent position with respect to the Liao. He hoped that making conquest, rather than peace, his goal would prove his imperial qualifications. Second, and more immediately, he eliminated the threat to his position posed by his younger brother and nephews by bringing about their deaths. Although it is true that he did not directly and openly order them killed, and that their deaths appeared to be either self-inflicted or natural, the three men's deaths so soon after

Taizong's failure fooled no one. Indeed, one of Taizong's own sons may well have been unhinged by his father's obvious fratricidal and nepoticidal actions. These personal considerations directly affected Taizong's policy decisions, and thus warrant some discussion.

Taizong's personal failure against the Liao was particularly serious because of the suspicious circumstances under which he assumed the throne. Even before his failure, an unknown, but significant, number of important people within the imperial family, army, and government already questioned whether Taizong should be emperor. His failure clearly demonstrated that he was not militarily qualified to be emperor, and raised the question of whether any of the other possible candidates for the throne would be better. Shortly after the Song army was defeated at the Gaoliang River (Gaoliang he) there was an aborted attempt to place his nephew Dezhao on the throne by some of the generals. Taizong discovered not only how shaky his own support was but also how replaceable he was in the eyes of the military. The generals were loyal to the dynasty, and to the Zhao family, but not to Taizong personally. His problem was therefore, on the one hand, to placate the military, and, on the other, to remove the option of turning to another Zhao family member to rule the dynasty.

Taizong believed that the best way to placate the military was to adopt an extremely belligerent policy with respect to the Liao. This was a direct expression of his continued faith in the army, as well as his continued support for generals and military action. Had he turned to a more conciliatory policy with the Liao, the military could reasonably have thought that the emperor trusted neither their competence nor their loyalty, and that their own opportunities for advancement would be diminished in a court favoring peace. Taizong was thus reassuring them that things had not changed from his brother's reign, when despite the installation of civil institutions, military men were still esteemed and could rise to the top of the government. But there were risks in this policy. In making the court's policy one of war, Taizong emphasized precisely that area in which he had failed so miserably. War with the Liao meant that military competence was an important imperial qualification. At the time, however, Taizong presumably expected that a future successful campaign would prove him worthy and free him to change policy. When his second campaign also ended in failure, he could not extricate himself from his aggressive war policy, and could not accept any measure that would appear to be defensive. He had painted himself into a corner by making the "recovery" of the Sixteen Prefectures a fundamental prop to his legitimacy.

Despite Taizong's legitimacy problems after his second defeat in 986, his position on the throne was much more secure than it had been after his 979 failure. In the wake of his earlier defeat, later in September of 979, his nephew Dezhao, "committed suicide" with a fruit knife[8]; his nephew Defang died suddenly on April 18, 981—without mention in the historical record of any cause[9]; his younger brother, Tingmei, died in exile on February 20, 984.[10] Taken together, these deaths removed the most obvious alternatives to Taizong's rule. Taizong had thus defused the most serious threats to his throne well before his second campaign began, removing all chance aside from the military outcome of glory or defeat.

But this outcome—the one variable he could not fully control—proved determinative. Taizong's second campaign not only failed, it also resulted in massive damage to the Song military. It was in this critical period that Taizong rejected He Chengju's explicit national defense policy of building the Great Ditch for fear of appearing weak, and yet he continued to allow local construction of it. Taizong was rhetorically unable for political reasons to promote the construction of a massive defense work precisely *because* the empire now, due to his military failures, so desperately needed it. This political constraint also demonstrates that no one at the Song court in favor of the project conceived of it as anything but a defensive work. Whereas the Liao was clear on its offensive potential, no one in the Song court ever argued that the Ditch was part of a plan to eventually conquer the Sixteen Prefectures, and therefore not a sign of weakness or defensive-mindedness. From the perspective of the Song court, the Great Ditch, the building of a massive defensive work to protect an entire region, was an acknowledgment of a defensive posture.

From a purely military perspective, openly adopting a defensive, even a passive-defensive, posture is not inherently bad; it is simply a strategic choice. One compares one's goals and one's means and arrives at an overall strategy that prioritizes some goals over others. The political ramifications of adopting a defensive strategy, however, can be great. Strategic military goals are predicated on political and cultural goals; they do not emerge in an abstracted, purely military realm. Taizong wanted to retake the Sixteen Prefectures not only to prove himself worthy to be emperor, but also to decisively defeat the Liao in order to establish the real or ritual dominance of the Song dynasty over every polity with which it was in contact. This politicocultural motive did not allow the Song court to accept the existence of another emperor, such as the Liao emperor, or the idea of strict boundaries upon its authority. There was only one Son of Heaven, and his responsibility and authority extended, in theory, to the entire world in ever-diminishing degrees. Even though it was understood that this was not true in reality, no Chinese dynasty ever willingly chose to explicitly abandon this principle. Building a giant defensive work would very clearly acknowledge the Song's limited authority. Hence, the Song's military goal, to capture the Sixteen Prefectures, was partly driven by a cultural goal, to subordinate the Liao politically to the Song. Taizong's failure to achieve either goal placed immense political pressure on him, which he responded to by simply refusing to accept the situation in which his failures had resulted.

Taizong's third son, Zhenzong, succeeded to the throne without any of his father's political problems but with a cultural background that was much the same. The political differences were, I believe, critical in allowing Zhenzong and his court to change their attitudes about making peace with the Liao. Zhenzong did not suffer from the legitimacy problems of Taizong, and thus was not driven to prove his right to rule through military conquest. He had not been defeated in the field as his father had, and so did not suffer from the same complex of personal humiliation. This is not to say that he was not deeply suspicious of the Liao, or that he could not manifest both belligerence and a strong desire for martial display. But Zhenzong ruled a vast empire with a serious border problem, and his goal was to solve that problem in any way possible. He could prove his worthiness as a ruler by solving the problem and ruling a peaceful empire, by neither expanding its borders nor forcing his subjects to support a war. Zhenzong was therefore disposed to seek a solution to the problem of war, which fundamentally meant peace, rather than a solution to his own personal political problems, which for Taizong had meant a military victory. Under these circumstances, the construction of the Great Ditch seemed a good first step in, at least, limiting the severity of the problem.

Deciding to finish the Great Ditch encouraged the sort of thinking that Taizong had been politically and temperamentally unable to accommodate. Yet, distinguishing between the military and mental effects of the Great Ditch is important. In the military sphere, the Great Ditch helped the Song army to demonstrate some real success in defeating Liao incursions. This was in contrast to the known problems of offense against the Liao, further emphasizing the positive value of defense. The choice was stark—failure in offense versus success in defense. In the mental sphere, that is, in the mentality of Zhenzong and his court, the changing military situation only reinforced their defensive-mindedness. Many officials had continued from Taizong's court, and had served alongside Zhenzong there when he was heir-apparent. All of these men therefore shared a common understanding of the military situation, and all also understood that while Taizong's military policy with respect to the Liao had been outwardly offensive, it had actually been defensive. Unencumbered by his father's political and personal problems with a conciliatory, or at least peace-oriented, foreign policy, Zhenzong was freer to openly acknowledge a defensive policy. This is not to say that circumstances required him to choose such a policy, only that he was not as constrained as Taizong in his range of options.

Nevertheless, there were still two factors that initially restrained Zhenzong in openly and wholeheartedly seeking peace with the Liao. First, he did not want to seek peace as the result of military defeat. Although he had not been personally defeated as his father had, he did not want to act from a perceived position of weakness. His great advantage was that he only needed to demonstrate strength in the face of Liao incursions to appear strong. An offensive victory would have been better, but it was unnecessary. Second, he was just as suspicious of the Liao as his father had been, and as many in his court were. Zhenzong did not and could not know whether or not the Liao court was intent upon destroying the Song dynasty. In hindsight it seems clear that the Liao had neither the intention nor the capability to do so, but no one in the Song court could be as certain, and the stakes were considerably higher for the Song Empire. These considerations, taken together with the disastrous results of the previous invasions of Liao territory, made building a strong defense system in Hebei a reasonable policy. The shift in mentality toward finding a way to make peace would only come later.

The war was not a one-sided affair, however, and the Liao altered its battlefield strategy in response to the stiffening Song defenses. The attacks of its armies had at first driven through the areas without water defenses. As those gaps were closed, the Liao court became increasingly anxious. In the summer of 1002, Liao forces surprised the Song by launching a campaign out of season, but very little was accomplished. They later shifted their efforts to the Guannan region, leaving most of the Song troops spread out and distant from the focus of their army. Yet even though the issue of the Guannan region was frequently raised, this was problematic for the Liao, since its goal was not territory but a political settlement.[11] Liao military efforts were directed at forcing the Song into diplomatic discussion. That goal was proving not just to be elusive, but possibly increasingly unlikely as Song defenses strengthened. The Liao court could not know for certain that Zhenzong wanted peace, and so had to act on the assumption that the Song would have to be forced to the negotiating table. It was therefore necessary for the Liao to increase its military pressure before the Song's defenses crippled its ability to do so without staggering losses. The Liao rulers may well have believed that the perfection of the Song's defense system such that they were really unable to penetrate it would mean more than the failure of their own enterprise. They would have lost the initiative and would be placed on the defensive themselves, waiting for the Song to work itself up to attack. There was therefore perhaps an increasing desperation in the Liao attacks leading up to the 1004 campaign. In that final campaign the Liao forces were badly overextended, and in serious danger of being cut off. Their military situation thus contributed to their swift negotiation and acceptance of an agreement.

Zhenzong and the Song court also changed their strategies over the course of the war. At the beginning, they were most concerned with building a strong defense that would defeat any Liao incursions into Hebei. This short-term strategy developed into a more long-term one of preparing a sustainable defense at as low a price as possible. To that end, large Song troop formation only moved up to the border to bolster the garrison forces only in the autumn and winter, when the steppe horses were strongest and the Liao army most likely to strike. The Liao took advantage of that in 1002, but the strategy was nonetheless effective over the long term. Indeed, Zhenzong's court did not have much of a strategy beyond foiling the Liao and turning an acute problem into a manageably chronic one. In effect, the Song was trying to simply diminish the value of the military initiative that the Liao held. But the court extended no diplomatic feelers, thus demonstrating that its overall policy with respect to the Liao remained purely military. When the Liao switched strategy, first concentrating on the Guannan area, and then striking southward toward the Song capital, Zhenzong's court panicked. These attacks provoked a serious crisis because they constituted a truly threatening campaign after years of improved defenses that had seemed to diminish the Liao threat. Already in a defensive mindset, the court felt vulnerable. Only the stalwart confidence of Kou Zhun (961–1023) was able to bolster the suddenly anxious Zhenzong. Zhenzong was induced to directly confront the threat, a move that, as imagined, helped convince the frontline troops that they were not being abandoned. In this act, Zhenzong switched from a passive defense, to an active one, moving up to face the Liao army. This move also marked the change in the Song stance from a long-term strategy to an immediate, short-term strategy, one with an incredible urgency to resolve the immediate threat.

The military situation in 1004 with the Liao army, led by the emperor and the dowager empress, overextended and desperate to achieve something political with the Song, and Zhenzong, shifting to an active defense and looking for a solution to the immediate military problem before him, yet worried that a military solution might fail, was extremely conducive to a peace agreement. Both sides were interested in shifting their interaction from the military sphere, since by then their disagreements lay in the political sphere. They had exhausted the productive possibilities of military action, leaving hope only in a political settlement. In a sense, this settlement had been both sides' goal from the very beginning, but they had been unable to conclude such a settlement as long as the military terms which underlay it were unresolved. And indeed, the fact that the agreement lasted for over a century indicates that it was more naturally in the interests of both sides to maintain the peace, and that neither side was interested in trying, or bold enough, to test whether the respective military realities had changed since 1004. The safest, most reliable solution in 1004 was peace, for which both sides were by then ready.

Conclusion

The Chanyuan Covenant of 1005 kept the peace between the Song and Liao Empires for over a century. During that time, the Great Ditch was allowed to break down, and the government's investment in that part of Hebei ceased. It had served its purpose. It had contributed directly and substantially to stabilizing and clarifying the military positions of the two empires, thus leading to the change in mentality that was the prerequisite for a peace agreement. It was therefore a successful work in two respects: first, from the Song perspective, it stabilized and enhanced their defenses in Hebei; second, it made peace possible by making war less effective for the Liao. Like the later Great Wall, it was not perfect, but unlike the Ming court, the Song court was still actively involved in trying to solve its northern border problem, and willing to find a peace which it could accept.

Without the desperate Liao invasion of 1004, peace might have been longer in coming. Liao losses had increased with each campaign, and the empire's economy was much less able to maintain the war that was shifting toward becoming a war of attrition on its part, rather than a war of annihilation of the enemy. The Song could sustain the conflict, and the Great Ditch shifted the ground rules more and more toward a war of attrition. It was just as the door was closing on the possibility of a war of annihilation that peace was made. Once that door closed, the Liao army would have suffered a slow process of grinding down which might have left it vulnerable to attack. Still, the Song army had proved poor at waging a war of annihilation against the Liao, finding that it could not destroy the Liao in a single or even sustained stroke. Song forces were thus always vulnerable to a counterattack. The very act of attacking would leave the Song army exposed to a Liao campaign of annihilation; that possibility could only be precluded by passive defense.

The Great Ditch helped to create the reality on the ground that brought peace, and created a stable border where none had been before, by changing the mentality of both the Song and Liao courts. When the Song acknowledged that it was building a vast defense system, it accepted, or admitted that it had come to accept, that its problem was a defensive one. Once the court had concluded that its policy had the negative goal of stopping Liao incursions, peace became a good solution to the problem. If it could achieve peace, its policy goal would be achieved. That was a change from Taizong's, and even Zhenzong's, earlier resistance to giving up the goal of conquering the Sixteen Prefectures. The change at the Liao court was subtler, but equally significant over the long run. The Liao court's initial goal was to establish a peaceful, stable border with the Song, and to manage that border through political pressure backed by the threat of force. The protracted, bloody campaigns in Hebei convinced the Liao leaders that they could not obtain such an uncertain, and uneven, strategic relationship. They were forced to engage in a much more equal, explicit political relationship with the Song Empire, and to accept that their military was not demonstrably superior to the Song military. The Chanyuan Covenant lasted for over a century because it was made between equals, who shared a common interest in maintaining peace. The Great Ditch was instrumental in establishing that equality on the battlefield, and also in the minds of the leadership in both courts.

Notes

1. Arthur Waldron, *The Great Wall: From History to Myth* (Cambridge, 1990), especially pp. 55–59. His argument is, of course, considerably more complex than I have abbreviated above. All translations are mine unless otherwise noted.
2. The designation "Great Ditch" is entirely my own, used here for convenience. There was no contemporary Song term for the extensive network of water defenses in Hebei.
3. My account of the Song's hydraulic defense system is based upon the following articles: Yan Qinheng, "Bei Song dui Liao tangdi sheshi zhi yanjiu," *Guoli Zhengzhi Daxue xuebao*, 8 (1963): 247–58; Lin Ruihan, "Bei Song zhi bianfang," *Guoli Taiwan Daxue wen shi zhe xuebao*, 10 (1970): 195–233, esp. pp. 197–201; Li Kewu, "Guanyu Bei Song Hebei tangli wenti," *Zhongzhou xuekan*, 4 (1987): 120–23; Nap-yin Lau, "Song-Yuan Chanyuan zhi meng xintan," pp. 722–25; Nap-yin Lau, "Waging War for Peace? The Peace Accord between the Song and the Liao in AD 1005" in *Warfare in Chinese History*, ed. Hans J. van de Ven (Leiden, 2000), pp. 180–221, esp. pp. 186–89 (This article is an abridged English version of his 1990 article in Chinese).

4. The Sixteen Prefectures constituted an area around present-day Beijing that encompassed the strategic passes controlling north-south access between the steppes and Hebei province. This territory was ceded to the Liao by Shi Jingtang, the Shatuo Türk founder of the third of five northern dynasties, the Later Jin, of the Five Dynasties period in 938 in return for military assistance.
5. For Zhou Shizong's Guannan campaign, see Peter Lorge, "War and the Creation of the Northern Song State" (Ph.D. diss., University of Pennsylvania, 1996), pp. 132–35.
6. Song Taizu used the capture of envoys from the kingdom of Later Shu (934–65), who were trying to get in touch with the Liao to coordinate efforts against the Song, as a pretext for invasion. See Lorge, "War and the Northern Song State," for the conquest of Shu, pp. 159–67; for the conquest of the Southern Han, pp. 177–83.
7. An earlier raid in 961 might also be considered an attempt to conquer the Northern Han, but it was broken off at a much earlier stage than the later two attempts after the Liao intervened.
8. Li Tao, *Xu Zizhi tongjian changbian* (Beijing, 1979), 20.460.
9. Li Tao, *Xu Zizhi tongjian changbian*, 22.490.
10. Li Tao, *Xu Zizhi tongjian changbian*, 25.572.
11. In this respect I differ from Nap-yin Lau, who believes that the Liao shift toward attacking the Guannan area was actually an attempt to capture that territory. I am not arguing that the Liao would not have been pleased to capture the Guannan area, only that their attacks were politically, rather than territorially, motivated.

Glossary

Bohai 渤海
Chanyuan zhi meng 澶淵之盟
Chengtian taihou 承天太后
Defang 德芳
Dezhao 德昭
Gaoliang he 高梁河
Guannan 關南
He Chengju 何承矩
Hebei 河北
Kou Zhun 寇準
Lulong 盧龍
Ming 明
Qidan 契丹
Shatuo 沙陀
Shi Jingtang 石敬瑭
Shiliu zhou 十六州
Song Taizu 宋太祖
Taihang shan 太行山
Taizong 太宗
Tingmei 廷美
Zhenzong 眞宗
Zhou Shizong 周世宗

Bibliography

Lau, Nap-yin. "Song-Yuan Chanyuan zhi meng xintan" 宋元澶淵之盟新談 [New Discussions on the Chanyuan Covenant of Song and Yuan Times]. *Lishi yuyan yanjiusuo jikan* 歷史語言研究所集刊 [Bulletin of the Institute of History and Philology (Taibei)] 61.3 (Sept. 1990):693–747.

———. "Waging War for Peace? The Peace Accord between the Song and the Liao in AD 1005." In *Warfare in Chinese History*, 84 vols. Sinica Leidensia, vol. 47, ed. Hans J. van de Ven. Leiden, Holland: E.J. Brill, 2000.

Li Kewu 李克武. "Guanyu Bei Song Hebei tangli wenti." 關於北宋河北塘立問提 [Concerning the Problems of Dike Establishment in Hebei province of the Northern Song]. *Zhongzhou xuekan* 中州學刊 [Zhongzhou Journal] 4 (1987): 120–23.

Li Tao 李燾. *Xu Zizhi tongjian changbian* 續資治通鑑長編 [Collected Data for the Continuation of Comprehensive Mirror for Aiding Government]. 25 vols. Beijing: Zhonghua shuju, 1979.

Lin Ruihan 林瑞翰. "Bei Song zhi bianfang" 北宋之邊防 [Border Defenses of the Northern Song]. *Guoli Taiwan Daxue wen shi zhe xuebao* 國立台灣大學文史折學報 [National Taiwan University Journal of Literature, History, and Philosophy] 10 (1970):195-233.

Lorge, Peter. "War and the Creation of the Northern Song State." Ph.D. diss. Philadelphia: University of Pennsylvania, 1996.

Waldron, Arthur. *The Great Wall: From History to Myth*. Cambridge: Cambridge University Press, 1990.

Yan Qinheng 閻沁恆. "Bei Song dui Liao tangdi sheshi zhi yanjiu" 北宋對遼塘堤設施之研究 [Research on Dike Construction by the Northern Song for Confronting the Liao]. *Guoli Zhengzhi Daxue xuebao* 國立政治大學學報 [National Zhengzhi University Journal], 8 (1963):247–58.

CHAPTER 4

IN PURSUIT OF THE GREAT PEACE: WANG DAN
AND THE EARLY SONG EVASION OF
THE "JUST WAR" DOCTRINE

Don J. Wyatt

The idea of the "just war" is a familiar one to Westerners, so much so that we are inclined to assign it an exclusively Western provenance.[1] However, the Chinese have also long espoused in writing the belief that resorting to "righteous armaments" or "just arms" (*yibing*) in order to prosecute war is sometimes inescapable and thus wholly justified.[2] Chinese notions of the "just war" indeed emerged at as early a stage in history as the beginning of the period of Warring States (ca. 480–220 BCE), when the concept no doubt paralleled the rising expectations of the emergence of the universal kingship that was used to anchor it.[3] By the time of the succeeding Qin (221–306 BCE) dynastic period, we can assume that the basic assumptions supporting the idea of the "just war" were already well in place and extremely pervasive.

To be sure, the Western and the Chinese notions of the "just war" stem from fundamentally dissimilar premises. In the West, we must attribute the conviction that some wars are more "justifiable" than others to assumptions deriving from the relatively uniform foundation of Christian religion. In China, this principle was more secularly based. But despite this difference of sacred versus secular bases, whether in China or in the West, two critical assumptions pertaining to the conception of the "just war" have persisted. First is the assumption that the "just war" is a legitimate strategy for inclusion in the defensive arsenal of any ruler. Second, and presupposing a well-ruled state, is the assumption that the "just war," by dint of becoming necessary only when confronted with annihilation, is always an irregular occurrence.

The fact that the Song period, which spans as an aggregate from CE 960 to 1279, offers particularly fertile exploratory ground for the whole question of when and under what circumstances war becomes necessary and justifiable should not surprise us. Although probably somewhat exaggerated, the relative military weakness of the Song Chinese state in relation to its surrounding enemies has become, more or less, an accepted fact. During the Song, the Chinese were threatened as in no previous time, and thus it would seem to have been a time most fitting for the waging of a "just war."

However, such a war was never prosecuted, and at no point during the Song—even as the dynasty confronted its complete termination at the hands of a foreign Mongol adversary—was the "just war"—understood as the *total* war—pursued. Much of the reason for this failure to prosecute the "just war" is that the strategy devoted to securing peace through diplomacy was, by and large, consistently favored over one for securing the same objective through war.[4] This almost unwavering favoritism toward the diplomatic rather than the military solution was established early in the history of the Song. Moreover, if we can believe the traditional accounts, we must attribute the inception of the elusion of the "just war" as policy most of all to a single individual. This individual was the influential high official and statesman Wang Dan (957–1017)—the putative original author of the early Song strategy for achieving peace through concerted resistance to what he perceived as the trap of the "just war." What follows is an examination, inasmuch as we can discern them across time, of his motives.

"Grand Councilor of Great Peace"

In his very person, Wang Dan epitomized all of the centralizing and civilizing tendencies set in motion by the Song dynastic founding. Born in 957, just three scant years before that crucial event, Wang Dan no doubt matured with the perception of himself as a participant in a great beginning, and his life story intersected and tracked—in an uncannily parallel manner—along with the fortunes and setbacks of the dynasty's formative first decades. We can assume that a ponderous weight of expectations rested heavily upon both the times and the man, and—at least at first—both flourished.

Wang Dan hailed from Daming (in extreme southern modern Hebei) via Xin county (in extreme western modern Shandong) and was born into a line of committed officials of ascending distinction—one spanning well back into the preceding chaotic Five Dynasties (907–60) and Ten Kingdoms (907–79) eras. His great-grandfather Wang Yan (fl. 900?) had served as magistrate of Liyang (in modern northern Henan). Under the Later Tang dynasty (923–36), his grandfather Wang Che, as a reminder of the left (*zuo shiyi*), had served in the national Chancellery (*menxia sheng*). His father Wang You (d. 980?), at the end of his life, obtained special appointment to serve as a vice minister in the Ministry of War (*bingbu shilang*) under the reign of Taizong (r. 976–97), the second Song emperor.[5] We must, therefore, deem the pressures to succeed that weighed upon Wan Dan to have been considerable and, in responding to them, he more than merely matched the achievements of his predecessors.

Wan Dan acquired the *jinshi* ("presented scholar") or doctoral degree in 980 at the still young but not prodigious age of twenty-three. Yet, if his profile within the context of the civil service examinations was somewhat ordinary, the subsequent arc of his career trajectory certainly was not. Wang Dan began his official career as the magistrate of Pingjiang county in Yue prefecture (in present-day northeastern Hunan). Thereafter, having already gained a sterling reputation as a capable and judicious administrator, he was promoted rapidly. After a period of a quarter century of official service in ever-changing capacities, his ascendancy culminated when, in 1006, he was chosen to succeed the reckless Kou Zhun (961–1023)—deviser of the successful but risky campaign at Chanyuan—as grand councilor.[6] However, highly significant and germane to the present discussion are Wang Dan's two distinct stints prior to this capstone achievement spent serving as examination administrator (*zhigong ju*). These appointments occurred in 992, when he served conjointly with his fellow official and recommender, Su Yijian (957–95), and in 1000—both of which were watershed years in the evolution of the civil service examination system.[7]

Upon reaching this summit of his career, Wang Dan served as grand councilor for an uninterrupted stretch of twelve years, from 1006 until 1017, and for a substantial interim period of five years within the twelve, from 1007 to 1011, he was unassisted as the sole grand councilor. Given the vicissitudes in the early Song political climate, only a man of extreme caution could have accomplished such a feat of longevity, and cautious indeed was Wang Dan. In all confrontations with China's two most predatory neighboring states—the Qidan Liao (947–1125) and the Tangut (Dangxiang or Tangguchang) Western Xia (1038–1227), Wang Dan sought to preserve the peace at all costs. For good or ill, our most persistent inherited image of him is that of a minister of state who felt that the benefits of peace were worth bearing any indignity suffered at the hands of Song's principal enemies of that time—the Qidan and the Tangut. For this reason and the fact that his policy actually worked—either forestalling or blunting the enemy onslaught for decades, Wang Dan has subsequently become remembered popularly as the "Grand Councilor of Great Peace" (*Taiping zaixiang*).

The instances in which Wang Dan—as grand councilor—exhibited his distinctive disinclination toward war are quite numerous. But, before subjecting crucial aspects of his behavior to thorough analysis, perhaps two glaring examples will suffice. At the end of the year 1010, when the Liao state mobilized a punitive invasion against the Kingdom of Korea, in advising the Emperor Zhenzong (r. 997–1022), Wang Dan recommended that, whether they were requested or not, Song forces should not be dispatched to intercede in behalf of Korea.[8] He justified offering no support in the defense of the Koreans on the basis that they themselves had, in 993, diverted their allegiance—and their regular payments of tribute—away from Song to Liao.[9] The fact that Korea, in defecting to the Liao, had confronted annihilation was inconsequential. Clearly, in Wang's view, the Song should continue not to recognize this switch in allegiance (just as it had not from the first), and—in its present war with Liao—Korea was now getting exactly what it deserved for its disloyalty. Conversely, the official Song History (*Songshi*) informs us that, when the Western Xia minister Zhao Deming (d. 1032) requested millions of pecks of grain beyond the tribute quota that the Song now regularly conveyed to the Tangut, Wang Dan granted the request.[10] The scholar Wang Pizhi (?–after 1096), writing in his nonofficial history Record of Banquet Conversations along the Sheng River (*Shengshui yantan lu*), affords us a more colorful—if idealized and even delusional—account of this same event:

> During the [Dazhong] xiangfu [1008–16] reign period, Zhao Deming petitioned the emperor, serving notice of his desire to come forth and borrow a million bushels of grain because of the famine in his [Xia] state. The great ministers all solicited a vow of defiance [from the throne] that Zhao would be punished for the audacity of his request. Only Wang Weigong Dan implored the emperor to have the grain collected in the capital region and its environs in the amount requested. It was then ordered that [Zhao] Deming should be permitted to enter the capital itself and fetch the grain. This display of magnanimity made Deming greatly ashamed for his past belligerence [toward the Song], and he was moreover compelled to express his appreciation [for the relief grain] to those at the court. All of this was to the delight of Zhenzong.[11]

The positions that Wang Dan took such as those related above were consistent, and they earned him a reputation as a peacemaker rather than a warmonger and, just as important is the fact that his sovereign Zhenzong invariably viewed Wang Dan's approach the most desirable course to pursue. Wang Dan thus became widely acclaimed as an official unmatched in his loyal to the emperor precisely because of his intractability whenever facing the threat of war and his refusal to plunge the empire headlong into any adversarial confrontation with the many warlike neighbors surrounding it. Thus from an early stage, to Wang Dan's mind, given the alternative of open warfare, peace, even if a bought peace, was the only option.

Reunifying Thought and Action

Although we may fail to uncover a dominating impetus behind it, we will surely find that certain factors were more important than others in shaping Wang Dan's antiwar stance. But even these quite discernible factors can defy easy quantification. Although timidity, for instance, no doubt played a role in bringing him to his position, we should not allow ourselves to believe that Wang's aversion to war was owing to timorousness alone. On the contrary, we should expect that Wang Dan, as a complex historical personality, was motivated by a complex of motivating factors and, upon subjection to our examination, such indeed seems to have been the case.

From the outset, we must also acknowledge that there are serious impediments to our full understanding of exactly what moved Wang Dan to oppose war in all forms and at all times. The main obstacle consists of either the choice or the failure of Wang himself to commit any views on this subject to writing. Consequently, in the matter of his opposition to war as well as in other related matters, we are largely dependent on opinions of Wang Dan's contemporaries and successors. Fortunately, the collateral evidence that these individuals supply is ample enough and compelling enough to prevent an impediment from becoming an impasse and thereby permits us to delve beyond the bare outlines of the views on the "just war" that Wang Dan is likely to have held. I therefore endeavor here to offer some insights regarding Wang Dan's motivations for opposing war, even though these motivations are not always so easily fathomed. We can measure success in this endeavor to the extent that we are enabled to answer certain key questions. Among the most obvious ones are why Wang Dan constantly eschewed war and why he was inclined to do whatever necessary to forestall and otherwise avoid interstate conflict.

Profiteer—Profound or Merely Petty?

In his avoidance of all military engagement and in his denial of war as even a potential means of resolving conflict between the Song and its rival states, Wang Dan is customarily depicted as preoccupied more with survival than victory and driven almost entirely by the quest for profit. There is much evidence to substantiate this depiction. Admittedly, inasmuch as he was the true originator of the Song strategy of so-called "appeasement," Wang Dan must also have been the deviser of a system in which peace was openly bought rather than gained through military threat, victory, or deterrence. But, in brokering a peace based on tribute between Song and Liao, Wang Dan was probably less the innovator than is frequently claimed. Indeed, as the late James T. C. Liu once astutely remarked of the Song Chinese state, "peace was bought from its aggressive new neighbor in the north, the Khitan Empire, through tribute, a practice common throughout Asia when a sedentary country was confronted by a horseback adversary."[12]

However, whether it was original or not, Wang Dan's strategy for deterrence based on the Song payment of tribute to the Liao did become the template for peaceful relations for the next century. Wang Dan was evidently convinced that— no matter what its price—the cost of peace would always pale in expense before the cost of war. We can see this view as a general reflection and a direct extension of his whole approach to statecraft. Wang was, at all times, cognizant of and concerned with the practicalities—the evaluation of the benefits of cost effectiveness and economies of scale in all matters related to state affairs. The example of an exchange recorded in the Song History between Wang and his like-minded sovereign Zhenzong underscores this point:[13]

> In the aftermath of a fire in the imperial quarters, Dan came rushing in [to see that the emperor was safe].
> The emperor said: "To cast away all that has been amassed over the course of two reigns is not to squander it. But to have nearly lost everything within the span a single reign, this is pitiful."

Dan replied: "The wealth of the throne includes the empire, and its riches are so sufficient that you should have no reason to worry. That which should be worried about is whether the dispensing of the directives of government or of rewards and punishments is amiss. If it is destined that Heaven will dispense such disasters as this [fire] because I, your servant, am serving you deficiently as steward of the state, then I am to be terminated and dismissed from office."[14]

Thus, we can conclude, from the foregoing passage, that an eye to the advantages conferred by profit was indeed a motive force both in Wang Dan's operative assumptions and even in his self-definition. Profit thus served as a kind of "constraining reality" for Wang Dan and it thereby became an internalized trait that distinguished him from those members of the war party like his predecessor as Grand Councilor Kou Zhun, who it was feared, with scant concern for the costs, would plunge the Song state rashly and headlong into war.

But, even if it was directed nominally in the interest of the state, for any official to be as obsessed with profit as Wang Dan reputedly was necessarily puts one's reputation at risk. For us as well as those much closer to him in time, such single-minded obsession raises the question of whether the primary concern of Wang Dan the "profiteer" was with profiting the state or solely with profiting his own person. Was he seeking the advancement of the imperial agenda or mere seeking his own advancement? Conclusiveness may continue to elude us but several accounts by his near-contemporaries, such as the one that follows by the poet and essayist Zhang Lei (1054–1114), suggest that even while perhaps meaning foremost to further the interests of the Song state, in attempting to do so, Wang was also disposed toward small-mindedness and pettiness. Zhang Lei's account in particular implies that Wang could often fail to see the potential larger benefits of getting seemingly small things right:

> The generations have transmitted that when the [construction of the Daoist temple] Jade-pure Palace (Yuqing gong) had just been completed Wang Weigong [Dan] had charge of the state. Ding Yaxiang [Wei] [962–1033] ordered that food and wine be lavishly prepared and that staff be arranged for the entertainment of visitors to the temple. Afterward, visitors to the temple frequently made complaints to Ding that spoiled food had been served. Making his way to the Secretariat (*zhongshu sheng*), Ding spoke to Wang Dan about the complaints but Wang did not reply. Ding repeated the complaints three or four times but, in the end, there was [still] nothing Wang would say. Flushing with anger [from his silence], Ding demanded to know why Wang would not answer. Wang [finally] said: "The Secretariat is not a marketplace where one expresses one's concerns about buns and cakes."[15]

Our latter-day reading of the foregoing anecdote invites a few interpretations. Wang Dan may well have been simply defending the legitimate gravitas associated with a vaunted institution. Or the above passage may indicate a negative attitude toward Daoism, though—for reasons to be discussed subsequently—Wang is unlikely to have expressed any such bias as openly as is suggested by the anecdote. Yet a final alternative is that Wang was merely an undisguised profiteer, and one with little capacity for either foresight or imagination. Viewed especially in accordance with this last alternative, Wang Dan emerges as someone who was willing to forsake the much greater sociopolitical good for the sake of what could be the trivial personal gain of advancing his reputation. To be sure, the question of whether such a foible was constitutional and habitual really does matter, for it unavoidably influenced his capacity for preserving the state with which he was entrusted. The kind of profiteer we choose to see Wang Dan as should rightly influence us markedly in formulating some conclusions on what was plausibly his own stance on the idea of the "just war."

Nurturer or Suppressor of the Talented?

Having considered the motive of profit, we are now well positioned to consider the implications of a likely second contributing factor to the anti-"just war" stance exhibited by Wang Dan—a factor that is no less controversial. Of his many skills as an administrator, none is more celebrated than Wang Dan's facility in the realm of what we may call human resources—chiefly, as an evaluator and selector of personnel. His deftness at discovering young men of talent and successfully recommending them to the posts appropriate for ensuring their future advancement was legendary and a source of much admiration and envy among his peers.[16] At least ten of the individuals he sponsored are said to have ascended to the post of grand councilor and we can definitely ascertain five of them—Kou Zhun, Li Di (967–1043), Wang Zeng (978–1083), Zhang Shixun (964–1049), and Lü Yijian (978–1043).[17] Wang Dan's two separate terms served as an examination administrator in 992 and in 1000 had doubtless helped in honing his abilities for detecting talent.

Given the residual importance of recommendation and sponsorship as vehicles to office in the late eleventh century, the whole question of whatever prescription Wang Dan might have employed to achieve the success he enjoyed in selecting the talented continues to be highly relevant to our discernment of his beliefs concerning who should be empowered by office. Yet, even while they are abundantly available, few of these laudatory accounts of Wang Dan's sponsorship activities supply specific descriptions of what his actual methods of personnel selection were. However, one report by the illustrious Sima Guang (1019–86) provides an exception. Moreover, its credibility can be little questioned, for Sima himself is renowned for having been especially gifted in this same capacity and openly desirous of aspiring to Wang Dan's unique level of competence in personnel selection.[18] Given his birth two years after Wang Dan's death, out of respect, we cannot expect that Sima would furnish a first-hand record of his forerunner's precise methodology that is in any way critical. But what Sima does provide—by describing the reputed manner of the grand councilor's reception and interview of candidates—is perhaps as close to an accurate approximation of Wang's procedures for scrutinizing talent as we are likely to get:

> During Zhenzong's time, when Wang Wenzheng Dan served as grand councilor, although [his office] might be filled to capacity with guests and visitors, there was never a time when he dared to interact with anyone on the basis of selfish interest. Upon withdrawing [to meet with anyone, Wang] would examine [the man's] capabilities, his speech, and the reputations of all those he had known for some time. If he intended to employ someone as an official, he would inquire about his place of residence.
>
> After the passage of several months, Wang would summon the man and question him by means of a lengthy but leisurely personal meeting, during which he would solicit the man's views on conditions within the empire in every direction. If he decided upon employing him, Wang would—commenting on what the man had said—tender an offer [of sponsorship]. He would then observe the talent's reaction, and confidentially record his name. On another day, the man would return to thank Wang [but] he would never thereafter return to see him again.
>
> There would always be omissions and deletions [but] Dan would first confidentially forward the names of three or four men to the emperor. If the emperor consented to employ them, the emperor would then—taking a brush—affix a number above each name in a ranking that was comparable [to Wang's]. No one would know [Zhenzong's] rankings. On the following day, in the hall, this matter was discussed and those ranked would vie with one another to be among those selected for employment. Dan daily required the employment of someone, and the ranked ones all strove to be that person. There was never an instance of someone refusing to report to the throne; never once was [Wang Dan] not capable of securing a ranked individual. Even though the person might be ill, he could not bring himself to remain idle.[19]

Provided that it is a reasonably accurate depiction, little comment is necessary on why Sima Guang and countless others were both impressed and influenced by the acumen and comportment above attributed to Wang Dan. In the minds of those seeking similar results, Wang Dan's methods for interrogating job-seekers became a template for success.

This particular portrait of Wang Dan in action furthermore reifies a crucial theme proposed earlier, for it exposes us to a man who—despite the overweening power he had accrued—exercised extreme caution with all those with whom he dealt. Wang Dan also demanded caution on the part of all subordinates and, on the basis of his reputed expertise as a personnel manager, he received it. As the following anecdote drawn from the writings of the scholar Wang Qi (1020–92)—much better known as Wang Junyu—indicates, Wang Dan believed caution even in the form of subterfuge could often be vital in preserving the image and—by extension—the security of the state:

> Near the end of [Dazhong] xiangfu [1008–16], when Wang Dan was overseeing the Secretariat-Chancellery (*zhongshu*), the Inner Treasury (*neitang*) suffered the

loss, due to damage, of its stores of fine silks—resulting in them becoming practically depleted. State Finance Commissioner Lin Te [fl. 1000] requested three times of the emperor that he be permitted to compensate for the loss by procuring silks from the markets of the grasslands beyond the [Yellow] River. [But] Dan completely quashed Lin's plan to do this, and Lin, leading subordinates [behind him], came forth to Wang Dan's own office to protest this decision. Speaking calmly, Dan said: "We indeed ought to naturally desire to acquire fine silks. [But] after you have exposed the weakness of our state to the four directions [in order to get them], then what?" Then, hardly more than several days had elapsed when four million bolts of silk were collected and received through the exchange of tribute between equals [with the Liao]. It seems that in bringing this matter to fruition Dan wanted foremost to advance the cause through secrecy.[20]

This anecdote provides a kind of postscript to the foregoing anecdote drawn from the Song History that details the occasion of the destructive fire in the imperial inner quarters, and there is no denying the cautionary flavor of both. However, in addition to differing in its specificity, this latter account also differs from the former in its purpose. Moreover, in either case, Wang is depicted as the spokesman for techniques of governance—in the former case, the dispersal of "the directives of government" and "rewards and punishments"; in the latter case, secrecy—that Chinese have, from time immemorial, viewed as the antitheses of recklessness and that have proven vital to the preservation of the state.

But there are still more layers to the image of Wang Dan as the manager or manipulator of men. Sima Guang, for example, further contributes to the portrayal of Wang Dan as exhibiting an implicit fairness amidst any secretiveness. Indeed, inasmuch as later scholars have subjected any aspect of his thought at all to scrutiny, the extent to which Wang Dan maintained and promoted a purely meritocratic outlook has commanded significant attention.[21] To be sure, we learn from such corroborating evidence as that provided only a bit more than a century after the fact by the scholar Fei Gun (*jinshi*, 1205) that Wang was by no means a nepotist:

> During the time that Wang Wenzhen [Dan] served as grand councilor, Han Zhongxian [Yi] [972–1044], the husband of his eldest daughter, because of the precedent requiring that relatives of high officials govern only in remote prefectures, was assigned to Yangzhou. Wang personally consoled his daughter, saying: "You need not worry. When your husband Han goes off to [Yang]chuan, you may then return to my house. [But] if I seek imperial dispensation in behalf of your husband Han, on another day [in the future], someone will reproach him and claim that, on the basis of a petition to the emperor by the father of his wife, he was able to avoid transferal to a remote assignment. Such would more than slightly harm him." When [Han] Zhongxian [later] learned of this [decision on his father-in-law's part not to interfere], he said: "Lord [Wang] has done me a great service."[22]

Moreover, no matter how compelled we are to question whether any moral criteria applied when he acted in his role as profiteer, we cannot easily overlook the overt presence of precepts that guided Wang Dan in appraisals of personnel. The following record extracted from the Song History, which involves Wang Dan's curiously ambivalent investment in a younger contemporary, serves as a case in point:

> Having gone twice to visit Wang Dan but, failing to see him, Grand Master of Remonstrance (*jianyi dafu*) Zhang Shide [*jinshi*, 1011] suspected that someone had slandered him. Thus, Zhang told Xiang Minzhong [949–1020], hoping that Xiang would casually inform Wang Dan [of his suspicion]. When subsequently discussing who should manage the Proclamation Drafting Section, [Wang] Dan said: "It is a pity about Zhang Shide." Minzhong then prodded him further regarding what he meant by this statement. Wang replied: "Before the emperor, I took the trouble to speak in his behalf as the son of a celebrated family, saying that he [potentially] had the deportment of an official. Then, unexpectedly, he twice appeared at my door. He is a top graduate in the examinations, having advanced with honors and [already] realized his ambitions. But he still ought to be [more] virtuous in his interactions with others. Instead, he resorts to clamoring after positions, acting like someone trying to advance without the benefit of a degree. What else should I have done [but not come forth when he came to visit me]?"
>
> [Xiang] Minzhong then communicated [Zhang] Shide's suspicion [of being slandered] to [Wang] Dan, who replied: "Am I one to put up with anyone who maligns and slanders someone else? It is merely that after Shide did advance [into the civil service] he treated me shabbily, that's all." Minzhong then truly commended Dan, saying: "Whenever there is a deficiency in what is appropriate, I can expect that you will not overlook it." Dan said: "But put off speaking of this matter to Shide. If he learns of it, then he will rely on advancing himself by trying to contain his greed, and this will [only] further provoke his contemptible habit [of insinuation]."[23]

If nothing else, the foregoing anecdote indicates that Wang Dan's regimen for the selection of the talented was not foolproof, and that he certainly sometimes seriously regretted some of his choices among the candidates he promoted for advancement—even if today we cannot always ascertain why.

But there may well be more than misgivings in judgment involved in the case of Zhang Shide, for there are additional contemporary and near-contemporary reports suggesting that Wang Dan could be guided less by virtue than by bias. The manifestations of this bias could appear quite capricious and extreme. One oft-cited example involves Wang's decision, while serving as education administrator, to fail one candidate for allegedly introducing a new interpretation of a specific word and yet advance another candidate who overtly erred in the examination fundamental of rhyming.[24] The candidate Wang chose to pass turns out to have been none other than Li Di, destined later to become grand councilor. It is of course possible to construe Wang's actions in this instance less as favoritism than a reinforcement of conservative early Song attitudes toward the examinations and an expression of the cautionary disapprobation toward scholarly innovation within their restrictive setting. Nevertheless, even so construed, there is no denying that this interpretation belies a certain unseemly proclivity for bias within what was theoretically the most meritocratic of cultural settings.

Wang Dan's misgivings about Zhang Shide in particular are, moreover, reflective of larger and deeper tensions—tensions that dwarfed either man. Within Chinese bureaucracy in any period, factionalism was rampant and infamous but—for numerous reasons, not the least of which being the documented ascendancy of the civilian official himself—this situation was especially true of the Song. We glean from this passage that Wang Dan may well felt himself ensnared in stalemates on two fronts—one, with the Qidan, *along* China's borders and a more personal one, with his ostensible compatriots, *within* them. We may venture to take Wang's concluding statement itself as his tacit recognition of being in such a plight. In addition to expressing his characteristic caution, it connotes just how firm the grip of this endemic factionalism really was. His concluding "But put off speaking of this to Shide" belies what must have been his awareness that there was no ironclad confidentiality on which to rely and that his views would eventually be found out by or even divulged to the other side. The porous and futile nature of such confidences is all the more exposed when we take into account that Xiang Minzhong—Wang Dan's interlocutor—was Zhang Shide's brother-in-law, the husband of his sister.[25] Furthermore, chiefly from this latter anecdote, we can intuit Wang Dan's entrenched scholarly conservatism as well as his very likely favoritism toward like-minded protégés, whom he sought to ensconce at the expense of less like-minded ones.

Noteworthy is the fact that Wang Dan did not succeed in waylaying Zhang Shide, and Zhang subsequently went on to enjoy Zhenzong's great confidence. Zhang Shide's official biography in the Song History conveys that: "When Qidan and Korean emissaries arrived [at court, the emperor] much employed Shide in managing them. At the beginning of the Tianxi reign period [1017], as a military commissioner, he pacified Huainan."[26]

Nevertheless, we should no less assuredly regard Zhang Shide as Wang Dan himself did—as a representative of the generation destined to succeed his own, who deserved to be either groomed for or barred from office. Given the perceived stakes, we may assume that Wang was moved to suppress the career prospects of any members of this succeeding generation who disagreed with him. But, within the tenuous context within which the Song imperial bureaucracy operated as a kind of increasingly threatened species, Wang Dan was able to use his numerous recommendation successes to absolve him of the charge of bias. Furthermore, in his efforts to expunge dissenting opinion from wherever possible within the civil service channel and to refuse to nurture potential opposition, Wang was hardly doing any more than any other chief minister had attempted to do—at any point before, during, or after the Song.

Thus, whether for good or ill, we cannot afford to ignore the conspicuous significance of the power that Wang Dan wielded in his recruitment activities. In this area of the Song civil enterprise, he may well have been unexcelled. The Song

History informs us that: "In general, those who Dan recommended were all men that had not been previously known. After his death, when the historians compiled the Veritable Records of Zhenzong (*Zhenzong shilu*), they acquired Wang Dan's internal memorials, and it began to become known just how many of the court's officials were those whom he had recommended."[27] Thus, in the area of personnel as well as in other aspects of the civil service (such as the examinations themselves), Wang Dan's contributions were both novel and singular.

Loyalism or Sycophancy?

Wang Dan's legacy of achievement in the personnel sphere may well be peerless. Unfortunately, however, his facility at stocking the bureaucracy with men of talent was not to constitute the final standard by which he has become historically judged. Instead, the question that has proven most controversial is that of precisely where Wang Dan's principal allegiances lay. Was he principally loyal to state, to sovereign, or to neither of these? Was he fundamentally loyal only to himself? The uncertainty surrounding Wang Dan's position on these questions has led to all manner of accusation being leveled against him and also led, consequently, to the permanent tarnishing of his legacy. Masterminding a strategy in which the enemy Qidan were paid off in order to keep them at bay was no cause for scorn. But being only as a self-aggrandizing opportunist who was loyal only to oneself certainly was. Therefore, determining the object of Wang Dan's allegiance has become the pivot on which his entire historical legacy has turned and, as is shown below, it has resulted in much mixed opinion.

On one level, to question whether Wang Dan privileged the emperor with his loyalty is unfair, for, in every age, the Chinese minister was necessarily beholden to the favor of his sovereign for his tenure. But one great irony of the Song is that, in what was ostensibly the newly emergent supreme age of the independent production of the civil official via the state bureaucracy, the particular occupant of any given post was perhaps never more expendable when compared to any prior time. Therefore, it is truly curious to note that later observers found Wang Dan's loyalty to Zhenzong, which was at least superficially of the archetypal sort demanded of all ministers by their sovereign, so suspect; it was this trait that they subjected to the harshest criticism. In an odd way, for many, the completeness with which Wang Dan vested his own interests in the flawed person of Zhenzong ensured that his sycophancy would become his largest defect in the unforgiving lens of the historical record.

Wang Dan served Emperor Zhenzong continuously and, whether feigned or not, with apparent faithfulness from the latter's succession in 997 until the death of the former in 1017—a full two decades. Both men prospered from the relationship, even if the degree to which the Song state prospered under them remains, even now, intensely debated. Peter Lorge's preceding description of Zhenzong's provocative sponsorship of the expensive and labor-intensive "Great Ditch" contradicts his natural apprehensiveness regarding matters of defense depicted here, and these contrasts complicate arriving at a balanced appraisal of the overall efficacy of his rule all the more. But there is no denying that the two men, Zhenzong and Wang Dan, were well suited to each other, and were united over the courses of both their careers by their shared reverence for caution at all costs. The emperor, like the minister, tended to view the amount of state revenue accrued or lost as the baseline for measuring the success or failure of what were fundamentally political undertakings, such as national defense. As grand councilor, Wang Dan, for his part, was a preservationist, who—unlike his predecessor Kou Zhun—seems never to have forced the emperor's hand on issues relating to the defense policy.[28] But Wang Dan was similarly passive in indulging imperial prerogative and caprice; this passivity would prove extremely costly for him personally.

The most fateful of Wang Dan's many excesses assumed the form of his contribution to the ostentatiously flamboyant and controversial resurrection of the Sacrifice to Heaven and Earth (*fengshan*) ceremony—beginning in late 1007—an event that requires at least some explanation of the context leading up to it. As with any change in the upper echelons of government, the fall from favor of Kou Zhun in 1006 precipitated much more than Wang Dan's succession to his position in the subsequent year. Kou's dismissal also provided his unscrupulous colleague and longstanding rival Wang Qinruo (962–1025) with much less obstructed access to the emperor. Having been removed, Kou could no longer couch his signature exploit—namely, that of having orchestrated the armed standoff and subsequent accord at Chanyuan in 1004–5—as a great victory and shield it from criticism. For his part, Wang Qinruo did his best to impress upon the insecure and equivocal Zhenzong a different reality—one that presented the Chanyuan Treaty as a most ignominious and demeaning embarrassment.[29] In relatively short order, Wang succeeded at undermining the agreement; he furthermore used his surging influence to convince the emperor that the most fitting way of expunging the defiling shame of this unequal accord with the enemy Qidan was by conducting the *fengshan* ceremony.

Tradition extols the Sacrifice to Heaven and Earth as one of the oldest ceremonies associated with the Chinese emperor. Yet, this attribution is really nothing more than presumption, for there is no mention of it as an imperial prerogative where one would expect some reference to be found—that is, in the Classic of Rites (*Lijing*), itself a likely product of a period as late as the early or Western Han dynasty (202 BCE–CE 9).[30] In times after the Western Han, when we can in fact verify its performance, the *fengshan* ceremony was also—perhaps in part because of the venerable status attributed to it—customarily one of the least frequently performed of imperial sacrifices.[31]

Originally, the Sacrifice to Heaven and Earth involved two distinct ceremonies that became merged at some indeterminate point in history. We can determine this distinction lexicographically, because *feng*, in this instance, denotes the sacrifices made by the emperor to Heaven from atop a greatly elevated stacked-earth ritual altar; *shan* denotes the emperor's act of purifying Earth and making sacrifices to the mountains and streams. Anciently, the emperor would embark on an imperial tour that would include four mountain peaks. Atop the greater mountains, he performed the *feng* sacrifice; atop the lesser mountains, the *shan* sacrifice. However, in succeeding eras, the ceremony became as much political as religious in its connotations, whereby it became a vehicle through which the ruler touted the empire's prestige as a national entity, ideally abroad as well as at home, and its original, more purely ritualistic functions were increasingly deemphasized.[32]

Thus, the ingenuity of Wang Qinruo's appropriation of the Sacrifice to Heaven and Earth lay in how he was able to successfully manipulate the emperor as well as an evolved rite identified with imperial person and commandeer both institutions for the purpose redressing an appropriate but largely concocted military grievance. But Wang Qinruo was well aware that still more embellishment was necessary for him to truly succeed. Tradition also dictated the appearance of auspicious signs that—in the form of missives or messages "dispensed by Heaven" (*tianshu*)—will augur the ceremony; upon receiving these signs, the emperor would then deem the ceremony ritually necessary. Unfortunately, no such messages were immediately forthcoming to Zhenzong. However, the absence of such messages did nothing to deter Wang Qinruo from simply fabricating them, which he did throughout the year 1008 and thus, by year's end, the stage was set for an excessively extravagant and, in the view of many, farcical revival of the Sacrifice to Heaven and Earth.[33]

For his part, Wang Dan, in the eleventh month of 1008, as commissioner of grand ceremonies (*dali shi*), was in the lead of the processional of more than 24,375 people who participated in the grandiloquent performance of the ceremony atop Mount Tai or Taishan.[34] Consequently, we have little choice on the basis of preliminary analysis but to view Wang Dan as having been a willing participant in what many contemporary and later observers regard as a massive charade. After all, Wang Dan had responded to the brazenly deceptive actions of Wang Qinruo mostly with inaction. Moreover, if his failure to expose or oppose the ruse voluntarily was not indefensible enough, when he later *was* impelled to act by imperial decree, rather than remonstrate against Wang Qinruo's chicanery, Wang Dan instead chose complicity. To be sure, especially in connection with the purported Heaven-dispatched messages, Wang was also guilty of knowingly condoning superstition. But, as modern rationalists, in accounting in hindsight for his tarnished legacy, we probably are moved to make too much of Wang's condoning the superstitious manipulation of the emperor and the masses. Perhaps even more egregious in the minds of his contemporary and subsequent critics was the fact that we must remember him as having played a full and frontal role in trivializing a rite that was vested with quasi-classical authority. Moreover, the great dismay of Wang Dan's later detractors is only compounded by the fact that the mockery of the Sacrifice to Heaven and Earth that he oversaw was the last documented performance of the ceremony in Chinese history.[35] In the minds of far too many observers of that time and since, the proper place for having taken a firmer stand was along the banks of the Yellow River—in and around Chanyuan—and not on the summit of Mount Tai.

But genuine attempts at fairness might also make us less condemnatory than his traditional critics were about Wang Dan's motives for participating in the Sacrifice to Heaven and Earth. We might be led to ask ourselves whether there was not something more on the plane of the self-sacrificial about his involvement. To do so reveals that while many later chroniclers have regarded it as reprehensible, Wang Dan's conduct as a coconspirator in the *fengshan* affair was not inexplicable to them. Nor should it be to us. We can start by observing that—in direct contrast to Kou Zhun's contentious relationship with Wang Qinruo—Wang Dan's relationship with Qinruo (who was no relation) was cordial and perhaps even approaching amicable.[36] We must also be mindful that, as has already been mentioned, Wang Dan was new in a post—the most exalted in the land—that he understandably desired to retain. Still, while his compliance in the *fengshan* episode is not inconsistent with what we have come to expect, whether he would have chosen to conduct himself in 1017 exactly as he had in 1007–8 still lingers as a legitimate question. Finally, the related question of the exact cast of his loyalty to Zhenzong deserves our deliberation. In other words, of what *variety* was it? Was Wang Dan a loyalist in the grand sense—as a protector of sovereign and country—or only in the small sense—as a protector mainly of his own self-interest?

Having been continually asked by his countrymen in the centuries following his death, these are not new questions about Wang Dan. In fact, among the most cogent assessments of Wang Dan and his actions is the one proffered by the man who was the outstanding philosophical nationalist of the seventeenth century—Wang Fuzhi (1619–92).[37] What is most noteworthy about his evaluation is the unexpected defense that Wang Fuzhi mounts for Wang Dan, which is all the more striking given Fuzhi's unremitting disparagement of other Song "just war" opponents, such as the much-reviled Qin Gui (1090–1155).[38] We should also note well the identity of the person to whom he attributes the real blame. Writing more than six centuries after the fact in his Deliberations on the Song (*Songlun*), Wang Fuzhi conveys a judicious appraisal that nonetheless begins with a most condemnatory allusion, one—putatively based on a real event—that exploits Wang Dan's reputation as a profiteer:

> Wang Dan received the gift of beautiful pearls, and then he slavishly complied with the falsehoods and delusions of Zhenzong. Accepting the loan of honors, he forsook vigilance. The situation of our not knowing about Dan is insufficient to excuse him. If the ruler desires that something should be done and he rewards and enriches his ministers in order to procure its success, then those executing the matter must demonstrate more than the kind of efficacy that only stops midway. If a minister does not achieve the goal, then he should be incapable of taking comfort in his position and he should resign. Yet, [if he does] then inferior men will be increasingly unrestrained, and the state will become increasingly imperiled.
>
> Dan resided in the post of prime minister; he remained tied to the fate of the state, even while the followers of Wang Qinruo, Ding Wei, and Chen Pengnian

[d. 1017]—with sidelong glances—sought his ouster. Even while irresolute and toadying, he held on to the Song reins of government. Surely there are instances in which less was achieved than in his case.[39]

In light of precedent, Wang Fuzhi's scathing assignment of fundamental blame to Zhenzong is stunning and stands in ironic contradistinction to what we would normally expect, especially when we take into account his likely (though not necessarily natural) proclivity always to identify and empathize with the figure of the emperor.[40] This instance notwithstanding, Wang Fuzhi by and large conformed to age-old conventions of imperial deference in that, much more frequently than not, he assigned blame to ministers for misleading or otherwise failing those with whom they were charged with serving. In writing, he avoided directly impugning the judgment or besmirching the authority of any monarch, but least of all one of a past as remote as the Song.

Wang Fuzhi's interpretation is also important for what it suggests about the cognizance and currency of a notion of the "just war" in the early Song period. Indeed, as he describes the passive and even servile expression of Wang Dan's loyalty to Zhenzong, Wang Fuzhi also raises the distinct possibility that the openly anti–"just war" stance often ascribed to Wang Dan in history was merely an extension of a position more furtively taken by his sovereign. According to this scenario, despite his many deficiencies and insecurities and regardless of the crippled and codependent nature of their relationship, Zhenzong really did lead and Wang Dan followed.

However, Wang Fuzhi's appraisal notwithstanding, there are also contrasting assessments and many of them come from individuals who were more proximate to Wang Dan in history and thus far better positioned to help us gauge the prevailing Song sentiment regarding him—at least insomuch as there was one at that given point in time. We can date one such revealing judgment to the period of only about one century following Wang Dan's death and it comes from the famed Southern Song raconteur Hong Mai (1123–1202).[41] Hong's opinion is contained his seminal Jottings of Rongzhai in Five Collections (*Rongzhai suibi wuji*), which he commenced writing in 1162.[42] Hong Mai specifically criticizes Wang Dan for his collusion in the fabrications related to the Heavenly-dispensed messages. But his brief critique, in general terms and through a concentration on character more than actions, nonetheless also embraces what is at the core of the "just war" question in the Song. It thereby indicates rather plainly how the descendants of the elite circle in which Wang Dan himself had once moved had come to regard his contributions on the war front. Within a generation of the seizure of the north by the Jurchen [Nüzhen] Jin dynasty (1115–1234) in 1126, Wang Dan had already become a much maligned and disparaged man:

> When Lord Wang Wenzheng Dan succeeded in becoming participant in determining government matters and grand councilor (*canzheng zaixiang*), there

was not a single thing he did not anticipate [receiving]. In officiating [throughout a career that spanned] from vice director (*shilang*) to grand guardian (*taibao*), whereas he engaged in displays of detached deliberation, his fault lay in his truly being obsessed [only] with the fear of worldly losses.

He was incapable of decisiveness. Yet, when he approached death, he desired to atone [for his past] by shaving his head and donning the robes of a Buddhist monk. But what manner of making amends is this?[43]

In comparison to that of Wang Fuzhi, Hong Mai's view of Wang Dan is clearly the harsher verdict. From Hong Mai's perspective of significantly greater historical immediacy in relation to the subject, a much less forgiving and wholly unflattering depiction of both Wang Dan and his motives emerges. From his remarks, Hong Mai—presumably, together with the bulk of his ill-fated contemporaries—obviously does not believe the putative "hundred years of peace"—one that was purchased so prominently by Wang Dan's many acts of concession—was worth the price.

Precedents Most Human

Having already touched on it several times obliquely, we now arrive at the point at which it is logical to confront and ponder the phenomenon of Wang Dan's peace-at-any-cost compulsion directly. To do so affords us enhanced insights regarding Wang Dan's place in the Chinese expression of that idea as well as properly complicates his motives as a political actor. It also broaches the question of pacifism and the appropriateness of its application to this case. To be sure, even raising the issue of pacifism in relation to traditional China generally tends to generate more problems than it solves. Far too commonly, Sinological scholars have had to suffer uninformed assertions of pacifism as explanations for some of the most baseless and stereotypical generalizations regarding Chinese military practice and the overall attitude of the Chinese historically toward war. Consequently, instead of pacifism, I have here opted to call the course pursued by Wang Dan and his likeminded cohort one of opposition to belligerence.

Whereas his subscription to pacifism remains an open question, there is no question at all that Wang Dan staunchly subscribed to a path that we might call nonbelligerent, if not anti-belligerent. But how did he arrive at this stance? In seeking answers, our deliberations are advanced by two revelations, which are examined below at length. The first is how contemporary the particular human precedent was that moved him to adopt his stance of evasion regarding war. No matter what we wish to call Wang Dan's eventual position, more than anything else, human influence moved him toward it and abetted him in unswervingly upholding it. The second is how very unlikely a candidate for anything resembling a nonbelligerent mantle Wang Dan originally was.

Whenever traditional China is concerned, one cannot be daunted to find precedents for any phenomenon, convention, act, or agent in remote and barely accessible antiquity. Thus, discovering the only discernible precedent near-at-hand and in extremely close temporal proximity to the subject under scrutiny can engender shock and even suspicion. Nevertheless, such is indeed the case for the most influential human precedent that emerges for Wang Dan, for it was none other than his contemporary and, in at least one way, crucial political prototype Li Hang (947–1004).

Li Hang was ten years senior to Wang Dan but to call the older man a mentor of the younger is probably to overstate the case. Both had in fact received the crucial doctorate in 980 and thus, as cograduates, they shared a bond of equivalence in achievement in the examinations that often made individuals either fast friends or determined enemies for life. Moreover, Li and Wang evinced startlingly similar career patterns, with the former, as we might expect on the basis of his chronological seniority, tracking slightly ahead of the latter. Both men, for example, served as examination administrators, with Li Hang serving in that post in 987, only five years prior to the first of Wang Dan's two stints in that capacity. This pattern of career correspondence of course culminated in both men ascending to serve in effect as grand councilors, with Li appointed as joint manager of affairs with the Secretariat-Chancellery (*tong zhongshu menxia pingzhang shi*) in 998—that is, eight years before Wang was to serve in a functionally equivalent capacity. Thus, their comparable if staggered career trajectories were decisive in drawing the two men into close association.

For his prowess as an evaluator of talent and selector of personnel, Li Hang achieved renown that rivaled that of Wang Dan. Moreover, in this connection, we are apprised of a factor that is far more elusive than in the case of Wang Dan because Li Hang actually appears to have derived his general principles from and attributed them to a specific text. Writing in his important collection of vignettes, perhaps no more than a century after the fact, the scholar Shao Bowen (1057–1134) records:[44]

> When he acted as grand councilor, Lord Li [Hang] Wenjing was [frequently] seen reading the *Analects* (*Lunyu*). When someone asked him about this, [he] said: "My manner of performing as grand councilor accords with [the two lines in the *Analects*]: 'Maintaining frugality and simplicity, always love the people; employ the people but only in ways appropriate to the season.' The excellence of these two lines has never been surpassed. Being the words of the sages, they are fit to be recited throughout one's entire life."[45]

Although its bearing on the matter of his approach to issues of personnel is obvious, we might assume Li Hang's reverence for a seemingly arbitrary exhortation by Kongzi or Confucius (551–479 BCE), plucked from the first book of the *Analects*, to have little bearing on either his attitudes toward war or his predisposition toward or against anything akin to nonbelligerence. Yet, a full quotation of the entire passage or chapter from which these two lines are extracted is perhaps subliminally revealing, for the sequence of lines in question is preceded by: "The Master said: 'In leading a thousand-chariot state, be respectful in performing your duties and resolute in standing by your words.'"[46] It is well known that, in ancient times, military capacity of a state was measured in the number of chariots it could mobilize, given that they represented the primary ordinance whereby warfare was conducted. It is clear that the leader that Confucius is addressing is at least the prospective prosecutor of war. Thus, especially the clause "employ the people but only in ways appropriate to the season" takes on new nuances of potentiality and becomes particularly provocative in terms of what it might have meant to Li Hang, not to mention whatever Confucius might have intended by it.

The directness of their experiences of war is in fact the one area in which the parity between Li Hang and Wang Dan diverged profoundly. As for Wang Dan, as has been established, he, in sum, had had very little real exposure to war. The situation for Li Hang was, however, starkly different. In the tenth month of 999, the Qidan encroachments into the north commenced and Zhenzong personally led Song armies in response. At that time, Li Hang was appointed to the additional post of vice director of the Secretariat (*zhongshu shilang*) and, serving conjointly as governor of the Eastern Capital (Bianliang or subsequently Kaifeng), he was ordered to organize measures specifically for its defense. Li was subsequently rewarded with the additional titles of vice director of the Chancellery (*menxia shilang*) and right vice director of the Department of State Affairs (*shangshu you puye*) precisely because of what was deemed his exemplary performance in this taxing and sensitive post. His experiences must have been in some manner transforming, because when clashes arose between the Song and what would eventually become the Western Xia at the turn of the eleventh century, ultimately precipitating the conflicts described by Michael McGrath in this volume, Li Hang consistently advocated the most extreme restraint. Believing the people along the western borderlands to be too impoverished to wage war effectively, he stressed—to no avail—that direct confrontation with the Tangut enemy was to be avoided. Whatever led Li Hang to recast his views remains unknown to us but he had clearly become—as Wang Dan would after him—the proponent of a strategy of peace, at all costs.

Nonbelligerence was not a strategy toward which Wang Dan was predisposed. On the contrary and somewhat surprisingly given his later commitment, Wang required convincing that it was the right course. We must credit Li Hang with exercising a kind of transformative suasion by example that made Wang Dan receptive enough to the nonbelligerence ideal such that he was eventually moved to incorporate that outlook fully and assume leadership of the peace party. In this important connection, Wang's admirer Sima Guang offers a brief but revealing account of the elder man's influence upon the younger:

> Once Zhenzong was already in the midst of discussing peace terms with the Qidan, Wang Wenzheng Dan inquired of Li Wenjing Hang, asking: "How are the peace discussions going?" Wenjing replied: "If they are good, then all will be good. If an end is put to these border concerns, then the fears of the people will

be allayed and the ruler of the people will gradually produce nothing less than an uplifting in their spirits."

[Wang] Wenzheng, for his part, was not persuaded by [Li's optimism] and [yet] when he was with Zhenzong during his latter years, [Wang Dan himself], on tours of inspection [in the aftermath of] the national crisis, supervised the major repair and restoration of [numerous imperial] palaces and Daoist observatories.

Wenzheng thereupon secretly praised [Li Hang], saying: "Lord Li must be said to have possessed an intelligence that came from prescience (*xianzhi*)."[47]

Sima Guang's record clearly articulates that the cause of peace was not one for which Wang Dan demonstrated either a natural or pronounced affinity. On the contrary, Wang Dan experienced the epiphany that brought him around to the peace perspective only because of his contact with Li Hang.

Although he was perhaps among the closest to Wang Dan temporally to make such an observation, Sima Guang was not the only one to note Li Hang's commandingly persuasive influence. Sima's contemporary Shao Bowen offers an even more detailed if somewhat more historically removed account of the relationship between Li and Wang when he apprises us that:

During the Xianping [998–1003] and Jingde [1004–7] reign periods, Lord Li Wenjing Hang occupied the post of grand councilor and Lord Wang Wenzheng Dan served as participant for determining government matters. At that time, neither the western nor the northern borders were pacified. There was no respite in the daily calls-to-arms [for troops to report to] and reports dispatched back from the fronts. [But] since the emperor was conscientious in performing his duties, the two lords could eat and sleep without anxiety.

Lord Wenzheng [Wang Dan], in exasperation, said: "How are we to achieve and witness a great peace? Our generation should be relieved [of this concern]." Lord Wenjing [Li Hang] replied: "It is fitting that we should be apprehensive and vigilant while our state is confronted by the external threat of powerful enemies. On some other day, although the empire will be at peace, the intentions of the emperor will [only] gradually be fulfilled. [Thus,] the situation still will not be one in which we can fold our hands and consider our work done."

"I am old and moreover will [soon] die. When you become grand councilor, it is fated that you yourself will realize all of this, without ever having to reflect deeply on what I have [just] said." Then the time arrived when the northern reaches were at peace and the western frontier compliant. Thereupon, the court performed the rites of visitation at the imperial tombs and a ceremony in celebration [of the accords] was conducted at Mount Feng. [On these occasions,] as for the grand and the obscure, the majestic and the minute—there was nothing to which particular attention was not paid.

Wenjing had already passed away, and Wenzheng [himself] was in decline. Yet, even in the feebleness with which he continued to lead and assist, commending [his predecessor], he always said: "Wenjing was sagacious." Therefore, at that time, Wenjing was said to be the sage-grand councilor.[48]

Albeit embellished, we have little reason to deem Shao Bowen's account less reliable than Sima Guang's. Moreover, the reference in this passage to the celebratory ceremony convened at Mount Feng (Fengshan; also called West Mountain or Xishan) is noteworthy for the symbolic connotations it likely denoted as a strategic and cultural boundary. Located in modern southwestern Hebei province, only some 13 kilometers west of the modern city of Xingtai (which was itself established during the Song), Mount Feng represented a site very near the northernmost extent of Song-controlled territory, pursuant to the redefinition of borders via the 1005 Chanyuan Peace Agreement. It thus exemplifies the claims of M. A. Butler in this book that Chinese middle-period borders were at times both physical and psychic.

Thus, in each instance, we must regard the essential thrust of the argument in the two foregoing records as being the same—namely, that Wang Dan came to subscribe to the mentality of nonbelligerence only *after* he was subjected to a humbling and personalized indoctrination delivered by an unimpeachable human agent. But there are several observations we can make that are assuredly larger than the fact that we here have two highly descriptive documents corroborating each other through this identical argument. Let us consider but a few of these observations in turn.

First, although it might really have evolved for other reasons already discussed in this study, the fact that history has accorded Li Hang status as an upright pillar of the state and Wang Dan a venal and largely unscrupulous functionary is one of the great ironies. Both men after all eventually promoted the same policies. But herein we can also discern an instance of one the harshest realities of the politics of personality that prevailed during the Song and of traditional Chinese political culture in general. Once one's moral capital had become, for whatever reasons, compromised or sullied, even the advocacy of the correct policies was unlikely to fully salvage it; one's reputation—largely in the form of one's past—had a persistent way of carrying over and beyond the current situation.

Second, through the means of these and similar documents, we find ourselves bearing witness to what, in all likelihood, was a curious but not uncommon political metamorphosis. Prior to his conversion experience, Wang Dan, stood much more in skepticism than in awe of Li Hang's nonbelligerent agenda. Only after it had begun to yield favorable results and, evidently, only after the death of its proponent, did Wang feel impelled to extend a grudging assent to Li and his platform. We of course cannot afford to accept these testimonies unquestioningly. Unavoidable is the possibility of bias against Wang Dan, though this factor is presumably reduced if not nonexistent in the reportage of Sima Guang, who greatly esteemed Wang Dan. We must also note that there is no explicit reference to the skeptic Wang Dan as ever having been an affiliate of the factions favoring war. The motives for his initial hesitancy in embracing Li Hang's orientation are simply not addressed. The fact that Wang Dan was not initially an advocate of peace does not necessarily make him originally a proponent of war. Nevertheless, in our speculations on what his pre-conversion leanings must likely have been, we are ultimately forced to ask ourselves how many alternatives to the pro-war stance could the Wang Dan who is depicted in these documents as not yet convinced of the virtues of peace have plausibly had.

Third and finally, such records as were produced by Sima Guang and Shao Bowen are no less valuable as commentaries on the times on which they focus than they are as descriptions of the actors who operated within those temporal parameters. Cautiously approached and judiciously used, these documents impart information that ranges from the transparently obvious to the marvelously revelatory. On the side of the obvious, we learn that nonbelligerence, if it existed at all as a mental construct for the Song ruling elite, remained a subconscious idea and phenomenon. This we can construe from the fact that, aside from the generic and ubiquitous term *wen* (civil or cultured), nonbelligerence existed both as a concept and an approach to statecraft without a real name. Yet, on the side of the strikingly revelatory, through such records, we can detect a self-consciousness of the Song as the age in which nonbelligerence clearly and unambiguously established itself as a legitimate and valued course of political action. Thus, in the hands of individuals like Li Hang, who never doubted its efficacy, and Wang Dan, who at first almost certainly did, the peace strategy—no longer to be confused with capitulation or treason— emerged during the Song not merely to distinguish itself as a policy but also to distinguish a significant number of its practitioners as advocates.

Where Peace Resides

In our consideration of a time when war was arguably the paramount preoccupation of the day, the minister Wang Dan has served us well as an intellectual portal through which to focus a penetrating light on the Song-period opposition to the long-established principle of the "just war." Wang Dan has unquestionably assisted us in better illuminating the scope and limits of the early Song capacity for confronting and engaging the "just war" concept in particular as well as the reality of war broadly. Moreover, Wang Dan's responses to the constant threat posed by war in China at the turn of the eleventh century are revealing in their own right. Through them, he fully exemplifies how the perpetual specter of war simultaneously simplified and complicated an astounding array of choices for the Song political actor. The words and deeds of Wang Dan and his many associates illustrate how Song ideas about the necessity for state solvency, government staffing and recruitment, and ritual ceremony, on the one hand, crucially determined and, on the other hand, were determined by the gravity of the threat of war.

Yet, employed as an informing lens of revelation, Wang Dan still remains somewhat opaque, considerably less than fully transparent and, with our still having failed to achieve full clarity, there remains at least one final and essential set of questions for us to ask: Can we really ascertain the concept of a "just war" as something that Wang Dan even recognized? At face value, for all intents and purposes, the foregoing discussion has surely described an individual representative of those elements in Song officialdom opposed in principle to the "just war." But how can we legitimately define Wang Dan as an opponent of this principle unless we can first confirm that he knew and appreciated the concept?

In the absence of writings on his part clearly certifying such knowledge and appreciation, we must resort to speculation to decide whether Wang Dan actually accepted the existence of a notion of "just war," let alone to decide whether he opposed it. But the speculation in which we must indulge is hardly groundless and, perhaps unsurprisingly, on the basis of it, I have come to believe that he did at least recognize the concept. As usual in the case of Wang Dan, the conclusive evidence for any such conviction is somewhat oblique. Nevertheless, it is both present and persuasive and, to uncover it, we must turn again—for the final time—to the most commended and redeeming facet of Wang Dan's legacy—that is, the sphere of the evaluation and procurement of personnel. Within it, in particular, we need to examine again his investment in and contributions to the systems of examination and sponsorship.

To date, the mid-twentieth-century scholarship of late Edward Kracke has made the most compelling case for Wang Dan having affixed the stamp of his personal influence on the Song examination and sponsorship systems. Writing in his landmark *Civil Service in Early Sung China, 960–1067*, Kracke maintained that— despite the absence of corroboration—we have little alternative but to make Wang Dan primarily responsible for the several innovations that occurred in the examination and sponsorship systems because they were instituted under his watch.[49] With all occurring between the years 1007 and 1017, precisely the years that Wang had ministerial charge of the state either jointly or singly, these innovations were several and well known. Just a few of the most noteworthy examples will suffice. In 1007, the practice of protecting the anonymity of examination candidates, already established in 992, was extended down to departmental-examination (*shengshi*) level.[50] In 1010, a proclamation of normalization aimed at institutionalizing controlled sponsorship on a par with the level already attained by the examinations was issued.[51] In 1015, a Bureau of Examination Copyists (*tenglu yuan*) was established with the expressed charge of copying examination papers to prevent the recognition of examinees' handwriting by examiners.[52] Although we are at a loss for confirming any of these developments as his direct initiative, Wang Dan was nonetheless the man in charge at the time of installation of each institution.

To this list of familiar developments, however, one more should be added that is considerably less familiar, less obvious, and, on a certain plane, less precisely datable. During Wang Dan's tenure as grand councilor, an irresolvable debate arose and raged over the content of the examination curriculum and, in particular, over the merits or detriments of the inclusion into it of a single work—the *Mencius (Mengzi)*.[53] As odd as it may seem to us now with the benefit of centuries of hindsight, the *Mencius* was a work not much studied before the tenth century and its value remained disputed over the entire course of the eleventh. Thus, at that time, few apparently thought of it as the definitive and indispensable companion to the *Analects* that it would become and, for many—if not most, the idea that it would—in less than two centuries—become included in the vaunted corpus that became known as the *Four Books* (*Sishu*) was virtually unthinkable.[54]

Nevertheless, in 1011, again on Wang Dan's watch, a fairly remarkable event occurred. In that year, heralded by the completion of Pronunciation and Meaning in Mencius (*Mengzi yinyi*) by the scholar Sun Shi (962–1033)—soon to become the most widely accepted commentary on the work, the *Mencius* was incorporated into the standard edition of the Thirteen Classics (*Shisan jing*).[55] Although it by no means points to the direct influence of Wang Dan, nevertheless, also worthy of note is the fact that Sun Shi's commentary resulted from his having been commissioned to revise the text of the *Mencius* by imperial order.[56] Interestingly, however, not even this encouraging development completely quelled the controversy concerning the *Mencius*, nor did it have the effect of establishing the text as a mandatory component of the examination curriculum, which it never did quite comfortably become during the Song.[57]

We cannot know whether Wang Dan was at the forefront of the debate over the *Mencius* or even whether he was in any way overtly involved. But, given his instructive and apparently creditable experience of having twice served as an examination administrator, it is extremely difficult to imagine that he was either ignorant of the debate or disinterested in its outcome. Similarly, and for many of the same reasons, we must assume that Wang Dan was well versed in the content of the *Mencius* and, being so versed, we should expect that the work did somehow inform his perspectives on war and, as importantly, on peace.

As a book, the *Mencius*—perhaps more conspicuously than any other Confucian text of the Warring States era—is replete with passages that disparage the pursuit of war, and these passages invariably describe war as the most wasteful, counterproductive, and misguided of all human enterprises.[58] Moreover, despite the claims made by such contemporary scholars as Thomas H. C. Lee, attributing to it a fascination with fighters and fighting,[59] *Mencius*, as a text, undeniably employs its imagery of the brave and courageous (*yong*) wholly and oftentimes militantly in the interest of a peaceful agenda. All passages in the *Mencius* concerning the pursuit and prosecution of war are couched in a language of unmistakable distaste. In my estimation, given the war-prone exigencies of Song times and context, it is difficult to conceive that this fact played absolutely no role in the controversy over the acceptance of the book.

Furthermore, among these many passages in the *Mencius* of expressly nonbelligerent bent, probably none is more salient the following one. In it, the historical Mencius (ca. 372–289 BCE), in the last *juan* or "chapter" of the book named for him, seizes upon the authority of the earlier classic of the Spring and Autumn Annals (*Chunqiu*) in order to make a stirring and what was no doubt, to men like Wang Dan, cogent point that all consideration of a war being called "just" must be balanced against the increasing awareness of the physical situation of the empire amidst an aggregation of contending states:

> Mencius said: "In the Spring and Autumn Annals, whereas there are instances of one war being better than another, *there are no just wars* (*yizhan*). One in authority

can wage a punitive expedition against his subordinates. But rival states do not punish one another by resorting to war."[60]

The above passage from the *Mencius*, at the very least, fixes the conceptual boundaries within which Wang Dan's cognizance of the idea of the "just war" becomes tenable. Mencius states that while a superior may, with impunity, wage war against an inferior (language with social as well as political ramifications), rival states (*diguo*)—evidently meaning states of approximate ethnocultural parity, which implicitly confront one another on a plane much closer to the level of equals, should not attempt to inflict punishment through such tactics. Mencius can only be thinking of interstate conflict mainly as he understood and experienced it in his time—that is, the predominantly "domestic" conflict between feudal *Chinese* states of his day. He understandably calls for a hierarchical resolution. He clearly states that conflict should be resolved much differently within a peerage of noble adversaries (the Chinese states) than it is between lord and vassals (the Chinese versus the non-Chinese).

Thus exposed is the inherent danger encountered in transposing the ancient standards of valuation of Mencius onto Wang Dan's markedly more complicated postfeudal context. Although contentious and increasingly deadly to one another, the "rival states" to which Mencius refers nonetheless comprised what was even then recognized as a proximate cultural bloc, being related—albeit, at times, remotely—by such ties as a roughly shared ethnic identity. To be sure, this situation no longer obtained in the world and times of Wang Dan, in which the sundry "rival states"—being almost exclusively non-Han and mostly beyond the boundaries of China proper—were as dissimilar from the Chinese as they were from each other in terms of their various elements of culture, including ethnicity.

We may also justifiably choose to question whether Wang Dan himself ever secretly harbored the thought, even for a fleeting instant, that the Liao—with whom there was a standing treaty in the form of the 1005 Chanyuan Accord—confronted the Song as such a state—as a *diguo* according to its classical articulation, with all of the rights and privileges seeming to pertain thereof within the Mencian framework of equality among rival states.[61] Indeed, by any standard that we might now apply, the fierce and protracted conflicts with the Qidan would seem to have confronted the Song with the cause for the pursuit of a "just war." But, in the end, to question of why Wang Dan, in his capacity as ministerial chief of the still fledgling Song state, chose not to regard the everyday reality of Liao provocations as grounds for such a war is perhaps to miss a vital point. Given our limited access to his inner reflections on the matter, we are ultimately forced to judge Wang Dan not so much by the thought he exhibited but by the actions he took—or, in many critical instances, did *not* take. In an age of consummate strife, Wang Dan's refusal—for any reason—to see the empire launched upon a course toward war clearly indicates his refusal even to entertain it as a serious option. Beyond this very plain truth, the continuance of his enigmatic silence on the matter may well end up being the best that we can ever expect of possible replies.

Notes

1. We can date the notion of the "just war" premise inherited by the West to at least the time when St. Augustine (354–430), as the Christian bishop of Hippo, discoursed on the subject in his renowned *The City of God* (*De civitate Dei*) and influential *Against Faustus* (*Contra Faustum*). Faustus was Augustine's Manichaean teacher prior to his recommitment to and baptism in Christianity. For a brief discussion of the significance of the articulation of the "just war" concept in this latter work of Augustine's as a factor in his rejection of Manichaeism, see Samuel N. C. Lieu, *Manichaeism in Central Asia and China* (Leiden, 1998), p. 141. For a succinct historical synopsis of the Western theoretical basis for the "just war," see Jean Bethke Elshtain, *Just War Against Terror: The Burden of American Power in a Violent World* (New York, 2003), pp. 46–58. All translations are mine unless otherwise noted.
2. This Chinese terminological equivalent to what we have familiarly come to call the doctrine of "just war" first appears in the Spring and Autumn Annals of Mister Lü (*Lüshi chunqiu*), a work at least initiated by the Minister of State Lü Buwei (d. 235 BCE). See Xu Weiyu, ed., *Lüshi chunqiu jishi* (Beijing, 1985), 8.10. See also John Knoblock and Jeffrey Riegel, *The Annals of Lü Buwei: A Complete Translation and Study* (Stanford, 2000), p. 199, wherein, as context demands, *yibing* is translated as "righteous armies": "As a general principle, one wants military positions and mountain passes to be advantageous, weaponry and armaments to be convenient, trained and honed fighters whose spirit is the very best, and the multitude of knights and people under one's command to be disciplined. These four are aids to righteous armies."
3. On the basis of this "righteous armies" passage, we can conclude that the "just war" concept was articulated anytime from half millennium to perhaps as much as a full millennium earlier in China than in the West. My exchanges with Mark Edward Lewis have much enhanced my understanding of the articulation of the "just war" concept during the pre-imperial period.
4. Modern European historian Sir Michael Howard has convincingly argued that the idea of peace is in fact an invented notion, maintaining that peace exists only against the backdrop of the ever-present threat of war. Such a view presents war or its likelihood—and *not* peace—as the normative modal assumption, at least in the history of the West. See Michael Howard, *The Invention of Peace* (New Haven, CT, 2001). Political scientist Robert Bates expresses very similar views to Howard's and links war integrally and indispensably to the whole history of state development. See Robert H. Bates, *Prosperity and Violence: The Political Economy of Development* (New York, 2001).
5. The constant threat of war made the defense of the Song state an inescapable concern for even the most civilian-minded of officials, and Wang Dan himself—despite his aversion—did not completely elude service of a military nature. In 996, he was appointed to serve briefly as a director in the Ministry of War (*bingbu langzhong*)—a position that was only slightly less elevated than that which his father had held in the same ministry and the last position that he held under the reign of Taizong. See Tuotuo, *Songshi* (Beijing, 1977), 282.9542–43. *Songshi* is hereafter designated by *SS*. For the translation of all official titles and institutions, I have primarily relied on Charles O. Hucker, *A Dictionary of Official Titles in Imperial China* (Stanford, 1985).

6. For a description of the conflict, which quickly devolved into a kind of grudging stalemate, see David C. Wright, "The Sung-Kitan War of A.D. 1004–1005 and the Treaty of Shanyüan," *Journal of Asian History* 32.1 (1998): 3–48. See also F. W. Mote, *Imperial China, 900–1800* (Cambridge, MA, 1999), pp. 70–71.
7. In 992, the Examination Office of the Ministry of Rites (*libu gongyuan*) revived the measure first practiced in a more limited form during the preceding Tang dynasty (618–907) of protecting the identities of examinees (*huming* or also *fengmi*). In the year 1000, of the 1,548 receiving the doctorate through the examination system, either 1,538 or 1,539 individuals were recruited into the bureaucracy—the highest number for any single year in the history of the Song. Still, neither of these developments is in any way directly traceable to Wang Dan himself. See Ma Duanlin, *Wenxian tongkao* (Beijing, 1986), 30.286. See also Wen-hsiung Hsü, "Wang Tan," in *Sung Biographies*, ed. Herbert Franke (Wiesbaden, 1976), pp. 1148–49 and E. A. Kracke, Jr., *Civil Service in Early Sung China, 960–1067* (Cambridge, MA, 1953), pp. 67, 60, 192.
8. *SS*, 7.144.
9. See Denis Twitchett and Klaus-Peter Tietze, "The Liao" in *The Cambridge History of China* vol. 6: *Alien Regimes and Border States, 907–1368*, ed. Herbert Franke and Denis Twitchett (Cambridge, 1994), pp. 103, 111.
10. *SS*, 282.9547.
11. Wang Pizhi, *Shengshui yantan lu* (Shanghai, 1935), 2.8. Especially for the literary histories of several of the Song works herein mentioned, I have closely consulted Balazs, Etienne, and Yves Hervouet, ed. *A Sung Bibliography (Bibliographie des Sung)* (Hong Kong, 1978).
12. James T. C. Liu, *China Turning Inward: Intellectual-Political Changes in the Early Twelfth Century* (Cambridge, MA, 1988), p. 2.
13. The reputation of Zhenzong for a tendency to quantify his political victories and losses perhaps exceeds that of any other Song monarch. See the unflattering portrayal of his role in negotiation of the Chanyuan Treaty in Mote, *Imperial China*, pp. 70–71.
14. *SS*, 282.9546. This particular passage is widely cited and probably originated in the effusively praise-extolling biographical record either written or compiled by Wang Dan's son Wang Su (1007–73). See Wang Su, *Wenzheng Wanggong yishi* (Shanghai, 1921), 1.4b–5. A nearly identical but somewhat embellished version of the same evidently much-admired passage appears in a work composed a century later by the scholar Li Yuan'gang (a. 1170). See Li Yuan'gang, *Houde lu* (Shanghai, 1921), 2.7a–b.
15. Zhang Lei, *Mingdao zazhi, xu* (Shanghai, 1920), 1.6b. See also *SS*, 8.157. Ding Wei was at this time participant in determining government matters (*canzhi zhengshi*). Beyond its tangibly reflecting Zhenzong's devotion to Daoism, the commencement of the construction of the Jade-pure Palace—officially the Jade-pure Palace of the Luminous Response (Yuqing zhaoying gong)—at the capital in 1014 evokes further questions about the legitimacy of Wang Dan's standing as profiteer. Did he approve of the extravagant facility or privately disapprove of it? The completed construction of the temple coincides with Wang's death in 1017 and, hence, by default, the termination of his influence as a bureaucrat. The Jade-pure Palace, as Frederick Mote states, "probably was the largest and most expensive imperial building project of the entire dynasty. Sadly enough, it was totally destroyed by fire in 1029, little more than ten years after it was

completed." See Mote, *Imperial China*, p. 163. For a detailed account of reaction at court to the destruction by fire of the temple, see Li Yuan'gang, *Houde lu*, 3.12b.
16. See Hsü, "Wang Tan," p. 1152.
17. The recommendation of Kou Zhun—the first of the individuals here listed—is representative as well as illustrative of Wang Dan's approach and style. An account appears in Li Yuan'gang, *Houde lu*, 1.4b–5.
18. The most current and thorough study of Sima Guang and his pervasive influence in such areas as personnel selection is Xiao-bin Ji, *Politics and Conservatism in Northern Song China: The Career and Thought of Sima Guang (A.D. 1019–1086)* (Hong Kong, 2005), pp. 41–43, 53–56, 179, 182.
19. Sima Guang, *Sushui jiwen* (Wuchang, 1877), 6.7b–8. An abbreviated and paraphrased version of this same passage is contained in *SS*, 282.9549.
20. Wang Junyu, *Guolao tanyuan* (Shanghai, 1921), 2.1.
21. A certain reverence for meritocracy was a value generally shared within Wang Dan's cohort but we should also note that the faith of at least some individuals lay more in the mechanics of the examination system than in the abstract values of equity underpinning it. See the opinion of Wang's younger contemporary Xia Song (984–1050), as presented in Thomas H. C. Lee, *Government Education and Examinations in Sung China* (Hong Kong; New York, 1985), pp. 203–4.
22. Fei Gun, "Wang Wenzhen xu ru Shu," *Liangxi manzhi* (1872 ed.), 3.7a–b. Yangzhou is today's modern Yang district, in southwestern Shaanxi province.
23. *SS*, 282.9550. Zhang Shide was the most favored among the ten sons of the prominent official Zhang Quhua (fl. 960–63), who had received the doctorate during the initial fifteen years of the Song when less than twenty per year were awarded. See Kracke, *Civil Service*, p. 58.
24. *SS*, 282.9550. See also Ma Duanlin, *Wenxian tongkao*, 30.286. See also Lee, *Government Education*, pp. 71–72.
25. *SS*, 282.9553.
26. *SS*, 306.10111.
27. *SS*, 282.9549.
28. Kou Zhun deployed several rash tactics, each of which contributed to his reputation for recklessness. They also no doubt factored into the abrupt curtailment of his term of service as grand councilor under Zhenzong. One extreme example was his insistence, during the Chanyuan conflict with the Liao in 1004, that Zhenzong personally lead Song forces north to confront the Qidan. Kou was convinced that seeing Zhenzong in the lead of his forces would overawe the enemy. By contrast, Wang Dan would never have risked endangering the person of the emperor by demanding such a maneuver, seeing any effectiveness it would render as trumped by its foolhardiness. See Mote, *Imperial China*, p. 115.
29. *SS*, 282.9544–45.
30. See Morohashi Tetsuji, comp. and ed., *Dai Kan-Wa jiten* (Tokyo, 1989–90), 4.10. An explanation of the Sacrifice to Heaven and Earth is contained in the late-Zhou or early-Han work *Guanzi*, wherein it is recorded that the primordial progenitor Wuhuaishi, who is a fixture figure in the *Guanzi*, began the practice of conducting the *feng* rites atop Mount Tai. The *Guanzi* describes the *shan* ceremony was successively performed since the times of the legendary sage-emperors Fu Xi, Shen Nong, Yan Di, and Huang Di, who all conducted it. However, the work *Wen Zhongzi* by Wang Tong (584–618) assigns the origins

of both the *feng* and the *shan* ceremonies to the period of the transition from the Qin to the Western Han dynasty. See Howard J. Wechsler, *Offerings of Jade and Silk: Ritual and Symbol in the Legitimation of the T'ang Dynasty* (New Haven, CT, 1985), pp. 170–94.

31. There was a gap of more than 500 years that separated the last later or Eastern Han-period performance of this sacrifice from its subsequent performances. Liu Xiu, canonized as Emperor Guangwu (r. CE 25–57), restorer of the Han dynasty in the form of the Eastern Han (CE 25–220), was the last to perform the rites in the Han before their resumption under three consecutive rulers in the early Tang. See Wechsler, *Offerings of Jade and Silk*, p. 175. See also Thomas H. C. Lee, *Education in Traditional China: A History* (Leiden, 2000), p. 249.
32. Morohashi, *Dai Kan-Wa jiten*, 4.10. See Wechsler, *Offerings of Jade and Silk*, pp. 176–94.
33. See Suzanne E. Cahill, "Taoism at the Sung Court: The Heavenly Text Affair of 1008," *Bulletin of Sung Yüan Studies* 16 (1980): 23–44. See also John W. Chaffee, *Branches of Heaven: A History of the Imperial Clan of Sung China* (Cambridge, MA, 1999), p. 37.
34. *SS*, 104.2527–28.
35. See Hsü, "Wang Tan," p. 1151.
36. *SS*, 282.9548–49.
37. For more especially on the intellectual outlook of Wang Fuzhi, see Alison Harley Black, *Man and Nature in the Philosophical Thought of Wang Fu-chih* (Seattle, 1989).
38. For the Song in particular as well as the imperial period in general, the much-maligned and much-studied Qin Gui is regarded as the archetypal traitor. For more on Qin Gui, see John E. Wills, Jr., *Mountain of Fame: Portraits in Chinese History* (Princeton, 1994), pp. 168–80.
39. Wang Fuzhi, *Songlun*, SBBY edn. (Shanghai, 1930), 3.9.
40. Wang Fuzhi's life circumstances contributed not only to making him a patriot but also an ardent monarchist. See S. H. Ch'i, "Wang Fu-chih" in *Eminent Chinese of the Ch'ing Period (1644–1912)*, ed. Arthur W. Hummel (Washington, DC, 1943–44), 2.817–19.
41. For more on Hong Mai, see Edward L. Davis, *Society and the Supernatural in Song China* (Honolulu, 2001).
42. See Chang Fu-jui, "Jung-chai sui-pi wu chi, 10 ch." in *A Sung Bibliography*, ed. Balazs and Hervouet, pp. 292, 296.
43. Hong Mai, "Wang Wenzheng gong," *Rongzhai suibi wuji* (Shanghai, 1935), 1.4.38.
44. Shao Bowen was a minor official and the son of the famous philosopher Shao Yong (1011–77).
45. Shao Bowen, *Henan Shaoshi wenjian qianlu* (Taibei, 1970), 7.13. The internal quotation from the *Analects* is contained in and extracted from *Lunyu*, 1.5.
46. *Lunyu*, 1.5.
47. Sima Guang, *Sushui jiwen*, 6.8b. For more on Wang Dan's eventual admiration for Li Hang as a model of foresight, see Ji, *Politics and Conservatism*, pp. 136–37.
48. Shao Bowen, *Henan Shaoshi wenjian qianlu*, 7.13a–b. Shao's statement closely approximates a passage in Wang Pizhi, *Shengshui yantan lu*, 2.9.
49. Kracke, *Civil Service*, pp. 32, 193.
50. Kracke, *Civil Service*, p. 192. See also Hsü, "Wang Tan," p. 1148.
51. Kracke, *Civil Service*, p. 193. See also Hsü, "Wang Tan," p. 1151.

52. Kracke, *Civil Service*, p. 192. See also Hsü, "Wang Tan," p. 1151.
53. Lee, *Education in Traditional China*, p. 379.
54. Lee, *Education in Traditional China*, p. 292.
55. See Tsien Tsuen-hsuin, *Paper and Printing* vol. 5 *(Chemistry and Chemical Technology)*, 1, *Science and Civilisation in China*, ed. Joseph Needham (Cambridge, 1985), pp. 162–63.
56. See Ichikawa Yasuji, "Meng-tzu yin-i, 2 ch.," tr., A. Albertat in *A Sung Bibliography*, ed. Balazs and Hervouet, p. 42.
57. Lee, *Education in Traditional China*, p. 292.
58. Seven examples seem to me to be of particular prominence. See *Mengzi*, 1.4b–5; 1.15b–16; 4.1b; 7.10; 12.10; 14.1a–b; 14.2b. For corresponding English-language translations, see D. C. Lau, tr., *Mencius* (London, 1970), pp. 51, 58, 85, 124, 177–78, 194, 195.
59. Lee, *Education in Traditional China*, p. 186.
60. *Mengzi*, 14.1b. For a translation alternative, see Lau, *Mencius*, p. 194. Emphasis added.
61. Interestingly, the middle-period Sinic geopolitical situation may well have produced an important lexicographical shift. In modern parlance, the term *di* now invariably means "enemy," not "rival," with the latter meaning having become archaic and regarded as the product of a much earlier time when the Han majority generally enjoyed the upper hand in its confrontations with its non-Han harassers. This power balance was to reverse definitively in the Song, and is perhaps reflected in and signified by this shift in the meaning of this term.

Glossary

Bianliang 汴梁
bingbu langzhong 兵部郎中
bingbu shilang 兵部侍郎
canzheng zaixiang 參政宰相
canzhi zhengshi 參知政事
Chanyuan 澶淵
Chen Pengnian 陳彭年
Chunqiu 春秋
dali shi 大禮使
Daming 大名
Dazhong xiangfu 大中祥符
Dangxiang 黨項 [Tangut]
di 敵
diguo 敵國
Ding Wei 丁謂
Ding Yaxiang 丁崖相
Fei Gun 費袞
fengmi 封彌
fengshan 封禪
Fengshan 封山
Fu Xi 伏羲
Guanzi 管子

Guangwu 光武
Han 漢
Han Yi 韓億
Han Zhongxian 韓忠憲
Hebei 河北
Henan 河南
Hong Mai 洪邁
huming 糊名
Hunan 湖南
Huainan 淮南
Huang Di 黃帝
jianyi dafu 諫議大夫
jinshi 進士
Jingde 景德
juan 卷
Kaifeng 開封
Kongzi 孔子 [Confucius]
Kou Zhun 寇準
Li Di 李迪
Li Hang 李沆
Li Yuan'gang 李元綱
libu gongyuan 禮部貢院
Lijing 禮經
Liyang 黎陽
Lin Te 林特
Liu Xiu 劉秀
Lü Buwei 呂不韋
Lü Yijian 呂夷簡
Lüshi chunqiu 呂氏春秋 呂
Lunyu 論語
menxia sheng 門下省
menxia shilang 門下侍郎
Mengzi 孟子
Mengzi yinyi 孟子音義
neitang 內帑
Nüzhen 女真 [Jurchen]
Pingjiang 平江
Qidan 契丹
Qin 秦
Qin Gui 秦檜
Rongzhai suibi wuji 容齋隨筆五集
Shaanxi 陝西
Shandong 山東
shangshu you puye 尚書右僕射
Shao Bowen 邵伯溫
Shao Yong 邵雍
Shen Nong 神農
shengshi 省試
Shengshui yantan lu 澠水燕談錄

shilang 侍郎
Shisan jing 十三經
Sima Guang 司馬光
Sishu 四書
Songlun 宋論
Songshi 宋史
Su Yijian 蘇易簡
Sun Shi 孫奭
taibao 太保
Taiping zaixiang 太平宰相
Taishan 泰山
Taizong 太宗
Tangguchang 唐古暢 [Tangut]
tenglu yuan 謄錄院
tianshu 天書
Tianxi 天禧
tong zhongshu menxia pingzhang shi 同中書門下平章事
Wang Che 王徹
Wang Dan 王旦
Wang Fuzhi 王夫之
Wang Junyu 王君玉
Wang Pizhi 王闢之
Wang Qi 王琪
Wang Qinruo 王欽若
Wang Su 王素
Wang Tong 王通
Wang Yan 王言
Wang You 王祐
Wang Zeng 王曾
Weigong 魏公
wen 文
Wen Zhongzi 文中子
Wenjing 文靖
Wenzhen 文貞
Wenzheng 文正
Wuhuaishi 無懷氏
Xishan 西山
Xia Song 夏竦
Xianping 咸平
xianzhi 先知
Xiang Minzhong 向敏中
Xin 莘
Xingtai 邢臺
Yan Di 炎帝
Yang 洋
Yangchuan 洋川
Yangzhou 洋州
yibing 義兵
yizhan 義戰

yong 勇
Yuqing gong 玉清宮
Yuqing zhaoying gong 玉清昭應宮
Yue 岳
Zhang Lei 張耒
Zhang Quhua 張去華
Zhang Shide 張師德
Zhang Shixun 張士遜
Zhao Deming 趙德明
Zhenzong 眞宗
Zhenzong shilu 眞宗實錄
zhigong ju 知貢擧
zhongshu 中書
zhongshu sheng 中書省
zhongshu shilang 中書侍郎
zuo shiyi 左拾遺

Bibliography

Balazs, Etienne and Yves Hervouet, ed. *A Sung Bibliography (Bibliographie des Sung).* Hong Kong: Chinese University Press, 1978.

Bates, Robert H. *Prosperity and Violence: The Political Economy of Development.* New York: W. W. Norton & Company, 2001.

Black, Alison Harley. *Man and Nature in the Philosophical Thought of Wang Fu-chih.* Seattle: University of Washington Press, 1989.

Cahill, Suzanne E. "Taoism at the Sung Court: The Heavenly Text Affair of 1008." *Bulletin of Sung Yüan Studies* 16 (1980):23–44.

Chaffee, John. *Branches of Heaven: A History of the Imperial Clan of Sung China.* Cambridge, MA: Harvard University Asia Center, 1999.

Chang Fu-jui. "Jung-chai sui-pi wu chi, 10 ch." In *A Sung Bibliography,* ed. Etienne Balazs and Yves Hervouet.

Ch'i, S. H. "Wang Fu-chih." In *Eminent Chinese of the Ch'ing Period (1644–1912),* ed. Arthur W. Hummel. 2 vols. Washington, DC: U. S. Government Printing Office, 1943–4.

Davis, Edward L. *Society and the Supernatural in Song China.* Honolulu: University of Hawai'i Press, 2001.

Elshtain, Jean Bethke. *Just War Against Terror: The Burden of American Power in a Violent World.* New York: Basic Books, 2003.

Fei Gun 費袞. "Wang Wenzhen xu ru Shu 王文貞婿入蜀 [Wang Dan's Son-in-law Enters Shu]." In *Liangxi manzhi* 梁谿漫志 [Rambling Annals of Liang Gorge], comp. Bao Tingbo 鮑廷博. *Zhibuzu zhai congshu* 知不足齋叢書 [Collected Books of the Studio of Insufficient Knowledge]. Tongzhi 同治 11 [1872] edn.

Hong Mai 洪邁. "Wang Wenzheng gong 王文正公 [Lord Wang Wenzheng]." *Rongzhai suibi wuji* 容齋隨筆五集 [Jottings of Rongzhai in Five Collections]. Shanghai: Shangwu yinshu guan [Commercial Press], 1935. *Guoxue jiben congshu* 國學基本叢書 [Foundations in National Learning Collected Books] edition.

Howard, Michael. *The Invention of Peace.* New Haven, CT: Yale University Press, 2001.

Hsü, Wen-hsiung. "Wang Tan." In *Sung Biographies,* ed. Herbert Franke. Wiesbaden, Germany: Franz Steiner Verlag, 1976.

Hucker, Charles O. *A Dictionary of Official Titles in Imperial China*. Stanford: Stanford University Press, 1985.
Ichikawa Yasuji. "Meng-tzu yin-i, 2 ch.," tr., A. Albertat. In *A Sung Bibliography* ed. Balazs and Hervouet.
Ji, Xiao-bin. *Politics and Conservatism in Northern Song China: The Career and Thought of Sima Guang (A.D. 1019–1086)*. Hong Kong: Chinese University Press, 2005.
Knoblock, John and Jeffrey Riegel. *The Annals of Lü Buwei: A Complete Translation and Study*. Stanford: Stanford University Press, 2000.
Kracke, Jr., E. A. *Civil Service in Early Sung China, 960–1067*. Cambridge, MA: Harvard University Press, 1953.
Lau, D. C., tr. *Mencius*. London: Penguin Books, 1970.
Lee, Thomas H. C. *Government Education and Examinations in Sung China*. Hong Kong and New York: Chinese University Press and St. Martin's Press, 1985.
———. *Education in Traditional China: A History*. Leiden, Holland: E. J. Brill, 2000.
Li Yuan'gang 李元綱. *Houde lu* 厚德錄 [Record of Virtue in Abundance], 20 vols., ed. Zuo Gui 左圭. *Baichuan xuehai* 百川學海 [Sea of Learning of a Hundred Streams], vol. 10. Shanghai: Bogu zhai, 1921.
Lieu, Samuel N. C. *Manichaeism in Central Asia and China*. Leiden, Holland: E. J. Brill, 1998.
Liu, James T. C. *China Turning Inward: Intellectual-Political Changes in the Early Twelfth Century*. Cambridge, MA: Council on East Asian Studies, Harvard University, 1988.
Lunyu 論語 [Analects].
Ma Duanlin 馬端臨. *Wenxian tongkao* 文獻通考 [Comprehensive Investigations into the Literary Inheritance]. 2 vols. Beijing: Zhonghua shuju, 1986.
Mengzi 孟子 [Mencius], annot. Zhao Qi 趙岐; ed. Jin Pan 金蟠. Shanghai: Zhonghua shuju, 1930. *Sibu beiyao* 四部備要 *(SBBY)* [Complete Essentials of the Four Divisions] edn.
Morohashi Tetsuji 諸橋轍次, comp. and ed. *Dai Kan-Wa jiten* 大漢和辭典 [Great Chinese-Japanese dictionary]. 2nd edition; 13 vols. Tokyo: Taishūkan shoten, 1989–90.
Mote, F. W. *Imperial China, 900–1800*. Cambridge, MA: Harvard University Press, 1999.
Shao Bowen 邵伯溫. *Henan Shaoshi wenjian qianlu* 河南邵氏聞見前錄 [Former Record of Things Heard and Seen by Mr. Shao of Henan]. Taibei: Guangwen shuju, 1970.
Sima Guang 司馬光. *Sushui jiwen* 涑水記聞 [Record of Rumors from the Man of Su River]. Wuchang: Hubei Chongwen shuju, 1877. *Hubei sanshisan zhong* 湖北三十三種 [Thirty-three Varieties of Hubei] edn.
Tsien Tsuen-hsuin. *Paper and Printing, Vol. 5 (Chemistry and Chemical Technology):1, Science and Civilisation in China*, ed. Joseph Needham. Cambridge: Cambridge University Press, 1985.
Tuotuo 脫脫. *Songshi* 宋史 [History of the Song Dynasty]. 40 vols. Beijing: Zhonghua shuju, 1977. Punctuated reproduction of 1345 prefaced edition.
Twitchett, Denis and Klaus-Peter Tietze. "The Liao." In *The Cambridge History of China, Vol. 6: Alien Regimes and Border States, 907–1368*, ed. Herbert Franke and Denis Twitchett. Cambridge: Cambridge University Press, 1994.
Wang Fuzhi 王夫之. *Songlun* 宋論 [Deliberations on the Song]. *Sibu beiyao* *(SBBY)* 四部備要 [Complete Essentials of the Four Divisions] edn. Shanghai: Zhonghua shuju, 1930.
Wang Junyu 王君玉 (also Wang Qi 王琪). *Guolao tanyuan* 國老談苑 [Garden for Discussing the National Heritage], ed. Zuo Gui 左圭. *Baichuan xuehai* 百川學海 [Sea of Learning of a Hundred Streams], vol. 13. Shanghai: Bogu zhai, 1921.

Wang Pizhi 王闢之. *Shengshui yantan lu* 澠水燕談錄 [Record of Banquet Conversations along the Sheng River]. Shanghai: Shangwu yinshu guan [Commercial Press], 1935. *Congshu jicheng chubian* 叢書集成初編 [Assembled First Editions of Collected Books] edition.

Wang Su 王素. *Wenzheng Wanggong yishi* 文正王公遺事 [Remnant Affairs of the Cultured and Upright Lord Wang], ed. Zuo Gui 左圭. *Baichuan xuehai* 百川學海 [Sea of Learning of a Hundred Streams], vol. 11. Shanghai: Bogu zhai, 1921.

Wechsler, Howard J. *Offerings of Jade and Silk: Ritual and Symbol in the Legitimation of the T'ang Dynasty*. New Haven, CT: Yale University Press, 1985.

Wills, Jr., John E. *Mountain of Fame: Portraits in Chinese History*. Princeton: Princeton University Press, 1994.

Wright, David C. "The Sung-Kitan War of A.D. 1004–1005 and the Treaty of Shanyüan." *Journal of Asian History* 32.1 (1998):3–48.

Xu Weiyu 許維遹, ed., *Lüshi chunqiu jishi* 呂氏春秋集釋 [Collected Interpretations of the Annals of Mr. Lü], 2 vols. Beijing: Beijing shi Zhongguo shudian, 1985.

Zhang Lei 張耒. *Mingdao zazhi* 明道雜志 [Miscellaneous Notes of Mingdao], *xu* 續 [Continuation]. Shanghai: Hanfenlou, 1920. *Xuehai leibian* 學海類編 [Arranged Compilation of the Sea of Learning] edn.

CHAPTER 5

HIDDEN TIME, HIDDEN SPACE: CROSSING BORDERS WITH OCCULT RITUAL IN THE SONG MILITARY

M. A. Butler

In 1104, the official Li Fuxian (fl. ca. 1100) lamented that, though in former times, battle was conducted according to ritual (*li*)[1], military practices of his time were not.[1] But, despite Li's complaint to the contrary, ritual remained an essential element of warfare in the Song dynasty (960–1279). The military was braided into the Song ritual network in many ways, both symbolically and practically. Great (that is, successful) military thinkers were oftentimes deified, after which court debates ensued on what were appropriate offerings for these strategists.[2] Loyal troops received bonus emoluments on the occasions of the suburban sacrifice ritual, performed once every three years.[3] Even weapons and equipment were manufactured and distributed according to a ritual hierarchy so that "the troops would respect ritual."[4] In addition to these means of ritual integration, military manuals of middle-period imperial China—Secret Classic of Venus, Planet of War (*Taibo yinjing*; ca. 759); Tiger Seal Classic (*Huqian jing*; submitted in 1005); and Comprehensive Military Essentials (*Wujing zongyao*; completed by court order in 1044)—document ritual practices. Such practices include prayer texts, instructions for sacrifice, moral admonitions, war initiation and conclusion rites, prognostication, divination, and other rituals that today would be termed occult.[5] This chapter is concerned with one of the latter ritual genres, a type of occult ritual based on the use of the cosmograph (*shi*), which gained great momentum during the Song.

The "Three Cosmographies" (*sanshi*) techniques refer collectively to the Six Water Cycles (*liuren*); the Supreme One (*taiyi*); and the Hidden Period (*dunjia*) techniques recorded in the manuals.[6] These techniques were performed on a compass-like device called a cosmograph or *shi* (figure 5.1), which was modeled after the heavens and their movements. In premodern literature, these techniques are

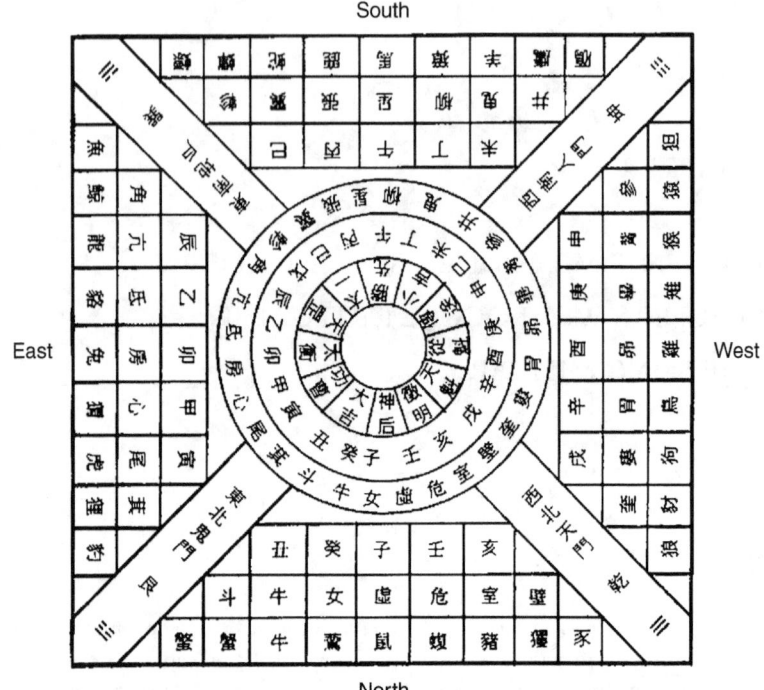

Figure 5.1 Six Water Cycles cosmograph (ca. late sixth century CE).
Source: Reconstructed from a rubbing of the excavated cosmograph and traditional sources.

most closely associated with a kind of sorcery practiced by the famous general Zhuge Liang (181–234). In modern times, the "Three Cosmographies" have become popularized in Hong Kong martial arts movies—in which the hero draws a circle on the ground, scribes a writ in the air, "paces the void," and then disappears by climbing through a rip in space-time.[7] Moreover, these techniques are still practiced in contemporary Taiwan, albeit in a somewhat different form.

The manuals mentioned above give a similar picture of the extraordinary potential of the "Three Cosmographies" techniques. By understanding the patterns of cosmic space and time, they tell us, one could use the Hidden Period to jump through time and space, change natural phenomena like weather, or disappear entirely.[8] One could not just know but "change good and evil fortune...by using the cosmograph."[9] It was also the means to esoteric knowledge: "Feng Hou performed the Hidden Period, thoroughly understanding ghosts and gods. The poles of the heavens and the obscure and profound, this is what is known as 'hidden' (*dun*)."[10] This statement places the techniques of the "Three Cosmographies" on the level of sorcery and the occult, marking them as more than simply a system of prognostication.

Such rituals may seem superficially the antithesis of military action. The use of these rituals has tended to be dismissed as symbolic and, therefore, tactically or strategically insignificant.[11] Scholars often oversimplify them as tools used merely to manipulate the warriors psychologically and emotionally.[12] It is possible that these rituals appear in military manuals through some historical quirk. Yet, these manuals devoted over half of their contents to ritual and belief. Most texts devote space to matters that their authors perceive as important. It seems likely, then, that the authors of these manuals believed in these rituals enough to commit them to writing. Moreover, as seen below, it is difficult to imagine creating rituals as complicated as the "Three Cosmographies" and not practice them.

Historical records also document the practice of these rituals. The courts of both the Tang (618–907) and the Song dynasties used the Six Water Cycles and Hidden Period techniques. Song emperors consulted "Three Cosmographies" diviners about affairs of state. At least eleven practitioners of the occult arts held positions prestigious enough to warrant biographies in the official histories of the Tang and Song. Unofficial sources suggest that these techniques were even more widespread than the official histories indicate.

The manuals specify not only the circumstances in which particular "Three Cosmographies" rituals should be performed but also the words and acts that constitute their content and performance. These words and acts and their invocation of the supernatural in the context of a social collectivity and a prescribed setting—in this case, being that of military personnel—constitute a system of belief. Understanding the ritual relations documented in these manuals tells us how the Song understood and used its military system, and ultimately, how the Song perceived conquest and put power into practice. From where does the supernatural power of these techniques come? What were the restrictions on this power? For answers, I look specifically at the role these rituals assumed during the Song in defining and creating borders.

Occult rituals found in Song dynasty military manuals defined either wholly or partially certain kinds of boundaries. Examined here are the relations of ritual action to various sorts of limits to determine not just how such rituals defined but also how they probed and transgressed these limits. During the Song, not the least important of these boundaries were those that scribed a symbolic or conceptual system, such as those thought to define the boundaries of nature, or authority and its role in governance, or knowledge and culture. Yet, these abstract boundaries were never divorced from practice, and practice itself was dependent upon and determined by such constraints as perceived boundaries. Thus, it would be cavalier to dismiss the links between occult rituals and the Song military system, and this situation is particularly true for what will be here defined as rituals of transgression.[13]

The Three Cosmographies techniques were both powerful and empowering in the Song period because they were thought to enable the performer to cross certain sorts of boundaries—time, space, the phenomenal universe. Rituals employing the cosmograph negated limits and order (especially as defined by *shu*—regularity, numbers, emblem, but other sorts of order, too) to create chaos and so produced supernatural power. The boundaries discussed here were constantly shifting, negotiated, and defined. Although operating as subversion (of the sorts of natural limits available to ordinary human action), and as transgression (of the same), the Three Cosmographies nevertheless operated within certain constraints of the "structure and rules" that it purported to "subvert and radically interrogate," what Peter Stallybrass and Allon White, in *The Politics and Poetics of Transgression*, call the "politics of transgression."[14]

Generally, ritual creates and maintains order through creating hierarchies, defining tabus, and so forth; generally, it creates an ideological ordering.[15] Yet at certain social intervals, according to Victor Turner, the creation of social order depends upon transitions. These transitions entail first disturbing or suspending order in some way prior to the new and different, usually higher, social status. Weddings, confirmations, childbirth, and the like are common examples. Turner calls the suspension of status, the period after the old and before the new, "liminal" states. Liminal states involve crossing certain sorts of boundaries to accommodate the transformed social state—infant to child, child to adult, citizen to warrior, and so on.[16] Likewise, Kristofer Schipper and Wang Hsiu-huei show the same to be true for the ritual definition of the Daoist altar and its reintegration with the cosmos. Using the example of the Hidden Period, a Three Cosmographies technique, they eloquently lay out the theme of progressing and regressing along time.[17]

Such crossings of boundaries are acts of *trans*gression, too; they overstep, trespass, violate, transcend, and permeate social, cultural, physical, or natural rules. Stallybrass and White discuss transgression in the context of the *carnivalesque*, a term originally borrowed from Mikhail Bakhtin (1895–1975), taking transgression to be synonymous with "symbolic inversion"; "broadly defined as any act of expressive behaviour which inverts, contradicts, abrogates, or in some fashion presents an alternative to commonly held cultural codes, values and norms be they linguistic, literary or artistic, religious, social and political."[18] It is precisely from this transgression—from the act of violating certain boundaries—that occult rituals like the Three Cosmographies derive their power.

To be sure, the Three Cosmographies constituted an alternative path, one that may have relied on a different moral code than that being defined at court. Thus, the issue of the social status of the military comes into play in relations between *shi* rituals and the authority to legitimate governance. Three Cosmographies techniques, originating outside the court, transgressed borders of the orthodox and orthodoxy. That is to say, the way that the Three Cosmographies mediated the authority of legitimate governance lies in the difference between the regulation of the cosmograph, or *shi*, as object and its performance.

In the same way, transgression enabled by the cosmograph techniques was ordered within a set of constraints. The constraints themselves were embedded in the continued practice and transmission of transgression. In other words, these methods were a kind of sanctioned transgression. Such a concept may not be so surprising: legitimacy and the authority to be considered legitimate stem from the ability, or the perceived right, of an individual, body, or institution to transgress (usually its own) laws, customs, and proclaimed or tacit morality.[19] The military system may be one of the best examples of such transgression.

But what were the limits that these rituals challenged? How were they defined and transgressed? How do "occult" systems invert, negate, or render permeable boundaries? Upon what kind of boundaries do such rituals act? The cosmograph produced power by and through its potential for transgression. I look at two of four related kinds of limits that the Three Cosmographies challenged: the limits of nature and phenomena, especially time and space; and the limits of authority and its role in legitimate governance.[20]

After discussing the rise of the Three Cosmographies during the Song, I evaluate the existence of these rituals as a "sanctioned" transgression, especially in light of two considerations. The first is the indeterminacy that is inscribed within the Hidden Period system itself, both as object (cosmograph) and the ritual techniques for using it. This indeterminacy enabled the user of the cosmograph to transgress the limits of nature. The second is the rise of paradoxical forms of the term *shi*—one being the cosmograph as an object, and another being its meaning of "specifications" as a legal category. Both of these forms restricted and transgressed the limits of authority, and commented on the dynamism between court and military during the Song.

The Rise of the Three Cosmographies during the Song

The techniques of the Three Cosmographies, especially the Irregular Opening/Hidden Period (*qimen dunjia*), were fully developed and refined during the Song.[21] Collectively, the Three Cosmographies represent some of the most complex, esoteric rituals disclosed in Chinese manuals, military and otherwise, that I have investigated so far.

Mentioned already in the History of the Latter Han (*Hou Hanshu*), an incipient form of the Hidden Period started to develop during the era of Northern and Southern Dynasties (420–589). The bibliography of the history of the Sui dynasty (581–618) records thirteen works on the Hidden Period, and many more on the Six Water Cycles. Beginning with Ge Hong (283–343), commentators repeatedly complained of the lack of good practitioners of these techniques, stating that the thorough understanding and transmission of these techniques was lost after *Huainanzi*.[22]

The Song went to great lengths to resurrect it. The Hidden Period went from geographically grounded system in the writings of Ge Hong to one more deified and star-oriented during the Song.[23] The Venus Classic of the late 750s documents eight methods; the Comprehensive Essentials lists twenty-four or so.[24] By the reign of Song emperor Renzong (r. 1022–63), seven different schools of the Hidden Period system had been established (apparently despite the proscriptions in place).[25]

Nevertheless, there are repeated warnings in the texts that discuss the Hidden Period as a technique for the specialist alone, and that it must only be practiced only in need. The Comprehensive Essentials warns that occult arts generally belong to the realm of ghosts and gods, and that, even those using them with restraint risk breaking tabus.[26]

These supernatural acts were accomplished via a system of cosmological openings and passages, based on a cosmological construct of worldly existence as one in a series of temporally and spatially nested universes.[27] Within the framework of the sexagenary calendrical cycle, coincidences and ruptures of the cycle and their convergence with alternate space constitute the mechanisms, or the key, by which the participants can tap into supernatural forces to produce a desired result. These mechanisms exist somewhat outside of the ordinary system of regularities of the cycle, in that they take advantage of cyclically impossible combinations of symbols that represented time.

Somewhat paradoxically, however, the mechanisms for crossing limits worked according to the rules and structures defined by the regularities of nature (*shu*). For instance, these ruptures were manipulated with number, the latter being an important Song contribution to Chinese philosophy. They closed and opened according to universal regularities and the visual representations of those regularities. In short, the Three Cosmographies rituals straddled the boundary between inside and outside, center and margin, empirical and true reality, the ordinary and the supernatural.

This system of the Three Cosmographies was widely practiced. Even some of the Song's foremost officials performed it, though skeptics claim otherwise and the official records do tend to be either somewhat indirect or terse about their subscription to it.[28] The three early Song officials Dou Yan (*jin shi*, late 930s; d. ca. late 960s?), Wang Pu (fl. 950s–60s), and Ma Shao (fl. late 960s–98?) were all claimed to have practiced one of the Three Cosmographies techniques. Others were involved less directly. If not participants, they often contributed to court discussions of one or another technique.[29] The involvement of these individuals is indicative of the broad popularity of the system. Why, after all, would the Song court discourage rituals that no one actually practiced?

Like all Chinese courts, the Song sought ways to control beliefs that the populace held, and it was the very popularity of the Three Cosmographies and similar techniques that led directly to their becoming proscribed.[30] But more worrisome to Song officialdom than the odd cosmograph secreted away were the practitioners of such arts and the associated sociopolitical collectivity they might inspire. Under the right conditions, individuals who were adept in occult arts could garner considerable authority in the commoner community, as magical acts are constituted by the belief of the social (or antisocial) collective. This situation could hold true whether the techniques produce results or not. By the same token, the inspired collectivity gave authority over to the practitioner, though it might sometimes be temporally or spatially bounded.[31] In the case of the Three Cosmographies, such authority was beyond court control or, worse still, even court awareness. The adepts in the Three Cosmographies were outside the established order because they worked against regularities, the accurate prediction of which formed the root of divination practices; because their techniques defied accurate categorization, spanning many types of knowledge and therefore, many departments of the government structure;[32] and because their techniques were apart from any textual tradition that was within the Song court's control, causing the state a great deal of trepidation, a point to which I shall return.

Possession of books on divination and other forms of magic became punishable by strangulation and sometimes death by slicing. Nevertheless, neither of these measures was very successful in deterring adepts from acquiring them.[33] The books indeed proliferated, and some of the most dramatic stories we possess involve diviners who openly flouted these proscriptions, thereby reputedly saving the empire (and, incidentally, earning spots in official history). Such was the case of Ma Shao, who openly transgressed court proscription of private practice of astronomical arts to inform Song emperor Taizong (r. 976–97) of a heavenly arrangement auspicious for his future success, if he made timely use of the opportunity (he did). Likewise, Xu Ji (850s–936), later an active official, was summoned out of reclusion by Zhaozong (r. 889–904) of the late Tang.[34] Zhou Taizu (r. 951–54) consulted Zhao Yanyi (894?–952?) about the fate of his rule.[35] Li Jing (571–649), a famous general of the Tang dynasty, was said to have used the cosmograph, no doubt referring to his military victories using weather and mists.[36] In the Qingli reign period (1041–48), Renzong summoned the recluse Xu Fu (n.d. over 70 years at death) to ask about recent incursions of the western nomads.[37] Paradoxically, the act of proscribing these techniques contributed to the social construction of these techniques as efficacious, powerful, and dangerous, unintentionally contributing to the fame and reputation of those who practiced them. Such was precisely the case with Xu Fu and Ma Shao.

The threat of the Three Cosmographies lay in the belief that the methods of the system gave the performer direct access to the divine, circumventing the mediating role of the emperor as "Son of Heaven." Aside from acquiring an extraordinary source of power through the techniques of Three Cosmographies, the practitioners of these methods potentially undermined the locus of the emperor's position as the sole representative of divine authority on earth. They posed the threat of not only directly interpreting Heaven's messages, but manipulating those messages, too. If these ritualists could access Heaven, what would stop others from doing so?

The Song court was also nervous about the performance of the Three Cosmographies for two other reasons. First, the court saw them as undermining the Way (*dao*) because, in the contexts of the new cosmology movement, the Three Cosmographies proponents who enacted them stood outside of philosophical factions. These individuals opted instead for direct, possibly amoral, techniques to achieve the Way. Though Li Quan (fl. 750s?–70s?) asserts in the Venus Classic that ultimately "auspiciousness and inauspiciousness, success and failure lie not in the

[Hidden Period] talisman but in the Dao" the implication is quite the opposite.[38] Second, the Song was concerned with the inconsistencies in calendrical prediction and empirical observations in the positions of the stars and other asterisms. These difficulties in time-telling methods likely both spurred the recovery and development of the Three Cosmographies techniques, while creating some anxiety about who might eventually possess them.[39]

Of the Three Cosmographies techniques, the Hidden Period (*dunjia*) in particular was expressly defined as a military technique; "being the art that one [uses] to mobilize troops while avoiding the enemy, and to conceal oneself while escaping material form; can it be considered anything but wondrous!"[40] The Official History of the Song (*Songshi*) calls it a military art, simultaneously describing it as a stage in the process of acquiring civilization.[41] The techniques utilizing the cosmographs linked time—especially as the progressions and regressions of heavenly bodies—with violence, as represented by the military. Time was considered violent, anyway, because it carried the potential to act outside of *shu* (regularities, number, emblem).[42] The role of the Three Cosmographies in relation to violence and legitimate authority is expressed in a Tang dynasty text, which relegates the Six Water Cycles method to the realm of popular practice, reserving the Hidden Period and Supreme One forms for the use of specialists only.[43] The "specialist" has presumably received some kind of official sanction to practice. A Song commentator, one Mr. Chao, defined the Hidden Period as the sole technique to be used for determining the fate of the country, ranking "the most well-known" occult arts of his time:

> The Six Water Cycles is for inferring the fate for one single time period. The celestial animal system, the five asterisms, figuring fortunes, and physiognomy—these categories of arts are for inferring the fate of the individual. Burial divining is good for inferring the destiny of the clan. Hidden Period method is for inferring the fate of the country. To know these arts is to know supernatural occurrences of the near and the far; sometimes they are accurate and sometimes they are not, but one cannot exhaust belief in only one of them.[44]

Posterity has interpreted Mr. Chao as meaning that the Hidden Period was an exclusively military technique. For this reason, the court closely guarded everything associated with it.

Many of the performances of the Three Cosmographies were directly related to military action.[45] He Gui (fl. 907–15?) used it to determine the strategy of conquest for Liang Taizu (r. 907–14).[46] Shi Kang (fl. ca. 1119–25) performed the Six Water Cycles to predict the fall of Daizhou—and, incidentally, his own death—to the Jin in 1125 (He and his two sons perished on the ramparts).[47] In earlier eras, Sang Daomou (fl. 766–80s?) used the Six Water Cycles in 758 to figure the outcome of a siege. The Tang court requested a copy of Li Quan's Venus Classic, receiving it from a mysterious Daoist adept in the late 750s.[48] Indeed, the references to the Three Cosmographies in official texts define the contours of a topography of major military episodes, and the examples cited coincide with the landmark military events either detailed or alluded to by several other authors in this volume: the Tang dynasty's An Lushan Rebellion of the 750s–60s (David Graff); the reunification of China proper under the Song founders in the 960s (Peter Lorge); the incursions of the Xi Xia in the 1030s and 1040s (Michael McGrath); the fall of the Northern Song in 1126 (James Anderson and Ruth Mostern); and later, when the court created oversight of the Three Cosmographies as an official position (Office of the Three Cosmographies; *sanshi guan*), the Mongol invasions, which lasted over the duration of the thirteenth century (Ruth Mostern and Michael Brose).[49]

Yet, until the compilation of the Comprehensive Essentials in 1044, *official* sources never really specify the content of these rituals. The privately authored Tang-dynasty work Venus Classic documents the Duke of Thunder (*Lei Gong*) method, the previous name for the Hidden Period. By 1005, Xu Dong (976–1015?) included some content of the technique in his manual, the Tiger Seal Classic. With these exceptions, there is a gap in writings that consciously discuss the Hidden Period until Yang Weide (?–after 1054) completed the sections of the Comprehensive Essentials and his Classic of the Talismanic Response of the Hidden Period (*Dunjia fuying jing*).

Official sources do note that the content of the Three Cosmographies was taxonomically independent. This categorical ambiguity distressed Zheng Qiao (1104–62), author of the early Song encyclopedia, the Comprehensive Treatise (*Tongzhi*). Noting that the Hidden Period appeared under four different categories in the imperial catalogue of the Four Treasuries (*Siku shumu*)—"Military Treatises," "Five Phases Divination," "Six Water Cycles Reckoning," and "Fortune-telling"—he argued for its definitive categorization as a subcategory of Six Water Cycles reckoning.[50] But his argument went unheeded. In the Official History of the Song, it appears in conjunction with the "Calendar," "Astronomy," "Nine Palaces Ritual," "Mathematics," "Military Arts," "Five Phases," and "Music."[51] In the encyclopedias of the late Song—early Yuan (1279–1368) dynasties, the General Investigation on Important Writings (*Wenxian tongkao*), Song commentators Mr. Chen and Mr. Chao raised the same argument that Zheng Qiao had.[52] Taxonomical indeterminacy was the hallmark of the Three Cosmographies generally, and the Hidden Period in particular was characterized as chaotic and disorderly, even anarchical.[53]

Given the early Song trepidations about the taxonomy of the techniques of the Three Cosmographies, the proscriptions around them, and the reorganization of the Song bureaucratic structure into the civil and military branches, the fact that the court sanctioned the practice of these techniques by military representatives is most remarkable. Practice of these rituals in the military environment, at least as prescribed by the manuals, meant that they were performed far from the court. It was probably the realization that such practices were taking place with or without sanction that motivated the court to include them in the Comprehensive Essentials in the first place. Possibly in a move for still more complete control, the institution of examinations in the Department of the Astrological Observation (*taishi ju*) for Three Cosmographies practitioners followed in 1104.[54]

The Three Cosmographies, especially the Hidden Period, assumed increasing importance over the course of the Song. The gradual slippage in accurate prediction of the motions of the heavenly bodies contributed to this elevation in status. Such astral discrepancies distressed the Song court because they were believed to reduce the accuracy of occult arts, the calendar, the ritual cycle, and the usefulness of the Three Cosmographies as a warfare technique. For identical reasons, possession of these occult techniques was highly desired not only by the Song but also by its neighbors. The proliferating texts written on the Three Cosmographies, the corresponding establishment of their seven different schools, their institutionalization through official venues such as the examination system, and their commitment to writing in imperially issued military manuals were all results of the Song court trying to recover legendary "lost" arts in order to gain control of a tradition practiced beyond its reach.

Cosmograph and the Boundaries of Nature

One of the most obvious types of boundaries that the Three Cosmographies transgressed was that of phenomenal boundaries, principally those of time and space. These cosmograph techniques exploit the rather odd phenomenon of a time-tracking system that employs ten heavenly stems crossed with twelve earthly branches yet produces only a 60-year, rather than 120-year, cycle. This meant that there were unused stems and branches at certain systemic intersections. By using cyclically impossible stem/branch combinations, metaphysical correspondences, and universal forces in conjunction with ritual performance, doors between series of nested universes opened at certain "time" locations.

This section explains how a characteristic indeterminacy inherent in the *shi* as object (cosmograph) and as ritual (occult technique) made transgression of phenomenal boundaries possible. The Three Cosmographies, and specifically the Hidden Period, crossed such phenomenal boundaries as presented by time, space, and the limits of the body. These techniques challenged the limits of nature and mediated how many Chinese of the Song conceptualized, constructed, and acted upon their universe. In what ways did such indeterminacy make crossing boundaries of space, time and other phenomena possible? The section below clarifies what these boundaries and markers were on the *shi* as object, and how, in conjunction with *shi* as occult method, manipulated these boundaries within a highly ordered, fixed, and complex set of restraints.

Elements of the Cosmograph

Like the Six Water Cycles and Supreme One techniques, the Hidden Period was performed on a device suitably called a cosmograph. Unfortunately, no cosmograph for the Irregular Opening/Hidden Period system (hereafter, Hidden Period) has been excavated. But the elements of the Six Water Cycles cosmograph—which, based on descriptions in extant manuals, those the Hidden Period closely resembled—provide visual clarity. (The Six Water Cycles has 720 possible "settings," compared to the Hidden Period's 1,800.) This device was traditionally composed of two plates, with the top round plate being moveable and called the Heaven plate and the bottom one fixed, square, and representing Earth.[55]

Figure 5.1 shows a drawing of an excavated Six Water Cycles cosmograph from the Six Dynasties (Liuchao) period (CE 222–589), probably dating to the late sixth century CE. It measures twelve centimeters square.[56] The design and layout of the cosmograph reflected *yin/yang* via the trigrams of the *Book of Change*, the Five Phases theory of mutual conquest and production, and a system of correspondences. The cosmograph models Heaven—the constellations, the moon, and the nine asterisms, and correlates these with time, the Five Phases, and earthly events.

The Heaven plate has three levels of markings, and the relationship of each ring to the other is fixed; that is, one moving plate contains all of the rings. On the square Earth plate, there is a pyramid arrangement intersected by four diagonal axes called the Four Secondary Cables (*siwei*) at the corners.[57] These axes interact with invisible "time" diagonals formed by "orphans and empties" that spin through the heaven plate. Thus, the image created is that of Heaven as a net holding the constellations and planets, and as a concrete, phenomenal structure on which time hangs.[58]

The cosmograph incorporates the heavenly branch—earthly stem system that the Chinese used for time-tracking on the sexagenary calendar. The ten heavenly Stems and the twelve earthly Branches combined to produce a sixty, not a 120-year cycle. (See figure 5.2.) Each branch is combined with a stem, and always the same set of stems, to determine the day of the year, the ten-day "week," and in certain situations, the month.[59]

The Hidden Period was derived from Heaven's "orphans and empties."[60] Kristofer Schipper and Wang Hsiu-huei explain the "orphans" and "empties" (*guxu*) as cyclically impossible stem and branch combinations. The disparities in number, time, and space made the Irregular Opening possible. The stems and branches combined with each other in the same pairs, leaving two unused branches in each cycle. For example, in the *jiazi* decade, *xu* and *hai* were unused. (See figure 5.2.) These are called "orphans." When the branches are laid out on a circle, the branches directly across from the two orphans are called the "empties." Each branch "corresponds to a given direction and hour of the day"; in this case, *xu* and *hai* are in the northwest and take up the hours from 7 to 9 pm and 9 to 11 pm, respectively.[61]

It was believed that these axial passages created by the orphans and the empties allowed one to travel backward and forward along time within the Hidden Period system.[62] To oversimplify somewhat, the object of the cosmograph reading is to line oneself up with one of the "Three Irregulars," the locations of the *yi*, *bing*, and *ding* heavenly Stems that float within the innermost circle of the cosmograph.[63] Then, depending on which of the Eight (Earth) Gates is open at the time (located

Ten Celestial Stems: jia 甲   yi 乙   bing 丙   ding 丁   mou 戊   ji 己   geng 庚
xin 辛   ren 壬   gui 癸

Twelve Earthly Branches: zi 子   chou 丑   yin 寅   mao 卯   chen 辰   si 巳   wu 午
wei 未   shen 申   you 酉   xu 戌   hai 亥

Sexagenary cycle by decade (reading down)

甲子 jiazi	甲戌 jiaxu	甲申 jiashen	甲午 jiawu	甲辰 jiachen	甲寅 jiayin
乙丑 yichou	乙亥 yihai	乙酉 yiyou	乙未 yiwei	乙巳 yisi	乙卯 yimao
丙寅 bingyin	丙子 bingzi	丙戌 bingxu	丙申 bingshen	丙午 bingwu	丙辰 bingyin
丁卯 dingmao	丁丑 dingchou	丁亥 dinghai	丁酉 dingyou	丁未 dingwei	丁巳 dingsi
戊辰 mouchen	戊寅 mouyin	戊子 mouzi	戊戌 mouxu	戊申 moushen	戊午 mouwu
己巳 jisi	己卯 jimao	己丑 jichou	己亥 jihai	己酉 jiyou	己未 jiwei
庚午 gengwu	庚辰 gengchen	庚寅 gengyin	庚子 gengzi	庚戌 gengxu	庚申 gengshen
辛未 xinwei	辛巳 xinsi	辛卯 xinmao	辛丑 xinchou	辛亥 xinhai	辛酉 xinyou
壬申 renshen	壬午 renwu	壬辰 renchen	壬寅 renyin	壬子 renzi	壬戌 renxu
癸酉 guiyou	癸未 guiwei	癸巳 guisi	癸卯 guimao	癸丑 guichou	癸亥 guihai

orphans: xu/hai   shen/you   wu/wei   chen/si   yin/mao   zi/chou

Figure 5.2 Showing elements of the sexagenary cycle.
Source: Chart created by M. A. Butler.

on the outer rings), one uses the Irregular Opening to its potential.[64] The following excerpt from the Comprehensive Essentials shows the lining up of super-phenomenal Heaven and Earth passages to locate the (always auspicious) deity, the Jade Maiden.

> This method relies on using tallies and enacting the scheme for finding the Heaven Gate and the Earth Door where the Jade Maiden is located. The head commander enters through the Earth Door and comes out the Heaven Gate; by obtaining the Jade Maiden's assistance, the army is united so that the enemy will be defeated. There will be nothing that will not bring certain victory.[65]

This passage gives the sense of the commander physically moving through the "wondrous" and "irregular" passage between Heaven and Earth, which is constructed from the disparities in the relative positions of the various cosmic elements.[66] As geometry, the cosmos behaved according to *shu*—number, regularities—yet superimposed onto "irregular" (*qi*[1]) or impossible configurations using "regular" time.[67] Using these disparities and their ability to produce power from potential is related to cultural views of space and time and changing views of phenomenal reality during the late Tang and early Song.

Finally, one of the Song innovations in the *shi* as cosmograph was to add a third layer to the Six Water Cycles design. The new design of the cosmograph reflected the Song interest in accurate time prediction, and their concern with more refined and detailed protocols (see next section). Perhaps more important, the addition of this layer had to do with the role of the Three Potentials (*sancai*; i.e., Heaven, human, and Earth) in Song cosmological revisions, in addition to its role in warfare, especially in reading landscape, *qi*[2] (universal essence), and heavenly timing.[68] "The top layer symbolizes Heaven and displays the Nine Asterisms; the middle layer symbolizes humans opening the Eight Gates; the bottom layer symbolizes Earth and is laid out with the Eight Trigrams for subduing the Eight Directions."[69] Thus, the Three Potentials organized the cosmograph and determined the ultimate efficacy of the end reading.

Transgressing Markers

Anthropologist Edmund Leach once wrote: "A boundary separates two zones of social space-time which are *normal, time-bound, clear-cut, central, secular*, but the spatial and temporal markers which actually serve as boundaries are themselves *abnormal, timeless, ambiguous, at the edge, sacred*."[70] Leach's statement could not be truer than when one considers the heavenly Stems and earthly Branches, markers that the Chinese used in their sexagenary calendar and key elements for the production of power in Three Cosmographies techniques. By manipulating these markers, the Three Cosmographies performer could influence nature and the heavens. The indeterminate attributes of these markers enabled such influence by making it possible for the performer to transgress phenomenal limits, and invert or "interrogate" the very same boundaries that they represent.[71]

Transgression via Three Cosmographies rituals was thought especially efficacious for crossing from the phenomenal into the supernatural world. The power of the Three Cosmographies for crossing the boundaries of nature, the power to perform supernatural acts such as jumping universes, and even disassembling the body (as in the "Duke of Thunder method" below) was possible by means of a series of markers that were themselves devoid of meaning. Their emptiness can take on many sorts of referents because they are void. *Jiazi*, a year or month in the calendrical cycle, for example, is often interpreted as highly auspicious, presumably because this pair heads the entire sexagenary cycle. In the form of an individual's Eight Characters (*bazi*); the four pairs of markers denoting the year, month, day, and hour when one is born, they stand in for all that comprises an individual—health, intellect, emotions, affect. This set of eight markers is at work in the "Duke of Thunder Method":

> Obtain the enemy commander's name, year, month, day and hour of birth. All in one breath (*qi*[2]), write them in red writing. According to [whichever] *Sha* deity governs the year, twist the cosmograph to the Ghost gate with the left hand, and with the right hand turn the cosmograph to the Heavenly Mainstay Cable (*tiangang*) and push on it. Using the Heavenly Mainstay Cable, command the enemy to submit [to us] out of terror; from this, they will be defeated.[72]

Just as the time markers can be used to create holes or gateways in an otherwise seamless universe, so these same markers, grouped as Eight Characters, can be used to penetrate or disassemble the physical and psychological components of the person in question. In this example, these signs take on meaning from a spectrum of possibilities that is embodied by all that stands behind the face of the cosmograph: the hexagrams of the *Book of Change*; the positions of the Nine Palaces; and the direction, color, element and so forth that corresponded with both. As separators and limina, as sacred and profane, these markers, because of their indeterminate nature, concretized time and collapsed space into time, so that both could be manipulated.

In the introduction to the Hidden Period, the Comprehensive Essentials states that the creation of the stems and branches resulted from inferring the "numbers" of Heaven and Earth.[73] The markers are powerful precisely because they are empty, as they can be invested with layered and indeterminate referents.[74] But, as they are produced from number, these markers are also emblematic. The patterns (*li*)[2] described above comprise a sort of immanence that ran through all things, concrete and abstract. That immanence links all things in the phenomenal world and manifests its representations via *shu*; that is, number as category and emblem, which are the means to work within and among patterns. By taking part in and "harmonizing with the patterns (*li*) of Heaven and human," all that is "damaging and bloodletting" will turn out auspiciously.[75] During the Song, warfare was seen as part of that pattern.[76]

The cosmograph techniques used disparity to produce power from potential. This was possible because of the views of phenomenal reality developed in the early Song. In particular, the Song concept of *li*, translated as "pattern" or "principle" and likened to the pattern in wood or jade, was meant to be something that all things possessed. Networks or matrices of patterns became available through the use of number as a quality, as a category, or as a regularity. In this light, the Hidden Period used differences in number as paths from one pattern to another.[77] The disparity in number apparent on the cosmograph drove the cosmograph techniques. Through the emblematic quality of number, the Hidden Period allowed one access to a series of heavenly qualities and enabled one to act on those qualities. Thus, we can view the system as actively patterning nature with number.

The traditional Chinese view that both time and space were relative and mobile also contributed to the development of cosmographic systems like the Hidden Period. Nathan Sivin has shown that time occurred cyclically and nested in ever-larger cycles, uniting at certain junctures of astronomical occurrences.[78] There was always a potential to connect the different layers of time and space, an especially salient feature of Chinese alchemy.[79] But the layering of associations and correlations of the Hidden Period system meant that time and space constituted their own peculiar geography, one that encompasses and is encompassed by other sorts of geography. Time-space was a nesting of patterns and *the* pattern itself, part of an all-encompassing cosmic pattern. The Hidden Period system resulted from the relative and varied views of time and space and the way they fit into the cosmic scheme. The visual component of the cosmograph system renders time palpable so that it can be transgressed, crossed over, manipulated, and violated.

Therefore, the underlying principles of the cosmograph are indeterminate, blurring boundaries that render power upon transgression. Time and space are collapsed, no longer really being separate media. Time is conceived of as a space—the portals are hidden, only becoming exposed at liminal times, when one marker is on the cusp of the next. One takes advantage of the cosmograph during times that do not belong to any markers, times that belong to none of the categories represented by the stems and branches. Only during a sort of non-time does the method works. Simultaneously, space is merely one of many levels of time, a place in a series of nested cycles; it is a backdrop for this schema, a patch of time as a key into another time.[80] The nature of the event (time) and its circumstances (the kind of action)—expressed as conjunctions and correspondences, and both of which are prescribed by the manuals—were dominant operators in reading the heavens and influencing their outcome.

Communication and the Limits of Authority

The layering of meaning of the term *shi* during the Song tested other sorts of boundaries. The conjunction of the two forms of *shi*—as cosmograph and its techniques and as legal, ritual protocols—arose during the Song. Therefore, they linguistically identified occult techniques performed on a cosmograph with a category of laws dealing with ritual communication and ritual objects. This section explores the underlying contradiction in the Song development of the *shi* (cosmograph, model, pattern) as an instrument for creative forms of occult practice and the closer association of *shi* (specification, model, regulation, protocol) with ritual instruments at the imperial level. It focuses on boundaries of authority, in particular, authority necessary to establish legitimate governance. The latter determines who can transgress moral and other sorts of codes that warfare entails.

This linguistic identification was an instrumental factor in the production of the military culture during the Song and at least one central factor in the Song concept of warfare. The social status of the military comes into play in the relations between *shi* rituals and the authority to legitimate governance. That is to say, the way that the Three Cosmographies mediated the authority of legitimate governance lies in the difference between the regulation of the *shi* as object and *shi* as performance.

The Layered Meaning of Shi

Brian McKnight has noted that laws radically changed their form during the Song dynasty.[81] At that time, a certain legal category, *shi*, "the least understood group [of four groups] of Song laws," arose. Orthographically identical to *shi* cosmograph, *shi*, as a legal category, meant "rules...[that] specified certain physical aspects of processes of communication."[82] *Shi* as a kind of legal rule changed emphasis from its Tang implications of action and behavior to *shi* as an object during the Song. This transformation from action to object, which occurred in the late Tang, "was accompanied by a narrowing in the focus of *shi* so that their connection with communication becomes unequivocal."[83] *Shi* belonged to a legal category and a ritual category, both of which came into play in the manufacture of objects. As "rules," *shi* were explications that refined the details of ritual propriety, especially the propriety regarding ritual objects and ritual communication. This propriety, McKnight says, comes not only from aesthetic concerns, but more important, stems from the idea that such details of propriety increased the efficacy of the ritual itself. If this is so, then the more specialized the concrete object, and the more limited the object became in outward appearance and function, the more efficacious the ritual performance. These details of physical objects with which *shi* as specification were concerned, then, were essential to ritual performance.

These protocols were concerned with the court—specifically with the emperor—and therefore represent official ritual. McKnight points out signal beacons as one example of *shi* found in the military. Although he does not cite them, occult rituals are the other, more prevalent type of *shi* noted in the manuals.[84] Aside from defining communication protocols, many of these *shi*, or regulations, dealt with plans and furnishings for ritual buildings and spaces, and ritual objects. McKnight points out that they emphasized the concrete aspects of ritual expressed in a range of regulations: "some idea of the vast size of these bodies of rules can be conveyed by noting that a collection of the rules concerning the Imperial Hall of Light, a ritual building used by the emperor, totaled twelve hundred volumes."[85]

At first glance, we can see how the cosmograph fits in nicely with *shi* as a legal category. Both types of *shi* are modes of communication. *Shi* as specifications specified how communication should be conducted, and the instruments with which it should be conducted. Both meanings of *shi*, as specifications and as cosmograph techniques, share the idea of ritual as a kind of communication. Similarly, the cosmograph as an object shares many characteristics of the *shi* as specification: it was highly specific, precise, and elaborately detailed. As an object, it was highly symbolic.

The Song revamped the cosmograph into three tiers, rather than two, to correspond to the Three Potentials (*sancai*) model of the cosmos. This revamped ritual object mediated communication with Heaven, reflecting the formulation of the relations of universal forces according to Zhou Dunyi (1017–73) and other thinkers of the early Song. As an attempt at using human as mediator of the Three Potentials, the cosmograph expanded human potential and their role in transcending and transgressing the limits of nature. These characteristics of the cosmograph stand in contradistinction to the restrictions of *shi* regulations: how words and objects mean, and the corresponding increasingly restricted spectrum of interpretations, the ultimate result of *shi* in its mode as specification.

In addition, the directness of communication with the cosmograph stands in contrast to the indirectness that arose from the increasingly detailed communication and ritual protocols of the *shi* specifications. The cosmograph bypassed the emperor to communicate directly with Heaven, and even made it possible for the performer to traverse Heaven's geography, talents the emperor simply did not possess. The transformation of the *shi* in the legal mode also contrasts with the institution of the cosmograph techniques. The latter was made to be performed: they were dependent on practice and action for their ritual efficacy. Conversely, we can interpret these as a higher level of refinement in communication, and the cosmograph itself as a refinement in receiving such communication.

The bifurcated meaning of *shi* was interpreted and acted upon differently according to court and military circumstances. As a new legal category, *shi* more closely defined communication, including that of the court with the general in the field and ad hoc imperial instructions. As Song innovations in occult forms, *shi* created a potential for transgression. Imperial protocols and ritual specifications arose to restrict their use. Yet the more restricted the ritual, the more power it garnered in actual performance.

The *shi* exemplifies the Song preoccupation with accurate, even sacred, communication.[86] Part of what underlay the rise of *shi* as "more closely defined communication" related to the Song policy that separated the civil and military branches of governance. The latter occurred concurrently with the rise of the *shi*, during the Five Dynasties—Song transition in the mid-to-late tenth century.

The more closely defined communication that resulted from *shi* in its legal mode characterizes ad hoc imperial instructions and the Song court's relations with the general in the field. Beginning in the early Song, the court restricted the range of decisions that the commander could make by requiring an extraordinary level of communication, in kind and degree, between the field command and the court prior to taking action on the battlefront. Furthermore, the Song court subjected the military system to an unprecedented degree of restriction.[87] This oppressive courtly circumscription of the field command, aside from contributing to the image of the Song military as ineffective, was incorporated into the entire military institution, expanded from *shi* as abstract rules to more concrete manufacture and distribution of equipment.

This expansion in the meaning of *shi* reflected an emerging difference between *fa* and *shi*. McKnight points out that the meaning of *fashi*, usually rendered as "method," is more fruitfully understood as two independent words during the

Song; *fa* being "organized, integrated bodies of rules on a particular topic" and *shi*, "legal rules" and specifications discussed above.⁸⁸

McKnight's distinction between *fa* and *shi*, between bodies of rules and specifications, sheds light on the dynamic between *shi* as cosmograph and *shi* as specifications and rules. In court discussions, *fa* and *shi* related to the manufacture of weapons and other equipment. There is a sense of *shi* as overall design, as outward appearance and as an aesthetic consideration of equipment. *Fa*, by contrast, suggests more objective physical attributes, such as precise dimensions of a particular object and the molds for casting it.⁸⁹ *Fa* refers to the system of how soldiers will occupy a place, also; for instance, the number of soldiers to a ten-household group (*bao*) and a hundred-household group (*jia*) in the local *baojia* defense system, the quantity and kind of payment soldiers receive for particular type of service, etc.⁹⁰ Not only did the court regulate military objects by incorporating them into a system of *fa* and *shi*, but these objects assumed a ritual aspect by that same incorporation.

The Song court used these integrated bodies of rule and specifications, for instance, to ritually define the hierarchy of the military organization and align its equipment accordingly. Military equipment manufacture and distribution followed an entire network of *fa* and *shi*.⁹¹ The court instituted punitive measures and more severe legal categories when *fa* and *shi* specifications and bodies of rules failed in certain manufacturing locales.⁹² In this network, which was closely debated in court, weapons, geography and battle arrays were categorized according to both *fa* and *shi*. Such results of *fa* and *shi* in their legal and manufacturing modes are especially apparent in battle array schema, in which the place of manufacture, the name of the schemata, and the type and quantity of equipment distributed was all highly specified and carefully aligned.⁹³ No doubt this reflected in part Song organization for equipping troops and measures to prevent weapons from falling into private hands, which appears to have been a problem.⁹⁴ But the distinction between *fa* and *shi* was important in incorporating the military into the ritual network. How?

Weapons and other equipment, such as armor and military vehicles, were viewed as ritual objects. In 1104, Li Fuxian spoke of the ritual aspects of warfare—in mounting war vehicles, to be specific—in connection with a debate about the *shi* that should be used to manufacture military vehicles.⁹⁵ Similarly, in 1117, Yuwen Cuizhong (n.d.) submitted a memorial in which he argued that Song Taizu and Taizong set aside weapons and equipment stored in the Imperial Martial Warehouse (*wuku*) so that the suburban army would respect ritual. They set them ahead of the other ritual implements, Yuwen said, so that there would be knowledge of the military arts.⁹⁶ In other words, ritual, *shi*, *fa*, and knowledge were all tied together in the martial context.

The distinction between *fa* and *shi* clarifies the relationship of equipment, specifications, and ritual to each other. It shows how deeply the Song wove such relations into the organization of the armed forces. This gives some insight into how the Song court constructed such ritual relations and the role those relations played in maintaining hierarchy; in this case, the court's own authority vis-à-vis the military organization.

Shi *at Court*

This distinction between *fa* and *shi* also appears in the court discussions of the cosmograph techniques. It first arose in the Tang, when the court built a cosmograph-like altar, requested and laid out by occult artist Su Jaiqing in 744. This event, documented in the Tang History, is quoted verbatim in the histories of the Five Dynasties, the Qidan Liao and the Song.[97] For the Song, the passage was invoked in 1035 by court scholars requesting that the *fa*—system or body of organized rules—for the "flying positions" (*feiyi weici zhi fa*) as part of the worship for the Noble Deities of the Nine Palaces be reinstated at the latter's own altar, located outside the eastern gates of the capital.[98] (The Tang had ceased the practice of rotating the positions of the deities circa 758.) The scholars' request recounts Su Jiaqing's *fa* for establishing an altar to these deities. This altar imitated the Nine Palace arrangement in the form of nine individual altars "accorded with the Hidden Period markings," each altar representing the deity that governed a particular (heavenly) palace. These deities changed from year to year, and this rotation around the altars was known as "flying positions" with "flying chessmen (*feiqi*)."[99] "Flying chessmen" tracked the positions, motions of heavenly bodies correlated with the Nine Palaces altars. The arrangement consisted of an incipient cosmograph with the deities performing the Paces of Yu via these "flying chessmen."

Instituting a system of rotating altar positions of the deities meant that the disasters and prosperities of the "nine provinces" would be better inferred. Should the rotating system be used, they argued, "when inferring and calculating fate, the deities at the rear would not be neglected, they would be enticed to protect against and eliminate miasmic *qi*[2] (vital universal essence), and *qi*[2] could be traced so that auspiciousness could be thoroughly plumbed."[100] These were not possible with a system of fixed positions. The request was granted. Later, in 1049, two levels were added to the Deities of the Nine Palace altar, which was 120 "feet" (*chi*; 27 cm/*chi*) on a side.

The dialogic nature of the way that *shi* defined boundaries is evident from looking at the transformation of the term during the Song. *Shi* took on layers of meanings, some paradoxical. Yet both meanings—specifications and cosmograph—corresponded to issues of the limits of authority, control and how these were shared. The relationship between such limits and *shi* lay in its contrasting meanings; *shi* as specification, rule, model, and object contrasted with its sense of occult ritual and the idea of event and performance that these rituals entailed. This divergence of meaning arose coincident with the separation of the civil and military branches of the government. In light of this development, the layered meaning of *shi* became invested with the limits of Song authority, especially as it related to methods of governance. The basis of the relationship of these two events lies in how each milieu—civil (*wen*) and military (*wu*)—interpreted and used *shi*.

Shi performances of the military and court differed in their motivation, dynamic, and result—that is, the dynamism of their methods and of how each produced power were dissimilar. *Shi* in its legal mode resulted in increasingly finer distinctions within the official bureaucracy. These distinctions were reified in the types and amount of communication between the court and the field command. The increasing ritual restrictions of *shi* were also an effort to regulate the hermeneutic of the sign, more closely defining object, image, and meaning. Prior to the Song, the quintessential hermeneute, who transmitted their arts privately and orally (which is to say, "secretly"), existed outside of the court. The oral and private training that dominated transmission of the military arts meant that many occult arts, which early Song rulers were so anxious to recoup, were kept alive in the network of martial training. The nature of the performance of the *shi* as it occurred in the military, the characterization of the military, and the military as a collective all point to this phenomenon.

Shi *in the Field*

The nature of the Hidden Period ritual is highly performative, usually including some sort of ritual body posturing, often the Paces of Yu, combined with incantations or chanting. For instance, in the Pacing the Potential Circumstance (*Ju*) Method, the performer holds stalk-like tallies (probably yarrow stalks) while hopping around a layout of the Big Dipper/Nine Palaces in the Paces of Yu sequence, chanting an incantation with each step, throwing a tally, turning, and then calling out below the constellation associated with that location.[101]

The oral and performative nature of the Hidden Period rituals points to an older tradition that was transmitted orally and therefore, "secretly." This is evident from the rhyming and seemingly nonsensical mnemonic devices for the performance layouts.[102] In the rituals, as in the founding myth, there is a tension between the magical authority of writing and the efficacy of the performance through gestures, incantation, and the manipulation of (magical) objects, as in "The Jade Maiden reverses and closes the Potential Circumstance":

> ...If the strength of the troops is flagging and it is desirable to retreat, call out praying to the Jade Maiden and go out the Earth Door. Holding a knife in the left hand, draw backhanded [on the ground] cutting through the Earth arteries; this will close the Earth Door. Still with the left hand, take hold of an inch of grass; shielding one's middle half [with it], without turning back to look, go out [the gate]. Neither human nor demon will be able to perceive or follow [your path].[103]

In the Venus Classic, the Hidden Period founding myth occurs as a talisman (directed to the eye of god and ghost), not a text. That it was delivered to the altar by a turtle and crocodile suggests that, like the River Chart and the Luo Writing, it was a magical schemata. The performance in the form of speech overrides writing; using the "the language for going in and coming out," it is clearly incantation that makes the method work.[104] The goal of getting language is to recite it, not read it; the goal of reciting it is to invoke action.[105]

Orally rhythmic but meaningless in writing, chants such as "the cow enters the rabbit garden and eats the sweet grass" are effective only when recited.[106] Lifted directly from alchemical meditation, the language of the Hidden Period suggests also the process of correspondence and harmony with *qi*[2].[107] Probably transliterations of Sanskrit, these incantations, like the Catholic Latin Mass, are magical precisely because they cannot be deciphered. These rituals in written form signaled the court's attempts to appropriate an oral and secret tradition. This fits with McKnight's suggestion that the Song instituted *shi* as legal rules in the tradition of Confucian "rectification of names" (*zhengming*), "straightening and clarifying" meaning, or a more precise correspondence between the sign and its referent. Similarly, Michel de Certeau suggests that those in power—in his example, the doctor and the priest—define the sorcerer as insane in order to replace her indecipherable discourse with the understood and orthodox, what he calls a "text-off."[108] Once written, of course, the rituals are static, controlled, and standardized. Such was the case when the Three Cosmographies were incorporated into the examination system in 1104, and later, in 1242, an official position at court was created for accomplished adepts in them.[109]

The various meanings of *shi* are not simply a matter of polarized opposites. Rather, *shi*/occult ritual stands as a symbolic inversion of specifications, yet simultaneously regulated by them. *Shi*-as-object displays characteristics of the legal mode. Yet as object, *shi* was ultimately interpretive because of its regulation via number as empty marker and emblem. The ritual performance of *shi* expresses this interpretive aspect. This collapsing of ritual object and legal specification ultimately increased its power to transgress. It no longer merely crosses phenomenal boundaries, but also the bounds and "rules" invested in it by the court.

The performance of *shi* rituals transgressed further by circumventing the cosmograph altogether:

> When the enemy [is planning] an ambush or mounting a surprise attack, and reckoning [on the cosmograph] there is no Gate to secret [oneself] within, the head commander of the army takes this as the method: Calling out to the gods, cast the tallies; first complete [this] for the Heaven Gate, then complete it for the Earth Gate. In the midst of the sixth secret call, invoke the Jade Maiden to come out of the gate. [Even if] the enemy has massed ten thousand or a hundred million, there is nothing they can do [to defeat us].[110]

This ritual performance dispenses with the cosmograph, resorting instead to other magical objects, number, and incantation, the human performer standing in for nature's correspondences. In a sense, these performances extract the essence of the cosmograph—its ability to align symbols, universal forces, and phenomena—to transgress and transcend, acting upon dire circumstances vis-à-vis the enemy. Symbolically, the performer escapes the control exerted remotely by the court, the latter intrinsic to the cosmograph as an object ritually and hierarchically aligned.

Descriptions of court uses of the Three Cosmographies emphasize its layout and its derivation from heavenly numbers. Military descriptions of the Three Cosmographies emphasize performance—how to throw or hold various objects (tallies, yarrow stalks, etc.), when to chant and from what position. These differences partially result from and reflect the historiographical practices of the imperial Chinese. Surely, however, the depictions of ritual content and its occult attributes in these sources that are associated with the martial and not the civil are significant. These depictions were effected by the differences we can detect in the rise of the civil official in contrast to that of the military official. The picture of the rise of the military man remains a murky one, while that of the civil servant is much clearer, both in fiction and in historical sources. During the Song, the civil servant became well entrenched, socially as well as politically. In many ways, this entrenchment of the civil official probably did contribute to the downgraded status of the soldier. How did the Song conceptualize the military as a system? To what degree did soldiers and officers and military practices stand outside of "ordinary" society and structures?

In order to engage these questions and address the issue of how *shi* might interrogate the limits of authority, one must look at the Chinese military vis-à-vis the civil side of Song governance. Secondary scholarship often suggests that the military occupied a marginal position within Chinese society, a disposition that first arose during the Song, and was related to the civil-military (*wen-wu*) split in the Song scheme of governance. Although some scholars claim that this distinction in the structure of the Song government was mostly only on paper (for instance, many posts remained unfilled throughout most of the dynasty), the Song court certainly took great pains to make sure individuals in the armed forces, especially at the command level, did not acquire enough autonomous power—that is, troop loyalty, wealth, equipment, and authority—to rebel.[111] The Song restructuring of the government, therefore, helped create the military as outside and marginal.

The military system was very much woven into the *shi* legal category. We have seen that the Song court made great efforts to incorporate the military organization into the ritual network. Through *fa* and *shi*, that organization was subjected to an inordinate number of rules and specifications. The "flying positions" and "flying chessmen" method that the court instituted in 1035, overtly directed at the heavens, smacked of control over its commanders at one remove, too. The compilation of the Comprehensive Essentials in 1044 resulted in part from an effort to restrain maverick transgression and to keep its ritual practices within the purview of the court. However, the incorporation of occult techniques into the Comprehensive Essentials, being a training manual among other things, officially condoned the practice of these rituals far afield from the court. Although this issue cannot be definitively settled here, there are two other points that bear on these events and the civil/military relationship during the Song.

First is the conceptualization of warfare as *guidao*. Writers of military treatises, beginning with the author(s) of Sunzi's *Art of War* (*Sunzi bingfa*), have consistently defined warfare as a *guidao*. Ralph Sawyer renders this idea as, "Warfare is the Way of deception (*gui*)." *Gui* is discussed in the manuals and other military treatises as a complement of *zheng*, regular or upright.[112] Commenting on this line, Cao Cao (155–220) wrote: "Warfare is without fixed form; it takes cunning and deceit (*guizha*) as its Way," an image of *gui* as water-like, flowing and flexible.[113] Construed in this sense, *gui* means mysterious or secret.[114] In its context of the Way (*dao*), *gui* suggests an affinity with occult, the reality that undergirds empirical reality.[115] Both the Comprehensive Essentials and the Tiger Seal Classic reiterate this conception of warfare as *guidao*. The Essentials emphasizes *gui* primarily as deception, responsiveness, and the unexpected.[116] The Tiger Seal, the earlier, privately authored work, tacitly elaborates *guidao* in relation to heavenly timing, yin and yang, empty and substantial.[117] The Three Cosmographies, in particular the Hidden Period, were also defined as a *guidao*.[118] In the sense of the unpredictable, *gui* techniques were a counterbalance to *shi* "specifications." By virtue of being recorded and imperially issued, *guidao* became part of the canon (*jing*) and the upright (*zheng*) Way. To incorporate the *guidao*—the deceptive, unpredictable and tricky—into a regularized set of behaviors and norms, such as that typified by canon, the upright Way, the Song bureaucracy and the examination system, suggests the social and epistemological formalization of alternate means of attaining the Way. The military organization was one of the few that could straddle such categories.

In and of itself, this conceptualization of the military arts and its organization was not decisive in determining attitudes toward or the status of its participants. But it does assume a greater meaning when considered in light of the unprivileged social context from which most of the troops and their leaders arose. For instance, Song recruits were often tattooed, a mark of identification they shared with many criminals during the time. Historian Fang Hao notes that recruits perceived tattooing practices to be onerous. Many recruits signed up for the food, money, and shelter but opted to run when faced with the brand. Believed to sear the bone, such practices affected not only the soldiers' social lives but also their physical health and their fates in the afterlife (as important, I argue elsewhere, it also affected their *yin* power). Troops tended also to be socially marginalized in numerous ways. Some were landless, poverty-stricken, or victims of famine, and enlisted merely as a survival strategy. Others were criminals, fugitives, escapees, and the deranged. These factors, combined with corrupt practices of the higher echelons of the military, sometimes predisposed soldiers toward social disintegration.[119]

Being always socially marginal to some degree, military troops potentially constituted their own collectivity. In Turner's theoretical scheme of ritual, liminal social states accommodate what he calls *communitas*, a sense of community "as a social modality" that arises from states of existence that are socially marginal. He proposes that long-term, relatively permanent relationships can form from mutual experience of such ritually or socially liminal states. Such is especially true when social reintegration of a ritual process fails to result, or when the individuals concerned hold a status that is marginal, denigrated or excluded from the main body of a social or ritual community.[120]

There are a few reasons that this *communitas* may have been the case for the Song troops. First, the troops were directly involved in at least some of the rituals of the Three Cosmographies. The Supreme One (*taiyi*), one of the Three Cosmographies, was acted out using troops with flags.[121] Battle arrays themselves were ritually constructed, incorporating over ten thousand troops. The collective engagement in these rituals meant that those within the organization were connected by a topography of belief. Second, the military was a group large enough to construct a charismatic leader. It appears from the military manuals that the diviners were usually high-level officers. They directly engaged the troops in ritual, and the commanders occupied a location constructed as sacred via battle array schema. Their position was officially appointed, but these commanders were collectively constructed, too.[122] Combined with the potential for corruption, it is not difficult to imagine that the commander as ritual specialist assumed the highly ambivalent position of magician; revered, feared, respected, despised, he nevertheless possessed powerful techniques for controlling the cosmos. Just as the taxonomic indeterminacy of the term *shi* and the Three Cosmographies was dangerous, so the commander/ magician, socially indeterminate, posed a danger all the more real for the human collectivity under their control. To return to my original point, the layering of meanings of *shi* signaled practices that related to differences in how the "specialist" was defined and constructed, and how their authority was constituted in the civil and military branches.

To return to the issue of *shi* and how it relates to the limits of authority: in the case of *shi*, symbols, ritual performance, and the objects associated with these rituals were coded and acted out according to varied circumstances and social groups. Both the symbolic manifestation of authority and the actual ritual trappings of authority are encompassed by the term *shi*. To move between cosmograph and protocols is to move from symbolic schema to more concrete aspects of authority and governance.

Song innovations in cosmographic occult forms (*shi*) created the potential for transgression of boundaries established by nature and by the court. One whole set of the latter manufactured boundaries consisted of the oppressive restrictions embodied by imperial protocols that resulted from increasing and perhaps even over-ritualized bureaucratization during the Song. These protocols were not opposed, but like *wen* and *wu* themselves, were deemed necessary components in the construction of authority and its delegation. The Song court sought to distribute power and authority through creating increasingly finer distinctions within its bureaucracy.

Our penetration of the linguistic layering of *shi* informs us that transgressing borders is authority-dependent. In the cosmograph techniques, the ritual performer was collectively constituted by the margins; intellectual, geographic, and social. Transgression (of tabus, etc.) usually results not in vilification of the transgressor but in an acquisition of new status; the thing or person transgressed upon is vilified, made superfluous, or even nullified.[123] Using the military organization as transgressed *upon*—that is, outside of the upright Way (*zhengdao*) and therefore, socially marginal—and as the transgress*or* of the upright Way, the court tried to create the cosmic power necessary for, if not success, at least avoiding defeat. By instituting ritual protocols, they hoped to ensure that that power could be only temporary.

Conclusion

Occult ritual such as the Three Cosmographies probed, interrogated and defined boundaries of phenomenal and symbolic realms that were expressed in practice, defining the borders of the Song universe. This is important because the set of relations involved in such practices, and the role transgression played in those relations, help us understand more clearly the production of power and culture, especially its approaches to warfare, during the Song dynasty. The cases of such systems as the Three Cosmographies and the increasing importance of the recreation of the rituals associated with them throughout the Song further distinguish that particular dynasty within China's imperial history. The distinctiveness of the Song is also evident in the area of authority, especially as it applied to governance, including the increasing alienation (at least in theory) between *wen* and *wu*.

The convergence between the age-old prescribed principles that the Three Cosmographies entail and the equally old but newly universalized constructions emerging during the Song—change, correspondence, mutual production and conquest, complementary forces of *yin/yang*, reciprocity of Heaven-human-Earth, number (*shu*), and patterns (*li*)—was reified by modifications made to the cosmograph instrument. The incorporation of a third plate reflected the importance of the Three Potentials to Song universal constructions, as did the rise of the Hidden Period, splitting time into ever more discrete units. Thus, boundaries and limina—sacred, ambiguous, indeterminate markers—between these units increased, affording more opportunities for communication with and physical apprehension of alternate universes, both phenomenal and divine. Such refinements in instruments that manipulated the phenomenal borders of the perceptible, human realm increased the inherent potential of the cosmography techniques to transgress those borders. Similarly, the more abundant transgressible thresholds inserted the human as a mediator of supernatural power in the Three Potentials triangle. Rituals of transgression ultimately connect complementary forces both natural and divine, in contradistinction to other sorts of ritual, which polarize and separate those forces (e.g., death rituals, divination, court rituals, and so forth). Rather than simply reading change and Heaven's portents, the Three Cosmographies established human control over these previously untapped powers.

The identification of the Three Cosmographies as a military technique stemmed precisely from its capacity for transgressing the borders between the readily perceptible, phenomenal world and realms thought to be imperceptible and sacred. The Three Cosmographies were, and still are, identified with sanctioned violence typified by *wu* (martial). In some senses, the cosmography techniques and *wu* shared characteristics that were similarly coded, both being vehicles of power that represented indeterminate states, a suspension of order, danger. As sanctioned violence, *wu* signifies conflict and a broken order, particularly in contrast to *wen* (literary, civilization). Although *wu* was necessary to establish order, it was order*ing*—temporary, active and performative. It was *wen*, however, that was order*ed*—stable, tranquil, mimetic, as characters on a page. Similarly, both *wu* and cosmography techniques incorporated transgression as its underlying operator.

The fact that the content of Three Cosmographies rituals was primarily documented in military manuals contoured the set of relations between the court and its military arm. During the Song, there was a greater effort to recover and refine these cosmograph rituals than in the past. This effort reflected the Song court's concern that these rituals might be used to subvert its own newly established state. Song proscriptions of the techniques were directed, at least initially, internally, at its own increasingly fluid society and especially at the army that had hoisted the dynasty to power. As the Song court coalesced and was increasingly bureaucratized, interest in the Three Cosmographies grew, resulting in its development into seven different schools by the mid-eleventh century.

Paralleling the bureaucratization of governance, comprehensive military manuals generated by the court represent the first official attempts to capture in writing what had been an oral ritual tradition, the content of which was effective only when performed. In its founding myth, the Hidden Period is based on talismans and drawings, not writing. The success of the Hidden Period depended on first "getting *language*." In the cosmograph rituals, writing as such is mentioned only as a combination of indeterminate and empty markers, the "eight characters" that signify only when invested with time and blood. Thus, in the act of documenting rituals in the manuals, then, there is a tension between the (legitimate) authority of writing and the power and efficacy of oral performance. In other words, these rituals in written form signaled the court's attempts to appropriate a tradition that was previously oral and therefore "secret." Once written down, the court of course believed it could standardize and control the Three Cosmographies.

The term *shi* assumed many layers of meaning during the Song. The contradictions inherent in those meanings and in its actual functions were instrumental in the production of the military culture and the Song idea of warfare. Paradoxical developments in *shi* as cosmography techniques and as legal and ritual protocols attested to court recognition of these rituals as efficacious and powerful. As protocols, *shi* were limits that the court wished to impose on ritual practitioners, especially those in the military. By instituting *shi* as a legal category, the court hoped to establish an active role in placing its own limits on military use of cosmography rituals, performance of which occurred outside their direct control. At the same time, such oppressive restrictions marked practitioners as both powerful (because transgression into the divine was the strict purview of the emperor and the transcendent) and socially separate. Given the status of the Three Cosmographies as proscribed and dangerous, practitioners could garner their own social collectives from within the military organization, collectives that were defined both by tradition and practice as being outside the upright Way. Song approaches to warfare, then, were not only territorially defined. Rather, the Chinese sphere of influence as defined by warfare extended to include the moral, ritual and cosmic spheres also. In other words, the military use of *shi* signifies not only the classical search for alternates to active warfare—typified by ancient military treatises such as Sunzi's, which emphasize stratagem over battle—but also the middle imperial conception of warfare as a sacred influence whose end results were more than physical.

Many questions remain. Did the Song court, in its efforts at control, unintentionally force "secret" methods like the Three Cosmographies out into the larger social milieu? To what extent did such rituals of transgression exist at other, rather less well-documented levels of Song society than the court? The perpetuity of the Three Cosmographies into the present day, and its endurance as a source of fascination in fiction, film, and romance suggest that these closely guarded and proscribed techniques did nonetheless find their way widely into popular practice. Although the precise dynamic of how that transferal came about remains obscure, I hope that this chapter may somehow contribute to future efforts at its discernment.

Notes

The author wishes to recognize and thank the Republic of China National Endowment for the Arts, the Fulbright Foundation, the Chiang Ching-kuo Foundation, and the Peace Studies and East Asia Programs at Cornell University for funding research at the Academia Sinica (hereafter AS) in Taiwan and in Ithaca, New York that made this project possible. Charles Peterson, David Holmberg, Naomi Standen, and the Cornell University Peace Studies Dinner Seminar read and commented on early drafts. I extend special thanks to Don Wyatt for his thorough reading and helpful comments on this chapter, and unflagging patience and grace throughout the revision process. All errors are, of course, my own. All translations are mine unless otherwise noted.

1. Tuo Tuo [Toghto], *Songshi* (Beijing, 1977) (hereafter *SS*), 197.4918. All dates noted are anno Domini (AD) or Common Era (CE) unless otherwise noted.
2. *SS*, 105.2556. This passage summarizes three such incidents, with the first to be discussed having occurred in 1112, under the reign of Emperor Huizong (r.1100–1125).
3. Wang Zengyu, *Songchao bingzhi chutan* (Beijing, 1983), p. 229.
4. *SS*, 197.4920.
5. These texts remain a repository—in some cases, the sole repository—of ritual practices of the era. Records of these rituals have been mined by scholars of Daoism but largely ignored by historians and other scholars of the Tang and Song periods.
6. On the translation of *liuren* as the "Six Water Cycles," see Henri Doré, *Researches into Chinese Superstitions* (Shanghai, 1917), 5:344 and Gu Jianqing, *Zhongguo fangshu da cidian* (Guangdong, 1991) (hereafter *FSDCD*), pp. 302–3. During the Song, the Hidden Period became synonymous with the Irregular Opening/Hidden Period (*qimen dunjia*) and its earlier name, Duke of Thunder (*Lei Gong*). I use Hidden Period and Irregular Opening/Hidden Period

interchangeably in this chapter. For more on the Three Cosmographies, individually or collectively, see: Yang Weide, *Dunjia fuying jing* (Shanghai, 1935) (hereafter *DJFYJ*); Cheng Daosheng, *Dunjia yanyi* (Shanghai, 1935) (hereafter *DJYY*); *FSDCD*; Chen Yinglue, comp. and ed., *Guiguzi qimen dafa* (Taibei, 1979); Duan Muyu, *Baihua qimen dunjia* (1986; rpr. Taibei, 1995); Fei Bingxun, *Qimen dunjia xinshu* (Changchun, 1991); Ho Peng Yoke, "Cong kexueshi guandian shitan 'Qimen dunjia,'" *Xibei daxue xuebao* 28.1 (1998): 1–4 and 28.2 (1998): 93–97; Marc Kalinowski, "Les Instruments Astro-calendériques des Han et la Méthode Liu Ren," *Bulletin École Francaise d'Extreme Orient* 62 (1983): 309–417; Marc Kalinowski, *Cosmologie et Divination dans la Chine Ancienne* (Paris, 1991); Kong Richang, *Qimen dunjia yanjiu* (Tainan, 1975); Liu Bowen, comp. and ed., *Qimen dunjia quanshu* (Hong Kong, n.d. [1915]); Kristofer Schipper and Wang Hsiu-huei, "Progressive and Regressive Time Cycles in Taoist Ritual" in *Time, Science and Society in China and the West* (The Study of Time, vol. 5), ed. J. T. Fraser, N. Lawrence, and F. C. Haber (Amherst, 1986); Yan Dunjie, "Guanyu Xihan chuqide shipan he zhanpan," *Kaogu* 5 (1978):334–37; Yan Dunjie, "Ba liuren shipan," *Wenwu cankao ziliao* 1958.7:20–23; Zhuge Wuhou (Liang), *Huopan qimen dunjia tongzong daquan (jingjiao ben)*, vols. 1 and 2 (Taizhong, 1965); and Ho Peng Yoke, *Chinese Mathematical Astrology: Reaching out to the Stars* (London, 2003). For the purposes of this chapter, the general concepts among the three methods were similar, and sometimes used in concert with each other during the Song. There are some differences between the cosmographs, and the events and circumstances for which each particular method should be used. All three are discussed in the manuals, but the Hidden Period and Six Water Cycles techniques dominate the manuals. Supreme One is sometimes discussed as one kind of Hidden Period.

7. *Qiannu youhun (A Chinese Ghost Story)*, directed by Ching Siu-tung [Cheng Xiaodong] (Hong Kong, 1987); the premodern novel attributed to Luo Guanzhong (ca. 1300–ca. 1400), *Romance of the Three Kingdoms*, tr. C. H. Brewitt-Taylor (Rutland, 1959), 2.251–53, 438–49.
8. Ho Peng Yoke, "Zhuge Liang yu *qimen dunjia*" (Singapore, 1998); Schipper and Wang, "Progressive and Regressive"; Zeng Gongliang and Ding Du, *Wujing zongyao* (Beijing; Shenyang, 1988) (hereafter *WJZY*), 21.2192; *DJYY*. All *WJZY* citations refer to the *houji* (latter section) unless otherwise noted as *qianji* (former section).
9. *WJZY*, 21.2174–75.
10. *WJZY*, 21.2192.
11. For a rather typical assessment, especially in Chinese secondary scholarship, see Xu Baolin, *Zhongguo bingshu tonglan* (Beijing, 1990), pp. 350–51.
12. See for example Brian Ferguson, "The General Consequences of War: An Amazonian Perspective" in *Studying War: Anthropological Perspectives*, ed. S. P. Reyna and R. E. Downs (Amsterdam, 1994), pp. 85–112, and esp. pp. 98–101.
13. On ritual as transgression, see Victor Turner, *Ritual Process* (Ithaca, 1969; rpr. 1977), pp. 94–130; Mary Douglas, *Purity and Danger* (London, 1966); Marshall Sahlins, *Historical Metaphors and Mythical Realities* (Ann Arbor, 1981); and James Boon, *Verging on Extra-vagence* (Princeton, 1999).
14. Peter Stallybrass and Allon White, *The Politics and Poetics of Transgression* (Ithaca, 1986), pp. 6–26 and "Conclusion"; and see James Boon's discussion in his *Verging*, p. 202.

15. Roy Rappaport, *Ritual and Religion in the Making of Humanity* (Cambridge, 1999).
16. Turner, *Process*, pp. 94–130.
17. Schipper and Wang, "Progressive and Regressive," pp. 188–201.
18. Stallybrass and White, *Transgression*, pp. 17–18. See the discussion of carnivalesque in Mikhail Bakhtin, *Rabelais and His World*, tr. Hélène Iswolsky (Bloomington, 1984).
19. See Boon, *Verging*, pp. 143–65, 200–202.
20. Both of these aspects of the cosmograph related to transgression of the two latter limits, geographical and cultural, which I discuss elsewhere.
21. The Irregular Opening, Hidden Period, and Six Water Cycles systems were sometimes conflated, and discussed as parts of the same genre of technique and used together; see *FSDCD*, p. 14. See n. 7 and Kristofer Marinus Schipper, *L'empereur Wu des Han dans la Legende taoiste* (Paris, 1965), pp. 34–39; Ngo Van Xuyet, *Divination, Magie et Politique dans la Chine Ancienne* (Paris, 1976), pp. 190–95; Ho Peng Yoke, "Cong kexue" and "Zhuge Liang."
22. Chen Menglei, comp. and ed., *Qinding gujin tushu jicheng* (Taibei, 1977) (hereafter *TSJC*), s.v. "Yishudian" 746.52b.
23. On Ge Hong's geographic emphasis, see James R. Ware, *Alchemy, Medicine and Religion in the China of AD 320. The Nei Pien of Ko Hung (Pao-p'u-tzu)* (New York, 1966), pp. 279–300.
24. Li Quan, *Taibo yinjing* (Taibei, 1957) (hereafter *TBYJ*), p. 9; *WJZY*, p. 21. Some of the *zashi* (miscellaneous cosmograph techniques) of the *TBYJ* are categorized as Hidden Period in *WJZY*. Xu Dong discusses Six Water Cycles, Hidden Period, and Orphans and Empties as parts of the same system in his *Huqian jing* (Shanghai, 1936) (hereafter *HQJ*).
25. *DJYY*, *Siku quanshu tiyao*, 2b–3.
26. *WJZY*, 16.1869.
27. Schipper and Wang, "Progressive and Regressive"; Nathan Sivin, *Cosmos and Computation in Early Chinese Mathematical Astronomy* (Leiden, 1969).
28. Chinese official documents are very rarely direct about the use of these techniques, a situation reflective of the nature of Chinese records of military encounters generally. See Charles Peterson, "Bibliographic Note" to "Regional Defense Against the Central Power: The Huai-hsi Campaign, 815–817" in *Chinese Ways on Warfare*, ed. Frank Kierman and John Fairbank (Cambridge, MA, 1974), p. 335.
29. Especially in the drawn out debates over the calibration of the pitch pipes that eventually culminated in the New Canon of the Essence of Music of the Jingyou Period [1034–37] (*Jingyou yuesui xinjing*) during Renzong's reign. Furthermore, it became increasingly popular throughout the Ming and especially in the Qing (1644–1912). See Yuan Shushan, *Zhongguo lidai buren zhuan* (1948; rpr. Taibei, 1998) (hereafter *LDBRZ*).
30. Proscription occurred in the ninth month of 972. *SS*, 461.13500; *WJZY*, 16.1869; see Christian Cochini and Anna Seidel, tr., *Chronique de la Dynastie des Sung (960–1279)* (Munich, 1968), p. 13. On proscription generally, see Brian E. McKnight and James T. C. Liu, tr., *The Enlightened Judgments: Ch'ing-ming chi: The Sung Dynasty Collection* (Albany, 1999).
31. Marcel Mauss, *A General Theory of Magic* (London, 1950; rpr. 1972); Turner, *Process*, pp. 108–9.

32. See Douglas, *Purity and Danger*.
33. McKnight and Liu, *Enlightened Judgments*, pp. 476–84.
34. Xue Juzheng, *Jiu Wudaishi* (Beijing, 1976) (hereafter *JWDS*), 71.944–45.
35. *JWDS*, 131.1730.
36. *DJYY*, *Siku quanshu tiyao*, 2b–3. For example, see the mist incident in which Li Jing routed the Türks, recounted in David A. Graff, "Early T'ang Generalship and the Textual Tradition" (Ph. D. diss., Princeton University, 1995), 2.499.
37. *SS*, 461.13500; *JWDS*, 71.944; *JWDS*, 131.1730; *TSJC*, s.v. "Yishudian," 746.50b; *LDBRZ*, p. 782.
38. *TBYJ*, 9.243.
39. For a fuller discussion of this, see Marcia Butler, "Reflections of a Military Medium" (Ph.D. diss., Cornell University, 2006), Chapter 5. The discussion of time and the cosmograph included such figures as Hong Mai, Shen Kuo, and Wang Fu. See *SS*, 461.13502; *TSJC*, s.v. "Yishudian," 745.43; Hong Mai, *Rongzhai suibi, sanbi*, 7.12; Cheng Minsheng and Li Xu, *Rongzhai suibi (baihuaban)* (Taibei, 1994), p. 416; and F. Richard Stephenson, "Chinese and Korean Star Maps and Catalogs" in *History of Cartography*, vol. 2, bk. 2, ed. J. B. Harley and David Woodward (Chicago, 1994), pp. 540–41.
40. *TSJC*, s.v. "Yishudian," 745.44.
41. *SS*, 461.13495.
42. Deborah Porter, *From Deluge to Discourse* (Albany, 1996), and Michael Loewe, *Divination, Mythology, and Monarchy in Han China* (Cambridge, 1994), p. 242.
43. *FSDCD*, 297 (*Sanshi*), citing *[Minghuang] Liudian*, 14.
44. *TSJC*, s.v. "Yishudian," 746.52b.
45. *TSJC*, s.v. "Yishudian," 746.52b; *DJYY*; Duan Muyu, *Qimen dunjia*; *DJFYJ*; Chen Yinglue, *Guiguzi qimen*; and Liu Bowen, *Qimen dunjia* all identify the Hidden Period to warfare.
46. Ouyang Xiu, *Xin Wudaishi*, 23.239.
47. *SS*, 446.13171.
48. *TBYJ* (*biao*).
49. *SS*, 157.3687. We might note that the pitch pipe debate, one of two incidents involving court use of the cosmograph, also coincided with hostilities on the Song periphery. In the first instance, in 1035, it corresponded with increasing tensions with the Xi Xia, and raids by the southwestern tribes—the Liao and the Yao—who plundered Leizhou and Huazhou; in 1049, with a rebellion by the Man peoples in the southwest. The Qidan Liao and later, the Jürchen Jin, shared with Song China this particular ideology. In this sense, then, the *shi* were very much a protocol that codified the approaches to governance, if not warfare.
50. Zheng Qiao, *Tongzhi*, 71.834.
51. *SS*, 23.2507; 24.1604; 126.2955; 165.3923; 260.5246.
52. *TSJC*, s.v. "Yishudian," 746.52b.
53. Furthering the theses of others, Victor Turner has commented on how unclassifiable bodies of knowledge, because they are construed as dangerous, invite constraints on their access and prohibitions on their practice. Such was clearly the case with the Three Cosmographies. See Turner, *Process*, p. 109, referring to Douglas, *Purity and Danger*.
54. *SS*, 157.3686–87; 165.3923.
55. This and the following are based on the discussions of the cosmograph in n. 7 above and: Christopher Cullen, "Some Further Points on the Shih." *Early China*

6 (1980–81): 31–46; Donald J. Harper, "The Han Cosmic Board (*shi*)." *Early China* 4 (1978–79): 1–10 and "The Han Cosmic Board. A Response to Christopher Cullen" *Early China* 6 (1980–81):47–56; Kalinowski, "Instruments Astro-calendériques" and *Cosmologie*; Michael Loewe, *Ways to Paradise* (London, 1979); John S. Major, *Heaven and Earth in Early Han Thought: Chapters 3, 4, and 5 of the* Huainanzi (Albany, 1993); and Chao Weipang, "The Chinese Science of Fate-calculation," *Folklore Studies* 5 (1946): 279–315, esp. pp. 288–91.
56. Kalinowski, "Instruments Astro-calendériques," pp. 353–81.
57. Kalinowski, "Instruments Astro-calendériques," pp. 374–81, calls these the Four Corners.
58. *Tiangang* is another name for the *jia* and *ji* stems, and combined with certain branches forms the main north-south axis on a "time circle." *HQJ*, 11.110; *WJZY*, 21.2196.
59. Joseph Needham, *Science and Civilisation in China* (hereafter *SCC*), 3:398.
60. *SS*, 461.13495.
61. *HQJ*, 11; Schipper and Wang, "Progressive and Regressive," p. 201. For a full explanation and an example of how the Six Ceremonies and the Three Irregulars are laid out, see the latter pp. 198–203.
62. This and the following are based on Schipper and Wang "Progressive and Regressive," pp. 198–203.
63. *DJYY*, *tiyao*, 1–2b; Schipper and Wang, "Progressive and Regressive," pp. 201–2.
64. In the most auspicious case, the performer lines up one of the Eight Gates with one of the Three Irregulars. For specific steps in reckoning on the cosmograph, see *TBYJ*, 9.248; *FSDCD*, 309; Fei Bingxun, *Qimen dunjia*, pp. 22–25; Duan, *Qimen dunjia*, pp. 15, 57, 120; *TBYJ*, 9.249–50 (*keshi*); Kalinowski, "Instruments Astro-calendériques"; and Ho Peng Yoke, "Cong kexue."
65. *WJZY*, 2219. There is another version involving tallies and chanting in *DJFYJ*, *xia*, 9a–b.
66. These include numerical disparities in divisions of eight (trigrams) and nine (palaces and asterisms) and their prime divisors; spatial disparities resulting from assigning twenty-two stems and branches onto nine palace locations; and disparities in the time of the lunar year of twelve months (the earthly branches), the solar seasons (twenty-four), and the lunar lodges (twenty-eight).
67. See Shen Kuo, *Mengxi bitan*, cited in *TSJC*, s.v. "Yishudian," 746.51a–b.
68. *HQJ*, 11 (*Tianshi*).
69. *DJFYJ*, *shang*, 1.
70. Edmund Leach, *Culture and Communication* (Cambridge, 1976), p. 35 (italics in the original); Boon, *Verging*, p. 202.
71. Boon, *Verging*, p. 202.
72. *WJZY*, 21.2173; see *HQJ*, 12.123 for another technique that uses the commander's birth year.
73. *WJZY*, 21.2192–93.
74. The founding myth of the Hidden Period as recounted in the *Venus Classic* is also fraught with indeterminate objects, animals, and ambitions, counterbalanced in the succeeding passage by unambiguous numerical prescriptions. *TBYJ*, 9.243.
75. *WJZY*, 21.2192–93. Taking *xiang* for *xian*.
76. *WJZY* (Renzong's Preface).

77. See Kidder Smith and Don J. Wyatt, "Shao Yung and Number" in Kidder Smith, Jr., *Sung Dynasty Uses of the* I Ching (Princeton, 1990), pp. 110–27.
78. Sivin, *Cosmos and Computation*.
79. Nathan Sivin and Joseph Needham, "On the Theoretical Background of Elixir Alchemy" in *SCC*, ed. Needham.
80. *HQJ*, 11.108–19.
81. Brian E. McKnight, "From Statute to Precedent: An Introduction to Song Law and its Transformation" in *Law and the State in Traditional East Asia*, ed. Brian E. McKnight (Honolulu, 1987), p. 112.
82. Brian E. McKnight, "Patterns of Law and Patterns of Thought: Notes on the Specifications (*shi*) of Song China," *Journal of the American Oriental Society* 102.2 (1982): 323–31, 322, 326; on the Song shift in laws generally, see McKnight, "From Statute to Precedent."
83. McKnight, "Patterns of Law," p. 330.
84. *WJZY, qianji*, 5.205. Compare with *shi* and *fa* as occult ritual in *WJZY*, 21.
85. McKnight and Liu, *Enlightened Judgments*, p. 15.
86. As McKnight asks: "Was communication more important to [the Song]? Or were they simply less confident of their ability to communicate accurately in the absence of clear guidelines?" McKnight, "Patterns of Law," p. 330.
87. *WJZY, qianji*, 14. Wang Zengyu, *Bingzhi chutan*, pp. 279–83, 302, 327.
88. During the Tang *fashi* is correctly understood as a binome when *fa* were major laws and *shi* minor by-laws. An example of the Song change in meaning, he asserts, is a more accurate rendering of the well-known text on buildings, the *Yingzao fashi*, as "The Specifications (*shi*) of the Organized Rules (*fa*) on Constructing Palaces (*yingzao*)." McKnight, "Patterns of Law," p. 326.
89. *SS*, 197.4918, 4919.
90. *SS*, 191.4749; referencing private *fa*.
91. *SS*, 193.4803; 197.4914–22.
92. In 1049, for instance, in a discussion of weapons, the *fa* and the *shi* for manufacturing and supplying weapons changed from a rule (*shi*) into a statute (*ling*) in those provinces manufacturing weapons that ignored *fa* and *shi* prescriptions. *SS*, 197.4919.
93. *SS*, 197.4912, 4918.
94. *SS*, 197.4910, 4912.
95. *SS*, 197.4918.
96. *SS*, 197.4920. The Martial Warehouse was part of the Court of Imperial Regalia (*weiwei si*). See *SS*, 6.164.2892–93; Chen Gaochun, *Zhongguo gudai junshi wenhua dacidian*, p. 957; Chang Fu-jui, *Fonctionnaires des Song* (Paris, 1962), p. 507, #855; Charles O. Hucker, *Dictionary of Official Titles in Imperial China* (Stanford, 1985), p. 565, #7683 and p. 571, #7779.
97. *JTS*, 24.929; *LSSY* 23.np; *SS*, 103.2507; *WXTK*, 80.731.
98. That is to say, these deities were considered outside deities, by virtue of their location. See Alfred Schinz, *The Magic Square: Cities in Ancient China* (Stuttgart, 1996), pp. 220–21.
99. *SS*, 103.2506–7; *WXTK*, 80.731.
100. *SS*, 103.2507.
101. *WJZY*, 21.2220–21. Similar rituals are described in *DJFYJ*, *xia*, 13b–18.
102. *DJFYJ*, *shang*, 2b (*bujufa*) gives a rhyming chant for laying out the *ju*. Similar technique was used for laying out the Nine Palaces.

103. *WJZY*, 21.2219. Similar versions show a grid of four verticals and five horizontals drawn on the ground with the knife and include the requirement of chanting as one draws; or the use of tallies and chanting. See *DJFYJ*, *xia*, 14b–15 and 9a–b, respectively.
104. *TBYJ*, 9.249.
105. On specifics of these symbols, see Kong Richang, *Qimen dunjia*, p. 5; Duan, *Qimen dunjia*, pp. 15, 57, 226.
106. *WJZY*, 21.2220–21.
107. Ware, *Nei Pien of Ko Hung*, pp. 279–300; Sivin and Needham, "Elixir Alchemy," pp. 264–68.
108. Michel de Certeau, *The Writing of History* (New York, 1975; rpr. 1988), pp. 244–55.
109. *SS*, 157.3686–87.
110. *WJZY*, 21.2219.
111. Wang Zengyu, *Bingzhi chutan*, Chapters 8–9.
112. Ralph Sawyer, tr., *Sun-tzu: Art of War* (Boulder, 1994), p. 168; Samuel Griffith, *Sun Tzu: the Art of War* (London, 1963), p. 66, #17.
113. *Sunzi bingfa* in *Zhongguo bingshu jicheng* (Beijing, 1987–), 7.421.
114. *ZWDZD*, 8.972: #36300, #36300.27, #36300.36.
115. Charles Poncé, *The Game of Wizards: Psyche, Science and Symbol in the Occult* (Baltimore, 1975), p. 12.
116. *WJZY*, 3.1284–90; Liu Lexian and Peng Mingzhe, ed., *Chuanshi cangshu: ziku; bingshu* (Haikou, 1995), pp. 503–4.
117. *HQJ*, *Biao*, 1; 4.30; 11.105–6.
118. *DJFYJ*, *shang*, 1; Duan, *Qimen dunjia*, p. 2.
119. Fang Hao, *Song shi* (Taibei, 1954), Chapter 4. Wang Zengyu, *Bingzhi chutan*, pp. 212–15.
120. Turner, *Process*, pp. 94–130.
121. *WJZY*, 18.2006–7; Liu and Peng, *Chuanshi cangshu*, p. 635.
122. On the collective construction of the sorcerer, see Mauss, *General Theory*.
123. As Sahlins articulates in his *Historical Metaphors*.

Glossary

bazi 八字
bao 保
baojia 保甲
Cao Cao 曹操
Chao 晁
Chen 陳
chi 尺
Daizhou 代州
dao 道
Dou Yan 竇儼
dun 遁
dunjia 遁甲
Dunjia fuying jing 遁甲符應經
fa 法

fashi 法式
feiqi 飛棋
feiyi weici zhi fa 飛移位次之法
Ge Hong 葛洪
guxu 孤虛
guidao 詭道
guizha 詭詐
He Gui 賀瑰
Hou Hanshu 後漢書
Huqian jing 虎鈐經
Huainanzi 淮南子
jia 甲
jing 經
Jingyou yuesui xinjing 景祐樂髓新經
ju 局
Lei Gong 雷公
li[1] 禮 [ritual]
li[2] 理 [pattern]
Li Fuxian 李復先
Li Jing 李靖
Li Quan 李筌
Liang Taizu 梁太祖
Liao 獠
ling 令
Liuchao 六朝
liuren 六壬
Ma Shao 馬韶
qi[1] 奇 [irregular]
qi[2] 氣 [vital universal essence, vapors, breath]
qimen dunjia 奇門遁甲
Qingli 慶曆
Renzong 仁宗
sancai 三才
sanshi 三式
sanshi guan 三式官
Sang Daomou 桑道茂
Sha 煞
Shen Kuo 沈括
shi 式
Shi Kang 史抗
shu 數
Siku shumu 四庫書目
siwei 四維
Song Taizu 宋太祖
Songshi 宋史
Su Jiaqing 蘇嘉慶
Sunzi bingfa 孫子兵法
Taibo yinjing 太白陰經
taishi ju 太史局

taiyi 太乙
Taizong 太宗
tiangang 天罡
Tongzhi 通志
Wang Fu 王黼
Wang Pu 王朴
weiwei si 衛尉司
wen 文
Wenxian tongkao 文獻通考
wu 武
Wujing zongyao 武經總要
wuku 武庫
Xu Dong 許洞
Xu Fu 徐復
Xu Ji 許寂
Yang Weide 楊維德
Yijing 易經
yin/yang 陰陽
Yu 禹
Yuwen Cuizhong 宇文粹中
Zhao Yanyi 趙延義
Zhaozong 昭宗
Zheng Qiao 鄭樵
zhengdao 正道
zhengming 正名
Zhou Dunyi 周敦頤
Zhou Taizu 周太祖
Zhuge Liang 諸葛亮

Bibliography

Bakhtin, Mikhail. *Rabelais and His World*, tr. Hélène Iswolsky. Bloomington: Indiana University Press, 1984.

Boon, James. *Verging on Extra-vagence*. Princeton: Princeton University Press, 1999.

Butler, Marcia. "Reflections of a Military Medium: Ritual and Magic in the Eleventh- and Twelfth-Century Chinese Military." Ph.D. diss. Ithaca, NY: Cornell University, 2006.

Chang Fu-jui. *Les Fonctionnaires des Song*. Paris: Mouton & Co., 1962.

Chao Weipang. "The Chinese Science of Fate-calculation." *Folklore Studies* 5 (1946):279–315.

Chen Gaochun 陳高春, ed. *Zhongguo gudai junshi wenhua dacidian* 中國古代軍事文化大辭典 [Great Dictionary of Ancient Chinese Military Affairs and Culture]. Beijing: Changzheng chubanshe, 1992.

Chen Menglei 陳夢雷, Jiang Tingxi 蔣廷錫, comp. and ed. *Qinding gujin tushu jicheng* 欽定古今圖書集成 [Imperially Commissioned Encyclopedia]. Taibei: Dingwen shuju, 1977.

Chen Yinglue 陳英略, comp. and ed. *Guiguzi qimen dafa* 鬼谷子奇門大法 [The Great Method of the Irregular Opening of Guiguzi]. Taibei: Guigu xianshi jiniantang, 1979.

Cheng Daosheng 程道生. *Dunjia yanyi* 遁甲演義 [The Practice and Meaning of the Hidden Period]. *Siku quanshu (SKQS)* 四庫全書 [Complete Books of the Four Treasuries] edn. Shanghai: Shangwu yinshuguan, 1935.

Cheng Minsheng 程民生 and Li Xu 李旭, ed. *Rongzhai suibi baihuaban* 容齋隨筆白話版 [A Vernacular Version of the Essays and Notes from Hong Mai's Brush]. Taibei: Hanqin wenhua shiye youxiangongsi, 1994.

Cochini, Christian and Anna Seidel, tr. *Chronique de la Dynastie des Sung (960–1279)*. Munich, Germany: Universität München Ostasiatisches Seminar, 1968.

Cullen, Christopher. "Some Further Points on the Shih." *Early China* 6 (1980–81):31–46.

De Certeau, Michel. *The Writing of History*. New York: Columbia University Press, 1975; rpr. 1988.

Doré, Henri. *Researches into Chinese Superstitions*, vol. 5. 8 vols. Shanghai: T'usewei Printing Press, 1917; 1914–26.

Douglas, Mary. *Purity and Danger*. London: Routledge and Kegan Paul, 1966.

Duan Muyu 端木譽. *Baihua qimen dunjia* 白話奇門遁甲 [The Vernacular Irregular Opening and the Hidden Period]. 1986. rpr. Taibei: Longyin wenhua shiye gufen youxian gongsi, 1995.

Fang Hao 方豪. *Song shi* 宋史 [A History of the Song]. Taibei: Zhonghua wenhua chubanshiye weiyuanhui, 1954.

Fei Bingxun 費秉勛. *Qimen dunjia xinshu* 奇門遁甲新述 [New Explications of the Irregular Opening and the Hidden Period]. Changchun: Shidai wenyi chubanshe, 1991.

Ferguson, Brian. "The General Consequences of War: An Amazonian Perspective." In *Studying War: Anthropological Perspectives*, ed. S. P. Reyna and R. E. Downs. Amsterdam, Holland: Gordon and Breach, 1994.

Fraser, J. T. and N. Lawrence and F. C. Haber, ed. *Time, Science and Society in China and the West*, 6 vols. The Study of Time, vol. 5. Amherst: University of Massachusetts Press, 1986.

Graff, David A. "Early T'ang Generalship and the Textual Tradition." 2 vols. Ph.D. diss. Princeton: Princeton University, 1995.

Griffith, Samuel. *Sun Tzu: The Art of War*. London: Oxford University Press, 1963.

Gu Jianqing 古健青. *Zhongguo fangshu da cidian* 中國方術大辭典 [Great Dictionary of the Chinese Occult Arts]. Guangzhou: Zhongshan daxue chubanshe, 1991.

Harley, J. B. and David Woodward, ed. *History of Cartography*. 2 vols. Chicago, Il: University of Chicago Press, 1994.

Harper, Donald J. "The Han Cosmic Board (shi)." *Early China* 4 (1978–79):1–10.

———. "The Han Cosmic Board. A response to Christopher Cullen." *Early China* 6 (1980–81):47–56.

Ho Peng Yoke 何丙郁. "Cong kexueshi guandian shitan *Qimen dunjia*" 從科學觀點試談奇門遁甲 [An Examination of the Traditional Chinese Secret Magical Art of *Qimen dunjia* from the Standpoint of History of Science], *Xibei daxue xuebao* 西北大學學報 [Northwest University Journal] 28.1 (1998):1–4; 28.2 (1998):93–7.

———. "Zhuge Liang yu *qimen dunjia*" 諸葛亮与奇門遁甲 [Zhuge Liang and His Magical Art of *Qimen Dunjia*] Singapore: *1997 Wu Teh Yao Memorial Lectures*, 1998.

———. *Chinese Mathematical Astrology: Reaching out to the Stars*. London: RoutledgeCurzon, 2003.

Hong Mai 洪邁. *Rongzhai suibi wuji* 容齋隨筆五集 [Essays and Notes from Hong Mai's Brush in Five Collections]. Changchun: Jilin wenshi chubanshe, 1991.

Huang, Zhunjie and Erik Zürcher, ed. *Time and Space in Chinese Culture*. Leiden, Holland: E. J. Brill, 1995.

Hucker, Charles O. *A Dictionary of Official Titles in Imperial China*. Stanford: Stanford University Press, 1985.

Kalinowski, Marc. "Les Instruments Astro-calendériques des Han et la Méthode Liu Ren." *Bulletin École Francaise d'Extreme Orient* 62 (1983):309–417.

———. *Cosmologie et Divination dans la Chine Ancienne*. Paris: École Francaise d'Extreme Orient, 1991.

Kong Richang 孔日昌. *Qimen dunjia yanjiu* 奇門遁甲研究 [Researches on the Irregular Opening and the Hidden Period]. Tainan: Xibei chubanshe, 1975.

Leach, Edmund. *Culture and Communication*. Cambridge: Cambridge University Press, 1976.

Li E 厲鶚. *Liaoshi shiyi* 遼史拾遺 [Supplements to the History of the Liao]. *Siku quanshu (SKQS)* 四庫全書 [Complete Works of the Four Treasuries] online edn.

Li Quan 李筌. *Taibo yinjing* 太白陰經 [Secret Classic of Venus, Planet of War] (*Shenji zhidi taibo yinjing* 神極制敵太白陰經 [Divinely Efficacious in Subduing the Enemy, Secret classic of Venus, Planet of War]). Zhongguo bingxue daxi 5. Taibei: Shijie bingxueshe, 1957.

Liu Bowen 劉佰溫, comp. and ed. [Zhang Liang 張良 and Zhuge Liang 諸葛亮]. *Qimen dunjia quanshu* 奇門遁甲全書 [Complete Works on the Irregular Opening and the Hidden period]. 1372 edition. Hong Kong: Kunlun chuban gongsi, n.d. (1915).

Liu Lexian 劉樂賢 and Peng Mingzhe 彭明哲, ed. *Chuanshi cangshu: ziku; bingshu* 傳世藏書:子庫兵書 [Hidden books Transmitted through the Generations: The philosophers Storehouse; Military Tracts]. Haikou: Hainan guoji xinwen chuban zhongxin; Chengcheng wenhua chuban youxian gongsi, 1995.

Liu Xianting 劉先廷. *Taibo yinjing yizhu* 太白陰經譯注 [Interpretations and commentaries on Secret Classic of Venus, Planet of War]. Beijing: Junshi kexue chubanshe, 1996.

Liu Xu 劉昫. *Jiu Tangshu* 舊唐書 [Old History of the Tang]. Taibei, Taiwan: AS (Academia Sinica) newly revised edn. Available at http:\\www.ihp.sinica.edu.tw\. Last accessed December 10, 2007.

Loewe, Michael. *Ways to Paradise*. London: George Allen and Unwin, 1979.

———. *Divination, Mythology, and Monarchy in Han China*. University of Cambridge Oriental Publications 48. Cambridge: Cambridge University Press, 1994.

Luo Guanzhong. *Romance of the Three Kingdoms*, tr. C. H. Brewitt-Taylor. 2 vols. Rutland, VT: Charles E. Tuttle, 1959.

Ma Duanlin 馬端臨. *Wenxian tongkao* 文獻通考 [General Investigation on Important Writings], 2 vols. Wanyou wenku, di 2 ji. Shitong di 7 zhong. Shanghai: Shangwu yinshuguan, 1936.

Major, John S. *Heaven and Earth in Early Han Thought: Chapters Three, Four, and Five of the Huainanzi with an Appendix by Christopher Cullen*. Albany, NY: SUNY Press, 1993.

Mauss, Marcel. *A General Theory of Magic*. London: Routledge and Kegan Paul, 1950; rpr. 1972.

McKnight, Brian E. "Patterns of Law and Patterns of Thought: Notes on the Specifications (*shi*) of Song China." *Journal of the American Oriental Society* 102.2 (1982):323–31.

———. "From Statute to Precedent: An Introduction to Song Law and its Transformation." In *Law and the State in Traditional East Asia*, ed. Brian McKnight. Honolulu: University of Hawai'i Press, 1987.

McKnight, Brian E. *Law and Order in Sung China*. Cambridge: Cambridge University Press, 1992.

McKnight, Brian E. and James T. C. Liu, tr. *The Enlightened Judgments: Ch'ing-ming chi: The Sung Dynasty Collection*. Albany, NY: SUNY Press, 1999.

Needham, Joseph. *Science and Civilisation in China*, 7 vols. Vol. 3; "Mathematics and the Sciences of the Heavens and the Earth." Cambridge: Cambridge University Press, 1959.

———. *Science and Civilisation in China*, vol. 5.4; "Chemistry and Chemical Technology: Spagyrical Discovery and Invention: Apparatus, Theories and Gifts." Cambridge: Cambridge University Press, 1980.

Ngo Van Xuyet. *Divination, Magie et Politique dans la Chine Ancienne*. Paris: Presses Universitaires de France, 1976.

Ouyang Xiu 歐陽修. *Xin Wudaishi* 新五代史 [New Official History of the Five Dynasties]. Taibei, Taiwan: AS. Available online at http:\\www.ihp.sinica.edu.tw\. Last accessed December 10, 2007.

Peterson, Charles. "Regional Defense Against the Central Power: The Huai-hsi Campaign, 815–817." In *Chinese Ways on Warfare*, ed. Frank Kierman and John Fairbank. Cambridge, MA: Harvard University Press, 1974.

Poncé, Charles. *The Game of Wizards: Psyche, Science and Symbol in the Occult*. Baltimore, MD: Penguin Books, 1975.

Porter, Deborah. *From Deluge to Discourse*. Albany, NY: SUNY Press, 1996.

Qiannu youhun 倩女幽魂 [*A Chinese Ghost Story*]. Directed by Ching Siu-tung 程小東 [Cheng Xiaodong]. Videotape. Hong Kong: Beijing dongfang yingyin gongsi, 1987.

Rappaport, Roy. *Ritual and Religion in the Making of Humanity*. Cambridge: Cambridge University Press, 1999.

Sahlins, Marshall. *Historical Metaphors and Mythical Realities*. Ann Arbor: University of Michigan Press, 1981.

Sawyer, Ralph, tr. *Sun-tzu: Art of War*. Boulder, CO: Westview Press, 1994.

Schinz, Alfred. *The Magic Square: Cities in Ancient China*. Stuttgart, Germany: Edition Axel Menges, 1996.

Schipper, Kristofer Marinus. *L'empereur Wu des Han dans la Legende taoiste*. Paris: École Francaise d'Extreme Orient, 1965.

Schipper, Kristofer and Wang Hsiu-huei. "Progressive and Regressive Time Cycles in Taoist Ritual." In *Time, Science and Society in China and the West*, ed. Fraser, Lawrence, and Haber.

Shen Kuo 沈括. *Mengxi bitan jiaozheng* 夢溪筆談校證 [Brush Strokes from Dream Creek, Annotated and Punctuated]. Taibei: Shijie shuju, 1961.

Sivin, Nathan. "On the Limits of Empirical Knowledge in the Traditional Chinese Sciences." In *Time, Science and Society in China and the West*, ed. Fraser, Lawrence, and Haber.

———. *Cosmos and Computation in Early Chinese Mathematical Astronomy*. Leiden, Holland: E. J. Brill, 1969.

Sivin, Nathan and Joseph Needham. "On the Theoretical Background of Elixir Alchemy." In *Science and Civilisation in China*, vol. 5. 4th edn. Needham.

Smith, Kidder and Don J. Wyatt. "Shao Yung and Number." In *Sung Dynasty Uses of the I Ching*, ed. Kidder Smith, Jr., Princeton: Princeton University Press, 1990.

Stallybrass, Peter and Allon White. *The Politics and Poetics of Transgression*. Ithaca, NY: Cornell University Press, 1986.

Stephenson, F. Richard. "Chinese and Korean Star Maps and Catalogs," In *History of Cartography*, ed. J. B. Harley and David Woodward.

Sunzi 孫子. *Sunzi bingfa shiyi jia zhu* 孫子兵法十一家注 [Sunzi's Art of War, with Eleven Commentaries]. vol. 7. In *Zhongguo bingshu jicheng* 中國兵書集成 [Encyclopedia of Chinese Military Works], 1987.
Tuo Tuo [Toghto] 脫脫. *Jinshi* 金史 [Official History of the Jin]. AS.
———. *Songshi* 宋史 [Official History of the Song]. 20 vols. Beijing: Zhonghua shuju, 1977 and AS (pagination identical).
Turner, Victor. *Ritual Process*. Ithaca, NY: Cornell University Press, 1969; rpr. 1977.
Wang Zengyu 王曾瑜. *Songchao bingzhi chutan* 宋朝兵制初探 [Initial Inquiries regarding the Military System of the Song Dynasty]. Beijing: Zhonghua shuju, 1983.
Ware, James R. *Alchemy, Medicine and Religion in the China of AD 320. The Nei Pien of Ko Hung (Pao-p'u-tzu)*. New York: Dover Publications, 1966.
Xu Baolin 許保林. *Zhongguo bingshu tonglan* 中國兵書通覽 [A Comprehensive Reading of the Chinese Military Works]. Beijing: Jiefangjun chubanshe, 1990.
Xu Dong 許洞. *Huqian jing* 虎鈐經 [Tiger Seal Classic]. Shanghai: Shangwu yinshuguan, 1936.
Xu Song 徐松, comp. *Song huiyao jigao* 宋會要輯稿 [Drafted Documents on Song State Matters]. Taibei, Taiwan: AS. Available online at http:\\www.ihp.sinica.edu.tw\. Last accessed December 10, 2007..
Xue Juzheng 薛居正. *Jiu Wudaishi* 舊五代史 [Old Official History of the Five Dynasties]. Beijing: Zhonghua shuju and AS, 1976 (pagination identical).
Yan Dunjie 嚴敦杰. "Ba liuren shipan." 跋六壬式盤 [Postscript to the Occult Practice of the Six Water Cycles]. *Wenwu cankao ziliao* 文物參考資料 [Reference Materials for Cultural Artifacts] 7 (1958):20–23.
———. "Guanyu Xi Han chuqide shipan he zhanpan." 關于西漢初期的式盤和占盤 [Concerning the Investigation of the Occult and Divination Practice at the Beginning of the Western Han]. *Kaogu* 考古 [Study of the Ancient] 5 (1978):334–37.
Yang Weide 楊維德. *Dunjia fuying jing* 遁甲符應經 [Classic of the Talismanic Response of the Hidden Period]. Shanghai: Shangwu yinshuguan, 1935.
Yuan Shushan 袁樹珊. *Zhongguo lidai buren zhuan* 中國歷代卜人傳 [Biographies of the Historical Prognosticators of China] (1948). Taibei: Xin wenfeng chuban gongsi, rpr. 1998.
Zeng Gongliang 曾公亮 and Ding Du 丁度. *Wujing zongyao* 武經總要 [Comprehensive Military Essentials]. In *Zhongguo bingshu jicheng* ed. Beijing; Shenyang: Jiefangjun chubanshe; Liao Shen shushe, 1988.
Zhang Wenru 張文儒. *Zhongguo bingxue wenhua* 中國古代兵學文化 [The culture of Ancient Chinese Military Study]. Beijing: Beijing daxue chubanshe, 1997.
Zheng Qiao 鄭樵. *Tongzhi* 通志 [Comprehensive Treatise]. Wanyou wenku, di 2 ji. Shitong di 4 zhong. Shanghai: Shangwu yinshuguan, 1935 edn.
"Zhongguo bingshu jicheng" bian weihui <中國兵書集成>編委會. *Zhongguo bingshu jicheng* 中國兵書集成 [Complete Collection of Chinese Military Works]. Beijing: Jiefangjun chubanshe, Liaoning shushe, 1987–.
Zhuge Wuhou [Liang] 諸葛武候. *Huopan qimen dunjia tongzong daquan (jingjiao ben)* 活盤奇門遁甲統綜大全 [Great and Complete Compendium of Extant Inquiries into the Irregular Opening and the Hidden Period]. 2 vols. Taizhong: Ruicheng shuju, 1965.

CHAPTER 6

FRUSTRATED EMPIRES: THE SONG–TANGUT XIA WAR OF 1038–44

Michael C. McGrath

As Chinese and Türkish imperial power waned in the late ninth century, new non-Chinese states emerged on the northern and northwestern frontiers of China, confronting Song dynasty (960–1279) with the Qidan Liao Empire to the north and the Tangut Xia Empire to the northwest.[1] The Liao dynasty (907–60), which predated the Chinese state by nearly fifty years, defeated the Song in 1004, from which it wrested gifts and recognition, and thereafter a peace. The Tangut Xia had been connected to the Song imperium since the beginning of the dynasty in 960.[2] The Xia ruler usually held a rank within the Chinese imperial bureaucracy and sometimes received gifts. The Xia also was in a tributary relationship with the Liao State. Although Tangut society practiced agriculture, herding, and trade, Li Yuanhao or also Zhao Yuanhao (r. 1032–48)—henceforth simply Yuanhao[3]—the ruler whose career defines the timeframe of this chapter—chose to use cavalry power to serve his imperial vision.[4]

Much as they have influenced development in other civilizations, the nomadic raids conducted by outsiders against the settled population of China, all for the purpose of extracting political and economic concessions (especially trading rights), present us with one of the fundamental features of Chinese traditional history.[5] When in possession of less than equivalent military strength, raiding could in fact serve a smaller polity as the most effective of all weapons in challenging a larger one. In a parallel comparison of a smaller state struggling with a larger state, Archer Jones commented: "In a war with so large a country as France, the English strategy [during the Hundred Years War] basically had relied on raids to extract political concessions."[6] In his time and in his setting, Yuanhao hoped to extract political recognition and trade from the Song by his attacks. But the ultimate results were neither like those imagined by Yuanhao nor like those imagined by the Chinese emperor Renzong (r. 1022–63) and his court in Kaifeng.

Hostilities in Escalation

Ever since 1007, the Song had enjoyed peace on its northern and western frontiers. Following a war between the Liao and the Song, the Xia ruler, Li Deming (r. 1005–32) had attacked the Song to gain concessions for the Xia as well.[7] For the next thirty years the northern and northwestern frontiers were quiet. Neither court nor province was moved out of its generation-long complacency until Yuanhao proclaimed his sovereignty in the tenth month of 1038. What followed for six years was an on-again, off-again war confined entirely inside the horseshoe bend of the Yellow River in the outer reaches of Shaanxi, with three major battles—all were defeats for the Song (Sanchuankou in early 1040, Haoshuichuan in early 1041, and Dingchuan in the fall of 1042).[8] Once peaceful relations were established (within a complex three-way diplomatic setting among Liao, Song, and Xia) in the twelfth month of 1044, there was no more war between the two states for another twenty-three years. From the point of view of Renzong and his entire government, the Xia identity was established and fixed—they were border tributaries who had horses to sell. But Yuanhao changed things, he founded a new dynastic state, Great Xia, according to the models and circumstances of his time and place, and this went in the face of the official Song image.[9]

Unlike his Song counterparts, Yuanhao imagined himself part of an imperial order in East Asia in which China was neither supreme nor dominant; his successors would continue to maintain this vision.[10] Chinese identity, Song identity as a state, was clearly defined from the emperor's viewpoint as extending to and including "all-under-Heaven" (*tianxia*). But the reality, of course, was multinational.[11] In the recently published large collection of documents concerning the Xia by the contemporary scholar Han Yincheng, we find that the terms for "state" (*guo*) and (*guojia*) are used hundreds of times, whereas the terms denoting "all-under-Heaven"; "the court" (*chaoting*); "clan ancestral temple" (*zongmiao*); and "gods of soil and grain" (*sheji*) appear fewer than twenty times in the Song-period sources relevant to the period under consideration, 1038–44.[12] Moreover, as Don Wyatt makes clear earlier in this volume, the court of Zhenzong (r. 998–1022) definitely recognized the Liao as *diguo*, an enemy state, establishing the fact that the Song already recognized the reality of a multinational order, even if it was repressed under the guise of a universal cultural order, *tianxia*.

Nevertheless, the Chinese Empire largely defined the international order. Even the diplomatic equality that existed between Liao and Song operated largely in terms of Chinese cultural and ritual forms.[13] Cultural influence seems mostly to have come from China to the Liao: Confucian texts and practices, writing, textiles and clothing, ritual and associated paraphernalia. The resultant push and pull of Chinese culture energized a fluctuating cultural and national identity. Yuanhao challenged the Song self-image of centrality and singleness, by declaring himself an emperor over a sovereign state, with its own calendar, reign period title, script, government organization, ranks and titles, regulations and laws, regulated hair style and clothing, and religious foundations.[14] The immediate affront was symbolic, not military. How Emperor Renzong,[15] his court, his military, and his regional officials responded to this challenge permits us to observe the two cultural accommodations from the Chinese viewpoint.

Between autumn 1038 and the end of 1044 Song and Xia were at odds and, for much of the time, at outright war. But because neither side wanted full-scale battles, wars were punctuated with long periods of the diplomatic exchange of memorials and negotiations between officials at the highest levels. On the ground, the situation meant raids, ambushes, armed patrols, and garrison defense,[16] with Chinese policy preferences for defensive rather than offensive strategies having become, as both Peter Lorge and Don Wyatt discuss, fully established during the reign of Zhenzong. The setting was thus a fluid zone, one that involved many non-Chinese peoples who were neither Chinese nor Tangut.[17] The 1044 military encyclopedia, Summary of Essentials Extracted from Military Classics (*Wujing zongyao*) reports that in 1041 Shaanxi had 670 tribes with a population of 155,600 people and 34,300 horses. The Song imperial army had 32,580 soldiers in 120 battalions with 9590 horses.[18] Several years later, Song imperial and provincial forces numbered just under 500 battalions, most of which were infantry.[19] The Song managed a fluctuating number of fortified outposts, ranging from the scale of motte-and-bailey to Roman military encampment to walled towns across a wide front. These fortified outposts were in the fluid tribal zone where they screened the inner prefectures of the Chinese circuits from the direct attack of the Xia cavalry.[20] In Renzong's time this front extended from the westernmost prefectures in Shaanxi (Deshun, Zhenrong, Wei[1], Yuan, Huan, Jing[1], Qing, and Yan[1] prefectures) eastward some 300 miles to the isolated, tiny prefectures of Lin and Fu[1] in Hedong. By 1043, this zone contained around 200 battalions of imperial troops and about 900 battalions of provincial troops and militias. Unlike the circumstances of the Hebei defense zone north of Kaifeng that faced the brunt of Liao forces and which herein are the foci of Lorge's chapter, the western zone of Shaanxi and Hedong was not an area of water obstacles.[21]

The Song side placed as many as 500,000 men under arms.[22] The total population of those living under the Xia was approximately 3 million. The Xia military numbered between 150,000 and 300,000, supported by revenue that came from taxing animal husbandry, irrigated agriculture, internal and external trade.[23] Xia cavalry was, of course, more mobile than Chinese infantry and operated with a shorter supply line. The Chinese did have cavalry, but not the pastures and breeding herds of the Xia, putting the Chinese always in need of more horses.[24] At this time only about one-third of Song imperial forces in Shaanxi and Hedong were cavalry units. The imperial forces of Hebei facing the Liao were 40 percent cavalry; each company or troop of cavalry had thirteen lancers and eighty archers.[25] China's long border zone with the steppe region always exposed China to the need for horses to fight cavalry attacks and incursions.[26] One of the first fact-finding reports after Yuanhao's "declaration of independence" came from the fiscal intendant (*zhuanyun shi*) of Shaanxi who said that the province needed five times as many horses as were now available to the military.[27]

In the late fall of 1038, while Renzong and his court were preparing for the triennial worship at the round altar to Heaven, Yuanhao had already conducted his own self-appointment as emperor of Xia at an outdoor altar.[28] The report of his rebellion reached court several weeks after he had finished the offerings, the report to Heaven and his ancestors, the receptions, announcements of promotions, honors, and gifts.[29] Thereby, the stage for the Xia challenge to Song hegemony was set.

Yuanhao's 1038 fait accompli did initiate more than a war with the Song. It also damaged the Tangut economy within the larger system of "transeurasian trade routes."[30] For the Song, this war provoked both immediate and long-term crises within the government and in the economy. China's status was deeply harmed as a consequence of the war, even though the Xia officially submitted. Both courts were forced to redefine their relationship to each other, to the Liao, and even redefine their own self-definitions.

Yuanhao in Ascendancy

Yuanhao's father had simultaneously acknowledged the Song and the Liao, sending tribute missions at the correct times to each. Even so, he began the active western expansion of the Tanguts. In 1028, Deming sent his son to capture Ganzhou, one of the Uyghur oasis states. In the far west, Yuanhao was fighting for empire and for his life. Although he was able to capture Guazhou, Shazhou, and Suzhou, he had spent 200 days of continuous fighting against a force of 100,000 led by one of the Kokonor generals. For his defense of Kokonor, the Song's contribution to Jue-si-luo (997–1065) was a promotion in official rank and associated gifts. Yuanhao's success confirmed him as Deming's heir. After three years of effort the Tanguts finally gained control of Liangzhou (another Uyghur oasis state), at the eastern side of the fertile plains area bounded on the west by Ganzhou. It took another few years to consolidate and extend these western conquests of Guazhou, Shazhou, and Suzhou, Lanzhou to other city-states of Qingtang, An'er, Zong'ge, and Daixingling.[31] After Yuanhao's conquests, Jue-si-luo, who had ruled over Kokonor since 1008, was forced to move his headquarters to the Qingtang area.

On several occasions Yuanhao had urged his father not to serve the Song and had rebutted his father's argument that the Tanguts had prospered because the Song had been good to them, saying that they were not Chinese to be cozened by silks.[32] As soon as Yuanhao inherited the rulership of the Xia at the end of 1032, he began to carve out a distinct political and cultural Tangut realm, spending the first year and a half consolidating his regime and transforming Tangut political and cultural organization.[33] Behind this effort was his early study of law and history, his own vision of what could be, his ferocity and violence, his excellent use of Chinese advisers, and his gifted brothers-in-law field generals. Yuanhao was striving to somehow absorb Chinese civilization without Sinification.[34] To some extent, he created a nativism to counteract Sinification, even dictating clothing, headgear, haircuts, and other sumptuary regulations, while he adopted some of the Chinese court practices. However, the most potent creation was a unique Tangut script, developed by a kinsman of Yuanhao's two great generals.[35]

Yuanhao went further down the path of imperial assertion by changing the reign-title name from the Song version to another one to avoid using the tabued name of his father within the Xia domain.[36] Testing the waters further in early 1034, he attacked Fu[1]zhouHedong. Renzong responded by ordering Linzhou and Fu[1]zhou to assist the starving Chinese and non-Chinese within their jurisdictions. As it turned out, the motive for the raids was not food, but war. Renzong sent prize tea to regional commandants, zone commanders, and military commanders (*dubushu, qianxia, jiangxiao*).[37]

In the spring weather of May, Renzong held one of the few three-day reviews he ever held of the imperial units in Kaifeng.[38] As a precaution, he ordered the Military Command (*dubushu*) of Fuyan circuit (Fuyan lu) to keep allied non-Chinese from raiding Xia territory. However, by June, locust had overrun all of north China, eating crops and grass alike. Yet, even by July, when Fu[1]zhou reported that Yuanhao had entered Song territory several times since the first month of the year, Renzong only ordered the Military Command of Bing district (Bingzhou) to be especially alert.[39] On September 12, 1034, Yuanhao led a very large retaliatory raid against Qingzhou in Huanqing circuit. Earlier a non-Chinese patrol leader had raided Xia territory destroying fortified settlements there. Yuanhao defeated the defending district commander (*dujian*), who had ignored an interpreter's warning of ambush. Demonstrating his superiority Yuanhao returned the Song officers and soldiers he had captured. On September 18, Renzong sent Zhou Weide, one of his eunuch troubleshooters, to Huanqing circuit to assess the situation. He also sent Liu Ping (d.1037), a general and prefectural administrator, as deputy general commandant (*dubushu*) for Huanqing. Liu Ping's earlier warning to Renzong that Yuanhao was preparing for cultural and political independence had been ignored. Now Renzong ordered Liu Ping to take care of the matter, giving him a million strings of cash to use as he saw fit. Renzong simply did not pay attention to this border problem. At that moment he was indisposed and took no action nor made any decision. When he had recovered his health, he immediately become preoccupied with the preparations for investiture of his new empress, Empress Cao (Cao taihou) (1016–79). Indeed, the only action taken by the Song was to cashier various eunuchs and generals in the circuit. Song Shou, one of the councilors of state, was more concerned about Renzong's banqueting, music, and women. Otherwise the empire was at peace.[40] Normal relations between the Song and the Xia states seem to have resumed by January 29, 1035, when Yuanhao sent fifty horses to the court and requested a copy of the Buddhist canon (*zangjing*), which was sent to him.[41] Until Yuanhao asked for recognition in September 1038, there was little further reaction on the Song side.[42]

During all this time, of course, Yuanhao was establishing the western end of his empire, which he sought to create along the lines of the Chinese imperial paradigm.

His efforts in this direction are not surprising. James Anderson in this volume refers to the comparable attempt of the Lý dynasty at making itself administratively "Chinese," and indeed such was the power of this model that the Liao, the Xia, the Vietnamese, the Koreans, and the Japanese at various times in their histories formed empires modeled on that of the Chinese. As of the end of 1037, Yuanhao's empire consisted of the following forts,[43] towns, and cities: Xia, Yin, Sui, Jing[2], You[1], Ling, Yan[2], Hui, Sheng, Gan, Liang, Gua, Sha, Su, Hong, Ting, Wei[2], Huai, and Long.[44] These comprised some 600 tribes and more than 300 fortified places.[45] Xingzhou, protected by the Yellow River and Helan Mountains was still his stronghold. Beyond establishing a Chinese-style central government for the militarized kingdom (which included sixteen bureaus), he also designated eighteen military control commissions spread among five military zones: (1) 70,000 soldiers to deal with the Liao, (2) 50,000 assigned to deal with Huan, Qing, Zhenrong, and Yuan prefectures, (3) 50,000 opposite Fuyan circuit and Lin and Fu[1] prefectures, (4) 30,000 to deal with the Xifan and Huige to the west, and (5) 50,000 in the eastern skirtlands of Helan Mountains, 50,000 at Ling, and 70,000 spread between Xing prefecture and Xingqing fu, or superior prefecture. Altogether Yuanhao had as many as 370,000 men under arms. These were mounted forces, which had been stretched thin by hard warfare and probably excessive use of non-warrior horsemen impressed to fill the army. He maintained a six-unit bodyguard of 5,000 and his elite cavalry force, Iron Cavalry (*tieqi*) of 3,000. It was a fearful concentration of military might overlaying a relatively shallow economic base.[46]

Preparing for campaigns in Song territory, Yuanhao requested permission from the Song in early 1038 to send a group to visit the five sacred Buddhist mountains via the official transport system. Even though Song border officials knew his real intention was to reconnoiter Hedong, permission was granted. Between Yuanhao's preliminary raids on Linzhou, Fu[1]zhou, Qingzhou, and Huanzhou in 1034 and his declaration of the Xia empire in 1038, Yuanhao had created a new cultural base, a new state, a new army, a new empire, a new dynasty. In the same time, the Song had responded with repairs to the Sanbai irrigation system in Shaanxi and reestablished the delivery system (*ruzhong*) to move grain and supplies into the border zone garrisons.[47] The Song court also distributed a compendium on military science, the Confidential Synopsis of Effective Military Strategy (*Shenwu milue*), and ordered secret repairs and construction of defensive works in Hebei and Hedong in the fall of 1037. This last measure was backed up by 1.5 million *liang* of silver and more than 300,000 bolts of silk.[48] Not until the tenth month of 1038, did the emperor's privy purse, represented by the Palace Storehouse or Inner Palace Treasury (*neicang ku*), begin disbursing resources for Shaanxi when 1 million bolts of silk were allocated for buying supplies.[49] Throughout the war with the Xia, Hebei and Hedong circuits continued to receive privy purse support because of the proximity to Liao and to the imperial capital.

Meanwhile, Yuanhao called the leading families together to discuss the attack on Song. Fuyan circuit was to be the first front with forces attacking along three main routes. Those chiefs who had criticized the plan were killed. Yuanhao's uncle, Weiming Shanyu (d. 1038), Yuanhao's senior war leader, had tried to stop Yuanhao from the war course several times without any success. Fearing he too would be killed, Shanyu kidnapped Yuanhao's wife and son to escape to the Song.[50] On October 16, the zone commander (*qianxia*) of Fuyan reported that Weiming Shanyu and thirty followers requested permission to surrender to the Song. The court ordered the local prefect not to accept the surrender. Shanyu and the others were sent back under military escort. Yuanhao had them all executed by massed archers.

By this time, Yuanhao had already begun calling himself by the Tangut title, Son of Blue Heaven (*wuzu*).[51] On November 10, he sent an envoy to the Song court to request recognition of his rule within the Xia State, including recognition of his own reign-period title "Heaven Confers Ritual Law and Continued Blessings" (*Tianshou lifa yanzuo*), as Emperor of Great Xia, (*Da Xia huangdi*). Yuanhao argued that he had descended from the Tuoba rulers of the Northern Wei (Bei Wei) dynasty (CE 386–534); that he had patterned script, clothing, rituals, and music, implements after the Chinese model; that the peoples of the region had all submitted to him; and that his people desired to form a state (*jian bangjia*). Thus, a month before Renzong conducted the worship of Heaven in the eleventh [lunar] month of 1038, Yuanhao had already constructed an altar to announce his self-appointment as "Emperor of the Xia." He had also ennobled his deceased grandfather and father as emperors. Now Yuanhao requested a patent of title from his majesty, the south-facing sovereign, and hoped for good relations. The timing of Yuanhao's worship on a round altar was intended as a clear affront to the Chinese ruler. In addition, Yuanhao did not send annual tribute from the Xia, emphasizing his new status.[52] But the Song minister Pang Ji (988–1063) persuaded Renzong that Yuanhao was not nearly as serious a problem as internal matters.[53]

In the four years from Yuanhao's elevation to emperor to his preliminary acceptance of peace at the end of 1042, the war was primarily driven by his actions and played out with Song reactions. Thus we could divide the war into five phases: (1) from late 1038 to the first month in 1040 when the Xia attacked Yan[1]zhou; (2) from early 1040 until early 1041 when the Song suffered a major defeat at Haoshuichuan; (3) from early 1041 to autumn of the same year when Yuanhao's forces attacked Yan[1]zhou; (4) from the autumn of 1041 to autumn 1042 when Song forces were defeated at Dingchuan near Wei[1]zhou; (5) from autumn 1042, when Yuanhao asked for peace, until summer 1044 when Yuanhao agreed to refer to himself as "subject" (*chen*) when addressing the Song.[54] This periodization emphasizes the major battles but ignores the accumulation of changes made by the Song and the accumulation of losses suffered by the Xia.

For our purposes, a better alternative is to divide the war in a way that focuses on the balance of initiative. After a preparatory stage, from 1024 to 1038, there was: (1) the first phase of the war was when Yuanhao had strategic and tactical advantage, from late 1038 to autumn 1040, as exemplified by the Xia victory in Yan[1]zhou with 20,000 Song dead and the Xia victory at Sanchuan in mid-February 1040, with more than 5,000 Song dead; (2) the second phase of the war occurred when Song and Xia strategic advantages were approaching a rough balance, as Song war responses accumulated from autumn 1040 to early 1041 and, despite the Xia maintaining the tactical advantage, Yuanhao twice asked for peace because he was suffering huge military losses; (3) the third phase of the war began with the Song having a slight advantage from early 1041 until early 1043 and there were Song attacks and victories, except for the battle of Haoshuichuan in which there were in excess of 6,000 Song dead compared to 7,400 Xia dead and, especially in light of a huge Xia cavalry advantage, Yuanhao's victory at Dingchuan in early November 1042 with several tens of thousands of Song dead; (4) the fourth, final, and relatively quiet phase of the war was from early 1043 until Yuanhao's formal acceptance and performance of ritual submission to the Song—including peace treaty, gifts, and enfeoffment and acceptance of office ceremonies conducted by Song ritualists—by the end of 1044, or even to his death in early 1048. In fact, thereafter, Song and Xia maintained relatively peaceful relations until 1067.[55] With the preparatory phase now well described, we can now examine the next four phases.

Phase One—Yuanhao with Strategic and Tactical Advantage

Consideration of how to respond to Yuanhao was postponed while Renzong and his officials prepared for the triennial cycle of worship of Heaven and Earth from the round altar was begun. Liu Ping was transferred from Huanqing to Fuyan circuit as deputy general commandant at the beginning of January. On January 9, 1039, border markets with the Xia were closed. Jue-si-luo was promoted to military governor (*jiedu shi*) for his support in fighting Yuanhao. A few months later, Jue-si-luo's two sons were given honorary ranks and his wife was given the official title of consort. A reward of 100,000 strings was offered for Yuanhao's capture. On January 14, Xia Song (985–1051) was also appointed pacification intendant (*anfu shi*), for Jingyuan and Qinfeng circuits, while Fan Yong (979–1046) was appointed pacification intendant for Fuyan and Huanqing circuits. So slowly did decisions get made that the court did not strip Yuanhao of his ranks, titles, and offices or the Song dynasty's Zhao imperial surname until July 16. A reward of official appointment and money was offered for his head. To bolster loyalty, money in varying amounts was given to troops in Shaanxi. Food and supplies were so scarce that men in Hedong and Shaanxi were drafted to deliver grain and supplies to the border zone garrisons. In addition to the drought in Shaanxi, Sichuan, which had had no rain since May, was suffering a serious famine.

In late October, soldiers in Linzhou and Fu[1]zhou, Sichuan and Shaanxi were given gifts of money. On the first day of the lunar month, November 19, 1038, pearls and jewels worth 300,000 strings were issued to the Finance Commission (*sansi*) to pay for border zone military provisions, both buttressing military preparations and easing the burden on local taxpayers. By controlling the crucial disbursements that paid for a war that were outside of and often a contribution to the illiquid government budget, Renzong kept control of the war. Because much of the revenue was pre-allocated, because the military costs of the west were absorbing ever-enlarging portions of the government's revenue, and because the emperor maintained a separate set of treasuries from the government, emperors were able to use their private treasuries to control the flow of money, much like the modern Bank of Japan does with "windowing."[56] The double-headed problem of budget-balancing and of liquidity once again produced a rash of money-saving measures. Renzong ordered the release of 270 palace women. In Hebei, strategy and economy were achieved simultaneously by giving the Hebei fiscal intendant overall direction of agricultural and military colonies in Hebei.

One common response to statecraft problems was to try to find the right men. Renzong formally ordered each of his close officials (*jinchen*) to recommend two men who had good plans for fighting the Xia and who had military ability. Later he asked for names of men who could help with the Xia border problem. The practice of recommendation was widespread at the time—an important feature of Song government, one of its chief problems, and intimately connected to social practices.[57]

Wang Deyong (987–1065) was dismissed as head of the Bureau of Military Affairs (*shumiyuan*) and replaced by Xia Shouyun (fl.1020s–40s), a high-ranking military official serving as military commander (*bushu*) in Hebei.[58] Wang was demoted again because of supposed irregularities in his horse dealings in Fu[1]zhou. Despite the various demotions, transfers, conferences, and disbursements, Renzong had not acted. Fu Bi (1004–83) pressed Renzong to deal with the Xia, pointedly critical of Xia Shouyun, the head of the Bureau of Military Affairs, as well as all the other councilors of state for the lack of preparedness.[59] Renzong was an indecisive man who allowed Lü Yijian (979–1044) to run the government for him. Lü was a conventionalist who practiced a do-nothing system of patronage and conventionalism.[60]

Song Qi (998–1061), an edict attendant (*daizhi*) of the Dragon Diagram Pavilion (*longtu ge*) and codirector of the Ritual Academy (*tong zhi liyiyuan*), submitted a memorial concerning the escalating rate of spending associated with the Shaanxi military problems. He noted that there were three excesses and three expenses: the excesses consisted of numbers of officials, of provincial troops (*xiangjun*), of Buddhists and Daoists; the expenses were comprised of ceaseless Buddhist and Daoist sacrifices, of maintaining ceremonial guard units at too many monasteries and temples, of maintaining imperial princes, commissioners of military affairs, and grand councilors holding nominal rank as military governor (*jiedu shi*).[61]

During late November 1039, Lu Shouqin (fl.1030s, 1040s), a zone commander in Fuyan circuit, repulsed the Xia attacks on Baoan military prefecture.[62] The Xia had also surrounded Chengping Fort (Chengping zhai) with some 30,000 mounted troops while Xu Huaide (fl.1030s, 1040s), the deputy circuit military commander (*fu bushu*) for Fuyan circuit was in the city. But he led a thousand or so troops to break through the encirclement and attack them, after which the Xia forces disengaged, after which some Song forces destroyed several Xia outposts. Lu Shouqin was promoted for his victory. Di Qing (1008–57) so distinguished himself that he was promoted four ranks from ordinary soldier to military official of fairly low rank. Subsequently, Di Qing would become a senior military official of the Song government and a successful expeditionary general.

In the following month, the last of the lunar year, Su Shen (fl. 1019–40s), a learned examination graduate, "presented scholar" (*jinshi*), who had also passed the decree examination (*xianlang fangzheng*), offered Renzong advice from his junior position of auxiliary in the Institute of History (*zhi shiguan*).[63] He warned Renzong to guard his health, and avoid overspending his energy and treasury on the distractions of sex. But his most significant advice was to urge Renzong to order his border zone generals and commanders to forward plans for an offensive war, as ten years of defense had not paid off. Fan Yong, prefect of Yan[1]zhou; the drafter Ye Qingchen (1000–1049); Liu Ping, deputy general commandant for Fuyan and Huanqing; Yang Jie (980–1049), prefect of Hezhongfu; and Xia Song submitted their appraisals and recommendations for dealing with the Xia.[64] Han Qi (1008–75) and Fu Bi also submitted memorials from their positions as policy critics.

No one advocated mounting an expedition against the Xia. The two basic issues were the difficulty of achieving a concentration of force and the insufficient time for effective training. Distances between settlements were so great that more fortifications, horses, mounted archers, local militias, and tribal allies were needed to counter Yuanhao's capability to bring large concentrations of mounted forces together for massive raids that easily bypassed sparsely guarded territory. The distances, terrain, and enemy required mounted warfare, which also requires considerable training. If Yang Jie's estimate was correct two or three years were needed to train forces to augment and replace detrained imperial garrison forces. A few months earlier Jia Changchao, one of Renzong's Hanlin advisers, had informed him that supporting the military and the court were absorbing the entire tribute grain delivery from Huainan, Liangzhe, and Jiangnan. Locally trained troops were less expensive than garrisons of imperial troops, which always included the infirm, old, and incapable.[65]

Liu Ping, the military commander for Huanqing circuit in Shaanxi asked Renzong to invite senior military officials, like Fan Yong and Xia Song to come to court to discuss with the councilors of state whether to pursue a policy of defense or of aggression. In Liu Ping's view, the Song could not fight on two fronts at once. The weaker of the two enemies had to be dealt with first. The military would follow the emperor's instructions.[66] Timidity as well as the reality that its military of 1038 consisted of undermanned units of mostly unfit or untrained soldiers may have motivated the Song reliance on defense, and defense has its uses. But, while Song defensive warfare was effective, it was clearly unlike the offensive warfare fought by Yuanhao. The issue of military weakness or effectiveness sometimes masks the deeper issue of national strength based on nonmilitary strengths.

Zhong Shiheng (985–1045), an official in Fu[1]zhou prefecture, received permission to reconstruct the walls of Kuanzhou to give better defensive coverage and offensive positioning against Yinzhou and Xiazhou. He was a man who had become a very important figure in the border zone, having been first recommended as a military leader in 1033.[67] After nine months, on October 16, 1040, the new city not only had a defensible water supply but had also held off Xia raids while rebuilding its walls.[68] This success must certainly have encouraged the extensive building or rebuilding of walls in Shaanxi and Hebei. So important was wall-building that, on the first day of the new year, all Shaanxi prefectures were ordered to build walls for defense.[69]

Phase Two—Tactical Advantage Retained, Strategic Advantage Lost

In February 1040, Yuanhao attacked Fort Chengping, Baoan, and Fort Jinming (which itself controlled twenty-four other fortified settlements) near Yan[1]zhou, where he captured the local commanding officer and his son, as a result of a cunning deception begun months before this action.[70] Yuanhao then moved in to encircle Yan[1]zhou which was unprepared because Yuanhao had duped the fearful prefect, Fan Yong.[71] Fighting continued throughout the spring and summer until autumn when Song imperial forces were defeated at Sanchuan, where the commanders Liu Ping and Shi Yuansun (dates unknown) were captured, and the seven-day siege of Yan[1]zhou was lifted because the Xia forces were not prepared to weather a heavy snow storm.

The Song lost approximately 20,000 men in one of the greatest military losses ever for the dynasty.[72] Although this was a large military defeat, there are three other matters to consider. First, the Song forces were vastly outnumbered— 100,000 versus only several tens of thousands (five to one in numbers, more still in terms of cavalry).[73] Second, the majority of the battle losses were caused by the General Liu Ping's lust for glory, careless forward movement contrary to standing orders against following Xia forces. Third, Liu Ping and his troops did kill 10 percent of Yuanhao's elite Iron Cavalry as well as others. A few days later Ren Fu (d. 1041) gave the Song a small victory when he and his forces defeated the Xia at Baibao.[74] Renzong was so angry that he changed the reign period name—from Baoyuan ("Treasured Prime") to Kangding ("Salubrious Fixity")—to avoid even sharing one character held in common with Yuanhao.[75] Renzong even listened to Fu Bi's suggestion to call for direct advice by lifting the ban on commenting outside one's jurisdiction. The gag order had been imposed approximately four years earlier when Fan Zhongyan (989–1052) was demoted and officials were ordered not to discuss matters outside their direct administrative purview.[76]

Thus, by early 1040, the military situation had already become so serious that the emperor ordered the Bureau of Military Affairs to deliberate with the chief councilors concerning the war with Yuanhao, overturning a longstanding dynastic policy to keep civil and military authority separate.[77] A few months later he expanded the deliberative group to include "participants" *can*,[78] and had a special meeting room set up by the Secretariat (*zhongshu menxia sheng*) just south of the Bureau of Military Affairs compound. Indeed, so desperate was the emperor that he permitted officials at court and on assignment in the provinces to comment on affairs of state. This was the first time since Fan Zhongyan had been demoted a little less than four years ago that officials were allowed to comment on matters outside their immediate jurisdiction of their offices.[79] A few weeks later, on April 15, 1040, Renzong ordered his senior officials to submit policy recommendations about whether to take a defensive or offensive approach to Shaanxi.[80]

In March of 1040, Han Qi, as a special drafting official, was sent out to Shaanxi to deal with the drought.[81] Following up on his survey of the repair and construction of walls and moats in Shaanxi, Han Qi was ordered to take charge of the repair and construction of walls and moats in Hebei. A month later, the Military Pacification Commission was ordered to inspect the various forts and walled towns in the border zone.

In early April, Yuanhao had already overrun Jinming Fort and attacked Anyuan, Saimen, and Yongping forts. Renzong ordered his officials to memorialize on deficiencies of the government and he dismissed his three military councilors because the Song had suffered a great defeat for which they had no advice. In their places, he appointed Yan Shu (991–1055), Song Shou (991–1040), and Wang Yiyong (fl.1026–55) (an imperial in-law) as administrators and co-administrator of the Bureau of Military Affairs.[82] Yan Shu, while serving as finance commissioner (*sansi shi*), made numerous recommendations to the emperor. Yan asked Renzong to discontinue using eunuchs as military supervisors (referring in particular to Lu Shouqin). He advised Renzong to require his field commanders to follow set-piece battle plans (because many field generals went their own way without coordinating or reconnoitering—like the recently defeated General Liu Ping). He urged Renzong to relinquish some of the treasures in the palace in order to pay for the war and draft and train archers.

In June, Han Qi convinced Renzong to restore Fan Zhongyan as a junior edict attendant (*daizhi*). Fan Zhongyan and Lü Yijian, with whom he had fallen out, made amends with each other.[83] Fan and Han Qi were appointed deputy military intendants (*jinglue fu shi*) of Shaanxi; Fan was also appointed prefect of Yan[1]zhou in September. Prior to his appointment, troops and commanders had been disposed as follows: each regional commandant (or circuit military commander) commanded 10,000 troops, each zone commander commanded 5,000 troops, and each district commander commanded 3,000. Whenever there was an incursion the lowest ranking commander had been sent in response. But Fan Zhongyan argued that this was an inappropriate way to respond to military threat and that it was a policy that led to defeat. He then divided the troops within Yan[1]zhou into six commands (*jiang*) each having 3,000 troops, and trained them within their commands, and responded to Xia incursions in terms of their numbers. His method worked, and the entire circuit adopted it. The Xia warned each other, "Don't attack Yan[1]zhou because nowadays Young Master Fan has several myriad soldiers and isn't as easy to dupe as Old Master Fan [Yong]."[84] The training commands established later during the chief ministry of Wang Anshi (1021–86) were similar attempts to solve the problem of continuous military training and preparedness at low cost for local troops.

The emperor's privy purse distributed 800,000 strings to buy food and fodder for the army in Shaanxi. The privy purse also paid out a store of pearls to pay for the purchase of horses appropriated in Jingdong, Jingxi, Huainan, and Shaanxi. Shaanxi was so hard-pressed economically, according to Han Qi's report, that its population was exempted from providing horses. In addition, tax remissions were granted in Shaanxi (20 percent of the autumn tax) and in Hedong. At the end of the year, 1 million pieces of thin silk were disbursed to pay for military stores. Price-regulating granaries (*changping cang*) were also ordered to buy military supplies. More dramatic was the use of iron coins and copper coins in Shaanxi. A bit later Hedong was also included. In both cases the policy was designed to make the region less attractive to invaders and to relieve the Song government of the burden of minting coinage as fast as it was demanded.

Casting about for someone to manage the war against Yuanhao, Renzong promoted and appointed Xia Shouyun, a senior military man with lifelong connections to the imperial family, as senior circuit military commander of the Shaanxi imperial infantry and cavalry as well as military pacification intendant (*Shaanxi dubushu jian jinglue anfu shi*). His deputy was Wang Shouzhong (dates unknown), a eunuch. Several days later Shouyun was given the additional appointment of border zone bandit suppression commissioner (*yuanbian zhaotao shi*).[85] Yuanhao overwhelmed Saimen and Anyuan forts in late June of 1040, killing one Song army commander. Immediately following the latest Song defeat the mediocre and timid Xia Shouyun was dismissed and recalled to Kaifeng and promoted to co-administrator of the Bureau of Military Affairs. In his place, Xia Song was appointed to every senior provincial office that involved command over imperial and provincial forces for offence and defense.[86]

More militia forces, especially archer units, were enrolled in Hedong, Shaanxi, and Hebei throughout the spring. Military and pacification intendants in Hebei and Shaanxi were variously made responsible for military colonies (*yingtian*), one of the standard ways to occupy border zone territory at minimal cost. The need for soldiers was so great that soldiers in prisoner units (*laocheng*) as well as convicts impressed into the military who were less than forty years old and still in good shape were to be transferred to imperial units rather than prefectural or local units.

In late June, Renzong replaced the ineffective Zhang Shixun (964–1044) with his old reliable Lü Yijian, who would serve as chief minister of state until 1043. In July, Hanlin academician Ding Du (990–1053) submitted Essential Readings for Border Preparations (*Beibian yaolan*) to the emperor.[87] The work emphasizes paying careful attention to fortification and protective walls (battlements), long-range patrolling, and control of critical locations.[88]

Concerned about the possibility of an alliance between the Xia and the Liao, Renzong sent an emissary to the Qidan in August to announce a campaign against

Yuanhao. Renzong and his councilors did little following the loss of approximately 5,000 men at Sanchuan near Wei[1]zhou, the third defeat of this year.[89] Expansion of imperial and regional military units increased the need for military officials and soldiers who had military skills. At this point, capable men were even asked to report themselves for appointment to command. In September, sixty-one experts in tactics were appointed in various grades.

At the end of the lunar year, January 29, 1041, Han Qi's widely shared policy of an expedition against the Xia was adopted. Fuyan and Jingyuan circuits were ordered to have their troops attack Yuanhao within two weeks. Advanced planning and military preparedness were features absent from Renzong's policies. Only after Fuyan and Jingyuan circuits were ordered to mount an attack on Yuanhao were the pack animals for supplies even assembled. Kaifeng, Jingdong, Jingxi, and Hedong were ordered to assemble 50,000 mules for the campaign in two weeks.[90]

Phase Three—Strategic Balance but Tactical Advantage Retained by the Xia (early 1041–summer 1041)

Hanlin academician Wang Yaochen (1003–58) and fifteen others were appointed as investigating pacification intendants (*tiliang anfu shi*) throughout the empire to deal with the widespread problems associated with famine, heavy taxation and service obligations, economic destitution, the war with the Xia, border zone conflicts in the north and south, as well as uprisings. Renzong accepted their recommendation to remit taxes for two years. This policy may have been acceptable because the Finance Commission had discovered a surplus of four million strings in the Finance Commission.[91] Whether there was a surplus or not, the emperor's privy purse disbursed 1 million strings of cash to the Finance Commission to help with military expenses in Shaanxi.[92] To help with the cash shortages in Shaanxi and Hebei, the fiscal intendants were authorized to allow merchants to deposit cash in border zone prefectures or interior prefectures in exchange for aromatics and spices, for ivory, salt or tea, or even imperial grace.[93] In the hopes of finding suitable officials to administer the troubled north, Renzong asked his close advisors to recommend officials suitable to serve as prefects, prefectural co-administrators, and district magistrates in Shaanxi and Hedong.

During the month of February 1041, Yuanhao sent an emissary to Jingyuan circuit asking for peace; he also sent another to Yan[1]zhou to negotiate an agreement with Fan Zhongyan. Fan dismissed it as an insincere offer.[94] While he dismissed Yuanhao's insincere offer of peace, Fan Zhongyan convinced Renzong to postpone the attack until the spring thaw, when Yuanhao's cavalry would be at its weakest for lack of fodder. Furthermore he asked for time to work on recruiting non-Chinese tribal allies, as Renzong had instructed him. Fuyan circuit would certainly be ready to counterattack. This exemption took the eastern wing out of any potential invasion front. Pursuing his long-term approach of deep defense based on a chain of walled and fortified settlements, Fan Zhongyan actively walled

Chengping and eleven other outposts where Chinese (*han*) and non-Chinese (*fan*) resumed their interrelated livelihoods.

In the second month, the defeat at Haoshuichuan was made even bitterer by the death of Renzong's second son. While the Song was still dawdling over the war, Yuanhao planned and mounted an attack against Wei[1]zhou. Ren Fu, the field commander for Huanqing circuit, a number of his subordinate generals including Wu Ying, Geng Fu, Sang Yi, and Wang Gui, all of whom were active throughout the 1030s until 1041, and more than 6,000 troops died in the ensuing battle of Haoshuichuan.[95] Han Qi, military intendant for Huanqing circuit, while traveling the border, went to Jing[1]zhou where his strategists said that Yuanhao would attack Wei[1]zhou. Han Qi sped to Zhenrong (about thirty miles north of Wei[1]) where he disposed all his troops and enlisted some 18,000 bravos (*ganyong*) and placed them under the command of Ren Fu so they could attack Yuanhao from a secured vantage or from ambush. Sang Yi was the vanguard commander. From his temporary encampment just outside the defensive moats of Zhenrong, Ren Fu rushed with several thousand light cavalry to Fort Huaiyuan (about thirty-five to forty miles due west of Zhenrong) where they fought a battle south of Zhangjia bao killing several hundred Xia soldiers.

The Xia abandoned horses, sheep, and loaded camels—feigning escape. Sang Yi gave chase and Ren Fu divided his troops, taking command of a portion also to chase after Xia troops. Near dusk, Ren Fu and Sang Yi combined forces and bivouacked at Haoshuichuan. Heedless of the Xia ruse they had diffused their forces in the chase. When they were north of Longgan cheng, the Xia forces met up with a large Xia army following the river, and attacked the Song army beneath Liupan shan (Liupan Mountain). At this point, the Song generals realized they had been tricked but were unable to regroup. Xia shock troops hit them in front and others ambushed the Song flank. The flash reports of Liu Ping, Ge Huaimin (d. 1042), and Ren Fu had already been in for more than ten days, but the chief councilors had deliberately delayed telling the emperor. Renzong learned of the defeat from an old soldier sweeping a courtyard who read from a letter. Renzong upbraided his chief councilors: "When things come to this and you speak of the emperor's kindness, you gentlemen really try my patience!"[96]

In May, Chen Zhizhong (991–1059), academician of the Aid-in-Governance Hall (*zizheng dian*), was appointed prefect of Yongxing and military pacification co-intendant and regional commandant of Shaanxi (*tong Shaanxi dubushu jian jingluehanfu yuanbian zhaotao shi*). Xia Song continued as supervising prefect of Yongxing. Fan Zhongyan, now prefect of Qingzhou, asked the court for permission to give gifts and rewards to the various Qiang tribal chiefs and to make treaties with them. Reliance on non-Chinese tribal allies had always been one of the mainstays of Chinese border zone relations with the non-Chinese.[97] Xia Song was ordered to station his army in Fu[2]zhou and Chen Zhizhong to station his army in Jing[1]zhou.

In July, the regional commands of Shaanxi were ordered to be especially alert and prepared to resist any Xia incursion, but were not to penetrate Xia territory.

The policy of mounting an expedition against the Xia was now in abeyance. Fan Yong, who had been serving as a military intendant in Shaanxi since 1038, was appointed prefect of Yongxing. By consolidating twenty battalions from among the best of three infantry regiments into a new one called "Ever Victorious" (*wansheng*), Renzong not only transferred some of the costs out of Kaifeng but also contributed to the defense against the Liao. These 12,000 troops, originally intended for Hebei, were then assigned to Lin and Fu[1] prefectures in late November.[98] In Shaanxi some efforts were made to train border zone garrison troops by transferring them to interior prefectures.[99]

At the height of summer, Yuanhao attacked Linzhou and Fu[1]zhou (both are near the top of the eastern leg of the Yellow River horseshoe). Reinforcements arrived from Fuyan after Zhe Jimin (d. 1050), the hereditary prefect of Fu[1]zhou, had repulsed the attack. Yuanhao also attacked Jinming (a defensive point about thirty-five miles north-northwest of Yan[1]zhou), destroyed Fort Ningyuan (a defensive position about thirty miles northeast of Linzhou), and overran Fengzhou (120 miles northeast of Linzhou, a northern outpost of Song control a few miles west of the eastern leg of the Yellow River horseshoe). Yuanhao bivouacked at Liuli Fort between Lin and Fu[1]. Zhang Kang (994–1056), the Bing-Dai zone commander attacked and chased away the Xia.[100] In addition Zhang Kang established some fortified settlements. Earlier ministerial requests for stationing some imperial troops went unanswered. After this attack the councilors of state considered protecting Lin and Fu[1] from Bing and Dai prefectures in Hedong. Twenty battalions originally intended for Hebei were reassigned to Hedong. As usual Yuanhao used up his troops profligately; this time his casualties numbered around 30,000.[101]

In October, large iron currency was circulated in Hedong. One reason was a rumor that the Qidan intended to invade the region. In March of 1042, Du Yan (978–1057), co-administrator of the Bureau of Military Affairs, was sent to Hedong with the authority of a pacification commissioner (*xuanfu shi*) to try to bring some discipline back into the troops stationed there.[102]

Despite Yuanhao's renewed attacks, the center of attention for the Song for the next few months would be Hebei and the Liao threat.[103] Responding to reports of a possible Qidan invasion, twenty-one prefectures in Hebei were ordered to repair their walls and moats as defensive preparations against the Liao.[104] Although matters between the Liao and the Song had been routine and peaceful for the past thirty years, the Song-Xia conflict provided an opportunity for the Liao to press for territorial gains after the stunning Xia defeat of the Song at Haoshuichuan.

Despite divided opinion among his senior advisors, Liao emperor Xingzong (1016–55, r. 1031–55) ordered troops to start assembling in You[2]zhou, one of major staging areas for invading Song territory.[105] However much the Song was unprepared to deal with the Xia, Renzong's seat of government was located where it was easily possible to have a unified command of the Hebei zone in contrast to the circumstances in Shaanxi. Furthermore, the four Hebei military districts

(Zhending fu, Dingzhou, Tianxiong jun, Chanzhou) each had reserves of 100,000 troops, 2 years of grain and fodder as well as 50,000 sets of armor and weapons. Sixty-four battalions of imperial troops (approximately 14,000) were assigned to Chanzhou.[106] Hebei defenses also included five hundred ships, which were secretly built in Jingdong and Jingxi.[107] Allocations for military expenses in Hebei included 1 million strings of cash and 2 million bolts of silk. Chen Zhizhong volunteered to serve as border zone pacification intendant for Hebei.[108]

Liao representatives Xiao Temo (dates unknown) and Liu Liufu (dates unknown) arrived in Kaifeng to demand cession of the ten districts (*xian*)[109] south of Waqiao guan (Waqiao Pass). They also demanded an explanation of why the Song was attacking the Xia and why it was violating the treaty of Chanyuan by building defensive works. For its part, the Song would finally demand an explanation from the Liao for the increase of its troops in Hebei.

LüYijian had earlier recommended Fu Bi to accompany the Qidan emissary from the northern border to Kaifeng. Along the route, Fu Bi challenged Xiao Temo, who tried to use illness as an excuse to refuse to make proper obeisances toward Renzong's official greeting. Xiao Temo and the others, full of fear, thereupon rose and made proper obeisances. Now Fu Bi was very open and Temo responded in kind, revealing what his ruler's intentions were. Fu Bi reported in full to Renzong, who was only willing to increase the annual subvention or marry an imperial princess to the Qidan emperor's son. While Lü Yijian did not particularly like Fu Bi, he nevertheless recommended him for the mission to the Qidan court to negotiate for the Song. The emperor was deeply moved by Fu Bi's expression of loyalty, offering to promote Fu Bi several ranks to be an auxiliary academician in the Bureau of Military Affairs, the offer of which Fu Bi declined.

Between the time Fu Bi left Kaifeng and the time he arrived at the Liao capital, the Qidan had assembled troops in You[2]zhou and You[3]zhou near the Hebei border. By July, Fu Bi convinced the Liao to agree to drop their territorial demands and accept instead an increase in the annual gift, now referred to as tribute (*na*).[110] Fu Bi and Liang Shi (1000–69) persuaded Liao emperor Xingzong with an offer of an extra 100,000 strings a year if he would convince the Xia to negotiate. Early in 1043, Xingzong pressured Yuanhao to negotiate with the Song, whereupon Yuanhao sent He Congxu (fl. 1040s) to negotiate.[111] Fu Bi was deeply shamed by the necessity of having to acquiesce to the lowering of Song status, not only because it was a patriotic shame but also because it was the personal shame of someone who lived in a deeply status-conscious society.[112]

By September, a treaty was agreed upon which not only increased the amounts the Song provided, but it also lowered the status of the Song by changing "gift-giving" (*zeng*) to "submitting an offering" (*na*). For the immediate strategic needs of the Song, this was sufficient. Attention could be redirected toward the west again. All ad hoc service in Hebei was discontinued as the region stood down from its military readiness. The Qidan ambassadors Xiao Temo and Liu Liufu came to Kaifeng to deliver the treaty of friendship. The Song agreed to add 100,000 bolts and 100,000 *liang* of silver per annum to their current amount, with the new total being 200,000 *liang* of silver and 300,000 bolts of silk. The treaty made Renzong elder brother to the Liao emperor, Xingzong.[113] This level of spending paled in comparison with spending in Hebei itself. In June 1042, Renzong allocated the equivalent of 12 million strings in silks to Hebei to assist in border expenses and reward its "righteous braves" (*yiyong*).[114]

Han Qi, Fan Zhongyan, and Pang Ji all offered advice on how to deal with the intermittent war in Shaanxi. All three were serving as prefects and military intendants in Shaanxi, and all three had concluded that the war would require two or three years to wear out Yuanhao. Pang Ji noted that Yuanhao usually only had ten days of supplies, did not do well with sieges, and took a lot of casualties. Pang Ji thus concluded that all fortified settlements should be prepared to withstand up to ten days of siege, which would give time for supporting Song forces to arrive.[115] Han Qi argued again for defense and offense by suggesting that a long-term defense would eventually defeat Yuanhao and, in any case, would be necessary to allow time for generals and troops to gain sufficient combat experience. Han Qi suggested adding 30,000 more troops to Fu[l]zhou, Qingzhou, and Wei[l]zhou. Expenses would not be a problem if the emperor were more temperate about his own expenses.[116] Fan Zhongyan deftly redefined attack as what was necessary to consolidate the empty spaces in Shaanxi through which Yuanhao moved his forces. Interlocking fortifications chosen for their control of the strategic space was the key to defeating Yuanhao. Fan Zhongyan also pleaded with the emperor to stop issuing secret orders because that kind of interference made it impossible to manage the war. Perhaps as important as anything, Fan argued that the Song should rely on the strength of its economy to defeat Yuanhao who stood at the head of a diminutive economy. In a calculus of interstate power, the size of the annual gift he extorted from the Song revealed not only the narrowness of his expectations but also the threat he posed to the Chinese. Lü Yijian sent the issue back for discussion among the Shaanxi military intendancies.[117] Earlier Fan Zhongyan had delivered a memorial from the Shaanxi Border Zone Military Intendancy comparing the advantages and disadvantages of offense versus defense in the hopes that Renzong and the councilors of state would choose.[118]

Conceding the failure of coordinating the four constituent circuits as one unified command, in mid-November 1041, Shaanxi was divided into four military circuits: Qinfeng, Jingyuan, Huanqing, and Fuyan whose seats were Qin, Wei[1], Qing, and Yan[1], respectively.[119] Shaanxi Agricultural Colony Offices for Qinfeng, Jingyuan, Huanqing, and Fuyan were established to help reduce military expenses. Each was to be under the intersecting direction of the circuit military commander and fiscal intendancy.[120] In addition to transferring imperial troops from Kaifeng, locals were drafted into additional militia battalions of archers.[121] According to one reckoning three million strings of cash were needed to pay for the additional 70,000 troops infused into Shaanxi over the preceding year. Jiangzhou, Raozhou, and Chizhou were ordered to mint 3 million strings of iron coins to help with the military campaign in Shaanxi.[122] Some relief from the tax burden was offered in Shaanxi and Lin and Fu[1].[123] Little was accomplished in the strategic direction of the Shaanxi war except that Renzong did not have to worry about a two-front war.

At the time of the triennial worship of Heaven on December 16, 1041, Renzong retroactively implemented a new reign title, Qingli ("Felicitous Chronometry").[124] Renzong wanted to change the unfavorable circumstances very much. While forgiving all owed taxes at the time of the worship of Heaven was not a pro forma act, Renzong assigned Ding Du and Liang Shi to work with the finance commissioner to forgive all owed taxes. A few months later, Renzong ordered censors and policy critics to work with the Finance Commission to eliminate all nonessential expenses. A preliminary measure to cut costs was to halve the gifts given to imperial clan and in-laws at the annual sacrifices to Heaven.[125]

Renzong asked for recommendations for field commanders from the Palace Command (*dianqian shiwei si*) as well as the eunuch service agencies. On the one hand, these were two obvious places to look for trustworthy military talent; on the other hand, selecting was an easy way of satisfying favorites, clansmen, and in-laws. Zhang Fangping (1007–91), director of the Remonstrance Bureau (*zhi jianyuan*) observed that in a period of fifty days some twenty eunuchs, in-laws, and physicians had been given various appointments and promotions.[126] The impulses creating favoritism and nepotism also drove away regular military and civil officials. The most distinctive measure taken to deal with the Shaanxi war was the brief attempt to abolish the Bureau of Military Affairs. Zhang Fangping produced the most dramatic advice, which created an escape for the emperor and his war-weary court. Zhang suggested that his majesty, as the father-mother to all, can neither bear the further suffering of the people nor even that of the tributary Yuanhao. His majesty can forgive Yuanhao and proceed with peace negotiations.[127]

In effect, Zhang's suggestion made it possible to accept peace proposals from Yuanhao that were not entirely proper in their language of deference. A secret emissary was sent to Yuanhao's chief councilor to let him know of the changed attitude of the Song. Fu Bi had initially suggested having the chief councilor act concurrently as the commissioner of Military Affairs. Renzong said Military Affairs ought to return to the Secretariat because the Bureau of Military Affairs was not a canonical office. However, not wanting to abolish the office, Renzong merely had the councilors of state deliberate with the senior officials of the Bureau. When Zhang Fangping suggested abolishing the Bureau, Renzong countered by suggesting that the chief councilors manage the Bureau.

Unbeknownst to anyone else at the time except the principal and his close associates was a covert deception operation run from the Song side, by the experienced, entrepreneurial, entrenched local administrator and leader, Zhong Shiheng, a tireless fighter against the Xia. He mounted his operation in mid-1042, using a wine-drinking, head-cutting, ex-monk, known as Monk Wang (Wang Heshang), to carry an open message and a concealed message to deceive Yuanhao into thinking that his general and strategist, Wangrong, was plotting against Yuanhao. The proof of the deception depended on Monk Wang's ability to suffer torture. As a result, Yuanhao forced Yeli Wangrong to commit suicide. The upshot was that Yuanhao lost the trust and full support of the tribal leaders who brought their horsemen and foot soldiers to form the hosts that descended upon the Chinese.[128] This wound to Yuanhao's ambition did not immediately stop him, but it surely reduced his capacity to force the Song to recognize him and trade with him.

The lull was shattered in early November 1042 when 100,000 Xia troops attacked the Dingchuan area in a complex of running battles and focused attacks during which the deputy circuit military commander, Ge Huaimin was killed along with thirteen other general officers and slightly more than 9,400 soldiers. His defeat was the result of reckless movement contrary to plans, not listening to the warnings of his subordinates and scouts, seeking glory, and underestimating the enemy.[129] Yuanhao now headed northeastward toward Wei[1], plundering and wasting along the way, when Fan Zhongyan, prefect of Qingzhou arrived with 6,000 troops from Binzhou and Jing[1]zhou, forcing the Xia to withdrew back into their own territory.[130]

Superior knowledge of the terrain and superior generalship were on Yuanhao's side, but numbers no longer were. Since his first victory at Yan[1]zhou in 1039, almost three years earlier, Yuanhao had lost half his forces.[131] Fuyan circuit now had 68,000 troops; Huanqing circuit 50,000; Jingyuan circuit 70,000; and Fengxiang circuit, 27,000; in addition there were almost 400,000 militiamen in Shaanxi. In 1042 and 1043, all the relevant prefects (Yongxing fu, Yan[1]zhou, Wei[1]zhou, Qingzhou, and Qinzhou) had been in office since 1041: Zheng Jian (992–1053), Pang Ji, Wang Yan (fl. 1034–44),[132] Fan Zhongyan, and Han Qi. Despite the talented administrators in Shaanxi, the Song did not have the initiative of choosing battle locations nor did it have a well-integrated defensive strategy.[133] In an effort to clarify the chain of command in Shaanxi, the Shaanxi circuit military commanders (Han Qi, Fan Zhongyan, and Pang Ji) held concurrent appointments as bandit suppression commissioners (*zhaotao shi*) giving them more authority than the military commanders of the four separate circuits of Shaanxi. Renzong also approved Fan Zhongyan's request that he and Han Qi share Jing[1]zhou as their joint seat for Jingyuan circuit, while Han Qi also would be the military intendant of Qinfeng and Fan Zhongyan also would be the military intendant of Huanqing. Han Qi, Fan Zhongyan, and Pang Ji, each, was given one million strings to carry out their program of armed settlement supported by reaction forces.[134] Naturally after the defeat more men were recruited. Following Han Qi's suggestion 185 battalions of Qinfeng archer militiamen were tattooed on the face, which, M. A. Butler as well as Anderson in their separate chapters herein observe, was a fairly common military practice meant to facilitate identification and bonding. In addition, 3,000 more men were impressed into the Baoyi militia. In order to prevent a repetition of Yuanhao's advantage 22,000 troops from Dingzhou in Hebei were transferred to Jingyuan circuit. An official was sent to help restore (*anfu*) Jingyuan circuit after the destruction of the invading army. The daughters and wives of slain generals and officers without support were brought into palace service.

Phase Four—Strategic Advantage to the Song but a Tactical Stalemate

At the start of 1043, Yuanhao sent He Congxu to negotiate,[135] and this time he meant to negotiate. We can deduce his intention because Yuanhao called his hosts together in mid-autumn and told them he could not attack the Song because he had agreed to Song demands and wanted peace.[136] In his letter of March 8, 1043 to Emperor Renzong, Yuanhao referred to Renzong as "father."[137] This ambiguous beginning culminated fifteen months later in late June 1044, when Yuanhao finally agreed to refer to himself as "subject" (*chen*).[138] The court was becoming increasingly weary of war just at the time when a Liao emissary informed them that Yuanhao was willing to negotiate but did not dare to initiate the negotiations. Earlier, at the end 1042 Pang Ji, who had replaced Fan Zhongyan as prefect of Yan[1]zhou, had been secretly instructed to discuss peace terms with the Xia.[139] As long as Yuanhao used the term *chen* when writing to the Song he could use his own title within Xia, or he could use other Tangut titles, such as *shanyu* or *kehan* (*khan*). Pang Ji went to the border town of Qingjian where he invited the Xia official, Li Wengui (dates unknown), instead of risking a direct refusal from Yuanhao.

Yuanhao decided to work this way because the continuous war with the Song was very hard on his country. Rumors circulating throughout the area included: Yuanhao had been defeated by the Xifan, that the Yeli clan had rebelled, that rats had eaten their grain stores, that there was a great famine, that Song gifts and border markets had stopped for a long time, that there was no more tea, that cloth was scarce, and that the people were weary.[140] By May, Shao Liangzuo (dates unknown), a staff officer at Baoan military prefecture knowledgeable in Tangut affairs, was authorized to negotiate with the Xia with the authority to offer enfeoffment as ruler of the Xia with an annual gift of 100,000 bolts of silk and 30,000 catties of tea if Yuanhao would call himself "subject" in letters to the Song. As Yuanhao was already engaged in a conflict with the Liao, and could not sustain a two-front war, Yuanhao had to negotiate.[141] Shao Liangzuo returned with Xia emissaries in late August, but Yuanhao still preferred to call himself "son." Han Qi was the only other adviser who opposed an agreement at this point. Renzong followed Han Qi. The next mission returned in early December. The economic significance of calling himself *chen* was being able to sell Tangut salt across the borders to the Song.

There were varying opinions within officialdom. Ouyang Xiu (1007–72) now believed Yuanhao was sincere. All along Sun Fu (998–1057) had been opposed to knuckling under to the great shame of China.[142] Yuanhao formally agreed to call himself *chen* in late June 1044.[143] Thereafter, Song and Xia relations were normalized until the 1070s, when the Song began a program of westward expansion that lasted until the Jin forces conquered the northern portion of the Song forty years later.[144]

Reversals of Fortune

What finally convinced Yuanhao to accept the Song peace offer? I believe that Song military and defense improvements had finally reached a point of effectiveness that Yuanhao's soldiers and resources could no longer match. On the Xia side, there were three factors leading to the peace settlement: (1) exhausted resources;[145] (2) Liao pressure;[146] and (3) loss of internal support (strongly influenced by Zhong Shiheng's deception operations). On the Song side, there were three major military factors and three nonmilitary factors. On the military side were: (1) the creation and training of local archer and crossbow militias, (2) the building and repairing walls of all prefectures, subprefectures, and forts for defensive protection; and (3) the use of non-Chinese allies to defend and fight for the Song side. The non-military factors were: (1) economic blockades, (2) the Song advantages in technology and production, and (3) the achievement of a minimal level of coordination among Song defense forces.

For the Song, all these developments were mostly routine, confirmed by long practice, and datable back to the periods of the Warring States (ca. 480–220 BCE) and the Han (206 BCE–CE 220). At the beginning of the official hostilities all of these elements of defense and offense were either non-existent, in disrepair, detrained, or unmanaged. But, by the beginning of 1043, the Song government had had three full years to set in place these six crucial military and nonmilitary elements of border defense and national security.[147]

By 1043, there were several hundred thousand trained local archer and crossbow militiamen in Shaanxi, and their archery skills were now generally effective.[148] Crucial to defense (or offense) was the use of local non-Chinese allies to screen Song from the monetary costs and social costs of full-scale war. By mid-1042, the accumulated efforts of men like Fan Zhongyan and others to entice the *fan* to settle in the in-between areas were paying off. The *fan* generally and the Qiang specifically were siding with the Song much more than with the Xia at this point.[149] By now, also, there were enough forts and walled cities to limit Yuanhao's maneuverability and to improve mutual support against him.

While archer militias, walls, and non-Chinese allies were crucial in the overall defense scheme, other elements figured in the final capitulation of Yuanhao. Economic blockades hurt the Xia, and eventually included a money embargo on the Xia.[150] Song China was technologically and economically superior to Xia. Weapons production eventually enabled the Chinese to use the power of iron and weapons production, culminating in large government arsenals where weapons were produced and developed.[151] Perhaps as important as anything else was coordination of all the combat units, city and prefectural archers, allies, and imperial troops. Coordination was very difficult because of overlapping, competing jurisdictions as well as slow communications between Kaifeng and Shaanxi. Han Qi and Fan Zhongyan relied on appointing staff officers to others' staffs, and they actively worked at coordinating operations with each other.[152] The overlap and cooperation among Fan Zhongyan, Han Qi, Fu Bi, and Wang Yaochen were crucial to orchestrating the multiyear, multicircuit defense and war effort.

As soon as negotiations had begun early in the year 1043, the court began reducing the level of spending in Shaanxi. Annual required sales of wood in Shaanxi fell by one-third. In February, Renzong asked his closest advisors to discuss eliminating and reducing taxes and required services for the entire empire based on reports from fiscal intendants to the Finance Commission.[153] In May, Wang Yaochen, the finance commissioner, submitted a report comparing income and spending levels before and after conflict with the Xia.[154] Shaanxi, Hebei, Hedong, and the capital district (*jingji*) increased income for the province by an average of 150 percent. Increases in expenditure levels varied more widely than increases in income levels. Expenditures doubled in Shaanxi, the province most affected by Yuanhao's incursions. Hedong expenditures increased 170 percent driven by the heavy recruitment of militias to support the war against Yuanhao and by the increased expenditures and recruitment to support firmer defense against the Liao. Since Hebei and the capital districts had already had the largest concentrations of imperial forces for the entire empire, the war with the Xia did not materially increase their local needs for more soldiers.

What was most striking about the report was that total spending in Shaanxi, Hedong, Hebei, and the capital district had increased from approximately 70 million strings to approximately 100 million strings.[155] Hartwell's investigation of government income and spending shows that the government operated on an accounting deficit from the founding until forty years later in CE 1000. Thereafter, for the next thirty-nine years, the government budget was in surplus. Then the decade of the 1040s suffered a drastic decline in income and expenditures through the government. Finally, the 1050s resumed the pattern of surpluses that had occurred specifically during the period 1020–39.[156] The emperor's privy purse always underwrote the deficits; furthermore, much of the provincial spending was covered by the provincial budgets of the various senior officials: prefectural administrators, fiscal intendants, regional military commanders, and military intendants.[157]

By late 1043, signs on the Song side that the war was over included the abolition of the customary frontier military colonies (*yingtian*) and the granting of permission to senior military officials to take mourning leave. Nevertheless, the provinces still needed looking after. Men like Fan Zhongyan and Ren Zhongshi (ca.969–ca.1046) were sent out as imperial *xuanfu* or pacification intendants not only to deal with the drought, famine, and destitution but also to address fears about a possible rekindling of hostilities with the Xia and the Liao, especially during the negotiations with the Xia.[158]

The war itself, when compared to others during the Song, revealed no more weaknesses than at other times. Compared to the Song defeats under Taizong (r. 976–97), Zhenzong and Shenzong (r. 1067–85), Renzong's losses of 20,000 troops to the Xia are relatively small.[159] Spending was much greater for the Shaanxi theater than the Hebei theater, because the war with the Xia was active while there had been no active hostilities, only the fear of hostilities, in Hebei. The power of the Xia to flummox the Song was largely the power of mobile horse warfare to ravage the greater economic power of an agriculturally based empire—a truth revealed in medieval Europe as well.[160] Warfare was directed by civil officials both at the policy level and at level of the theater of military operations. Civilian predominance, indifference to military preparedness, and easy reliance of non-Chinese tribal allies, at first reduced Song military effectiveness. But military deficiencies were offset with economic resources and large-scale static defense.

An enemy like Yuanhao had neither the resources to penetrate geographical obstacles nor the population to settle, conquer, or hold any central territory. In the four years of fighting, Yuanhao launched only five major attacks: in late 1039, mid-1040, early 1041, mid-1041 and late 1042, all of them on the northwestern periphery of the empire. The Song court seems almost always to have been more concerned about Hedong and Hebei than Shaanxi. Indeed, the war with the Xia was peripheral enough that a northern capital was designated in Hebei, but no western capital was established at Loyang. The difference in level of annual gifts delivered to the Liao and to the Xia also reveals the priority of the two as threats to the Song.

Renzong and his civilian court dithered away the war—never fully accepting the policy of aggression because of its implications for the growth of regional and military organizations.[161] Despite the already high levels of taxation and spending, an active military policy would be even more expensive. Probably even more relevant to the course of the war were Renzong's lack of ambition and his palace-bound leisurely lifestyle. Naturally there was also strong capital-centered bureaucratic interest in preventing the growth of competing provincial power centers. These factors and others—such as ambition and lifestyle of the emperor—led the Song to only practice a particularly skewed form of warfare: almost exclusively defensive warfare.

By contrast, the Xia practiced an almost exclusively offensive warfare.[162] Using categories developed in Trevor Dupuy's *Evolution of Weapons and Warfare*, we can see that the Song embodied: "(2) defensive strength is greater than offensive strength, (3) defensive posture is necessary when successful offense impossible, (6) defenders' chances of success are directly proportional to fortification strength, (8) successful defense requires depth and reserves, (9) superior strength always wins." But the Xia embodied: "(1) offensive action is essential to positive combat results, (4) flank or rear attack is more likely to succeed than frontal attack, (5) initiative permits application of preponderant combat power, (7) an attacker willing to pay the price can always penetrate the strongest defenses, (10) surprise substantially enhances combat power."[163] The remaining principles (11, 12–13) express the ideas that the more arrows coming your way, the more you should spread out and that wars are always messed up (as expressed in the military acronym—SNAFU, situation normal, all fouled up).

The exaggerated forms of warfare that each side practiced contributed to the frustrations each ruler faced in his pursuit of empire. Renzong inherited his throne after a ten-year regency under his stepmother. Yuanhao was his father's expeditionary commander who conquered an empire, invented a new, hybrid Tangut-Chinese-Buddhist culture and society. For Renzong, maintaining the empire required that no one raise a formal, open challenge to its legitimacy. The Liao leaders were complicit with their support to Chinese cultural superiority. Even as Yuanhao's imperial, territorial, cultural, and economic vision challenged the Song vision of the world, the initial cost to the Song was only annual gifts and missions to the Liao court. Yuanhao explicitly assumed the title of emperor based on the ritual of Heaven-bestowed legitimacy following an outdoor rite of worship on a raised, round altar. For the Song to maintain this vision of empire required that Yuanhao refer to himself as *chen*, literally "servant," not as emperor. Ironically, the Liao intervened because the Song appeared weak enough to extort. Thus because the Song pursued such a passive and defensive approach to maintaining *tianxia* based on a commitment to Confucian, civilian, *wen* values, the Song ended up having to submit to the Liao and offer tribute each year rather than the former gifts. Renzong's empire was diminished, but the Song was arguably not any weaker for it.[164] The fact is that the Song had enjoyed decades of peace through treaty and annual gifts.

Yuanhao ended up with larger annual payments of silver and silk, but he did not gain the profits from the horse or salt trade that he had anticipated. The Song under Renzong shifted its horse-buying to the Tibetans (Qiang), and it absolutely refused to allow Tangut salt into China.[165] During the course of the recently concluded war, both states had wasted their wealth in pursuing goals they could never quite achieve. In the end, both emperors had to accept narrower conceptions of empire than the ones they had dreamed of having.

Notes

1. Luc Kwanten, *Imperial Nomads: A History of Central Asia, 500–1500* (Philadelphia, 1979), p. 69; Sechin Jagchid and Van Jay Symons, *Peace, War, and Trade along the Great Wall: Nomadic-Chinese Interactions through Two Millennia* (Bloomington, 1989), p. 123; Herbert Franke and Denis Twitchett, "Introduction" in *The Cambridge History of China*, vol. 6: *Alien Regimes and Border States, 907–1368*, ed. Herbert Franke and Denis Twitchett (Cambridge, 1994), p. 4. One Chinese rendering of the name Tangut is *Dangxiang*. All translations are mine unless otherwise noted.
2. F. W. Mote, *Imperial China, 900–1800* (Cambridge, MA, 1999), p. 171; Franke and Twitchett, "Introduction," p. 13; Gari Ledyard, "Yin and Yang in the China-Manchuria-Korea Triangle" in *China among Equals: The Middle Kingdom and Its Neighbors, 10th–14th Centuries*, ed. Morris Rossabi (Berkeley, 1983), p. 322.
3. Yuanhao carried the Tang imperial surname, Li, and also the Song imperial surname, Zhao. He renamed himself Weiming Niangxiao to emphasize his Tangut identity. He is also known as the Jingzong emperor (r. 1032–48) of the Xia dynasty (1032–1227). Yuanhao was "the third ruler of the autonomous Ordos

state founded in 981 by his grandfather, Li Jiqian." Ruth W. Dunnell, *The Great State of White and High: Buddhism and State Formation in Eleventh-Century Xia* (Honolulu, 1996), p. 27.
4. Mote, *Imperial China*, p. 190.
5. William H. McNeill, *The Pursuit of Power: Technology, Armed Forces, and Society since A.D. 1000* (Chicago, 1982), pp. 15–16; David C. Wright, "The Northern Frontier" in *A Military History of China*, ed. David A. Graff and Robin Higham (Boulder, 2002), pp. 57–63; Jagchid and Symons, *Peace, War, and Trade*, pp. 11–16; Li Huarui, *Song Xia guanxi shi* (Shijiazhuang, Hebei, 1998), pp. 328–42; Arthur Waldron, *The Great Wall of China: From History to Myth* (Cambridge, 1990), p. 35; J. R. McNeill and William H. McNeill, *The Human Web: A Bird's-eye View of World History* (New York, 2003), p. 58.
6. Archer Jones, *The Art of War in the Western World* (Oxford, 1987), p. 168.
7. Li, *Song Xia guanxi shi*, pp. 434–36.
8. Li Tao, *Xu Zizhi tongjian changbian* (hereafter *XCB*) (Beijing, 1979–95), 126.2966–70; 131.3100–3103; 137.3302.
9. Ruth W. Dunnell, "Tanguts and the Tangut State of Ta Hsia" (Ph.D. diss., Princeton University, 1983), pp. 113–36.
10. See Ruth W. Dunnell, "Biography of Weiming (Li) Renxiao (1124–1193): Fifth Emperor of the Xia," *Journal of Sung-Yuan Studies* 25 (1995): 226.
11. Nap-yin Lau, "Waging War for Peace? The Peace Accord between the Song and the Liao in AD 1005" in *Warfare in Chinese History*, ed. Hans J. van de Ven (Leiden, 2000), p. 214.
12. Han Yincheng, *Dangxiang yu Xi Xia ziliao huibian* (Yinchuan, 2000), vol. 2, parts.1–3. The material relevant to the years 1032 to 1044 is found in pp. 1689–3018; see also Kwanten, *Imperial Nomads*, pp. 76, 312.
13. Ledyard, "Yin and Yang," p. 324; Franke and Twitchett, "Introduction," pp. 20, 21; Mote, *Imperial China*, p. 118.
14. See especially Ruth Dunnell's *Great State of White and High*, pp. 27–49 and her "The Hsi Hsia" in *The Cambridge History of China*, vol. 6, pp. 180–186. The Song went to war to preserve its identity. As Wyatt observes in the introduction to this work, "war implies identity."
15. For details about Renzong (1010–63), consult Michael C. McGrath, "Jen-tsung (r. 1023–1063) and Ying-tsung (r. 1063–1067)," draft chapter, in *The Cambridge History of China*, vol. 5, Part 1: *The Sung Dynasty and Its Precursors, 906–1279*, ed. Denis C. Twitchett and Paul Jakov Smith (Cambridge, forthcoming) and Huang Yansheng, *Song Renzong Song Yingzong* (Changchun, 1997), pp. 1–271.
16. Jones, *Art of War in the Western World*, pp. 55–56.
17. Chiang T'ien-chien [Jiang Tianjian], *Pei Sung tui-yü Hsi-Hsia pienfang yenchiu lunchi* (Taipei, 1993), pp. 136–46.
18. Han, *Dangxiang yu Xi Xia ziliao huibian*, p. 2299, quoting from the eighteenth of the twenty early chapters (*qianji*) of the Summary of Essentials Extracted from Military Classics (*Wujing zongyao*) of Zeng Gongliang (999–1078).
19. Michael C. McGrath, "Military and Regional Administration in Northern Sung China" (Ph.D. diss., Princeton University, 1982), pp. 171, 172.
20. McGrath, "Military and Regional Administration," pp. 182–84; Li Huarui, *Song Xia guanxi shi*, pp. 221–312.
21. See Lorge's chapter 3, for his description and analysis of the "Great Ditch" in the Hebei defense zone, especially p. 63.

22. Michael C. McGrath, "Jen-tsung (r. 1023–1063) and Ying-tsung (r. 1063–1067)," pp. 116–117. Ouyang Xiu commented on the huge numbers even in 1040. Han, *Dangxiang yu Xi Xia ziliao huibian*, pp. 2122–23; see also *XCB*, 129.3064.
23. Dunnell, "The Hsi Hsia," pp. 154, 183.
24. Morris Rossabi, "Introduction" in *China among Equals*, p. 8.
25. By comparison an infantry company had eight swordsmen, sixteen long-spearmen, and seventy crossbowmen. See McGrath, "Regional and Military Administration," pp. 171, 173. In the chapter 2 of this volume, David Graff offers a roughly comparable figure regarding the typical percentage of the Tang cavalry. He cites his own work, "Early T'ang Generalship and the Textual Tradition," vol. 1 (Ph.D. diss., Princeton University, 1995), pp. 170–75.
26. Wright, "Northern Frontier," p. 58.
27. Han, *Dangxiang yu Xi Xia ziliao huibian*, p. 1876.
28. *XCB*, 122.2882–83.
29. *XCB*, 122.2887.
30. Yoshinobu Shiba, "Sung Foreign Trade: Its Scope and Organization" in *China among Equals*, pp. 94–101.
31. Tuotuo, *Songshi* (hereafter *SS*)(Beijing, 1977), 485.13994.
32. See Dunnell, "Tanguts and the Tangut State," pp. 100, 105, 106.
33. Bi Yuan, *Xu Zizhi tongjian* (Beijing, 1957), 39, p. 907. Hereafter referred to as *XTJ*. For a full account of Yuan-hao, see Dunnell, "The Hsi Hsia," pp. 180–89 and Tsien Tsuen-hsuin. *Paper and Printing*, vol. 5 *(Chemistry and Chemical Technology)*, 1, *Science and Civilisation in China*, ed. Joseph Needham (Cambridge, 1985), p. 169.
34. Mote, *Imperial China*, pp. 189–90.
35. Dunnell, "The Hsi Hsia," p. 182.
36. *XCB*, 115.2704. In order to avoid insulting Yuanhao, the Song did not change the Mingdao reign title. See *XCB*, 113.2654.
37. Military authority was fragmented by overlapping jurisdictions and spotty coordination as a way of preventing undue concentration of military authority. *Dubushu* and *qianxia* are senior military commanders of approximately 10,000 and 5,000, respectively. Jiangxiao refer to generals, colonels, and captains—the men who actually command field units in the field. Potentially separate chains of command existed under prefectural administrators and under circuit military intendants. Most of the time, they were not well coordinated.
38. See McGrath, "Jen-tsung (r. 1023–1063) and Ying-tsung (r. 1063–1067)," p. 21. *XCB*, 105.2440; 108.2524; 117.2754; 123.2900; 126.2985; 128.3030; 128.3045; 137.3280; 140.3358; 157.3804; 159.3854; 177.4287; *SS*, 11.215.
39. Bingzhou was on the site of modern Taiyuan.
40. *XCB*, 115.2694.
41. See Dunnell, *Great State of White and High*, for the significance of Buddhism to the Tangut people and to Yuanhao.
42. Such was the case despite the fact that there were reports about Yuanhao's ambitions as early as the end of 1032. See *SS*, 467.13635. For information on the Song knowledge of Yuanhao in 1034, see *XCB* 115.2704 and also Han, *Dangxiang yu Xi Xia ziliao huibian*, p. 1706.
43. The Tanguts and the Chinese both made use of fortified settlements ranging from stockades to walled cities. In general, the term *fort* is here used loosely to

include any and all types of fortified towns, outposts, stockades, motte and bailey fortifications, and other forms of dispersed settlements in the border zone where Chinese abutted non-Chinese tribes and societies.

44. Han, *Dangxiang yu Xi Xia ziliao huibian*, p. 1737; *XCB*, 120.2845.
45. Han, *Dangxiang yu Xi Xia ziliao huibian*, p. 2271, 2273.
46. *XCB*, 119.2813–14, 2845.
47. See Peter J. Golas, "Sung Financial Administration," draft chapter, in *The Cambridge History of China*, vol. 5, part 1 (forthcoming), pp. 76–78.
48. A *liang* of silver in Song times was approximately two ounces.
49. *XCB*, 122.2879. *Neicang* is translated as "Palace Storehouse" in Charles O. Hucker *A Dictionary of Official Titles in Imperial China* (Stanford, 1985), p. 353, #4276. However, Robert Hartwell consistently referred to it as "the privy purse," as being the collective function of the Palace Storehouse and all the other storehouses, warehouses, and offices under the direct control of the emperor. See Robert M. Hartwell, "The Imperial Treasuries: Finance and Power in Song China," *Bulletin of Sung Yüan Studies* 20 (1988): 18–89. The term "privy purse" is used throughout this chapter.
50. Han, *Dangxiang yu Xi Xia ziliao huibian*, pp. 1744, 1745.
51. *XCB*, 122.2880–81. The title conveys the Tangut word for *khaghan* or "emperor," which is translated as "blue son of heaven" or "son of blue heaven." See Dunnell, "The Hsi Hsia," p. 181. One reason this title was problematic for the Song was that the pronunciation rhymed with the Chinese term for "our ancestor." See Dunnell, "Tanguts and the Tangut State," p. 115.
52. *XCB*, 122.2888.
53. Zhao Ruyu, ed., *[Guochao]zhuchen zouyi*. Songshi ziliao cuibian, no. 2; rpr. of a Ming edn. of the 1186 edn. (Taibei, 1970), 131.4437–41. Hereafter ZCZY. Han Qi reminded the emperor that external problems such as Yuanhao's incursions were caused by internal failures of Song government. Han, *Dangxiang yu Xi Xia ziliao huibian*, p. 1766.
54. *XCB*, 149.3616–17.
55. Dunnell, "The Hsi Hsia," p. 192.
56. Chalmers Johnson, *MITI and the Japanese Miracle, 1925–1975* (Stanford, 1982) and David Flath, *The Japanese Economy* (Oxford, 2000), pp. 118, 201.
57. Winston W. Lo, *An Introduction of the Civil Service of Sung China* (Honolulu, 1987), pp. 191–200; E. A. Kracke, Jr., *Civil Service in Early Sung China, 960–1067* (Cambridge, MA, 1953), pp. 102–98; Mote, *Imperial China*, pp. 134–35.
58. *SS*, 290.9715–17.
59. *ZCZY*, 131.4444–75; *XCB*, 124.2925–34.
60. Han, *Dangxiang yu Xi Xia ziliao huibian*, p.1962–63 (3/40); 2029 (6/40); 2117 (12/40); 2335 (8/41); 2490 (5/42); 2562 (10/42); and 2766 (8/43) are examples of various officials admonishing the emperor to act, to take charge of the government. See McGrath, "Jen-tsung (r. 1023–1063) and Ying-tsung (r. 1063–1067)," p. 43; *XCB* 141.3373 (6/43) and *XCB* 160.3865 (3/47).
61. *SS*, 284.9594–95.
62. *XCB*, 125.2944.
63. *XCB*, 125.2950–53.
64. *XCB*, 125.2953–60; *ZCZY*, 132.4477–80.
65. *XCB*, 123.2905–6.

66. *XCB*, 125.2956–58.
67. Han, *Dangxiang yu Xi Xia ziliao huibian*, p. 1694; *SS*, 287.9654; *SS*, 335.10741–44.
68. *XCB*, 128.3043.
69. See Han, *Dangxiang yu Xi Xia ziliao huibian*, pp. 1789, 1810, 1940, 2604, 2816; *SS*, 331.10667.
70. Han, *Dangxiang yu Xi Xia ziliao huibian*, pp. 1880–81. *XCB*, 126.2965–68.
71. *XCB*, 126.2965–70.
72. *XCB*, 128.3042.
73. Han, *Dangxiang yu Xi Xia ziliao huibian*, pp. 1880–81, 1891–92, 1911, 2038; *SS*, 324.10128.
74. *XCB*, 128.3044.
75. Han, *Dangxiang yu Xi Xia ziliao huibian*, p. 1931.
76. *XCB*, 118.2783–86, 2788.
77. McGrath, "Military and Regional Administration," p. 125; *SS*, 162.3800–3801; *SS*, 10.207; *XCB*, 126.2975–76, 2992.
78. The *can* were the second-level civil councilors of state. For the scope of their authority and functions, see Hucker, *Dictionary of Official Titles*, p. 517.
79. *XCB*, 126.2986.
80. *XCB*, 126.2982.
81. The drought resulted in famine, which was widespread. The Sichuan, Liangzhe, and Jiangnan regions all suffered from famine, and the famine led to localized peasant uprisings in areas such as Jingdong, Huainan, and elsewhere. One of the ways in which the Song government sought to help with famine was by recruiting from among those areas suffering from famine or other forms of natural disaster. For example, in early 1042, provincial militia units were established in Jingdong, Jingxi, Huainan, Liangzhe, Jiangnan, and elsewhere, totaling more than a hundred thousand men enrolled. *SS*, 11.211.
82. *XCB*, 128.2987–88.
83. *XCB*, 127.3013–14.
84. *XCB*, 128.3035–36.
85. *XCB*, 126.2971–72, 2973.
86. *XCB*, 127.3013.
87. Together with Zeng Gongliang, Ding Du was co-compiler and coeditor of the military encyclopedia, *Summary of Essentials Extracted from Military Classics*, which was presented to the emperor in 1044. *XCB*, 127.3021–22; *XCB*, 144.3484.
88. *XTJ*, 42.1012; *XCB*, 127.3021–22.
89. *XCB*, 128.3041.
90. *XTJ*, 42.1021.
91. *XCB*, 128.3037–38; 130.3083; 132.3148.
92. *XCB*, 132.3127.
93. *XCB*, 135.3215.
94. *XCB*, 130.3085–89. See Janet McCracken Novey, "Yü Ching, a Northern Sung Statesman, and His Treatise on the Ch'i-tan Bureaucracy" (Ph.D. diss., Indiana University, 1983), pp. 53–58. Near the end of the year, Zhang Fangping suggested a policy that any offer or communication should be sent to Kaifeng for evaluation rather than being rejected outright on the spot. *XCB*, 134.3187.
95. *XCB*, 131.3100–103, 3110–12.

96. Ding Chuanjing, comp. and ed., *Songren yishi leibian* (Beijing 1981), 1:26. This was not the only time information was withheld from Renzong: reports of the uprising of Wang Lun in 1043 and the Nong Zhigao (Nùng Trí Cao) insurrection of 1052 were also delayed. See Klaus Flessel, "Early Chinese Newspapers (Tenth to Thirteenth Centuries)" in *Collected Papers of the 29th Congress of Chinese Studies, Sept. 10–15, 1984, University of Tubingen*, ed. Tilemann Grimm, Peter M. Kuhfus, and Gudrun Wacker (Stuttgart, 1988), p. 65.
97. See Lo Ch'iu-ch'ing [Luo Qiuqing], "Pei Sung ping-chih yen-chiu," *Hsin-ya hsüeh-pao*, 3.1 (Aug. 1957):169–270, and "Sung Hsia chan-cheng chung te fan-pu yu pao-chai," *Ch'ung-chi hsüeh-pao*, 6.2 (May 1967):223–43.
98. *XCB*, 132.3151; 134.3195–96.
99. *XCB*, 3149.
100. *XCB*, 133.3180–81.
101. *XCB*, 132.3154; 133.3160, 3163–64, 3168, 3169, 3172, 3179–82; 134.3196–97, 3205.
102. *XCB*, 135.3227. See Hucker, *Dictionary of Official Titles*, p. 251.
103. See Denis Twitchett and Klaus-Peter Tietze, "The Liao" in *The Cambridge History of China, Vol. 6*, pp. 114–23 and the Map on pp. 118–19. See also Melvin Thlick-Len Ang, "Sung-Liao Diplomacy in Eleventh- and Twelfth-Century China: A Study of the Social and Political Determinants of Foreign Policy" (Ph.D. diss., University of Pennsylvania, 1983), esp. pp. 83–88; Jing-shen Tao, *Two Sons of Heaven* (Tucson, 1988), pp. 53–67; Tao Jing-shen, "Yu Ching and Sung Policies Toward Liao and Hsia, 1042–1044," *Journal of Asian History* 6 (1972): 114–22.
104. *XCB*, 134.3187.
105. *XCB*, 136.3265.
106. Chanzhou is the prefecture where the Chanyuan Accord between Song and Liao was signed in early 1005. This river city guarded a crucial bridge connecting to Kaifeng.
107. *XCB*, 135.3226.
108. *XCB*, 135.3226.
109. A *xian* is the smallest standard level of government administration, often translated as county, subprefecture, or district.
110. *XCB*, 135.3229–31, 3234–36; 137.3283–87; Jing-shen Tao, *Two Sons of Heaven*, pp. 60–62; Ang, "Sung-Liao Diplomacy," p. 87.
111. Tao Jing-shen, "Yu Ching and Sung Policies," p. 116; *XCB*, 139.3343; see Jing-shen Tao, *Two Sons of Heaven*, p. 30: "From the 1040s onward, the Khitans often intervened in Sung–Hsi Hsia relations."
112. *XCB*, 138.3309.
113. Jing-shen Tao, *Two Sons of Heaven*, pp. 17, 107.
114. Hartwell, "The Imperial Treasuries," p. 57; *XCB*, 137.3276.
115. *XCB*, 135.3222.
116. *XCB*, 133.3176–78.
117. *XCB*, 135.3218.
118. *XCB*, 134.3216–18.
119. *XCB*, 134.3191, 3205.
120. *XCB*, 134.3192, 3197, 3205, 3206.
121. *XCB*, 132.3150; 134.3196; 137.3291.
122. *XCB*, 134.3196.

123. *XCB*, 134.3198.
124. *XCB*, 134.3198.
125. Robert M. Hartwell, "Financial Expertise, Examinations, and the Formulation of Economic Policy in Northern Sung China," *Journal of Asian Studies* 30 (1971), p. 294; *XCB*, 134.3205.
126. *XCB*, 133.3165.
127. Han, *Dangxiang yu Xi Xia ziliao huibian*, p. 2376.
128. Han, *Dangxiang yu Xi Xia ziliao huibian*, pp. 2461–62 (4/42), 2626–27 (12/42).
129. Han, *Dangxiang yu Xi Xia ziliao huibian*, p. 2621.
130. *XCB*, 137.3300–3303; 138.3310.
131. See Li Chen and Ch'en T'ing-yuan, *Chung-kuo li-tai chan-cheng shih* (Taipei, 1976), 11:297; Han, *Dangxiang yu Xi Xia ziliao huibian*, pp. 2177, 2197, 2331, 2340, 2376; *SS*, 485.13998.
132. He was later demoted for responsibility in the then recent defeat as the responsible prefect; later demoted further. See *XCB*, 138.3316, 3321.
133. *XCB*, 138.3311; 139.3345.
134. One is reminded of the strategic hamlets program in South Vietnam during the United States war against the Vietnamese Communists during the 1960s and 1970s.
135. *XCB*, 138.3330–3303; 139.3343; 140.3358, 3361, 3362; 142.3403–5, 3408; 145.3500–3501, 3507–8, 3513, 3514–15; 146.3536–37; 149.3613, 3616.
136. Han, *Dangxiang yu Xi Xia ziliao huibian*, p. 2787.
137. *XCB*, 139.3343–44.
138. *XCB*, 149.3616.
139. *XCB*, 138.3332.
140. *XCB*, 138.3330.
141. Dunnell, "Tanguts and the Tangut State," pp. 126–28; Jing-shen Tao, *Two Sons of Heaven*, pp. 62–63.
142. *XCB*, 145.3500–3501, 3507, 3514–15.
143. *XCB*, 149.3616.
144. Dunnell, "The Hsi Hsia," pp. 179, 180, 192, 193.
145. Jagchid and Symons, *Peace, War, and Trade*, p. 133.
146. Jagchid and Symons, *Peace, War, and Trade*, pp. 115–16, 130–32.
147. Han, *Dangxiang yu Xi Xia ziliao huibian*, pp. 1789 (4/39); 1810 (6/39); 1885 (1/40); 1940 (2/40); 1955 (3/40); 2005 (5/40); 2028 (6/40); 2084 (9/40); 2504 (5/42); 2604 (10/42); 2797 (11/43); 2816 (12/43).
148. Han, *Dangxiang yu Xi Xia ziliao huibian*, p. 2447. See also pp. 1766 (12/38); 1795 (6/39); 1819 (8/39); 1842 (10/39); 1923 (2/40); 1980 (3/40); 1989 (4/40); 2031 (6/40); 2035 (6/40); 2052 (8/40); 2115 (11/40); 2319 (11/41); 2567 (10/42); 2728 (6/43); 2797 (11/43); 2904 (5/44).
149. Han, *Dangxiang yu Xi Xia ziliao huibian*, pp.1921 (2/40); 1926 (2/40); 2157; 2262 (5/41); 2300 (7/41); 2420 (1/42); 2512 (5/42); 2603 (10/42); 2785 (10/43); 3001 (10/44).
150. Han, *Dangxiang yu Xi Xia ziliao huibian*, pp. 1762 (12/38); 1780 (2/39); 2140 (12/40); 2262 (5/41); 2378 (10/41); 2630 (12/42).
151. Han, *Dangxiang yu Xi Xia ziliao huibian*, pp. 2000 (4/40); 2039 (7/40); 2280 (5/41); 2640 (12/42).
152. Han, *Dangxiang yu Xi Xia ziliao huibian*, pp. 2036 (1/40); 2119 (12/40); 2161 (1/41); 2611 (11/42); 2702 (re 11/42). Concerning this lack of

coordination, see pp. 1997 (4/40); 2036–39 (7/40); 2045 (7/40); 2304 (7/41); 2310 (7/41).
153. *XCB*, 139.3341; 141.3374.
154. *ZCZY*, 13.621–24. See also *XCB*, 140.3366.
155. Accounts were kept in equivalents of strings of cash by converting all the commodities that were offered as tax payments into a single accounting unit. Although these conversion rates were loosely tied to market values, the Finance Commission nonetheless determined them. One can get a sense of the scale of these expenditures by comparing them with figures from three years for which we have both income and expenditure figures for the central government budget (1048, 1049, and 1065 respectively): 122,000,000 in, 111,000,000 out; 126,000,000 in, 126,000,000 out; 116,000,000 in, 131,000,000 out.
156. Hartwell, "The Imperial Treasuries," pp. 20, 62.
157. Hartwell, "The Imperial Treasuries," pp. 61, 81.
158. *XCB*, 142.3421.
159. Chen Bangchan, *Songshi jishi benmo* (Beijing, 1977), 1:80 notes losses of 10,000. See Twitchett and Tietze, "The Liao," p. 86. See also Paul Smith's draft chapter, n. 435, on the reign of Shen-tsung [Shenzong], in *The Cambridge History of China*, vol. 5, part 1 (forthcoming), which notes losses into the hundreds of thousands.
160. McNeill and McNeill, *Human Web*, p. 58, 88; Owen Lattimore, *Inner Asian Frontiers of China* (Boston, 1962), pp. 63–65, 75, 465; Michael S. Neiberg, *Warfare in World History* (London, 2001), p. 22; Mote, *Imperial China*, pp. 393, 410.
161. Li and Ch'en, *Chung-kuo li-tai chan-cheng shih*, 11.290.
162. Trevor N. Dupuy, *The Evolution of Weapons and Warfare* (Cambridge, MA, 1984), pp. 326–33. See also Jones, *Art of War in the Western World*, pp. 613–716; James Fallows, *National Defense* (New York, 1981), pp. 3–19; Harry G. Summers, Jr., *On Strategy: A Critical Analysis of the Vietnam War* (New York, 1995); Field Manual 31–21, *Guerilla Warfare and Special Forces Operations* (Department of the Army, Sept. 1961).
163. Dupuy, *Weapons and Warfare*, pp. 326–33.
164. Mote, *Imperial China*, p. 380.
165. Dunnell, "The Hsi Hsia," p. 179.

Glossary

An'er 安二
anfu 安撫
anfu shi 安撫使
Anyuan 安遠
Baibao 白豹
Baoan (jun) 保安軍
Baoyi 保毅
Baoyuan 寶元
Bei Wei 北魏
Beibian yaolan 備邊要覽
Bin(zhou) 邠州
Bingzhou 并州

bushu 部署
can 參
Cao taihou 曹皇后
Chanyuan 澶淵
Chanzhou 澶州
changping cang 常平倉
chaoting 朝廷
chen 臣
Chen Zhizhong 陳執中
Chengping zhai 承平寨
Chi(zhou) 池州
Da Xia huangdi 大夏皇帝
Daixingling 帶星嶺
daizhi 待制
Dangxiang 黨項 [Tangut]
Deshun 德順
Di Qing 狄青
dianqian shiwei si 殿前侍衛司
Ding(zhou) 定州
Ding Du 丁度
Dingchuan 定川
dubushu 都部署
dujian 都監
Du Yan 杜衍
fan 蕃
Fan Yong 范雍
Fan Zhongyan 范仲淹
Feng(zhou) 豐州
Fengxiang 鳳翔
Fu[1](zhou) 府州
Fu[2](zhou) 鄜州
Fu Bi 富弼
fu bushu 副部署
Fuyan lu 鄜延路
ganyong 敢勇
Ganzhou 甘州
Ge Huaimin 葛懷敏
Geng Fu 耿傅
Guazhou 瓜州
guo 國
guojia 國家
han 漢 [Han]
Han 漢
Han Qi 韓琦
Han Yincheng 韓蔭晟
Hanlin 翰林
Haoshuichuan 好水川
He Congxu 賀從勖
Hebei 河北

Hedong 河東
Helan 賀蘭
Hong(zhou) 洪州
Huai(zhou) 懷州
Huainan 淮南
Huaiyuan 懷遠
Huan(zhou) 環州
Huanqing lu 環慶路
Hui(zhou) 會州
Huige 回紇
Jia Changchao 賈昌朝
jian bangjia 建邦家
jiang 將
Jiang(zhou) 江州
Jiangnan 江南
jiangxiao 將校
jiedu shi 節都使
jinchen 近臣
Jinming 金明
jinshi 進士
Jing[1](zhou) 涇州
Jing[2](zhou) 靜州
Jingdong 京東
jingji 京畿
jinglue anfu shi 經略安撫使
Jingxi 京西
Jingyuan lu 涇原路
Jingzong 景宗
Jue-si-luo 厥斯羅
Kaifeng 開封
Kangding 康定
kehan (khan) 可汗
Kuan(zhou) 寬州
laocheng 牢城
Li 李
Li Deming 李德明
Li Jiqian 李繼遷
Li Wengui 李文貴
Li Yuanhao 李元昊
liang 兩
Liang Shi 梁適
Liangzhe 兩浙
Liang(zhou) 涼州
Lin(zhou) 麟州
Ling(zhou) 靈州
Liu Liufu 劉六符
Liupan shan 六盤山
Liu Ping 劉平
Longgan cheng 龍竿城

longtu ge 龍圖閣
Long(zhou) 龍州
lu 路
Lu Shouqin 廬守懃
Lü Yijian 呂夷建
Ming 明
Mingdao 明道
na 納
neicang ku 內藏庫
Ningyuan 寧遠
Ouyang Xiu 歐陽修
Pang Ji 龐籍
Qidan 契丹
qianxia 黔轄
Qiang 羌
Qin 秦
Qinfeng 秦鳳
Qing(zhou) 慶州
Qingjian 清澗
Qingli 慶歷
Qingtang 青堂
Rao(zhou) 饒州
Ren Fu 任福
Ren Zhongshi 任中師
Renzong 仁宗
ruzhong 入中
Saimen 塞門
Sanbai 三白
Sanchuankou 三川口
sansi 三司
sansi shi 三司使
Sang Yi 桑懌
Shazhou 沙州
Shaanxi 陝西
Shaanxi dubushu jian jinglue anfu shi 陝西都部署兼經略安撫使
shanyu 單于
Shao Liangzuo 邵良佐
sheji 社稷
Shenwu milue 神武密略
Shenzong 神宗
Sheng(zhou) 勝州
Shi Yuansun 石元孫
shumiyuan 樞密院
Sichuan 四川
Song Qi 宋祁
Song Shou 宋綬
Su(zhou) 肅州
Su Shen 蘇紳
Sui(zhou) 綏州

Sun Fu 孫甫
Taiyuan 太原
Taizong 太宗
tiliang anfu shi 體量安撫使
Tianshou lifa yanzuo 天授禮法延祚
tianxia 天下
Tianxiong jun 天雄軍
tieqi 鐵騎
tong Shaanxi dubushu jian jingluehanfu yuanbian zhaotao shi
    同陝西都部署兼經略安撫緣邊招討使
tong zhi liyiyuan 同知禮儀院
Tuoba 拓跋
Waqiao guan 瓦橋關
wansheng 萬勝
Wang Anshi 王安石
Wang Deyong 王德用
Wang Gui 王珪
Wang Heshang 王和尚
Wang Shouzhong 王守忠
Wang Yan 王沿
Wang Yaochen 王堯臣
Wang Yiyong 王貽永
Wei[1](zhou) 渭州
Wei[2](zhou) 威州
Weiming Shanyu 嵬名山遇
wen 文
Wu Ying 武英
Wujing zongyao 武經總要
wuzu 兀卒
Xifan 西蕃
Xia(zhou) 夏州
Xia Shouyun 夏守贇
Xia Song 夏竦
xian 縣
xianlang fangzheng 賢郎方正
xiangjun 廂軍
Xiao Temo 蕭特默
Xing(zhou) 興州
Xingqing fu 興慶府
Xingzong 興宗
Xu Huaide 許懷德
xuanfu 宣撫
xuanfu shi 宣撫使
Yan[1](zhou) 延州
Yan[2](zhou) 鹽州
Yang Jie 楊偕
Ye Qingchen 葉清臣
Yeli Wangrong 野利旺榮

yiyong 義勇
Yin(zhou) 銀州
yingtian 營田
Yongping 永平
Yongxing 永興
You[1](zhou) 宥州
You[2](zhou) 幽州
You[3](zhou) 郁州
Yuan(zhou) 原州
yuanbian zhaotao shi 緣邊招討使
Yuanhao 元昊
zangjing 藏經
zeng 贈
Zeng Gongliang 曾公亮
Zhang Fangping 張方平
Zhang Kang 張亢
Zhang Shixun 張士遜
Zhangjia bao 張家堡
Zhao 趙
Zhao Yuanhao 趙元昊
zhaotao shi 招討使
Zhe Jimin 折繼閔
Zhending fu 鎮定府
Zhenrong 鎮戎
Zhenzong 眞宗
Zheng Jian 鄭戩
zhi jianyuan 知諫院
zhi shiguan 直史館
Zhong Shiheng 种世衡
zhongshu menxia sheng 中書門下省
Zhou Weide 周惟德
zhuanyun shi 轉運使
zizheng dian 資政殿
Zong'ge 宗哥
zongmiao 宗廟

Bibliography

Ang, Melvin Thlick-Len. "Sung-Liao Diplomacy in Eleventh- and Twelfth-Century China: A Study of the Social and Political Determinants of Foreign Policy." Ph.D. diss. Philadelphia: University of Pennsylvania, 1983.
Army, Department of. *Guerilla Warfare and Special Forces Operations*. Field Manual 31-21. Department of the Army, September 1961.
Bi Yuan 畢沅. *Xu Zizhi tongjian* 續資治通鑑 [Continuation of the Comprehensive Mirror for Aid in Governing]. Punctuated 1796 edn. 12 vols. Beijing: Zhonghua shudian, 1957.

Chen Bangchan 陳邦瞻. *Songshi jishi benmo* 宋史紀事本末 [Exhaustive account of the Events in the History of the Song]. Punctuated 1606 edn. 3 vols. Beijing: Zhonghua shuju, 1977.
Chiang T'ien-chien [Jiang Tianjian] 江天健. *Pei Sung tui-yü Hsi Hsia pienfang yenchiu lunchi* 北宋對於西夏邊防研究論集 [Collected Essays on Research into the Defense of the Northern Sung against the Western Hsia]. Taipei: Hua-shih ch'u-pan-she, 1993.
Ding Chuanjing 丁傳靖, comp and ed. *Songren yishi leibian* 宋人軼事彙編 [Compilation of Anecdotes of Song Personalities]. 3 vols. Beijing: Zhonghua shuju, 1981.
Dunnell, Ruth W. "Tanguts and the Tangut State of Ta Hsia." Ph.D. diss. Princeton: Princeton University, 1983.
———. "The Hsi Hsia." In *The Cambridge History of China, Vol. 6: Alien Regimes and Border States, 907–1368*, ed. Herbert Franke and Denis Twitchett. Cambridge: Cambridge University Press, 1994.
———. "Biography of Weiming (Li) Renxiao (1124–1193): Fifth Emperor of the Xia." *Journal of Sung-Yuan Studies* 25 (1995):219–28.
———. *The Great State of White and High: Buddhism and State Formation in Eleventh-Century Xia*. Honolulu: University of Hawai'i Press, 1996.
Dupuy, Trevor N. *The Evolution of Weapons and Warfare*. Cambridge, MA: Da Capo Press, 1984.
Fallows, James. *National Defense*. New York: Random House, 1981.
Flath, David. *The Japanese Economy*. Oxford: Oxford University Press, 2000.
Flessel, Klaus. "Early Chinese Newspapers (Tenth to Thirteenth Centuries)." In *Collected Papers of the 29th Congress of Chinese Studies, Sept. 10–15, 1984, University of Tubingen*, ed. Tilemann Grimm, Peter M. Kuhfus, and Gudrun Wacker. Stuttgart, Germany: Attempto, 1988.
Franke, Herbert and Denis Twitchett. "Introduction." In *The Cambridge History of China, Vol. 6: Alien Regimes and Border States, 907–1368*, ed. Herbert Franke and Denis Twitchett. Cambridge: Cambridge University Press, 1994.
Golas, Peter J. "Sung Financial Administration." Draft chapter for *The Cambridge History of China Vol. 5, Part 1: The Sung Dynasty and Its Precursors, 906–1279*, ed. Denis Twitchett and Paul Jakov Smith. Cambridge: Cambridge University Press, forthcoming.
Graff, David A. "Early T'ang Generalship and the Textual Tradition." 2 vols. Ph.D. diss. Princeton: Princeton University, 1995.
Han Yincheng 韓蔭晟. *Dangxiang yu Xi Xia ziliao huibian* 党項與西夏資料匯編 [Collection of Materials Concerning the Dangxiang and the Western Xia]. 4 vols. Yinchuan: Ningxia renmin chubanshe, 2000.
Hartwell, Robert M. "Financial Expertise, Examinations, and the Formulation of Economic Policy in Northern Sung China." *Journal of Asian Studies* 30 (1970–71):281–314.
———. "The Imperial Treasuries: Finance and Power in Song China." *Bulletin of Sung Yuan Studies* 20 (1988):18–89.
Huang Yansheng 黃燕生. *Song Renzong Song Yingzong* 宋仁宗 宋英宗 [Song Renzong, Song Yingzong]. Changchun: Jilin wenshi chubanshe, 1997.
Hucker, Charles O. *A Dictionary of Official Titles in Imperial China*. Stanford: Stanford University Press, 1985.
Jagchid, Sechin and Van Jay Symons. *Peace, War, and Trade Along the Great Wall: Nomadic-Chinese Interactions through Two Millennia*. Bloomington: Indiana University Press, 1989.

Johnson, Chalmers. *MITI and the Japanese Miracle, 1925–1975*. Stanford: Stanford University Press, 1982.
Jones, Archer. *The Art of War in the Western World*. Oxford: Oxford University Press, 1987.
Kracke, E. A., Jr. *Civil Service in Early Sung China 960–1067*. Cambridge, MA: Harvard University Press, 1953.
Kwanten, Luc. *Imperial Nomads: A History of Central Asia, 500–1500*. Philadelphia: University of Pennsylvania Press, 1979.
Lattimore, Owen. *Inner Asian Frontiers of China*. [New York: American Geographical Society of New York, 1940] Boston: Beacon Press, 1962.
Lau, Nap-yin. "Waging War for Peace? The Peace Accord between the Song and the Liao in AD 1005." In *Warfare in Chinese History*, 84 vols. Sinica Leidensia, vol. 47, ed. Hans J. van de Ven. Leiden, Holland: E.J. Brill, 2000.
Ledyard, Gari. "Yin and Yang in the China-Manchuria-Korea Triangle." In *China among Equals: The Middle Kingdom and Its Neighbors, 10th–14th Centuries*, ed. Morris Rossabi. Berkeley: University of California Press, 1983.
Li Chen [Li Zhen] 李震 and Ch'en T'ing-yuan [Chen Tingyuan] 陳廷元. *Chung-guo li-tai chan-cheng shih* 中國歷代戰爭史 [A History of Warfare in the Historical Periods of China]. 13 vols. Taipei: Li-ming wen-hua, 1976.
Li Huarui 李华瑞. *Song Xia guanxi shi* 宋夏关系史 [A History of Song and Xia Relations]. Shijiazhuang, Hebei: Hebei renmin chubanshe, 1998.
Li Tao 李燾. *Xu Zizhi tongjian changbian* 續資治通鑑長篇 [Collected data for the Continuation of the Comprehensive Mirror to Aid in Governing]. Collated and Punctuated 1183 edn. 34 vols.; 520 chaps. Beijing: Zhonghua shuju, 1979–95.
Lo Ch'iu-ch'ing [Luo Qiuqing] 羅球慶. "Pei Sung ping-chih yen-chiu" 北宋兵制研究 [Research on the Northern Sung military system]. *Hsin-ya hsüeh-pao* 新亞學報 [New Asia Journal] 3.1 (Aug. 1957):169–270.
———. "Sung Hsia chan-cheng chung te fan-pu yü pao-chai" 宋夏戰爭中的蕃部與堡寨 [Frontier Outposts and Fortified Compounds during the Warfare between Sung and Hsia]. *Ch'ung-chi hsüeh-pao* 崇基學報 [Revering the Fundamentals Journal] 6:2 (May 1967): 223–43.
Lo, Winston W. *An Introduction to the Civil Service of Sung China*. Cambridge, MA: Harvard University Press, 1987.
McGrath, Michael C. "Military and Regional Administration in Northern Sung China (960–1126)." Ph.D. diss. Princeton: Princeton University, 1982.
———. "Jen-tsung (r. 1023–1063) and Ying-tsung (r. 1063–1067)." Draft chapter for *The Cambridge History of China Vol. 5, Part 1: The Sung Dynasty and Its Precursors, 906–1279*, ed. Denis Twitchett and Paul Jakov Smith. Cambridge: Cambridge University Press, forthcoming.
McNeill, William H. *The Pursuit of Power: Technology, Armed Forces, and Society since A.D. 1000*. Chicago, IL: University of Chicago Press, 1982.
McNeill, J. R. and William H. McNeill. *The Human Web: A Bird's-Eye View of World History*. New York: W. W. Norton & Company, 2003.
Mote, F. W. *Imperial China, 900–1800*. Cambridge, MA: Harvard University Press, 1999.
Neiberg, Michael S. *Warfare in World History*. London: Routledge, 2001.
Novey, Janet McCracken. "Yü Ching, a Northern Song Statesman, and His Treatise on the Ch'i-tan Bureaucracy." Ph.D. diss. Bloomington: Indiana University, 1983.
Rossabi, Morris. "Introduction." In *China among Equals: The Middle Kingdom and Its Neighbors, 10th–14th Centuries*, ed. Morris Rossabi. Berkeley: University of California Press, 1983.

Shiba, Yoshinobu. "Sung Foreign Trade: Its Scope and Organization." In *China among Equals: The Middle Kingdom and Its Neighbors, 10th–14th Centuries*, ed. Morris Rossabi. Berkeley: University of California Press, 1983.

Smith, Paul Jakov. "Shen-tsung's Reign (1068–1085)." Draft chapter for *The Cambridge History of China* Vol. 5, Part 1: *The Sung Dynasty and Its Precursors, 906–1279*, ed. Denis Twitchett and Paul Jakov Smith. Cambridge: Cambridge University Press, forthcoming.

Summers, Harry G., Jr. On Strategy: *A Critical Analysis of the Vietnam War*. Reissue ed. New York: Presidio Press, 1995.

Tao Jing-shen. "Yü Ching and Sung policies toward Liao and Hsia, 1042–1044." *Journal of Asian History* 6 (1972):114–22.

Tao, Jing-shen. *Two Sons of Heaven: Studies in Sung-Liao Relations*. Tucson: University of Arizona Press, 1988.

Tsien Tsuen-hsuin. *Paper and Printing*, Vol. 5 *(Chemistry and Chemical Technology):1, Science and Civilisation in China*, ed. Joseph Needham. Cambridge: Cambridge University Press, 1985.

Tuotuo 脱脱. *Songshi* 宋史 [History of the Song]. Punctuated; compiled 1343–45 ed. 40 vols. Beijing: Zhonghua shuju, 1977.

Twitchett, Denis and Klaus-Peter Tietze, "The Liao." In *The Cambridge History of China*, Vol 6: *Alien Regimes and Border States, 907–1368*, ed. Herbert Franke and Denis Twitchett. Cambridge: Cambridge University Press, 1994.

Waldron, Arthur. *The Great Wall of China: From History to Myth*. Cambridge: Cambridge University Press, 1990.

Wright, David C. "The Northern Frontier." In *A Military History of China*, ed. David A. Graff and Robin Higham. Boulder, CO: Westview Press, 2002.

Zhao Ruyu 趙汝愚, ed. *[Guochao]zhuchen zouyi* 國朝諸臣奏議 [Memorials of the Various Ministers (of the Song Dynasty)]. Songshi ziliao cuibian 宋史資料萃編 [Song Historical Materials Series] no. 2; rpr. of a Ming edition of the 1186 edn. 10 vols. Taibei: Wenhai chubanshe, 1970.

CHAPTER 7

"TREACHEROUS FACTIONS": SHIFTING
FRONTIER ALLIANCES IN THE BREAKDOWN OF
SINO-VIETNAMESE RELATIONS ON THE EVE
OF THE 1075 BORDER WAR

James A. Anderson

Neither the Vietnamese court in Thăng Long nor the Chinese court in Kaifeng could likely have imagined that the suppression of the insurgency of Nùng Trí Cao (Nong Zhigao) (1025–53) would lead to war. However, the official containment of the frontier chieftain's three ambitious attempts to establish a frontier kingdom in 1042, 1048 and 1052, eventually had the effect of escalating tensions along the Sino-Vietnamese frontier region to the point of major conflict. Indeed, the pacification campaign launched against Nùng Trí Cao's followers in the 1050s and the subsequent submissions of strategic Tai-speaking frontier communities to direct control of the Song dynasty (960–1279), contributed directly to the outbreak of the Sino-Vietnamese border war of 1075–77.

In the breakdown in relations leading to warfare between the Chinese and Vietnamese states, the factor of shifting alliances between the two courts and their respective frontier communities was key but hardly all-determinative. Among the other crucial influences were the Chinese court's efforts to increase frontier economic activity under the Song court–sponsored reforms of the New Policies (*xinfa*) (1068–85) that were authored by its grand councilor Wang Anshi (1021–86) and the consolidation of peripheral fiefdoms by the Vietnamese Lý (1010–1225) court during an accelerated period of state-building. Nevertheless, despite these other factors that exacerbated regional tensions, in the aftermath of open hostilities, the two courts ultimately did conduct talks to negotiate a fixed border between the Đại Việt kingdom and the Song Empire.[1] These talks and the establishment of a fixed border marked a diplomatic watershed in middle-period Sino-Vietnamese relations. In these negotiations one must consider the role the frontier Tai-speaking communities played in shaping this firm dividing line between Chinese and Vietnamese domains. Control of these communities and their resources was an important consideration in the positions taken by both the Song and Lý negotiators. Moreover, the line of demarcation established upon the conclusion of these talks would largely remain in place through to the present day.

However, a preliminary reading of existing historical sources mostly reveals only a struggle between two imperial powers staged among dispossessed Tai-speaking communities. Thus, discerning the true nature of frontier relations in this period proves to be a difficult task. The available Chinese sources do not readily disclose local concerns, because most of the language used even by Song frontier officials in their memorials to the court couched matters in court-centered contexts. Likewise, extant imperial Vietnamese sources view this period from the perspective of the Lý ruler and his closest advisors at court. In our efforts to gain a clearer understanding of regional interaction along the frontier in the premodern period, we owe a great deal to Vietnamese scholars working in the Democratic Republic of Vietnam after 1954. These scholars were the first to question the paradigm of a Chinese political and cultural monolith that was inherited from French colonial writers. As Patricia Pelley notes, "by emphasizing the ethnic heterogeneity of China, by underscoring the tenacity of regional politics in China, and by calling attention to South China's historic links to Southeast Asia, revolutionary scholars managed to reduce the apparently monolithic and overwhelmingly Han dimensions of China."[2] However, whereas they saw a diversity of interests among the subjects of Chinese rulers, these historians unfortunately often also chose to see the subjects of Vietnamese kings as unified in their interests. It is foremost their almost invariant depiction of an eleventh-century Vietnamese society filled with Kinh and non-Kinh engaged in a "United Front" against Chinese aggression from the north with which this chapter takes issue.

These same scholars have also assumed that the Lý court prevailed in its efforts to woo the Tai-speaking communities of the region over to the Vietnamese. One can easily draw this conclusion from existing sources, but there is no denying a strong nationalist bias to these findings. Patriotic Vietnamese scholars in the twentieth century have long been interested in countering the picture of Vietnamese regional and ethnic disunity promoted in earlier French colonial scholarship. Shortly after the seizure and colonization of Vietnam in the late nineteenth century, much French colonial academic effort was devoted to the reconstruction of Vietnamese premodern society and this fact helps in explaining the relative ease with which Vietnam fell to French domination.

Pelley further observes that, "to overcome this characterization, revolutionary writers were supposed to recite haranguing clichés about the essential unity and homogeneity of (Vietnam) and its indomitable spirit in the fight against foreign aggression."[3] Regarding the eleventh century, an influential voice that inspired this group of revolutionary scholars was the historian Hoàng Xuân Hãn (1908–96), who had argued in his 1949 seminal work *Lý Thường Kiệt* that the Lý court had a special ability in "giving heart to (phủ dụ)" the uplands peoples, promoting the Lý court's prestige among "the mountain dwellers" further north and helping to maintain peace along the Đại Việt kingdom's inland frontier.[4] Later when Thăng Long sought to attract supporters among Tai-speaking communities on the eve of the general Lý Thường Kiệt's (1019–1105) invasion of the Song frontier, Hoàng Xuân Hãn argued that the Vietnamese court soon benefited from the local knowledge and logistical support provided by these communities.[5]

In his book, the late Professor Hãn described the Nùng clan as the local representatives of the Lý court and the lands they occupied as sovereign Vietnamese territory. At one point he wrote that although the frontier leader and Nùng Trí Cao's kinsman Nùng Tông Đán (1013–?) and his relatives had approached the Song court and had offered the local động settlements of Lôi Hỏa and Kế Thành, both of which would later be incorporated into the Song's "Pacified Prefecture" (*shun'an zhou*) on the northern side of the frontier, to the Song authorities, "the family of Tông Đán still maintained control of his old territory, which therefore was territory that still belonged to Vietnam."[6] Following the publication of *Lý Thường Kiệt*, Hoàng Xuân Hãn's opinions continued to influence future generations of Vietnamese scholars, who saw an undeniable unity of purpose between the Vietnamese court and the uplands frontier peoples in the face of Chinese aggression of the mid-eleventh century.

Other Vietnamese historians have emphasized Nùng Tông Đán's participation in Lý Thường Kiệt's preemptive attack on Song territory as a clear sign that the Lý court had wisely cultivated strong relations with its Tai-speaking neighbors. Conservative scholar and former prime minister Trần Trọng Kim (1883–1953) noted in his influential historical survey *Việt Nam Sử Lược* that Tông Đán held a high leadership position in the Lý military force, perhaps even ranking him on par with Lý Thường Kiệt.[7] Nguyễn Ngọc Huy (b. 1924) notes in his work on the Lê Code that "one result of (the Lý court's) benevolent policy toward minority leaders was their effective support for the dynasty in the successful campaigns against the Sung."[8] Lê Thành Khôi contends that the Lý policy of fostering alliances with the uplands communities eventually "bore its fruits," and he notes Tông Đán's leadership role in Lý Thường Kiệt's military force as a prime example of this success.[9] Professor Phan Huy Lê of Hà Nội National University, in turn quoting Hoàng Xuân Hãn, has written, "Generally speaking, all of the Lý court's wise policies (regarding local chieftains) were successful and they held a important significance during preparations for the victorious battle with the Song during the years 1075–77."[10] In another recent study produced by the Bureau for National Defense in the Vietnamese Institute of Military History Lê Đình Sỹ writes, "The Lý were concerned to protect 'the silk and brocade' (i.e. our beautiful) fatherland's territorial integrity, as well as the independence and the autonomy of our people."[11] Ethnologists working on the history of Tai-speaking groups in Vietnam have voiced similar opinions. Hà Văn Thư and Lã Văn Lô wrote in 1984 that "when the

Song invaded our country, all of the local militia (comprised of uplands people) joined together in the cause at strategically important sites, carrying out surprise attacks on the military gatherings and supply lines of the enemy."[12] A more recent ethnographic work reiterates this same event in the historical introduction.[13]

I believe that the abovementioned historiographical imperative for solidarity has unduly influenced many of these Vietnamese scholars to claim that, when the two courts clashed in open conflict in 1075, the Lý leadership benefited more from uplands support than did the Song leadership. On the contrary, I maintain that the Chinese authorities successfully cultivated relations with these uplands communities, particularly with the declared followers of Nùng Trí Cao and his clan, and that this change in frontier policy alarmed the lowlands Vietnamese court and its uplands supporters to such a degree that the "offense as the best defense" military strategy promoted by the Lý military aide Lý Thường Kiệt was eventually adopted.

Growing Chinese Interest in the South

Through the 1060s, longstanding political institutions shaped the respective frontier policies of the Song and Lý courts. For the Chinese leadership, frontier policy served the "centering" function of the traditional tribute system.[14] Ideally, the Chinese court's frontier administration, known as the system of ruling with "loose reins" (*jimi*), sought to introduce to its "uncultured" inhabitants all the benefits of life at the "civilized" center.[15] This zone system of frontier management had served the Chinese leadership adequately in the southwest since the Tang dynasty (618–907), and there had been little incentive to change the status quo. The Đại Việt leadership, unlike the Song, did not follow a center-periphery zonal arrangement, but instead maintained personalized "patron-client" relationships with each of its "satellite" partners along the frontier region.[16] Moreover, for economic and political purposes, Vietnamese leaders depended on controlling the resources of the frontier, whether material and human. To achieve this control, they employed a combination of marriage alliances and military excursions to ensure their supremacy in the region. Moreover, successive Vietnamese courts took the projection of influence along the frontier as indicative of their efficacy, which was measured primarily in resources extracted rather than the "centering" of loyalty among frontier vassals.

However, by the eleventh century, both Chinese and Vietnamese courts viewed these frontier communities as a ready pool of able personnel to contribute to what Jeffery Barlow has termed the "military labor market."[17] Chinese regimes had in the past used militia assembled from the Tai-speaking frontier communities in their armed conflicts with Vietnamese forces based in the Hồng River Delta region. During the period of the Five Dynasties (907–60) and Ten Kingdoms (907–79), the Southern Han (907–71) founder Liu Yin (r. 907–11) recruited troops from the southern Guangxi region, among them archers, for assist in the war then being waged against the kingdom of Chu (927–56).[18] These troops were well known for their ferocity. In 930, the Southern Han ruler Liu Gong (r. 911–42) recruited more local militia to help with the invasion of northern Vietnam, then under the command of the Vietnamese strongman Khúc Thừa Mỹ (917–30). Fifty years later, when the Song court launched its punitive attack on Lê Hoàn (r. 980–1005), the Chinese army gathered up another contingent of southern militia from the frontier region to supplement its northern forces.[19] Given the reputation for bravery in battle, this Tai-speaking militia was considered a valuable military asset and a worthy ally in frontier conflicts. By 1065, some 44,500 militia soldiers from these communities were enlisted by local Song authorities.[20] These numbers could suggest that the Chinese court was eager to tap this source of military manpower. However, this increase in recruitment could also reflect a rapid shift in political loyalties in the region.

The successful expedition of the Song general Di Qing (1008–61) against the Nùng Trí Cao's rebel army and the Lý court's refusal to intervene on either side brought a tentative peace to the frontier region. For nearly twenty years after Nùng Trí Cao's defeat, frontier disturbances rarely occurred, and Chinese and Vietnamese military resources contained whatever disorder that did occur swiftly. Han homesteaders and discharged soldiers also moved to the area at this time, and settled in existing Chinese communities and on the outskirts of *jimi* regions. Simultaneously, new local leaders took control of the decimated but still remaining frontier communities. However, the regional peace would not last. The ethnic balance along the frontier was changing and the Song imperial presence along the edges of a frontier that the Lý leadership itself desired to control was growing. Several influential Nùng leaders sided with the Vietnamese court in the emerging confrontation and, in the ensuing conflict, Kaifeng realized that an entirely new arrangement for frontier relations had to be established.

Manipulating the Frontier

Although it was unsuccessful in establishing an autonomous frontier state equal in political resilience to the late Tang-period Uyghur state of the Tarim Basin alluded to by Michael Brose in this volume, the revolt of the 1050s Tai-speaking leader Nùng Trí Cao's had nonetheless exposed weaknesses in the Song administration of its southern region. Furthermore, frontier unrest threatened to begin anew with a new generation of Nùng leadership. In tenth month of 1060, the frontier administrator Wang Han (fl. 1043–63) memorialized the throne, stating that Nùng Trí Cao's fellow clansman, Nùng Tông Đán had already crossed back into Song territory in 1057.[21] Tông Đán had since assembled a following and was now threatening to plunder the region. Following rumors that Nùng Trí Cao was actually still alive, Wang visited Tông Đán's camp at Lôi Hỏa, and spoke with Trí Cao's son Nùng Nhật Tân (fl. 1050–78). According to the History of the Song (*Songshi*), Wang said the following to the frontier leader's son," If you seek "Interior Dependency" (*neifu*) status with the Song court, the Vietnamese will see you as an enemy. If you remain outside (China proper) as a loyal frontier militia leader, you can expect to be rewarded with tempting profit. Therefore, there is no need for scheming. Now, return home to report this news to your father, and then to choose the path that offers the greatest benefit."[22]

As the Guangnan West circuit Fiscal Commissioner (*zhuanyunshi*) Wang Han feared that the Nùng clan's resurgence could spell the end to peace on the frontier. Therefore, he requested that a new policy be enacted. The Song court responded by ignoring Wang's specific recommendation and instead requesting that the Nùng communities, along with other ethnic groups, be made interior dependencies of the Song Empire. In this manner, the troubles between the Song and its frontier temporarily subsided. Nùng Trí Cao's followers had achieved the elevated "Interior Dependency" status Trí Cao and his father had initially been seeking, although at the cost of many lives. However, Nùng Trí Cao had later fought for no less than his own kingdom stretching across southern China. Such an independent polity within China's borders would not emerge until the "Warlord Period" (1916–28) of the early twentieth century.

Moreover, the Song court acknowledged the Nùng clan's continued regional influence by accepting Tông Đán's renewed local leadership. Xiao Gu, then the court-appointed military commissioner (*jinglueshi*), advised the court to return Tông Đán's followers to official service by peaceful means, including a treaty alliance and new honorary titles. By the summer of 1061, however, even the emperor was lamenting the fact that the "Nùng Bandit (Tông Đán)" and his family had strayed so far from the observance of their frontier duties that the Chinese ruler thought they might never really return to the imperial fold.[23] Yet, when Tông Đán in 1062 requested that the territories under his authority be incorporated into the Chinese empire, Emperor Renzong (r. 1022–63) accommodated this request.

The Chinese ruler then extended a new set of titles and nominal positions to leading members of frontier communities, at a level of authority below the titles granted to the Vietnamese court and its officials. The Draft of Documents Pertaining to Song Official Matters (*Song huiyao*) records that the "Loyal Warrior" (*wuzong jiangjun*) Tông Đán, regarded by the Song court to be the prefect of Lôi Hỏa, recently renamed "Pacified Prefecture" (*shun'an zhou*), was granted the title "Personal Guardian General of the Right" (*you qianniu weijiangjun*).[24] Nùng Trí Cao's younger brother Nùng Trí Hội (fl.1062–85) received the title "Personal Guardian General of the Left" (*zuo qianniu weijiangjun*). Other members of the Nùng clan, and former followers of Trí Cao, also received official recognition. Nùng Binh (?–?), Nùng Lượng (?–?), Nùng Hạ Khanh (?–?), local leaders from the Temo *jimi* prefecture, which encompassed territory from modern-day Wenshan in eastern Yunnan to Jingxi in southern Guangxi, swore their loyalty to the Song court.[25] Nùng Hạ Khanh was almost certainly Nùng Trí Cao's mother A Nùng's third husband, a fact that may or may not have been known to Xiao Go and the other Song officials, who adminsitered the area. However, Trí Cao's own former rebel commanders Lư Báo (?–?), Lê Mạo (?–?), and Hoàng Trọng Khanh (?–?) were all granted official titles that denoted service at the local level to the Song court.²⁶ In all of these titles, there is an element of reorienting local authority to a position much more dependent on the centralized authority of the Song court, suggesting integration that was similar to the alliances of local Uyghur military leaders and Tang military officials that David Graff describes in his chapter. These titles were granted with the condition that they might be withdrawn at any point that their holders do no live up to the official obligations that these titles implied.

In the wake of all these administrative appointments, the *jimi* prefectures had lost their autonomous status in the eyes of the Song leadership. The change was not limited to new titles alone. Local militia along the southwestern frontier were reorganized and trained to comply with new court standards for frontier defense. In 1065, the local military commission (*anfu si*) of Guangnan West circuit (*Guangnan xilu*), under the direction of the new Guizhou prefect Lu Shen (1012–70), took charge of the organization of communities along the southwestern frontier.²⁷ The forty-five grotto settlements in the Left and Right Rivers (Zuoyou jiang) region were all appointed a grotto militia leader (*dongjiang*). The commissioner then surveyed the region's population of able-bodied men, from which he selected groups to be led by a guard commander (*xiaochang*) from the area's prominent households. Each guard commander then received a specific signal banner (*qihao*) for his group's distinction. Groups of thirty men were organized into self-regulating units of local governance known as "tithings (*jia*)."²⁸ Tithings received different leaders when they were organized in groups of five led by a troop commandant (*dutou*), groups of ten led by an aboriginal commander (*zhijunshi*), and groups of fifty led by a commander-in-chief (*duzhijunshi*).

As noted above, some 44,500 local men along the southwestern frontier may have been registered under this new system. At least on paper, these efforts to organize frontier militia went far beyond any previous attempts under the existing *jimi* frontier system of management. The military reorganization of the frontier and the recruitment of local militia resembled what Michael McGrath herein describes as the 1041 efforts of Emperor Renzong to fortify Shaanxi against military attack by the neighboring Tanguts. Perhaps for that reason, this tightening of frontier defenses on the Song side did not bode well with the Vietnamese court, which saw its own flexible and personally orientated systems of local control being gradually undermined.

Moreover, greater numbers of Song subjects from the north were moving into the region during this period. Scholars have noted a sharp increase in population numbers along China's southwest frontier by the end of the eleventh century. During the period 976–84, the total population of the prefectures of Yongzhou, Binzhou, Xiangzhou (modern-day Xiangzhou county in central Guangxi), Rongzhou (modern-day Rongan county in Guangxi), Hengzhou, Liuzhou (modern-day Liuzhou city) and Yizhou was estimated to be in the area of 17,760 households, and by the period 1078–85 populations for the same area had increased to 56,596 households.²⁹ Moreover, figures for the entire Guangnan West circuit for 1080 place the region's population at 287,723 households, a 133 percent increase from an earlier Tang census in 742.³⁰ One should note that these figures included both indigenous communities and the more recent Han settlements. Moreover, improved methods of recording household registration may indeed accord for some of the increase. However, the trend toward increased Han settlement remains clear through these changes; an increase accounted for by both the community of soldiers who had followed Di Qing in his campaign against Nùng Trí Cao's forces, and the merchants who provided support for the Song military.

The Republican period gazetteer A Record of Fengshan County (*Fengshan xianzhi*) makes this point; "Before the Tang, this county was settled by the Miao barbarian people. There were no traces of Han settlers. In 1053, The 'Great Martial Leader' Di (Qing) put down the rebellion of the Quang Nguyên barbarian Nùng Trí Cao, the troops following the general's expedition remained in the region to open up and settle the wasteland. Their settlements extended throughout this county."³¹

Li Wenxiong in his early-twentieth-century gazetteer A Record of Longjin County (*Longjin xianzhi*) (modern-day Longzhou county in Guangxi) extends this population shift right down to the frontier in his observations:

> Longjin county before the Tang was a part of Giao Chỉ (or Vietnamese) territory. Its inhabitants were subjects of Giao Chỉ. In 1052, Zhao Ding (?–?),³² following the success of the Di (Wuxiang) Qing in his campaign against the barbarians, was appointed to the hereditary position of local administrator. A division of General Di's soldiers from the Shandong region entered the area to settle down. Because of this event, many settlers from north of the Yangzi River moved into the area to live. After the barbarian wastelands had started to be controlled (by the Song court), settlers from Fujian (*min*), Jiangxi (*gan*), Hunan (*xiang*), and the Guangdong (*yue*) region daily flocked to the region. Some came to take positions as local officials, and they married into the local community. Some came as merchants, marrying into the region as well. Most of these Han homesteaders settled in the larger towns or the marketplaces. However, there were certainly those gathered in the rural villages to conduct their business.³³

Throughout the Song Empire the word had spread that new opportunities could now be found in this southernmost outpost of imperial control, and many now were more than willing to try their luck in its settlement.

A cultural shift had also begun to take place in the region, with an increased emphasis on North Chinese or "Central Plain" (*zhongyuan*) practices. A Record of the Empire's Borders and Dimensions during the Taiping Period (*Taiping huanyuji*) by Yue Shi (930–1007) describes the earliest signs of change. Huang Xianfan contends that this trend accelerated during the period after the fall of North China to Jürchen armies, as noted in A Record of This Region's Merits (*Yudi jisheng*) by Wang Xiangzhi (d. after 1221); "following the Song's 'Southern Push' (*nandu*), i.e., fall to the Jin, when many northerners moved south to escape their homelands, clothing styles, ceremonials caps, rituals and music then became the same as those practices in North China."[34] However, these social practices were actually brought into the region by Di Qing's troops and the accompanying cadre of local officials. If the Guangnan region had not had strong ties with court culture during the early Song period, these ties were laid in place and strengthened with each wave of northern settlers that poured into the frontier.

Meanwhile, the Vietnamese court pursued a policy of expansion, with military expeditions to the south against neighboring Champa, along with pacification campaigns to assert direct court control over indigenous communities located along the northern frontier. Lý Phật Mã died late in 1054, and the Khai Hoàng prince Lý Nhật Tôn ascended the throne to preside over a Vietnamese Kingdom that had become increasingly "united and self-assured."[35] Lý Phật Mã had already started a court-organized movement toward frontier settlement and control, and this trend continued unabated throughout the period of unrest involving Nùng Trí Cao.

Soon there was more evidence of Viet expansion in the frontier region. In 1059 the Lý court made the additional effort to take direct control of its frontier and the local manpower. The court divided the northern frontier in the Left and Right Rivers region into the new administrative units; Ngự Long, Vũ Thắng, Long Dực, Thần Điện, Bổng Thánh, Bảo Thắng (Bảo Thắng county in modern-day Lào Cai province), Hùng Lược, and Vạn Tiệp.[36] To each of these units the court assigned an official serving Thăng Long's interest. In the most expressive gesture on regional dominance, Lý Nhật Tôn ordered that militia units be established among the local communities and that conscripts all have the characters "Army of the Son of Heaven" (*tianzi jun*) tattooed on their foreheads.[37] This practice had existed since early times, and had last been practiced by Lê Hoàn in assembling his own militia forces. The emphasis on the control of regional manpower reflects a distinctly Southeast Asian system of statecraft.[38] Most importantly, it indicated that the Lý desired to tap its frontier resources in a novel manner to fuel efforts at regional expansion. Resources at this point in time largely referred to human resources.

During the early 1060s, the Sino-Vietnamese frontier experienced numerous local disturbances among the indigenous communities, in response perhaps to the influx of settlers from the north. Moreover, there were clashes between troops serving both the Chinese and Vietnamese courts. In the spring of 1060, the elderly chieftain of the frontier prefecture Lạng Châu and imperial in-law through a marriage alliance Thân Thiệu Thái (?–?) crossed into Song territory to raid frontier settlements for cattle and new militia recruits.[39] Thiệu Thái also captured the local Song military leader Yang Baocai (?–?) in the attack. In the autumn of 1060, Song troops crossed the frontier. However, the Chinese were unsuccessful in their attempt to bring Yang back.[40]

Kaifeng soon dispatched the newly appointed military commissioner (*anfu shi*) Yu Jing (1000–1064) to the Guangnan region to quell unrest stirred up by Giap Đồng natives led by Thiệu Thái. Fighting there had already claimed the lives of five military inspectors (*xunjian*).⁴¹ Once he reached the south, Yu Jing also sent a court representative secretly to Champa to enlist Cham support for a possible allied attack on Vietnamese communities in Guangnan.⁴² This increased activity along the frontier naturally caught the attention of the Vietnamese court, which reportedly had also caught wind of the Cham plot. As the Song court took a greater interest in the frontier region, a new court policy emerged of courting local leaders directly, rather than relying on the assistance of their tribute representative in the Vietnamese court. Such a shift in behavior undercut the local authority that official tributary relations with the Chinese had once afforded Thăng Long. As the Song court began to seek local leaders to implement its regional interests, even in opposition to Vietnamese interests, the Đại Cồ Việt court sought ways to make their own presence felt along the frontier.

However, the Lý court likely saw merit in defusing what had become a tense relationship with the Song. In the following year, a delegation from Thăng Long led by Bi Gia Dụ (?–?) traveled to Yongzhou to negotiate terms for peace with Yu Qing himself.⁴³ Lý Nhật Tôn instructed his court "send an envoy into China to convey thanks (for quelling the earlier disturbances), but continue to collect more intelligence on Cham troops, Yu Qing's forces, and other troops stationed in the Guangnan Western circuit."⁴⁴ The Chinese delegation again requested the return of Yang Baocai, but this requested was denied.⁴⁵ Given the recent unrest, however, the Chinese emperor Renzong hesitated to raise tensions further along the southern frontier, and he ordered his delegated military leaders of his local military commissions to refrain from assembling troops in the region. The Song ruler then allowed a tribute mission from Thăng Long to travel to Kaifeng for an imperial audience. On February 8, 1063 (by the Western calendar), the two Vietnamese envoys offered tribute to the Song emperor that included nine tamed elephants, a gift that the Vietnamese leaders then considered their most precious offering.⁴⁶ Sino-Vietnamese relations appeared at this stage to have reached a new equilibrium.

However, within months, the relationship between the two courts had changed once again. On March 30, 1063 the Song emperor Renzong passed away, and the heir-apparent Zhao Shu (Yingzong, r. 1063–67) came to power. Vietnamese envoys soon arrived in Kaifeng to congratulate the ascension of the new emperor. On April 7, 1063 Yingzong made an important imperial gesture by sending gifts, such as calligraphic compositions in the hand of the late ruler Renzong, to the Vietnamese court. Such gift was likely an acknowledgment that the Vietnamese ruler and his advisors were learned enough to appreciate the literary refinement of these works and that they fell within the wider circle of *zhongyuan* culture. Yingzong also granted the ruler Lý Nhật Tôn the post concurrent manager of governmental affairs in the Secretariat-Chancellery (*tongzhong shumen xiaping zhangshi*).⁴⁷ The Song emperor's purpose for granting this office was likely to reinforce from the outset of his reign the image of the Vietnamese court as an extension of the Chinese central court and to preserve the position of Lý Nhật Tôn as both a frontier official and a participant in the formulation of central court policy. However, this gesture on the part of the Song court did not completely ameliorate tensions on the frontier.

On the same day that the Vietnamese envoy Lý Kế Tiên (?–?) prepared to depart Kaifeng, news arrived from the south that a frontier militia under the leadership of errant clan leader Thàn Thiệu Thái had engaged in yet another attack on settlements within Guangnan West circuit.[48] A Guangnan official sent an urgent plea to Kaifeng for an immediate punitive attack on the southern intruders. However, Chinese sources record that the Song court had come to the conclusion that Thàn Thiệu Thái was "reckless and mad," perhaps as a conscious effort to divorce his actions from those of the Vietnamese court. In any case, an envoy from Thăng Long had already been dispatched to Kaifeng to ask forgiveness for the attack. Yingzong, therefore, did not raise an army to deal with this problem. Local Song officials may have wanted a stronger response from Kaifeng, but the Song ruler maintained that his vassals were still capable of self-regulation.

More than a year passed before any further troubles arose. On November 18, 1064, the Guizhou prefect Lu Shen memorialized the throne during a court visit by Vietnamese envoys. Lu reported a military delegation from Thăng Long had allegedly come across the frontier in search of Nùng Tông Đán's son Nùng Nhật Tân and his followers, but this same delegation show an interest in taking control of a section of Song territory, including the Wenmen dong (Wenmen Grotto, located near Hurun village in modern-day Jingxi county) *jimi* district.[49] Although the court took no specific action as a result of this memorial, Lu appeared determined to expand the Song's military presence in the south.

After delivering his memorial, Lu Shen set out along the frontier to Yongzhou. As mentioned earlier in this chapter, he commissioned forty-five local aboriginal leaders from the Left and Right River region as military officers in his growing militia. When he had assembled the abovementioned 44,500 seasoned troops, he ordered his force to repair and fortify military installations in the region. He also requested that local Song administrators cast special seals for his militia leaders. Lu also petitioned the Song court with a request that the Left and Right River region be exempted from the payment of all back taxes.[50] Lu took all these measures to gain the loyalties of those communities that one generation previously had joined Nùng Trí Cao in his rebellion against the throne. The effort to provide military training for the leaders of this frontier militia was a variation on existing court policy, but Lu's methods built on Kaifeng's growing interest in a more direct incorporation of these frontier areas.

After witnessing these events along the frontier, Vietnamese officials became quite concerned. Thăng Long immediately sent a tribute-bearing envoy to Kaifeng to "send their greetings" as well as to remind the Chinese court of the precedent of relying on Vietnamese authorities to settle frontier matters. Meanwhile, Lu had again memorialized the throne, requesting that the court offer special training and indoctrination to one local chieftain (*tuding*) each year. Following this training regime, after three years this chieftain would be made a member of the official bureaucracy.[51]

At about this same time, it appears that Nùng Tông Đán had decided to switch allegiances. It may have been that the local chieftain saw his traditional base of power eroding rapidly under the new system of frontier management set in place by Lu Shen. The evidence is rather scanty; however, according to the *Songshi*, at some point after late 1065, Tông Đán made overtures to join in an alliance with Lý Nhật Tôn and the Quảng Nguyên chieftain Lưu Ký (?–?).[52] Fearing a potentially hostile coalition so close to home, Lu Shen sent an envoy to announce this news to the Song court. Emperor Yingzong, a mentally weak and distracted ruler by this point, apparently took no other action than to reassign Tông Đán his honorific titles. This lack of attention from the center was to have a harmful effect regarding the vitality of the Song presence along the frontier. As highlighted in the Vietnamese sources, at this point, Tông Đán became a willing and able ally of the Lý court to perform a key military role in the 1075–77 conflict.

This alliance between Tông Đán and the Quảng Nguyên chieftain Lưu Ký had its roots in the third rebellion of Nùng Trí Cao. Shen Kua argues in *Mengxi bitan* that among Trí Cao's chief supporters for his initial assault on the Hengshan Garrison prior to the attack on Yongzhou were Lư Báo, Lê Mạo and Hoàng Trọng Khanh and Liệu Thông (?–?).[53] When the rebellion was finally suppressed, Lư Báo called together Trí Cao's disbanded rebel army and eventually returned to Quảng Nguyên, where the entire group had pledged its loyalty to Lưu Ký. As mentioned earlier in this chapter, the Song court rewarded this group with official titles, despite their direct participation in Nùng Trí Cao's insurrection and their ties to Lưu Ký. The Song support for these local leaders would have mixed results. By 1069, Lư Báo and another of Trí Cao's kin Nùng Trí Hội had announced their support for the Song court, while Nùng Tông Đán and Lưu Ký would cast their lot with the Vietnamese court. The greatest change in the balance of relations in this period came with the rise in Kaifeng of the young emperor Shenzong, who ushered in a new approach to frontier management.

On January 8, 1067, Yingzong passed away and his son Zhao Xu, posthumously known as Song emperor Shenzong. (r. 1067–85), ascended to the throne. Shenzong followed his father by rewarding all well-wishers generously during the first days of his reign. However, he appeared to pay special attention to the Vietnamese delegation. When Thăng Long dispatched a mission to greet the new emperor, Shenzong presented the envoys with a lavish array of gifts: set of official robes for the Lý household, a golden belt, 200 *liang* of silver ingots, three hundred bolts of silk, two horses, and a saddle inlaid with gold and silver plating.[54] On February 9, 1067, Shenzong decreed that Lý Nhật Tôn should be granted the title "King of the Southern Pacified Region" (*nanping wang*). Reestablishing the tribute relations between the two courts according to terms set at the beginning of the dynasty appears to have been the initial aim of the young emperor. However, Chinese frontier officials in the emperor's service at the same time were training for military action along the southern edge of the empire.

By late 1067, there was more movement on the Song side of the frontier region. The new Guizhou prefect Zhang Tian (fl. 1068–77) reported that "through interviews I have heard that the Quảng Nguyên Châu official Lưu Kỷ maintains ties with Lư Báo, despite the fact that Lưu Kỷ is an official in the service of Lý Nhật Tôn. Lư Báo is a member of Nùng Trí Cao's treacherous faction, still located in Quảng Nguyên Châu. Lưu Kỷ is currently planning to cause mischief of some sort, and Lư Báo now intends to seek personal glory by crossing over into Chinese territory. I want to halt Lư Báo and crush his followers."[55] The Song court's Bureau of Military Affairs (*qumiyuan*) replied to this report with the following,

> Lư Báo is certainly a member of Nùng Trí Cao's treacherous faction. However, any action against Lưu Kỷ cannot be allowed. If commoners chose to cross the frontier (into Song territory), they will be targeted and executed. However, it is not necessary to send military officials to pursue their leaders and the Vietnamese army. The court does not treat prisoners according to the ritual protocol expected of outer barbarians (*waiyi*). If this Lưu Kỷ chooses to transfer the administration of his prefecture back to China, such action ought to be accepted. Therefore, it is not necessary to attract these people, but instead officials should record the fact that Lưu Kỷ is approaching, and that Quảng Nguyên has no other leader. It is not necessary to launch a defense of our territory until Lưu Kỷ has advanced into Han-controlled territory. If he doesn't, then let the situation settle and the problem will fade.[56]

The Song court chose to follow this policy, suddenly abandoning the balance of power along the frontier that the court had always advocated in its tribute relations with the Vietnamese leadership.

By 1069, however, Lư Báo had instead offered his allegiances to the Song court, while Lưu Kỷ had remained in the Quảng Nguyên region, nominally under the control of Thăng Long.[57] In the late summer, the Vietnamese court sent a tribute mission north to maintain good relations with the court at Kaifeng. Shortly thereafter, perhaps to counter Tông Đán's defection, the young Chinese emperor confirmed the Nùng clan's frontier status by conferring on Nùng Trí Hội, now seen by the Chinese as the sole leader of Quảng Nguyên's adjoining settlements of Guwu and Shun'an (Lôi Hỏa), a variation on Tông Đán's former title "Great General and Personal Guardian General of the Right" (*dajiangjun wei youqianniu*).[58] The Chinese leadership hoped to maintain a solid ally in the region, even through this period of rapid change.

In late 1071, local Song officials again appraised the court of the shifting allegiances among local leaders. The Guangnan military commissioner Xiao Gu reported to Kaifeng, "the Vietnamese official Lưu Kỷ has been sighted at the head of more than two hundred men in the vicinity of Shun'an prefecture. We have not yet determined how many Vietnamese have joined his entourage."[59] Lưu Kỷ's action had been deemed as particularly interesting, given his earlier overtures and the recent alliance forged with Quảng Nguyên's other influential leader Nùng Trí Hội. The Song court responded to Xiao Gu's memorial, "Recently I have received repeated reports that Quảng Nguyên's "barbarian bandits (*manzei*)" have been gathering (for unlawful reasons), and there seems to be no end in sight for these occurrences. These disturbances have now unsettled the general populace in the grotto settlements. However, I'm concerned that the bandits cannot help but to act in a crafty manner."[60] The Song court was well aware of the effect that locally influential leaders still had in a region that Kaifeng now wished to have some say. However, the only effective strategy appeared to be the manipulation of chieftains with significant followings, and hope that these individuals would not one day switch sides.

Political changes on the Vietnamese side of the frontier resulted in further changes to the extant network of relations, and, by the 1060s, Lý rulers had become more comfortable viewing themselves as a dynastic power with the imperial authority and apparatus of power needed to maintain a long-term command over their expanding territory. Lý Phật Mã, second ruler of the dynasty, had set an important precedent for his successors with his ambitious efforts in territorial expansion and the court's establishment of regional dominance over the leaders of local communities, and his son sought to follow and improve upon his father's reign.

An important aspect of regional dominance was the maintenance of free passage through the frontier region. On November 26, 1068, Lý Nhật Tôn made this declaration at court,

> The military commanders of Guangnan and Jiangnan prefectures always make their presence known along the main route by which we carry memorials to the Song court. Persons travelling this route face difficult obstacles. The high official Nguy Trọng Hòa (?–?) reports that people taking this route face disruption in many counties and prefectures, including all kinds of fees that they must pay. I have ordered the commander of the Sea-based Second Circuit Prefectural Army to act according to ancient rules of protocol when receiving persons along this major thoroughfare. However, in the event that this route is disrupted or cut off, we must not show fear, but instead launch a vigorous defense of the Việt Kingdom.[61]

In that year, Lý Nhật Tôn established new offices for his own government to strengthen the institutional control of his family. Lý dynastic power would remain strong through the end of his reign.

However, with Lý Nhật Tôn's death on February 2, 1072, a succession crisis in the imperial household nearly broke down the imperial authority that the earlier generations had managed to build up. The Crown Prince Lý Can Đức (r. 1072–1127), son of a commoner consort Ỷ Lan (1044–1117) was only six years old when he took the throne.[62] The young Vietnamese ruler and his regents, including the defender-in-chief (*thái úy*) Lý Thường Kiệt, were soon busy consolidating his authority in the face of court opposition from Lý Nhât Tôn's principal wives. Toward this end, the young ruler turned to the frontier for political backing. The court of Can Đức soon announced a general amnesty for all "outlaws (*tù*)" in the "protected prefectures (*đô hộ phủ*)," referring to the frontier region.[63] The anonymously authored thirteenth-century court chronicle A Survey of the History of Việt (*Việt Sử Lược*) records that, in gratitude, the local chieftain of Lạng Châu Dương Cảnh Thông (?–?) presented a white deer to the court as tribute followed by numerous officials paying their respects.[64] The emperor ordered that Cảnh Thông be granted the title Grand Guardian (*thái bảo*), following the precedent by Lý Phật Mã of cementing ties with frontier officials with this ancient Chinese honorific title. By the late summer of 1072, Can Đức appears to have felt that his mandate to rule was clear, and he embarked on numerous imperial activities, all of which culminated in the construction of five additions to the imperial palace complex.

Wang Anshi's Economic Activism and a New Vision of the Frontier

By early 1073, some of the most important changes in the Sino-Vietnamese relationship during the Song period were now just beyond the horizon. These changes were influenced by two main factors; the increasing self-confidence of the Lý court in the projection of its autonomous regional authority, and the elements of Song court-sponsored programs of economic activism and military enhancement, at the urging of reform-minded official Wang Anshi, that touched on the frontier region. Wang's vision of a single centrally directed state enterprise for the management of the empire's resources eventually came into conflict with the Vietnamese court's notion that it should manage the frontier as its rulers saw fit. When the Song leadership was no longer content to administer frontier matters from a distance through its vassal representative, conflicts along the frontier quickly escalated into open, armed hostilities.

Wang Anshi had a vision for an economically and militarily revived Song imperial order that could once again make manifest the grand principles of "original intent" proclaimed by the sage rulers of antiquity.[65] As Peter Bol observes, because Wang Anshi maintained, "all things are in principle part of the greater whole," it became necessary for the state to reconcile and ultimately unite the individual interests of various social groups under the court's leadership. As Bol further notes, where conservatives such as Sima Guang saw a distortion of underlying principle in the trend toward greater commercialization of Song society, for example, Wang Anshi saw an opportunity to use this trend to combine the energies of public and private interest in a more efficient and constructive manner. Extending the state's reach to the frontier region was an extension of Wang's vision of holistic order to the Song Empire and a rationalization of that empires' potential.

What had changed in the interim between Nùng Trí Cao's rebellion and these events was that the Song court had been forced to reevaluate its traditional frontier policy, and the choice was made for more direct administration of the area. Recent scholarship has identified the personal political ambitions of the Shenzong emperor as the motivational forces behind most changes in frontier management during this period. As Paul Smith writes, "fanned as they were by imperial passion, irredentism and frontier adventure emerged during (Shenzong's) reign as a potent form of political capital that swept a new constellation of men—including general, eunuchs, and hawkish bureaucrats—into power."[66] Vietnamese scholarship for this period has traditionally fixed the blame on Wang Anshi and his immediate supporters for territorial expansion in the Sino-Vietnamese frontier region. However, the emperor himself had called for a more aggressive frontier policy wherever the Song bordered on lands formerly under Han Chinese control. Throughout the 1060s military officials were dispatched from Kaifeng to the prefectures of southeastern Guangxi to take up positions as local administrators. Imperial troops were transferred to the region, and the number of war-horses was increased considerably.[67] During this same period, Shenzong's court had closed down the border markets along the Song frontier with the Tangut-led Xi Xia kingdom, and the emperor himself had commended a Song general who had led an unprovoked attack on a Xi Xia border town.[68] The emperor's own desire to recover "lost" territory opened the possibility for experimentation with Wang Anshi's policy for strengthened frontier administration.

One aspect of Wang Anshi's 1060s program of "economic activism" that affected this general region was the court's extended reach into the frontier area for new sources of revenue and strategically valuable items. As Paul Smith notes in a discussion of the Tea and Horse Agency (*duda tiju chama si*) in Sichuan, "by grafting native recruitment onto the strategy of bureaucratic entrepreneurship, reform policymakers decentralized operational and personnel authority to the men who had most to gain from state economic activism and thus acquired for the state unprecedented access to Szechwan's surplus product."[69] Although the Guangnan West circuit region had less to offer the court economically, horses and precious minerals either passed through or were found in close proximity to this are. One of Wang's earliest reform measures in mid-1069 was to grant fiscal intendants in six of the Song's southern circuits the right to disregard local quotas on tribute items, and instead to fill government orders by buying and selling these items according to their prices on the open market.[70] Under Wang Anshi's New Policies reforms, greater attention was paid to seeking out loyal supporters of the Song Empire who could assist with the systematic extraction of these resources.

As historians have explored quite extensively in the past, Wang Anshi's policies did not proceed uncontested at court, and this news spread beyond the frontier. Chinese officials also heard the news that Lý Thường Kiệt had argued publicly in Thăng Long that Wang Anshi, in his plans to expand the training of militias into the frontier region, had already demonstrated that the Song court desired to take control of the frontier, and ignore the precedent of tribute responsibilities. Wang had recently sent a memorial to the Song emperor Shenzong, calling for action from Song imperial troops.[71] For these reasons, Chinese officials announced that the Vietnamese court was once again in danger of losing legitimacy. Cross-frontier tensions had reached a breaking point, and any single event could have sparked a violent reaction.

In 1075, the Quảng Nguyên chieftain Lưu Kỷ unexpectedly launched an attack on Yongzhou; however, Nùng Trí Hội, now ruling from Guihua prefecture (or Wuyang grotto settlement), was able to ward off the attackers.[72] As a result of this attack, or perhaps to preempt future disturbance, emperor Shenzong issued an edict that the members of the native "Five Clans" (*wu xingfan*) of northern Guangnan should present tribute to the court every five years.[73] In 1073, a group from these communities had made a large tribute offering to the Chinese court, and thereafter missions had continued on an erratic schedule. The Song emperor likely desired to standardize relations with these communities without alienating them, given the defection of other groups across the frontier in this period. The *Songshi* estimates that the Five Clans amounted to a sizable population, because they were able to muster a delegation of eight hundred and ninety for their 1073 tribute mission.[74] The Chinese emperor would need a large number of local allies, if he chose to mount a successful attack in the region.

Given the changing conditions and shifting alliances along the frontier, by 1075 relations between Song and Đại Việt authorities had soured considerably. One local indication of deteriorating relations was the Chinese court's interest in further militarizing the frontier region north of the Nùng clan's home region. In the spring of 1075, Shenzong sent two officials, Hanlin Academy member and director in the Ministry of Justice (*xingbu langzhong*) Shen Qi (1017–88) and former prefect of Qianzhou (today located in southern Jiangxi) Liu Yi (1017–86) to take up the administration of Guizhou, at the site of modern-day Guilin.[75] Shen and Liu were instructed by the court to train the local militia in techniques of riverine warfare. Moreover, the court ordered the local people to cease all trade with subjects of the Đại Việt court, further insolating communities that lay on the northern and southern edges of the frontier.

The Vietnamese court was well aware of these activities, and it prepared a response. As is well known to Vietnamese readers, Lý Thường Kiệt had anticipated an attack from the north, and he chose what later Vietnamese historians would call an "attack in self-defense." He divided his army into two groups. The objective of the first unit, under the control of his new frontier ally Tông Đán and with a strong contingent of uplands inhabitants, was to invade Guangxi to attract Song troops stationed at Yongzhou south into the frontier.[76] At this same time, the principal army, under the command of Lý Thường Kiệt himself, would deploy along the South China coast to occupy those places then left defenseless.

In the autumn of 1075, Tông Đán took control of the Guwan, Taiping, Yongping, and Qianlong garrisons.[77] During advance of Tông Đán's forces, the fleet of Lý Thường Kiệt, having seized the two prefectures of Qinzhou and Lianzhou, advanced further into Song territory.[78] To alleviate fear and to keep (local Song subjects) off on his rearguard, Thường Kiệt proclaimed that he came only to apprehend a rebel (Lưu Kỷ perhaps?) who had taken refuge in China and whom the Chinese prefect had refused to repatriate. Thường Kiệt also was presented as a liberator of the Chinese people, who had been impoverished and oppressed by the reforms of Wang Anshi.[79]

Lý Thường Kiệt, with Tông Đán, arrived in the early spring of 1076 at Yongzhou and devastated a local Song militia force under the leadership of Zhang Shoujie (d. 1076), the governor-general (*dudu*) of Guangnan West circuit. Zhang himself was beheaded in the fighting at the Kunlun guan (Kunlun Pass).[80] After forty-two days of intense resistance and at the end of their resources, the defenders of the Yongzhou succumbed under a furious attack. Thousands had died in the fighting. The city fortress was completely razed to the ground, and its commander Su Jian (fl. 1071–76) had killed his own family and committed suicide by refusing to leave the blazing building.[81] However, a large unit of the Song army soon approached, and the Lý forces withdrew, taking along an enormous amount of spoils and thousands of prisoners.[82]

Shortly before launching the attack of the Song, Lý Thường Kiệt had also led a successful campaign in 1069 against the southern Cham Kingdom. Therefore, the Song court called on Cham and Khmer forces to join the Chinese in retaliating against Vietnamese aggression.[83] In late 1076, the combined forces under the command of Guo Kui (1022–88), acting as the Annan circuit punitive expedition officer (*Annandao zhaotaoshi*) and his assisting officer Zhao Di (?–?) launched a counter-attack.[84] The combined Chinese army included more than 100,000 men.[85] One hundred mounted cavalrymen under the command of Tao Bi (1015–78) entered the frontier by way of the Left River region.[86] The frontier was penetrated at three points. The Song force quickly took possession of the Quảng Nguyên prefecture, crushing resistance among the Đại Việt loyalists and capturing the region's leader, the aforementioned Lưu Kỷ, and setting fire to the *dong* dwellings.[87]

By the beginning of 1077, the combined Song land forces had crushed Lý resistance from Cơ Lang and Quyết Lý, and the Chinese forces were rapidly approaching Thăng Long. The Song armies met on northern bank of the Như Nguyệt (or Cầu) River, also known in Chinese sources as the Fuliang River, in modern Bắc Ninh Province.[88] Lý Thường Kiệt regarded the defense of this river to be absolutely crucial to the Vietnamese cause, not only because the Nhu Nguyệt provided the last possible opportunity to protect the delta region in which the capital was located, but also because this region contained the home village of the dynasty's founder, as well as the tombs of former rulers at Thiên Đức.[89] Lý Thường Kiệt had ordered his men to construct on the river's southern bank a wide earthen rampart protected by several lines constructed from piles of bamboo. Most of his fleet crossed at the mouth of the Bạch Đằng River in order to prevent the Chinese fleet from joining its supporting infantry units.[90]

Nevertheless, the Song front line was able to cross the river, and soon their cavalry riders were no more than several miles from Thăng Long. To encourage the counter-attack, Lý Thường Kiệt ordered one of his officers to hide in the temple of the god of the river, Trương Hát, and to recite the following stanza, known to Vietnamese schoolchildren worldwide:

> Over the peaks and rivers of the South reigns the emperor of the South.
> Such is the destiny fixed forever on the Celestial Book.
> How dare the Barbarians invade our land?
> Their foolish audacity will witness their bloody rout![91]

As legend has it, Thường Kiệt's troops were so inspired by this stirring verse; they held their ground to beat back the first wave of Song attackers. The Chinese tried again to cross the river and were again pushed back, sustaining one thousand casualties.[92] Meanwhile the invading naval fleet was held back by Vietnamese defenders at the coast, and so was prevented from providing the necessary backing to continue the attack. The Song foray into Vietnamese territory came to a standstill.

At this point, the two opposing forces faced each other on the banks of the river. The Song forces bombarded Lý positions and their supporting junks. When Lý Thường Kiệt tried to take the offensive, he suffered a significant defeat, in which two Lý princes perished, at the Kháo Túc River.[93] However, logistical problems, the tropical climate, and disease had decimated the Song army, which had lost more than half of its effectiveness. On the other side of the conflict, the Vietnamese court feared that a prolonged war would not produce any positive result. At this point Lý Thường Kiệt made peace overtures. The Song agree to withdraw their troops, but it retained control of five disputed regions of Quảng Nguyên (then renamed Shun'anzhou, as mentioned earlier), Tư Lang Châu, Môn Châu, Tô Mậu Châu, and Quang Lang, which comprised a major part of the modern Vietnamese provinces of Cao Bằng and Lạng Sơn. The leader of the Chinese assault Guo Kui had left Shun'anzhou under the administration of his cavalry commander Tao Bi.[94] Chinese sources note that the Vietnamese had seized a section of Song territory along the frontier as well. The war had lasted fifteen months. When the dust had settled, the Đại Việt armies had managed once again to hold off a well-equipped Song military force.

Border Negotiations and Demarcation

After a long period of strained silence between the two courts, Thăng Long agreed in 1082 to return the captured prefectures of Yong, Qin, and Lian, along with their inhabitants and prisoners-of-war, to Kaifeng. In return, Chinese authorities returned four prefectures and one county seized from the Vietnamese court, including Nùng Trí Cao's birthplace and the Nùng clan home base Quảng Nguyên.[95] In the aftermath of these concessions, a poem circulated throughout the

Song Empire, one line of which read "Because we had a hankering for Giao Chỉ elephants, we gave up Quảng Nguyên gold (*Pin Jiaozhi xiang, que shi Guangyuan jin*)."[96]

This resolution of the border dispute did not come without a few revengeful acts by both courts. In the late spring of 1079, Song authorities in Guangnan captured and beheaded Nùng Trí Xuân (d.1079) and took his wife and children as hostages.[97] In 1083, under the pretence of pursuing Nùng Trí Hội, Vietnamese troops attacked his home prefecture Guihua. The *Songshi* reports that when Trí Hội approached the military commissioner (*jinglueshi*) Xiong Ben (1026–91) to plead for fresh troops to fight off the Vietnamese, Xiong instead had the chieftain brought into custody for questioning. Lý Can Đức then assembled for troops to "thank" Xiong Ben, and to request the return of "the eight động," that is, the six counties of Bảo Lạc and the two aboriginal settlements of Susang.

However, the two courts soon recognized that the time had come to resolve their differences regarding sovereignty over the border regions of Quảng Nguyên and Guihua. In 1084 the Vietnamese court sent the Director of Military Personnel (*binh bộ thị lang*) Lê Văn Thịnh (fl. 1075–96) to negotiate border issues with the Chinese. Xiong Ben sent the Left River Region's military inspector and a Wang Anshi supporter Cheng Zhuo (?–?) to argue the Song's case. In the vicinity of the Left River, surveying delegations from both courts inspected the area separately and then convened at the Song-held Yongping garrison in southernmost Guangnan.[98]

Negotiations proceeded from July 6 to August 8, 1084. The Vietnamese delegation spoke of designating Quảng Nguyên and Guihua prefectures as two sides of a fixed border (*qiangjie*) region between the two states. Lê Văn Hưu's History of the Great Viet (*Đại Việt Sử Ký*) contains these comments about the Vietnamese negotiator: "Lê Van Thình should be regarded as a good official. He was someone who got along with others. He did not seek to vex (his Chinese counterparts) or cause trouble, and so he was able to change the attitude of the Song emperor. As for the six counties that Đại Việt troops had invaded, the resources of this territory had not yet been utilized by anyone. The leader of the Vietnamese delegation chose a negotiation strategy that avoided the ill-will which might have emerged from China's defeat at the hands of Vietnamese troops."[99]

However, Lê Van Thình proved also to be a tough negotiator, and the Chinese officials present found it very difficult to challenge his points.[100] When the Song emperor heard of the proposal made by the Vietnamese court, he ordered his officials to look into Lê Van Thình's reasons for wanting to retain control of Quảng Nguyên. He then offered Lê Van Thình the lavish gift of an ornamental belt, a robe, and five hundred bolts of thick silk. By the end of the negotiations, however, Lê Van Thình had retained control for the Vietnamese court of the area beyond the Eight Passes (*bát ải*), that is, Bảo Lạc and Susang. With the successful conclusion of the negotiations, the *Songshi* compilers noted, "the South's turmoil was thus quelled."[101]

The Song court quickly placed the overtures for negotiations in the context of tribute protocol. Concerning the prefectures and counties seized by Song troops, the Chinese emperor issued the following edict,

> You, my nobleman, as the administrator of the southern kingdom of Giao Chỉ (Nanjiao), have for generations maintained hegemony over this region. However, you have now lapsed in virtue by disobeying my orders and by robbing the frontier towns. You have cast aside the notions of paying heed to your ancestors and to assumptions of loyalty and obedience. And you have added annoyance for this court by launching your attack. Your troops have advanced deep into Song territory, and they are on the verge of heading home only after becoming exhausted. The signs of their crimes are many, and there is no need to list more of your transgressions. Now you are sending envoys to reestablish tribute relations. I have examined your messages, and opinions. Clearly, you have repented. I am in charge of a myriad of kingdoms, and I do not distinguish between those kingdoms close at hand and those far away. However, I see the people of Yongzhou and Qinzhou, displaced by fire and theft, long ago lost their native lands. I will wait until I have sent these people back to their border region before I give Quảng Nguyên and the other lands back to Giao Châu.[102]

The *Songshi* compilers had this comment, regarding the territory, considered during the negotiations:

> Shunzhou (or Quảng Nguyên) is located in the extreme southern region, and this region was used to defend (the Song Empire's) frontier. Due to the dense fog and pestilent conditions, and many of the region's inhabitants died of illness. Tao Bi actually died while posted here. The court knew that this area was of no use, so the Chinese negotiator returned a total of four prefectures and one county. However, Quảng Nguyên was formerly attached to the Yongzhou administration region as a *loose rein* aboriginal district. It originally did not belong to Giao Chỉ.[103]

Although all Song rulers through the period described above had allowed Vietnamese leaders to regulate frontier affairs in this region, the thirteenth-century Yuan-period compilers of the *Songshi* had already altered this perception to claim a precedent for direct control of this territory in question by Chinese authorities.

By the end of the Northern Song in 1126, rulers in Kaifeng understood that the Đại Việt region occupied a place one step further away from the influence of the Chinese central court. According to the map An Illustration of Prefectures and Commanderies Beyond the Influence of Our Dynasty (*Benchao huawai zhoujun tu*), the region labeled An Nam on this map is clearly left within the Song Empire, the prefectures making up the Đại Việt territory are placed outside of China, retaining the same status the well-known Sixteen Prefectures (Shiliu zhou) that had once been lost to the Liao.[104]

Conclusion

Historians have certainly not been in total agreement when describing the state of affairs along the frontier in the aftermath of Nùng Trí Cao's rebellion. The clearest discernable "school" of scholarship may be found among modern Vietnamese historians, who argue that the frontier communities rallied in support of the nation-building efforts of the Lý leadership. Much of this scholarship begins with the assumption that the Sino-Vietnamese frontier region had remained vaguely defined with the advent of the Đại Việt Kingdom and its recognition by China.[105] However such a statement depends heavily on very modern notions of political boundaries and the rights and responsibilities of nation-states, which maintain these boundaries. As I have argued in this study, a premodern frontier can lack a clearly delineated physical demarcation, and still be divided into unambiguously understood spheres of administration. In the case of the Sino-Vietnamese frontier before Nùng Trí Cao's revolt, the Song court through the precepts of tribute protocol expected the Vietnamese court to manage affairs in the Chinese court's name in this region. When disturbances arose, the Chinese leadership would turn to Vietnamese authorities for rectification.

However, the Nùng Trí Cao rebellion and its aftermath would change everything. The Chinese court's response to the regional tensions also reflected the increased interest of Kaifeng in the resources of the Guangnan region. The Song court, facing border opposition both in the northern and southern regions of the young empire, implemented new policies that emphasized the stricter definition and regulation of its internal territory.[106] Changes even in the content of questions for the civil service examinations reflected this shift toward a more aggressive border policy.[107] The Vietnamese court, however, viewed Nùng Trí Cao's insurgence as an interruption in the orderly conduct of tribute relations. Drawing specifically on the Chinese model of tribute as signifier of political submission, the Đại Việt emperor saw Nùng Trí Cao and his followers as disloyal subjects of his domain, worthy of punishment for this reason.

In his summary of changes to frontier policy in the late Northern Song, Okada Koji has argued that between 1068 and Song Huizong's Chongning reign period (1102–6), through the border negotiations with the Lý court, the Song court attempted to pursue a more assertive frontier policy by abandoning the *jimi* prefecture system in favor of opening up *jimi* territories for economic development, but that is new policy ultimately failed.[108] Okada attributes the failure to two factors. First, abandoning the existing *jimi* system necessarily involved the establishment of a formal administrative arrangement that included the posting of officials to these outlying areas. The funding of such new positions put a greater strain on court resources at a time when Kaifeng could not afford the extra financial burden.[109] Secondly, the Song court for purposes of taxation treated similarly Han settlers and non-Han frontier inhabitants outside *jimi* administrative regions. These non-Han communities were soon expected to should the greater tax burden that resulted from the construction of new fortification and road systems along the frontier. For this reason, the Tai-speaking residents of the frontier protested violently when large groups of Han settlers began to flood into the region.[110] By the beginning of the twelfth century, this shift in policy was suspended and the earlier *jimi* administration was reinvigorated.

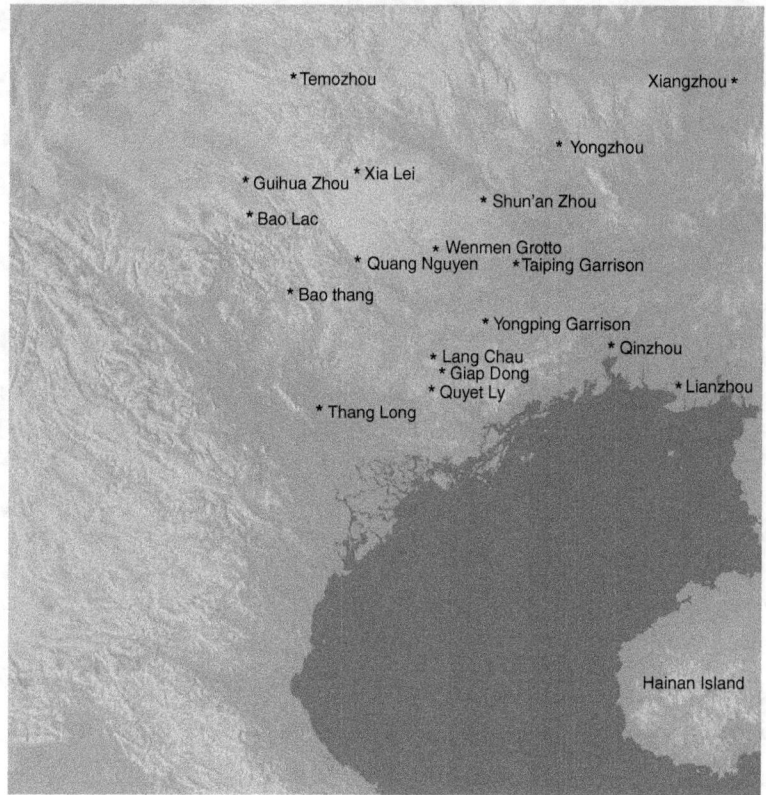

Figure 7.1 Map of 1075 Song-Lý frontier war (including contested territories).
Source: Map created by James Anderson.

To the south of these *jimi* areas, the Vietnamese leadership also changed its frontier policy to adopt a less territorially aggressive approach. Thăng Long's northern expansion was reversed after the 1075 conflict, which altered the Vietnamese court's direct control over local communities as well. The *Songshi* notes that soon after the frontier war Lý Nhân Tôn agreed in 1082 to return the three captured Song prefectures Yongzhou, Qinzhou and Lianzhou along with one thousand prisoners-of-war, he also sent a group of 221 persons to the Song. Men over the age of fifteen all bore the aforementioned tattoo saying "Army of the Son of Heaven" and men over twenty bore the mark "conscripts of the Southern Court" (*tou nanchao*). Women bore the tattoo "official guests" (*guanke*) on their left hands.[111] While the Vietnamese court had earlier regarded this population as servants in the Lý cause of expansion, turning them over to the Chinese authorities

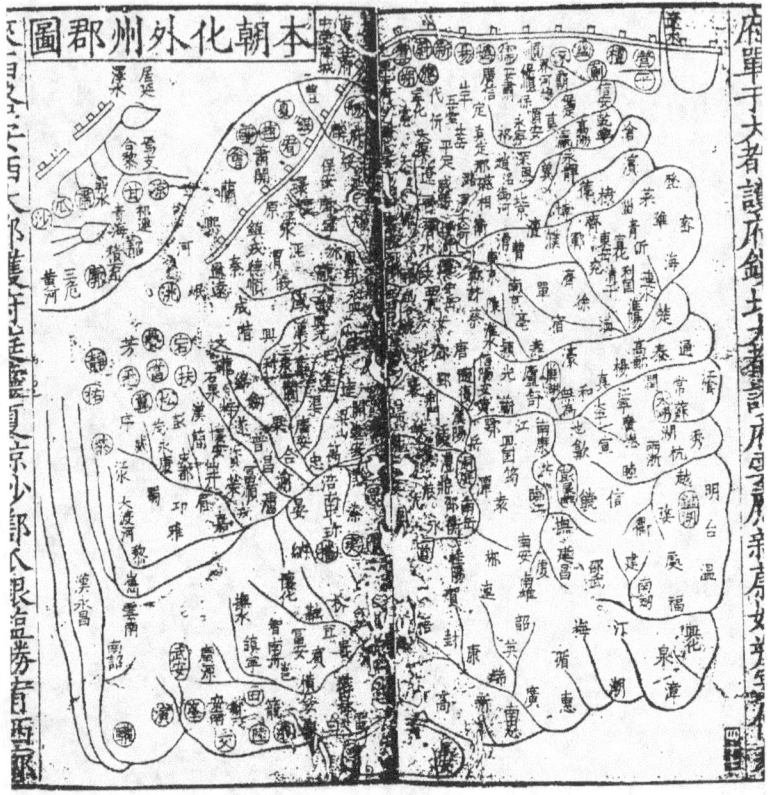

Figure 7.2 An Illustration of Prefectures and Commanderies Beyond the Influence of Our Dynasty *(Benchao huawai zhoujun tu)* from a Song-period edition historical atlas.
Source: Tôyô Bunko edition; Shanghai: Guji, 1989, pp. 80–81.

as a gesture of goodwill was also a sign that these frontier communities no longer held great importance by the 1080s.

However, the successful conclusion of border negotiations was indicative of more than a provisional resolution of differences between the three parties along the frontier. Chinese imperial might no longer served as a strong deterrent in the face of the Vietnamese court's expansion of regional power, and the Song could do little to control or impede the refashioning of the Lý in the image of the Chinese imperial model. Nevertheless, the Chinese remained the stronger of the two parties, and Vietnamese leadership carefully maintained its tributary ties with the Song court out of the conviction that this system was, in the final analysis, the best option available. Once clear boundaries had been drawn, major military tensions quickly subsided. Trade issues, and not border conflict, would define the Sino-Vietnamese exchanges by the late eleventh century. The bonds of the tribute system would remain strong, but both sides now regarded the material benefits of close ties to be more important than the quest to iron out political differences. Ly leaders, for their part, turned their attention inward, concentrating on the expansion and elaboration of their own empire. The Chinese leaders also redirected their attention, now having more than enough to occupy their concerns along their northern, rather than southern, frontier.

Notes

This chapter is adapted from the corresponding chapter in the author's *The Rebel Den of Nùng Trí Cao: Loyalty and Identity along the Sino-Vietnamese Frontier* (Seattle; Singapore, 2007). All translations are mine unless otherwise noted.

1. Đinh Bộ Lĩnh (923–80) founded his independent Vietnamese Kingdom with the title Đại Cồ Việt (968–1054). The Lý dynasty ruler Lý Nhật Tôn (b. 1023) would later rename the kingdom Đại Việt (1054–1400). This title would remain in use until the end of the Trần dynasty (1225–1400).
2. Patricia Pelley, "'Barbarians' and 'Younger Brothers': The Remaking of Race in Postcolonial Vietnam," *Journal of Southeast Asian Studies* 29.2 (Sept. 1998), p. 376.
3. Ibid.
4. Hoàng Xuân Hãn, *Lý Thường Kiệt: Lịch Sử Ngoại Giao Trều Lý* (Hanoi, 1949), p. 94.
5. Hoàng Xuân Hãn, *Lý Thường Kiệt*, p. 260.
6. Hoàng Xuân Hãn, *Lý Thường Kiệt*, p. 122.
7. Trần Trọng Kim, *Việt Nam Sử Lược* (rpr. Glendale, CA, 1982), 1:103.
8. Nguyen Ngoc Huy, *The Le Code: Law in Traditional Vietnam: A Comparative Sino-Vietnamese Legal Study with Historical-Juridical Analysis and Annotations*, vol. 1 (Athens, OH, 1987), p. 10.
9. Le Thanh Khoi, *Histoire du Viet Nam* (Paris, 1981), pp. 158, 160.
10. Phan Huy Lê, "Nùng Trí Cao Nhân Vật Lịch Sử và Biểu Tượng Văn Hóa" in *Nùng Trí Cao: kỷ yếu hội thảo khoa học*, ed. Trần Văn Phượng (Cao Bằng, 1995), p. 178. See also Hoàng Xuân Hãn, *Lý Thường Kiệt*, pp. 81–97.
11. Lê Đình Sỹ, *Kế sách giữ nước thời Lý-Trần* (Hanoi, 1994), p. 9.
12. Hà Văn Thư and Lã Văn Lô, *Văn hóa Tày Nùng* (Hanoi, 1984), p. 9.
13. Bế Viết Đẳng, *Các dân tộc Tày, Nùng ở Việt Nam* (Hanoi, 1992), p. 54.
14. James L. Hevia, *Cherishing Men from Afar: Qing Guest Ritual and the Macartney Embassy of 1793* (Durham, 1995), p. 123.
15. I have located the first recorded reference to this institution of frontier management in the Confucian classic Book of History (*Shangshu*) in the following passage: "Beyond the Nine Principalities (i.e., the North China Central Plain) was barbarian territory. Here the (Zhou) ruler had installed barbarians who ruled with a loose rein and nothing else. This was because these people could not be made the same as those who accepted Central Plain (Hua Xia) ways." Cited in Ruan Yuan, *Shisan jing zhu* (Beijing, 1980).
16. Although this statement refers to Wolters's work, I nonetheless note that in the second edition of *History, Culture, and Region in Southeast Asian Perspectives*,

Wolters does not contend that premodern Vietnam followed his well-known "mandala" model of Southeast Asian political organization. Cited in O.W. Wolters, *History, Culture, and Region in Southeast Asian Perspectives* (Ithaca; Singapore, 1999), pp. 143–44.
17. Jeffery G. Barlow. *The Zhuang* [online]. Pacific University, 2000. [Cited July 16, 2001]. Available from World Wide Web: (http://mcel.pacificu.edu/as/resources/zhuang/zhuang8.htm).
18. Barlow. *The Zhuang* [online], [Cited July 4, 2001].
19. Li Tao, *Xu Zizhi tongjian changbian* (Beijing, 1985), 22.490–91. This work is hereafter referred to as *XZZTJCB*.
20. Toghto [Tuotuo], *Songshi* (Beijing, 1983), 191.4746. This work is hereafter referred to as *SS*.
21. *SS*, 12.241.
22. *SS*, 312.10244.
23. *SS*, 12.247.
24. Xu Song, *Song huiyao jiben* (Taibei, 1964), 198.7799. This work is hereafter referred to as *SHY*.
25. *SHY*, 198.7799. An interesting question involves whether these Nùng leaders were expressing personal loyalty to Emperor Yingzong. The *SHY* account is ambiguous and therefore does not provide us with a clear answer to this question.
26. The *SHY* account mistakenly conflates the names of Lư Báo and Li Mao as "Lu Mao." See Shen Kua's account for the proper listing of names. Shen Kua, *Mengxi bitan* in *Wenbai duizhao Mengxi bitan quanyi*.
27. *SS*, 191.4746.
28. See Charles Hucker, *A Dictionary of Official Titles in Imperial China* (Stanford, 1985), p. 137. Hucker contends that the leaders of "tithings" were known as "tithing chiefs" (*jiazhang*) or "tithing heads" (*jiatou*), while the *SS* account uses an older Han-period title "guard commander" (*xiaozhang*). See Hucker, *Dictionary of Official Titles*, p. 234.
29. The Taiping xingguo period figures may be found in Yue Shi, *Taiping huanyu ji* (Record of the Empire's Borders and Dimensions during the Taiping Period). The Yuanfeng period figures may be found in Wang Cun, *Yuanfeng jiuyu ji*. This information is cited in Huang Xianfan, *Nong Zhigao* (Nanning, 1983), p. 91.
30. These regional figures are cited in Huang Xianfan, *Zhuangzu tongshi* (Nanning, 1988), p. 52. The Song number is contained in Wang Cun's *Yuanfeng jiuyu ji*, while the Tang figure is available in the "geography" (*dili*) section of the New History of the Tang (*Xin Tangshu*) of Ouyang Xiu (1007–72). A graph in Huang's book (p. 53) offers a Song population figure of 387,723 households, which appears to be a mistake.
31. Fengshan county in this gazetteer entry was comprised of today's Donglan and Fengshan counties, located in northwestern Guangxi province. This information is cited in Huang Xianfan, *Nong Zhigao*, pp. 91–92.
32. Li Wenxiong may have been mistaken about Zhao Ding's participation. Zhao was a Song official, but he lived from 1085 to 1147.
33. Li Wenxiong, *Longjin xianzhi* (hand-etched rpr. Nanning, 1960), p. 39. Longjin county was the early-twentieth-century name for today's Longzhou county.
34. Wang Xiangzhi, *Yudi jisheng* in Huang Xianfan, *Zhuangzu tongshi*, p. 50.
35. Keith Taylor, "Madagascar in the Ancient Malayo-Polynesian Myths" in *Explorations in Early Southeast Asian History: The Origins of Southeast Asian Statecraft*, ed. Kenneth Hall and John Whitmore (Ann Arbor, 1976), p. 179.

36. Ngô Si Liên, *Đai Việt sử ký toàn Tập* IV. Quyển 3.2b. Chính Hòa thu' 18 (1697) ed. Vietnamese tr. and annot. Phan Huy Lê, Ngô Đức Tho and Hà Văn Tân (Hanoi, 1993), p. 129. Hereafter referred to as *DVSKTT*.
37. Phan Huy Chu, *Lịch triều hiến chương loại chí*. Tap 4. *Binh Che Chi*. (Hanoi, 1960–61), p. 5. *DVSKTT* (1993), 3.2b.
38. Wolters, *History, Culture, and Region*, pp. 113–14.
39. *DVSKTT* (1984), 3:242.
40. *DVSKTT* (1984), 3:242.
41. Yi Xingguang, *Yu Jing puzhuan zhilue* (Guangzhou, 1993), p. 78. Military officers of the military inspector rank were often used to patrol frontier regions, and these officials (including Yang) may have been in the area to train the local militia.
42. *SS*, 288.14068.
43. *DVSKTT* (1984), 3:242.
44. *SHY*, 197.7730.
45. *DVSKTT* (1984), 3:242.
46. *SHY*, 197.7730.
47. During the Tang and Song dynasties, the Chinese court granted this title to high officials at court who, along with their prescribed official duties, also participated in decision-making sessions as Grand Councilors. See Hucker, *Dictionary of Official Titles*, p. 554.
48. *SS*, 488.14068. Hucker notes that the title of administrative aide was granted in the Song to palace eunuchs assigned to special tasks outside of the imperial household. Lý Kế Tiên had earlier traveled to Kaifeng with Mai Cảnh Tiên, who had also been labeled with a title commonly granted to eunuchs at the Song court. The Vietnamese court in this period was not known to have employed eunuchs at court, and so this title reflects perhaps a Song scholarly inclination to label as eunuchs any rogue officials misappropriating court authority.
49. *SS*, 488.14068.
50. *XZZTJCB*, 203.4923.
51. *XZZTJCB*, 203.4923.
52. *SS*, 495.14218.
53. Shen Kua, *Mengxi bitan*, annot. Li Wenze and Wu Hongze (Chengdu, 1996), p. 347.
54. *SHY*, 197.7730.
55. *SHY*, 197.7730.
56. *SHY*, 197.7730–31.
57. Shen Kua, *Mengxi bitan quanyi*, p. 347.
58. *SS*, 14.272.
59. *XZZTJCB*, 228.
60. *XZZTJCB*, 228.
61. *SHY*, 197.7731.
62. Lý Can Đức would be known posthumously as Lý Nhân Tông.
63. Anon., *Việt Sử Lược*, annot., Chen Chinghe (Tokyo, 1987) 2:61.
64. Anon., *Việt Sử Lược*, annot., Qian Xizuo (Taibei, 1968), p. 38.
65. Peter K. Bol, "Government, Society and State: On the Political Visions of Ssuma Kuang and Wang An-shih" in *Ordering the World: Approaches to State and Society in Sung Dynasty China*, ed. Robert P. Hymes and Conrad Schirokauer (Berkeley, 1993), p. 186.
66. Paul Jakov Smith, "Introduction," draft chapter, in *The Cambridge History of China*, vol. 5, part 1: *The Sung Dynasty and Its Precursors, 906–1279*, ed. Denis C. Twitchett and Paul Jakov Smith (Cambridge, forthcoming), p. 24.

67. Huang Xianfan, *Nong Zhigao*, p. 101.
68. *SS*, 471.13712, 494.14189–90. Smith, "Introduction," pp. 22–23.
69. Paul J. Smith, "State Power and Economic Activism during the New Policies, 1068–1085: The Tea and Horse Trade and the 'Green Sprouts' Loan Policy" in *Ordering the World*, ed. Hymes and Schirokauer, p. 110.
70. Peter K. Bol, "Government, Society and State," p. 168.
71. Wang Anshi, "Chibang Jiaozhi" in *Wang Wengong wenji* (Shanghai, 1974), 1:108–9.
72. *SS*, 15.288.
73. The "Five Clans" included the Long Fan, Fang Fan, Zhang Fan, Shi Fan, and the Luo Fan. Their home region would be located near modern Guilin. Cited in *SS*, 496.14241.
74. *SS*, 496.14241.
75. *DVSKTT* (1993), 3.8. *SS*, 334.10728. Shen had had experience training frontier militia elsewhere in the empire, and Liu was known to the court for his book Methods of Distinguishing the Orthodox from the Heterodox (*Zhengsu fang*), in which the scholar-official described a strategy for encouraging common people to turn from local practices to court-sanctioned ways.
76. Le Thanh Khoi, *Histoire du Viet Nam: des origines à 1858* (Paris, 1981), p. 159.
77. Guwan prefecture's location is not easily determined. The Taiping garrison was located in Thât Khê prefecture in modern-day northern Cao Bằng. The Yongping garrison was located between Siming prefecture and Môn Châu or modern-day Na Cham. The Qianlong garrison was located at modern-day Shangsi county in southern Guangxi.
78. *DVSKTT* (1993), 3.8b.
79. Le Thanh Khoi, *Histoire du Viet Nam*, p. 159.
80. Phan Huy Chú, *Lịch triều hiến chương loại chí*. Tập II. Nhân Vật Chí, 2b.
81. *SS*, 446.13157.
82. *DVSKTT* (1993), 3.8b.
83. *SS*, 15.290.
84. Phan Huy Chú *Lịch triều hiến chương loại chí*, 2b. See also *SS*, 15.290. The compilers of the *SS*'s "Basic Annals" (*benji*) appear to believe that Thường Kiệt's name was Lý Hiến.
85. *SS*, 303.10051.
86. *SS*, 334.10736.
87. *XZZTJCB*, 279.6831.
88. *XZZTJCB*, 279.6843.
89. Hoàng Xuân Hãn, *Lý Thường Kiệt*, p. 285.
90. Ibid., p. 285.
91. The Vietnamese text reads: "Nam quốc sơn hà Nam đế cư, Tiệt nhiên định phân tại thiên thư, Như hà nghịch lỗ lai xâm pham, Nhữ đẳng hành khan thủ bại hư." Cited in Editorial Board of the Institute of Literature in the Committee for the Social Sciences of Viet Nam. *Tho van Ly-Tran* (Hanoi, 1977–88), p. 321.
92. *DVSKTT* (1993), 3.9b.
93. Hoàng Xuân Hãn, *Lý Thường Kiệt*, p. 291.
94. *SS*, 334.10736.
95. Li Tao, *Xu Zizhi tongjian changbian* (Taibei, 1961), 297.15.
96. *DVSKTT* (1984), 3:251.
97. *SS*, 15.297.

98. *DVSKTT* (1993), 3.11.
99. Lê Văn Hưu, *Đại Việt Sử Ký* (Hanoi, n.d.), A. 1272/1, p. 140.
100. Hoàng Xuân Hãn, *Lý Thường Kiệt*, p. 338.
101. *SS*, 334.10732.
102. *SS*, 488.14069.
103. *SS*, 488.14069.
104. According to the legend on the Ming edition of this map, the "lost" southwestern prefectures include Giao, Phong, Nhương, Nghiêm, Điền, Ái, Hoan, Lục, Phúc Lộc, Trường, Việt, Ôn, Diễn, Lâm, Cảnh, Hoàn, Bình, Cầm, Sơn, and Vũ An. The home region of Nùng Trí Cao, Quảng Nguyên, has been placed back within Song territory. For a useful source on Vietnamese historical geography, see Nguyễn Văn Siêu, *Đại Việt địa dư toàn biên* (Hanoi, 1997).
105. See Le Thanh Khoi, *Histoire du Viet Nam*, p. 158.
106. Okada Koji, *Chûgoku kanan minzoku shakaishi kenkyu* (Tokyo, 1993), p. 246.
107. Okada, *Chûgoku kanan minzoku shakaishi kenkyu*, p. 249.
108. Okada, *Chûgoku kanan minzoku shakaishi kenkyu*, p. 20.
109. Okada, *Chûgoku kanan minzoku shakaishi kenkyu*, p. 20.
110. Okada, *Chûgoku kanan minzoku shakaishi kenkyu*, p. 20.
111. *SS*, 488.14069.

Glossary

Ái 愛
anfu shi 安撫使
anfu si 安撫司
Annandao zhaotaoshi 安南道招討使
Bảo Lạc 保樂
Bảo Thắng 保勝
bát ải 八隘
Benchao huawai zhoujun tu 本朝化外州郡圖
benji 本紀
Bi Gia Dụ 費嘉祐
binh bộ thị lang 兵部侍郎
Bình 平
Binzhou 賓州
Bổng Thánh 棒聖
Cầm 笒
Cảnh 景
Cheng Zhuo 成卓
Chongning 崇寧
Cơ Lang 機郎
Đại Cồ Việt 大瞿越
Đại Việt 大越
dajiangjun wei youqianniu 大將軍為右千牛
Di Qing 狄青
dili 地理
Diễn 演
Điền 田

Đinh Bộ Lĩnh 丁部領
đô hộ phủ 都護府
dongjiang 洞將
Donglan 東蘭
duda tiju chama si 都大提舉茶馬司
dudu 都督
Dương Cảnh Thông 楊景通
dutou 都頭
duzhijunshi 都指揮使
Fang Fan 方著
Fengshan 風山
Fengshan xianzhi 風山縣志
gan 贛
Giao Chỉ 交趾
Giap Đồng 甲峒
guanke 官客
Guangxi 廣西
Guihua 歸化
Guilin 桂林
Guizhou 桂州
Guo Kui 郭逵
Guwan 古萬
Guwu 古勿
Han 漢
Hengzhou 橫州
Hoan 驩
Hoàn 環
Hoàng Trọng Khanh 黃仲卿
Hurun 湖潤
Hua Xia 華夏
Hùng Lược 雄略
jimi 羈縻
jia 甲
jiatou 甲頭
jiazhang 甲長
Jiangxi 江西
jinglueshi 經略使
Jingxi 靖西
Kaifeng 開封
Khai Hoàng 開皇
Khúc Thừa Mỹ 曲承美
Kunlun guan 崑崙關
Lâm 林
Lạng Châu 諒州
Lê Hoàn 黎桓
Lê Mạo 黎貌
Lê Van Thình 黎文盛
Li Wenxiong 李文雄

Lianzhou 廉州
Liệu Thông 廖通
Liu Gong 劉龔
Liu Yi 劉䶮
Liu Yin 劉隱
Liuzhou 柳州
Long Dực 龍翼
Long Fan 龍蕃
Longjin xianzhi 龍僅縣志
Longzhou 龍州
Lư Báo 盧豹
Lu Shen 陸詵
Lục 陸
Luo Fan 羅蕃
Lưu Ký 劉紀
Lý 李
Lý Can Đức 李乾德
Lý Hiến 李憲
Lý Kế Tiên 李繼先
Lý Nhân Tông 李仁宗
Lý Nhật Tôn 李日尊
Lý Phật Mã 李佛瑪
Lý Thường Kiệt 李常傑
Mai Cảnh Tiên 梅景先
manzei 蠻賊
Mengxi bitan 夢溪筆談
Miao 苗
min 閩
Ming 明
Môn Châu 門州
nandu 南度
Nanjiao 南交
nanping wang 南平王
neifu 內附
Nghiêm 嚴
Ngự Long 馭龍
Nguy Trọng Hòa 魏仲和
Như Nguyệt 如月
Nhương 瀼
Nùng Binh 儂兵
Nùng Hạ Khanh 儂夏卿
Nùng Lượng 儂亮
Nùng Nhật Tân 儂日新
Nùng Tông Đán 儂宗旦
Nùng Trí Cao (Nong Zhigao 儂智高)
Nùng Trí Hội 儂智會
Nùng Trí Xuân 儂智春
Okada Koji 岡田宏二

Ôn 溫
Ouyang Xiu 歐陽修
Phong 峰
Phúc Lộc 福祿
Pin Jiaozhi xiang, que shi Guangyuan jin 貧交趾象, 卻失廣源金
qiangjie 強界
Qianlong 遷隆
Qianzhou 虔州
qihao 旗號
Qinzhou 欽州
Quang Lang 桄榔
Quảng Nguyên 廣源
qumiyuan 樞密院
Quyết Lý 決裡
Renzong 仁宗
Rongan 融安
Rongzhou 融州
Ruan Yuan 阮元
Shangshu 尚書
Shangsi 上思
Shen Kuo 沈括
Shen Qi 沈起
Shenzong 神宗
Shi Fan 石蕃
Shiliu zhou 十六州
Shun'anzhou 順安州
Shunzhou 順州
Sichuan 四川
Siming 思明
Sơn 山
Songshi 宋史
Su Jian 蘇緘
Susang 宿桑
Taiping 太平
Taiping huanyu ji 太平寰宇記
Tao Bi 陶弼
Temo 特磨
thái bảo 太保
thái úy 太尉
Thần Điện 神電
Thăng Long 升龍
Thiên Đức 天德
tianzi jun 天子軍
Tô Mậu Châu 蘇茂州
tongzhong shumen xiaping zhangshi 同中書門下平章事
Trường 長
Trương Hát 張喝

tù 囚
Tư Lang Châu 思琅州
tuding 土丁
Vạn Tiệp 萬捷
Việt Sử Lược 越史略
Việt 越
Vũ An 武安
Vũ Thắng 武勝
waiyi 外夷
Wang Anshi 王安石
Wang Han 王罕
Wang Wengong wenji 王文公文集
Wang Xiangzhi 王象之
Wenmen dong 溫悶洞
Wenshan 文山
wu xingfan 五姓蕃
Wuyang 勿陽
wuzong jiangjun 武總將軍
xiang 湘
Xiangzhou 象州
Xiao Gu 蕭固
xiaozhang 校長
xinfa 新法
xingbu langzhong 刑部郎中
Xiong Ben 熊本
xunjian 巡檢
Ỷ Lan 倚蘭
Yang Baocai 楊保材
Yizhou 宜州
Yingzong 英宗
Yongping 永平
Yongzhou 邕州
you qianniu weijiangjun 右千牛衛將軍
Yu Jing 余靖
Yudi jisheng 輿地紀勝
yue 粵
Yue Shi 樂史
Zhang Fan 張蕃
Zhang Shoujie 張守節
Zhang Tian 張田
Zhao Di 趙諦
Zhao Ding 趙鼎
Zhao Shu 趙署
Zhao Xu 趙頊
Zhengsu fang 正俗方
zhijunshi 指揮使
zhongyuan 中原

zhuanyunshi 轉運使
zuo qianniu weijiangjun 左千牛衛將軍
Zuoyou jiang 左右江

Bibliography

Anderson, James A. *The Rebel Den of Nùng Trí Cao: Loyalty and Identity along the Sino-Vietnamese Frontier*. Seattle: University of Washington Press; Singapore: National Singapore University Press, 2007.
Anon. *Việt Sử Lược* 越史略 [A Survey of the History of Việt], annot., Qian Xizuo 錢熙祚. Taibei: Guangwen shuju, 1968.
———. *Việt Sử Lược* 越史略 [A Survey of the History of Việt], annot., Chen Chinghe 陳景河. Tokyo: Soka University, 1987.
Barlow, Jeffery G. *The Zhuang* [online]. Pacific University, 2000. Available online at http://mcel.pacificu.edu/as/resources/zhuang/zhuang8.htm. Last accessed December 10, 2007.
Bế Viết Đẳng. *Các dân tộc Tây, Nùng ở Vietnam* [Tay and Nung Nationalities in Vietnam]. Hanoi, Vietnam: Viên khoa học xả hội Việt Nam, Viên dân tộc học, 1992.
Bol, Peter K. "Government, Society and State: On the Political Visions of Ssu-ma Kuang and Wang An-shih." In *Ordering the World: Approaches to State and Society in Sung Dynasty China*, ed. Robert P. Hymes and Conrad Schirokauer. Studies on China 16. Berkeley: University of California Press, 1993.
Editorial Board of the Institute of Literature in the Committee for the Social Sciences of Viet Nam. *Thơ Văn Lý Trần* [Poetry and Prose of the Lý and Trần Dynasties]. Hanoi, Vietnam: Khoa học Xã hội, 1977–88.
Hà Văn Thư and Lã Văn Lô. *Văn hóa Tày Nùng* [Tay and Nung Cultures]. Hanoi: Nhà Xuất Bản Văn hóa, 1984.
Hall, Kenneth and John Whitmore. *Explorations in Early Southeast Asian History: The Origins of Southeast Asian Statecraft*. Ann Arbor: Michigan Papers on South and Southeast Asia, 11, 1976.
Hevia, James L. *Cherishing Men from Afar: Qing Guest Ritual and the Macartney Embassy of 1793*. Durham, NC: Duke University Press, 1995.
Hoàng Xuân Hãn. *Lý Thường Kiệt: Lịch Sử Ngoại Giao Trều Lý*. [Lý Thường Kiệt: A History of Ly Foreign Relations], Hanoi: Sông Nhị, 1949.
Huang Xianfan 黄現璠. *Nong Zhigao* 儂智高 [Nong Zhigao]. Nanning: Guangxi renmin chubanshe, 1983.
———. *Zhuangzu tongshi* 狀族通史 [Survey of Zhuang History]. Nanning: Guangxi minzu, 1988.
Hucker, Charles O. *A Dictionary of Official Titles in Imperial China*. Stanford: Stanford University Press, 1985.
Lê Đình Sỹ. *Kế sách giữ nước thời Lý-Trần* [Means of National Defense in the Ly-Tran period]. Hanoi: Chính trị quốc gia, 1994.
Le Thanh Khoi. *Histoire du Viet Nam*. Paris: Sudestasie, 1981.
Lê Văn Hưu. *Đại Việt Sử Ký* 大越史記 [History of the Great Viet]. Hanoi: Viên Hán Nôm ms., A. 1272/1.
Li Tao 李燾. *Xu Zizhi tongjian changbian* 續資治通鑑長編 [Collected Data for the Continuation of the Comprehensive Mirror for Aid in Government]. Taibei: Shijie shuju, 1961.

———. *Xu Zizhi tongjian changbian* 續資治通鑑長編 [Collected Data for the Continuation of the Comprehensive Mirror for Aid in Government]. Beijing: Zhonghua shuju, 1985.

Li Wenxiong 李文雄. *Longjin xianzhi* 龍津縣志 [Record of Longjin County]. Minguo 35 (1946). Hand-etched rpr. Nanning: Guangxi #2 Provincial Library, 1960.

Ngô Si Liên. *Đại Việt Sử Ký toan thư* 大越史記全書 [Complete History of the Great Viet]. 1697 Woodblock Edn. Hanoi, Vietnam: Nhà Xuất Bản Khoa Học Xã Hội, 1993.

Nguyễn Ngọc Huy. *The Le Code: Law in Traditional Vietnam: A Comparative Sino-Vietnamese Legal Study with Historical-Juridical Analysis and Annotations*, vol. 1. 3 vols. Athens: Ohio University Press, 1987.

Nguyễn Văn Siêu. *Đại Việt địa dư toàn biên* [Complete Atlas of the Đại Việt Kingdom]. Hanoi Viên sử học: Văn hóa, 1997.

Okada Koji 岡田宏二. *Chûgoku kanan minzoku shakaishi kenkyu* 中国華南民族社会史研究 [Studies of the Ethnic and Social History of South China]. Tokyo: Kyuko Shoin, 1993.

Pelley, Patricia. " 'Barbarians' and 'Younger Brothers': The Remaking of Race in Postcolonial Vietnam." *Journal of Southeast Asian Studies* 29.2 (Sept. 1998):374–91.

Phan Huy Chú 潘輝注 (1782–1840). *Lịch triều hiến chương loại chí* 歷朝憲章類誌 [Encyclopedia of Institutions from Successive Courts]. Saigon, Vietnam: Phủ Quốc vụ khanh đặc trách văn hóa, 1972.

Phan Huy Lê. "Nùng Trí Cao Nhân Vật Lịch Sử và Biểu Tương Văn Hóa" [Nùng Trí Cao as Historical Figure and Cultural Phenomenon]. In *Nùng Trí Cao: kỷ yếu hội thảo khoa học* [Nùng Trí Cao: annals of a meeting for scientific study], ed. Trần Văn Phượng. Cao Bằng: Sở Văn hóa thông tin, 1995.

Ruan Yuan 阮元. *Shisan jing zhu* 十三經注 [Annotated Edition of the Thirteen Classics]. Beijing: Zhonghua shuju, 1980.

Shen Kua. 沈 括. *Mengxi bitan* 夢溪筆談 [Notes from Dream Brook]. In *Wenbai duizhao Mengxi bitan quanyi* 文白對照夢溪筆談全譯 [Complete Classical-Colloquial Rendition of Notes from Dream Brook], annot. Li Wenze 李文澤 and Wu Hongze 吳洪澤. Chengdu: Ba Shu shushe, 1996.

Smith, Paul J. "State Power and Economic Activism during the New Policies, 1068-1085: The Tea and Horse Trade and the 'Green Sprouts' Loan Policy." In *Ordering the World: Approaches to State and Society in Sung Dynasty China*, ed. Robert P. Hymes and Conrad Schirokauer. Studies on China 16. Berkeley: University of California, 1993.

Smith, Paul J. "Introduction." Draft chapter for *The Cambridge History of China Vol. 5, Part 1: The Sung Dynasty and Its Precursors, 906–1279*, ed. Denis C. Twitchett and Paul Jakov Smith. Cambridge: Cambridge University Press, forthcoming.

Taylor, Keith. "Madagascar in the Ancient Malayo-Polynesian Myths." In *Explorations in Early Southeast Asian History: The Origins of Southeast Asian Statecraft*, ed. Kenneth Hall and John Whitmore. Ann Arbor: Michigan Papers on South and Southeast Asia, 11, 1976.

Toghto [Tuotuo] 脫脫. *Songshi* 宋史 [Official History of the Song Dynasty]. Beijing: Zhonghua shuju, 1983.

Trần Trọng Kim. *Vietnam Sử Lược* [Survey History of Vietnam], vol. 1. 2 vols. rpr. Glendale, CA: Đại Nam Pub., 1982.

Wang Anshi 王安石. "Chibang Jiaozhi" 敕牓交趾 [An Official Statement concerning Jiaozhi]. In *Wang Wengong wenji* 王文公文集 [Writings of Wang Wengong]. 2 vols. Shanghai: Shanghai renmin chubanshe, 1974.

Wang Xiangzhi 王象之. *Yudi jisheng* 與地紀勝 [A Record of This Region's Merits]. In Huang Xianfan, *Zhuangzu tongshi*. Nanning: Guangxi minzu, 1988.

Wolters, O.W. *History, Culture, and Region in Southeast Asian Perspectives* (Ithaca, NY: Southeast Asia Program, Cornell University; in cooperation with Singapore: Institute of Southeast Asian Studies, 1999).

Xu Song 徐松. *Song huiyao jiben* 宋會要輯本 [Draft of Documents Pertaining to Song Official Matters]. 1809 edn. Taibei: Shijie shuju, 1964.

Yi Xingguang 易行廣. *Yu Jing puzhuan zhilue* 余靖譜傳誌略 [Biographical Chronological Outline of Yu Jing]. Guangzhou: Jinan daxue, 1993.

CHAPTER 8

FROM BATTLEFIELDS TO COUNTIES: WAR, BORDER, AND STATE POWER IN SOUTHERN SONG HUAINAN

Ruth Mostern

Beginning in 1128, troops from the state of Jin, who had recently toppled the Song capital at Kaifeng, invaded the circuits of Huainan in an attempt to eradicate the remnant state to the south. In the early 1130s, a Song counteroffensive was staged from the same region. Fighting was fierce in Huainan, and the effects of the battles were devastating. The two circuits of Huainan East and West (Huainan dong; Huainan xi), with a combined population of more than 1 million households in 1102, had only about 150,000 households in 1162. Even a century after the Jin invasion, the population had rebounded to only one-third of its prewar level. Huainan was a "real" battlefield in the twelfth century. By the time the Song and the Jin signed a peace treaty in 1142, Huainan, once some 500 miles from the nearest interstate border, had become a frontier province.

This chapter chronicles the emergence of a new role for this devastated border region. In particular, how did the court govern a region that had been so thoroughly ravaged? How did the remaining population respond to attempts by the state to restore authority and extract tax revenue? The capacity of the region to provide funds for state activities was uncertain, and sovereign control was in doubt. Indeed there was initially no way to know whether this land was even going to be a part of the Song Empire. In this atmosphere, in the twelfth century, how did the court, local and regional officials, and locally and regionally powerful residents manage the organization of territory and allow Huainan to function as a frontier for the first time?

Space, War, and Empire in the Song

My point of entry for answering these questions is to examine Huainan's political geography. In the Song era, manipulating the number and the distribution of counties (*xian*) and prefectures (*zhou, fu, jun,* and *jian*) allowed the court to regulate the circulation of revenue and personnel that served as the foundation of imperial control over the realm.[1] In Huainan, these procedures turned the two provinces of Huainan from civil into military space. Counties were required to remit a set quota of commercial, alcohol monopoly, and land taxes to both the prefecture and the circuit (*lu*) in which they were located.[2] In addition, they were sometimes also required to contribute to supporting troops billeted in their territory—either in kind, or by allowing agricultural land in the county to be used as state farms (*tuntian*).[3] In times and regions of rising commercial activity, tax receipts could be quite significant, and surplus beyond the state quotas was considerable. Yet, on frontiers, which were often regions that were impoverished or sparsely populated, or prosperous regions that had suffered from wars or environmental disasters that interrupted harvests and commerce, local taxes were often insufficient to meet local needs. When local resources had to be used to support locally stationed troops, the burden was exacerbated further.[4] Nevertheless, the quota of receipts to the prefecture was not normally eased in these cases, nor was relief or subsidy from the prefecture, circuit, or court generally available. Fiscally autarkic, counties were on their own when it came to managing both surplus and deficit.[5]

One of the main demands on the prefectural revenue assembled from county taxes was for defense funding. Prefectures paid the salaries of troops stationed within their borders. They also paid for armies stationed in border garrisons in their regions. For instance, during the Northern Song (960–1126), prefectures in the northwest and Sichuan were required to send tax revenue to armies on the frontier, but prefectures in the south were not. Prefectures, like counties, had extremely unequal resources, and yet, all were required to fund local activities from local sources. Many prefectures were unable to sustain their financial role, especially as the places with the highest military expenses often had among the lowest tax revenues. In many regions of the empire, prefectures were frequently in deficit.[6] In the mid-eleventh century, on the remote yet strategically essential Northern Song Shaanxi frontier discussed by Michael McGrath in this volume (chapter 6), prefectures were established and abolished frequently as court officials weighed insolvent populations against military imperatives.[7]

Even when foreign invasion was at stake, there was a contradiction between the ideal of centralization and the reality of local fiscal autonomy. Territories along interstate borders, which were of the greatest strategic importance to the state, maintained large numbers of troops, on marginal land, with small local populations. They were often the territories least equipped to play their designated role. Defensive troops were strictly associated with administrative regions. In the mid-1040s, one commentator attributed the Song defeat by Xi Xia to the fact that troops stationed along the border had not been permitted to cross prefectural boundaries, and were too dispersed to withstand Xia cavalry attacks. Song China was a centralized bureaucratic empire, with fiscally autonomous local government units. The way that the court resolved the contradiction at the core of its field administration was to regularly increase and decrease the number of counties and prefectures as conditions required. Early Southern Song Huainan was one time and place where field administration became untenable in a way that necessitated that response. When the empire became relatively stable once again after the 1142 peace treaty, Huainan had become a frontier province, and its spatial organization evolved in accordance with its new functions.

Counties and prefectures were sustainable only when their tax revenue was adequate. That is, they required a large enough number of residents, sufficiently compliant with demands from the state, to tender surplus grain, cash, or labor to support imperial authority. When these conditions were not met, jurisdictions could be abolished. At the same time, when events like war and rebellion called for a more significant civil or military administration and a more dense state presence, new administrative units had to be created to anchor state activities. War called the integrity of the empire into question in the Song, both because of invasion itself and also because it challenged the fiscal assumptions on which territorial administration rested. The case of Southern Song Huainan illustrates both of those outcomes.

Battlefronts such as Huainan's met criteria both for increasing and for reducing jurisdictions. On the one hand, as populations contracted during and after the war, counties and prefectures full of troops were unable to meet tax obligations. According to standard Song practice, they ought to be abolished. On the other hand, the numerous soldiers and civil officials dispersed along the Song-Jin frontier required administrative homes in existing or new jurisdictions.[8] The war threw Huainan into the jaws of this contradiction, and as a result, its Southern Song spatial organization was unstable for some time.

Political Economy and Geography in Huainan before the Southern Song

Throughout the Northern Song era (960–1127), Huainan was far away from the frontier. It was among those parts of the empire with a significant and rising agricultural and trade surplus. Grain and money remitted to the court from Huainan helped to underwrite costs such as those incurred in combating the Xi Xia in the 1040s and extending the presence of the state on its southwestern perimeter in Hunan and Sichuan. According to the description in the geography monograph in the Song History (*Songshi*), Huainan stretched east to the sea, west to the Huan River (Huan he), south to the Bin and the Yangzi, and north to the Qing and the Huai rivers. It produced tea, salt, silk, and other cloth as well as grain.

It was also strategically located between the capital and the borders in the north, and the centers of commerce and agricultural productivity in the south. Two prefectures were designated as "powerful jurisdictions" (*juzhen*)—Yang and Shou. Key transportation routes bisected many additional prefectures. These included even the Grand Canal, which carried grain and other commodities from the southern rice producing regions to the north.[9] Huainan's devastation in the twelfth century was a loss to the stability, security, and wealth of Song China, and it was a prize contended for between Song and the Jürchen Jin throughout their hostilities.

Eastern Huainan, of the "water margin" fame from Chinese literary history, was historically a region full of marshes. Beginning before the Song, wetlands were drained for fields and water was guided into canals.[10] During the Northern Song, government policy, advances in hydraulic technology, and population growth all supported significant construction of polders and levees.[11] Contemporary historical economic geographer Cheng Minsheng describes the significant features of Huainan in the Song. The land was fertile, and the capacity for irrigation was excellent. Pisciculture was well developed in regions that remained too marshy or saline to support agriculture, and the level of productivity was high. In the 1070s, irrigation initiatives in Yang prefecture elevated agricultural productivity by an order of magnitude.[12] Huainan's water resources were exploited not only for irrigation but also for transportation. The canal system was extensive and highly developed. Huainan was a commercialized area of the empire highly integrated with regional economies in both the north and in the southeast. The marshy, eastern, coastal part of Huainan had a highly advanced salt industry; the eastern prefectures of Yang, Tong, and Lianshui were the center of salt production for the entire empire. During the course of the Northern Song, dike-building and swamp-draining initiatives allowed saline land in the east to be claimed for agriculture as well, and populations and incomes rose.[13] As Southern Song commentator Sun Yingshi (1154–1206) remarked, "In times of peace, Huainan's flourishing beauty (*shengli*) is first in the realm."[14]

War, Politics, and Territory in Southern Song Huainan

In 1127, the newly risen Jürchen state of Jin toppled the city of Kaifeng, the capital of the Chinese Song dynasty for more than 150 years. The emperor and his lately abdicated father were captured and marched to Manchuria with their ladies and courtiers, and the remnants of the Song court fled south. They finally established a new capital at Lin'an (now modern Hangzhou), south of the Yangzi River and over a thousand miles from Kaifeng, in 1138.

The late 1120s and 1130s saw offensive and counteroffensive as the Jin armies tried repeatedly to gain a strategic foothold in South China, and the Song tried to establish a defensible boundary. Following several major battles and almost incessant skirmishing, an 1142 treaty set the boundary at the Huai River. Though the peace was interrupted twice, by a Jin invasion in 1161 and a Song invasion in 1205, the border held until the fall of the Southern Song to the Mongol Yuan dynasty in 1276.

The battles were devastating. Observers of that period write of cities and monasteries laid waste, fields and villages abandoned, dikes breached and valleys flooded, and census and taxation records lost forever. The most sustained fighting of the war occurred in Huainan East and West. Huainan's traditional role as a conduit between northern and southern China, which had been largely responsible for its prosperity, was now its undoing. The regional metropolis of Yang prefecture alone was lost and recaptured five times during the Southern Song, and a number of other prefectural seats—Chu[1], Tong, Gaoyou, Huaiyuan, and others—met similar fates.

Huainan was destroyed in the wars of the late 1120s and early 1130s. Most of its fields, polders, and dikes were ruined, and most of the population that survived the battles fled to other regions of the empire. When Kaifeng fell, Song troops retreated with Jin troops in pursuit, crossing the Huai River and the plains between the Huai and the Yangzi. The emperor and his court took refuge in Huainan's Yang prefecture on the Grand Canal in 1128, but, besieged there, abandoned it for Hang prefecture further south in Liangzhe the following year. Huainan rice was banned from export to other regions of China, lest this diminish vital military resources available for armies there.[15]

Both sides were menaces to the remaining Huainan population. Song troops pillaged the countryside for provisions; Jin troops looted and burned the prefectural and county seats and other towns as they passed through them. In 1129, Jin efforts to topple the court in its third southern refuge, Jiankang (modern Nanjing), in Jiangnan, precipitated the dispatching of flanking forces east and west through the Huainan circuits to reach the Yangzi. As the troops passed through Huainan, they attacked Shou, Chu[1], Lu, He, and Wuwei prefectures to the west of Jiankang, and Zhen prefecture to the east. Subsequent engagements focused on the wealthy Huainan prefectural seats where the Grand Canal met the Huai River in the north and the Yangzi in the south: Chu[2] and Yang.[16] Lawless retreating Song troops ravaged the land as much as the Jin troops did, and Song commanders broke dikes and flooded fields in an attempt to slow the Jin onslaught.[17]

The extent of the destruction was remarkable. Waves of people fled to central China; others were killed by troops or died in the famines and epidemics that followed in their wake.[18] The population of Huainan East, 324,193 households in 1102, dropped to 110,897 at the time of the next census in 1162. The population of Huainan West declined by 92.5 percent, from 700,174 to 52,174 households.[19] The staff size of counties was pegged to population and tax revenue. A demographic crisis like the one the Jin wars engendered wreaked havoc on a system designed according to such principles.

During the battles and their aftermath, as Huainan devolved into a frontier region, the process of founding, abolishing, and transferring territories became an important tool in the Song statecraft arsenal. Even excluding cases in which whole jurisdictions were captured by one side or another, there were more than fifty instances of territorial change in Huainan over the course of the Southern Song. Indeed, about a third of all territorial changes in the empire during the Southern Song were in Huainan, and this situation very much reflects the position of this emerging frontier territory as the epicenter of the war.

Why did the court prioritize the drawing and redrawing of the domestic political landscape during this time of upheaval? Effectively managing the map of the empire was a key to successful field administration in the Song. Let us consider that counties and prefectures were likely to be created at times and in places of acute military conflict in order to serve as containers for the staffing and funding necessary to support large armies. However, the geographical system presumed that they would be abolished in the aftermath of fighting when, having lost population by the tens of thousands to flight, disease, conscription, massacre, or famine, there was no tax revenue to support a local government, and no offices available for such a government to perform. The system was inherently unstable because these two impulses were contradictory.

Thus, many territorial changes on the Huainan battlefields in the early Southern Song were never intended to be permanent. A large number of the field reports suggesting territorial changes, and court edicts ordering them, explicitly call for changes to be reversed as soon as conditions permitted. These "conditional" (*quan*) abolitions evolved as a solution to turmoil in the size of population and harvests, allowing counties and prefectures to be abolished when they were fiscally unsustainable, and then reestablished as soon as conditions permitted.

The use of temporary abolition as a rhetorical and administrative tactic was new in the Southern Song. Although territories had been abolished and subsequently reestablished before, especially at the end of the Northern Song, it had been a result of factional disputes and policy reversals. In the Southern Song, by contrast, the intention to reestablish territories was explicitly stated in the same edicts that called for their abolition. Territories were abolished after battles, and slated for reestablishment when circumstances permitted.[20]

Officials who wished to propose the temporary abolition of devastated counties and prefectures deployed the concept of *quan*. In this charged atmosphere, territories switched hands rapidly and frequently. Those that remained in Song hands in the wake of devastating battles were often left with little resident population, little land under cultivation, and inadequate infrastructure for the delivery of taxes or the provision of government services. The use of *quan*, a statecraft keyword with classical origins, may have helped early Southern Song planners to justify politically difficult abolitions when counties and prefectures could no longer support themselves. As places were reestablished, this policy also allowed Huainan to emerge as a stable frontier region, in much the same way as the Hebei waterworks and Shaanxi garrisons discussed in this volume did on the northern frontier.

From Battlefield to Borderland: A Provisional Landscape for Huainan

This section of the chapter examines the changes in spatial organization that began to transform Huainan from a wealthy domestic province of the empire into a frontier during the 1130s and 1140s. According to the Song History, there were a total of thirty changes in the distribution of counties and prefectures in Huainan between 1127 and 1142. Four prefectures fell to Jin at the beginning of the

Southern Song. Of these, three were regained prior to 1142. In addition to the thirty changes noted in the Song History, the Drafted Documents on Song State Matters (*Song huiyao jigao*) preserves a number of documents concerning additional changes that lasted only a short time and that were not recorded in the official Song History. Jurisdictions were abolished and reestablished at such a rapid pace that, as one late-eighteenth-century geographer complained, the canonical Song guides to administrative jurisdictions, the Song History and the General Investigation on Important Writings (*Wenxian tongkao*), had errors, inconsistencies, and elisions in their geographical records of the most volatile places in the early Southern Song.[21] The documents themselves—edicts from the court commanding abolitions across the region, as well as memorials from local officials—all explain that short-term abolitions were a response to the demographic collapse engendered by fighting and looting in the heartland of the empire. The court temporarily abolished counties and prefectures in an attempt to manage sudden and calamitous changes in the circumstances of jurisdictions that were supposed to be self-supporting, under conditions of local pressure and limited information.

At first, the territorial changes in Huainan, which began when the court was based at Yang prefecture in 1127–28, served to make the presence of the state on this new frontier denser. Yang's Jiangdu county was split in half to form two new counties, Guangling and Taixing, creating more jurisdictions close to the new court.[22] The same year, Yang prefecture, where the court was situated, and Lu, adjacent to it, were made into commandery prefectures (*shuaifu*), prefectures with added military authority.[23] Yizhen prefecture (later known as Zhen), west of Yang, was changed from civil *zhou* status to military *jun*.[24] Shanyang county, in Chu[2] prefecture, on the Grand Canal just south of the Huai River, was made into Huai'an prefecture.[25] This earliest phase of territorial change in Huainan, before the 1131 Jin invasion, laid the foundation for a permanent court at Yang. It increased the military presence in Huainan by increasing the number of prefectures, which commanded their own troops and military officers.[26] In addition, several Huainan jurisdictions were traded back and forth between Song and Jin in 1131 as Jin assaults on Song territory increased.[27]

As the war continued, Huainan's formerly domestic territories became a frontier. The circumstances of Huainan's border prefectures were similar in some ways to those of late Tang Lulong, discussed in this volume by David Graff (chapter 2), as locally powerful individuals and the court negotiated differing ideas about frontier policy. Locally powerful resident patrons, not just court officials, played a role in determining the spatial organization of the new Huainan frontier. One such case occurred in Zhaoxin county, which had been in the jurisdiction of Si prefecture. During the Northern Song, Si was a fairly large prefecture, with a population of 53,965 households in the 1070s.[28] However, Si was split in half by the war, when the part of its territory that lay north of the Huai River fell under Jin control. In 1131, Zhaoxin was moved out of the truncated Si prefecture and into the adjacent Hao prefecture based on a petition by the acting county magistrate (*zhixian*), Liu Gang (d. 1160), a native of Zhaoxin.

Liu Gang's 1131 petition offers a rare look into the details of the relationship between war, population movement, territory, and personnel politics. During this tumultuous time, in violation of conventional regulations forbidding officials from serving in their home jurisdictions, Liu led a state-recognized militia, and also ran the civil administration of Zhaoxin.[29] He explained that, at the direction of the court, he had commanded 10,000 troops, most of them locals (*turen*) of Zhaoxin county. After the northern half of Si fell to the Jin and its remaining counties were placed under the jurisdiction of a new special administrative district (*zhenfu*), the troops that had been under his personal command were to have been dispersed far from home to Chu[1] and Hao prefectures. Liu Gang pleaded with the court on behalf of his men, "who yearn to return to the [previous] situation" (*si gui shi*), to move the county out of the jurisdiction of the Si prefecture special district, and into the adjacent Hao prefecture to the west, so that the deployment of his troops would not be subject to the commands of the new special district.[30] The minister (*shangshu*), a high level administrator who answered directly to the emperor, responded personally to Liu Gang's complaint. He recommended: "Liu Gang has lived in Zhaoxin for a long time, and it is fitting for him to manage the divisions and jurisdictions [of territory]." An edict was issued placing Zhaoxin under the jurisdiction of Hao prefecture.[31]

Although several of the changes to spatial organization that created the frontier in Huainan occurred during the peak of the fighting, it was actually in the years immediately after the war ended that Huainan's borderland geography emerged. When the fighting in Huainan subsided in the mid-1130s, the demographic consequences of the war became evident to civil officials attempting to create a manageable postwar landscape. The destruction of Huainan motivated a round of court-ordered conditional abolitions of territories there in the mid- and late-1130s. In the winter of 1133, the emperor commanded that civil and military offices throughout the counties and prefectures of Huainan should be abolished.[32] It was a clear policy directive from the court: the massive decline in tax revenue and population as a result of the war made some territories temporarily unsustainable. According to the edict, the state presence in the circuit was to be reduced, and it was in this context that the *quan* strategy of conditional territorial reduction came into its own over the next few years.

The first documented case of a conditional abolition occurred in Lianshui prefecture near the mouth of the Huai River. Lianshui prefecture, which had been restored only three years earlier, was provisionally abolished in the spring of 1134. As one circuit level military official wrote, "the territory of Lianshui prefecture is not large. The population is declining, and so by order of grace it should be amalgamated [with an adjacent territory] and abolished."[33] The implementation of this order explicitly called for the abolition of Lianshui prefecture to be temporary. The official proposed the following: marshy and coastal Yancheng county, then under the jurisdiction of the adjacent Chu[2] prefecture, was a salt-producing place, not a farming region. For that reason, it was capable of generating tax revenue despite the war. If Lianshui prefecture were temporarily made into a county and put under the jurisdiction of Chu[2] prefecture, it could be subsidized by revenue from Yancheng. The arrangement only needed to be maintained until Lianshui's farms could recover. The suggestion was granted, and Lianshui became a county of Chu[2] prefecture under the governance of the Huai Coastal Military Commission.[34] The war did not affect all of Huainan's economy to the same extent. Conditional abolitions allowed the court to maximize the efficacy of places that continued to prosper.

The same year, the coastal Wucheng county, Chu[2] prefecture, was abolished—also with the stipulation that the change be temporary—after it was reported that its population had declined to only eighty-eight households. It was made into a garrison-market of Huaiyin prefecture.[35] Conditionally revising the map of the empire allowed the court to leverage revenue from places on the Huainan frontier that remained relatively more intact after the war and to support their neighbors, whose decline in fortunes were related to the war and were likely to be temporary.

The conditional abolitions of Lianshui and Wucheng were only the beginning. The following year, in 1134, the court issued an edict proposing the widespread adoption of this approach in Huainan. In the wake of the demographic collapse of Huainan, the court proposed provisional abolition of counties and prefectures throughout both of its constituent circuits as a systematic policy. Local officials were solicited to select the territories that ought to be abolished. In 1134, the central government proposed the temporary abolition of jurisdictions across all parts of Huainan East and West circuits:[36]

> The Huai region has repeatedly been subject to great destruction. It is appropriate to conditionally abolish [some territories]. Now an itemized proposal: Cheng prefecture should be provisionally abolished and reconstituted as Gaoyou county, under the jurisdiction of Yang prefecture. Xinghua county should as before be placed under the jurisdiction of Tai prefecture. Shu prefecture should abolish three counties. Ji prefecture should abolish two counties. He, Chu[1], Chu[2], and Wuwei prefectures should each abolish one county. Each prefect should be ordered to survey the size of the population and the distances between places and propose which counties should be abolished. They should write a report to the Military Commission, who will endorse the proposal and submit it to the Department of State Affairs. As for those places that are to be abolished or amalgamated, for each one we should appoint one supervisory garrison official.[37]

This passage again makes explicit the relationship between the devastation wrought by the war and the need to conditionally abolish territories. Officials in the field played a key role in gathering and analyzing information about postwar conditions and social geography. On the basis of their reports, decisions about which places to abolish were made with reference to their total population and the spatial distribution of settlements. The emperor approved the proposal and the abolitions commenced.

Edicts and memorials concerning the repercussions of this mandate continued for months, as court and local officials negotiated a provisional postwar field administration.[38] In the end, only three Huainan county abolitions in 1135 were recorded in the Song History geography monograph. We can only speculate about the cases that are documented in the Drafted Documents but not recorded in the Song History. They may never have been implemented, or implemented so briefly as to have seemed irrelevant to the fourteenth century authors of the Song History. As Yao Wentian complained in the eighteenth century, it is impossible to construct the geography of this period with complete precision. Nevertheless, the records in the Drafted Documents are quite revealing about the creation of a border region in wartime Huainan. Regardless of their effect on the map of the empire, they deserve due consideration as texts about Song frontier ideology as war reached the heartland of the empire.

Only a month after the order to survey possible abolitions in the Huai region, one unnamed Huainan East circuit official issued a report about the extent of the devastation in Chu[1] prefecture. On the basis of a survey of the size and distribution of the population of the prefecture, he proposed that it abolish a county and reduce staff:

> Chu[1] prefecture ought to abolish one county. This is based on a personal visit by acting prefect (*quan zhi junzhou shi*) He Yang: This prefecture governs three counties—Qingliu, Laian, and Quanjiao. The size and distribution of the population have been surveyed. Among them, Laian county has been totally ravaged, and the population is small. Now I recommend abolishing it and amalgamating it with Qingliu. Laian county only needs one garrison-level official. The currently dispatched Gentleman for Fostering Temperance (*chengjie lang*)[39] and acting Laian District Defender (*xianwei*) Zhang Zhongwu can fill the post of supervisor for garrison affairs, manage public matters for the garrison, and concurrently manage taxes. All the other official posts are abolished.[40]

Once again, this document explains that a jurisdiction was abolished because it had been devastated in the war and had lost population. There were no state funded reconstruction efforts on the Huainan frontier. Refugees had to return to their homes, cultivate their fields, and pay taxes *before* the state could resume a more dense presence in any area.

As we have already seen with respect to the salt-producing Chu[2] prefecture, one solution to the impasse was to pair the jurisdictions that had suffered the most damage with others whose population and infrastructure were relatively more intact. In a similar case, in the spring of 1135, the emperor issued an edict to move Taixing county from Tai prefecture to Yang prefecture in order to aid the reconstruction of Yang. The edict was based on a report from Yang prefect Ye Huan (fl.1136):

> When Tang Chenye and Song Xiao served here, they received a directive to move Taixing county into Yang prefecture, along with the single canton of Daohua in

Chaixu garrison. Because of the invasion of the slaves [Jin] (*luren*), [Taixing] was under the provisional jurisdiction of Tai prefecture. The abovementioned county, garrison, and canton did not have slaves pass through their territory, so their tax revenue can go to help with the expenses for Yang prefecture.[41]

Taixing, a county that still bore revenue, was prized, and was deployed to support Yang, the prefecture where its surplus was needed the most. Not only could a whole county be moved for this reason, but even an individual canton, Daohua, was transferred to Yang as well.

Many mid-1130s planners saw the abolition of counties and prefectures as a solution to wartime devastation. However, they and their colleagues soon discovered that the situation was more complicated than they had originally believed. Two edicts from 1135 called for the restoration of Huainan counties.[42] The employment and commerce associated with government business were considerable, and abolishing a territory could devastate the local economy rather than improve it. Vested interests of officials or other constituents may also have played a role. In 1138, Wujiang garrison-market was restored to its status as a county of He prefecture on the grounds that it was after the county was abolished, not before, that the population started to decline.[43]

Yet, as imperial and state functions were restored to the wartorn southern empire, and state power was asserted throughout the new realm, the status of rapidly changing jurisdictions on the frontier was not always clear. At the beginning of 1136, the superintendent for public affairs for the two Huainan circuits (*tidian Huainan lianglu gongshi*) recommended the abolition of Guangji county, Jin prefecture, following the precedent of Taihu and Susong counties in Shu prefecture. He was perhaps unaware that Taihu and Susong had been reestablished five months earlier. Nevertheless, the recommendation to abolish Guangji was approved.[44] This case signals the confusion and faulty information under which officials seem to have operated at this time.

To recap, there were three subperiods during the decade of the 1130s on the Huainan frontier: the war itself at the beginning of the decade, stocktaking and temporary abolition in the middle of the decade, and then a gradual return to the status quo ante. During the war itself, some territories, when occupied by Jin, left the roster of Song territories. These were restored when they returned to Song hands. In 1134–35, many counties and prefectures were abolished because they did not produce enough tax revenue to support even a small administration. The fiscal structure of Song local government units did not allow for places to be maintained under such circumstances. The final years of the decade were devoted to restoring places for two reasons: because their populations and fields had recovered, and because the abolitions had been counterproductive to commerce and to certain peoples' livelihoods. Although it might seem surprising that border populations could recover so quickly, other contemporary sources reveal consistent information. Li Chunnian (d. 1160), architect of a cadastral (*jingjie*) land surveying initiative in the 1140s, found landowners and tenants back in their fields by the time he proposed a mapping and surveying program in 1142. With county landownership records destroyed, they were struggling with each other over property relations, filing lawsuits, and devising schemes to remove land from the tax rolls.[45]

The war began to wind down by the late 1130s. The first Jürchen peace envoys arrived in Lin'an in 1138, and an initial amnesty was declared the following year. It took two more years to arrive at a final treaty. Geography was the sticking point. Jin and Song diplomats were negotiating the determination and demarcation of the border, and the establishment of border crossing and border maintenance procedures. In October 1141, the Jin emperor signaled that peace would be possible if the Song negotiators would agree to make the middle reaches of the Huai River the borderline. Two months later, the Song court agreed in principle, and the treaty was signed at the end of 1141. The counties and prefectures of Huainan that were split in two by the interstate border would not be reunited, and the provisional extent of their jurisdiction was finalized.

From 1142 onward, Song paid annual tributes of silver and silk amounting to 250,000 ounces and bolts to Jin. Other treaty provisions concerned security: fugitives from Song to the north could not be pursued, and no large garrisons could be stationed in the border prefectures. The language of the treaty established Song as a vassal state of Jin. A system of trenches marked the location of the border on the ground.[46] Licensed border markets were established with the most important of them being at Si prefecture in Huainan. With a stable, territorially clear treaty in place, Huainan's Northern Song role as a conduit between north and south as restored, and trade began to flourish.[47] As with the negotiation of the Song-Liao border discussed by Peter Lorge in this volume (chapter 3), it seems likely that stability on the ground in the frontier zone is part of what made the treaty possible.

With the finalization of the peace treaty recognizing the Jin dynasty and establishing a border between the two states, the Song court was in a position to turn its attention to domestic affairs. The Jin war had dealt a heavy blow to the Song tax base. The well-surveyed lands of the north were lost altogether. In the south, farmland was ravaged, cultivators had fled, and tax records and land deeds were destroyed. The large landowners, strongmen, and corrupt clerks who had been a scourge of reform efforts throughout the Northern Song were more powerful than ever, positioned to exploit the lack of records, absence of cultivators, and administrative vacuum of the region.

The pace of territorial change slowed significantly after 1137 as battles and refugee movements diminished. After the signing of the 1142 treaty, the spatial organization of the Huainan frontier was revised slightly, as the court attempted to create a landscape for its truncated and ravaged territories. A stable geography, for an empire that had survived war and invasion, was coming into effect. A postwar frontier emerged by the mid-1140s, and the next fifteen years were a period of stabilization and reconstruction in the Huainan borderland.

The Huainan Borderland between the Wars

In contrast to Song interstate borders in the Shaanxi deserts, the Hebei grasslands, and the Guangnan jungles, the Huainan border cut through the middle of a province in a region that had been prosperous and densely populated before the war. Officials in the 1140s needed to sponsor mapmaking and surveying initiatives to evaluate and record the condition of Huainan. Particularly noteworthy was the cadastral (*jingjie*) survey with its objective of restoring effective records of landownership and gathering the land tax. They also paid renewed attention to Huainan's status in regional transportation, which was especially critical given its location along the new interstate border. Counties and prefectures were realigned in support of that role. Creating a stable border and supplying the troops stationed along it depended on developing and describing a sustainable administrative and economic infrastructure. Following the war, official buildings, moats, dikes, roads, schools, and shrines were in disrepair; maps, registers, and guides to local affairs for officials had been destroyed, and most officials were demoralized.[48]

Throughout the empire, tax remittances, including those from wealthy Jiangnan, had decreased. Those that were collected were often extracted from the poor and powerless. According to *jingjie* architect Li Chunnian, powerful landowners were able to encroach on neighboring property while leaving the original owners with the tax responsibility, register land in the name of their tenants, and engage in other ploys to dodge taxes. As we have seen in the previous section of this chapter, magistrates and prefects were mandated to survey the populations and lands of their jurisdictions so that the court could assess whether the territories remained fiscally viable. *Jingjie* was a way to assist with this task. The *jingjie* survey called for each landowner to create sketch maps of his or her holding and register them at the canton. Each county was to create a giant wall map of all its constituent landholdings. The *jingjie* survey was a mixed success, but it and local successor programs were associated with significant local mapmaking.[49] At the end of the century, Zhao Fan (fl. 1190), prefect of Yang, commissioned "rapid surveys" (*sudiao*) of troop positions throughout Huainan West circuit, and used them to create a circuit map. Zhao also used internal-use maps from the court (*shi chaoting you neitu*) in order to construct dikes and embankments around the prefecture for defense and irrigation.[50] *Jingjie* and other surveying and cartography initiatives in Huainan illustrate the extensive scrutiny that was required for both defense and postwar reconstruction there. Without improved maps and records, it was difficult to manage the frontier.

Creating an effective transportation network for Huainan, where certain routes were taking on new importance, was also important to its emergence as a new frontier. The staff needed to police and manage trade routes in Huainan also needed to be contained in counties and prefectures. In 1143, Tianchang prefecture, which had been demoted to a county of Yang prefecture in 966, was reestablished. Two counties from neighboring Si prefecture were brought under Tianchang's jurisdiction.[51] Nine months later, neighboring Yutai county became a prefecture and Tianchang, demoted to a county once again, was placed under Yutai's jurisdiction. As the Secretariat-Chancellery explained, an important route for official travel to the border at the Huai River passed through Yutai. There were many dignitaries in the region, and the need for security was high. That is why the emperor responded with an edict to raise Yutai county to prefectural status, and make Tianchang prefecture a county as it was before, under its jurisdiction.[52] Shen Gai (fl. 1162), prefect of the newly established Yutai, was put in charge of extensively redeploying the existing officials in the region. His mandate was to accommodate the territorial changes without burdening the state's coffers.[53]

A long document from 1161 retrospectively explains frontier-planning considerations in Huainan after the 1142 peace treaty. It relates in particular to Gaoyou, a jurisdiction that had already been established and abolished repeatedly. It is from Yang Hang (fl. 1165), the provisionally deputed Huainan vice fiscal commissioner (*zhuanyun fushi*):

> Gaoyou county in Yang prefecture originally occupied prefectural status. Recently, on occasion of the battles, it was temporarily changed into a county. Now it has become the place with the largest population in Huai[nan] East. However, it is very far from Yang prefecture [seat], and it is not convenient for people to [go there and] pay their taxes. Moreover the canals and dikes that the county is in charge of are linked with lakes that occupy a large area. Local magnates and ruffians get together for profit and I am worried that this will give rise to problems. Let's change it back to Gaoyou prefecture as it was before. . .Moreover let us have an order sent down that the affected places should be sent 20,000 strings of cash and 3,000 piculs (*shi*) of grain in order to meet expenses.[54]

An edict followed: "Send the prefect to get the money from Yang prefecture that was put in the treasury earlier this year. The grain should come from the ever-normal granary and be dispersed. Everything else is approved as you said."[55] Places were reestablished as fast as their restored population permitted or when troop deployment (defense against domestic insurgents or foreign invaders) required it. The vested interests of local people militated in favor of preserving or increasing jurisdictions even when resources were limited. This was true whether they were militia leaders or gentlemen with the ear of the court, venal functionaries, or, as in this case, magnates and ruffians whose power had to be counterbalanced by state officials.

The Huainan Frontier in the Last Century of the Song

The 1142 treaty did not ensure an impermeable border. Merchants smuggled goods, and troops encroached the boundary. In the 1150s, an aggressive regime came to power at the Jin court, and in 1159, the Jin ruler, the hawkish Prince of Hailing (*Hailing wang*) (r. 1149–61), began preparing for an all-out attack on Song.[56] In the summer of 1161, warned of an impending attack, Song generals strengthened the border defenses. Troops on both sides massed along the Huai River. In mid-fall, Jin forces crossed the Huai, occupied much of Huainan, and advanced south toward the Yangzi. Song troops on the southern banks of the Yangzi held the Jin advance in check. Other Song armies conquered some Jin prefectures along the western part of the border, while Jin efforts were concentrated in the east. The final engagement of the war occurred on the banks of the Huai, and Song troops held Jin forces north of the Yangzi.[57] Soon after, the Prince of Hailing was murdered by a group of Jin officers, and his successor Shizong (r. 1161–89), faced with domestic unrest and an inconclusive war, withdrew troops from the front. He sent envoys to Song asking for a resumption of normal relations, but he did not demobilize his forces, and there were border skirmishes both in the Huai region and on the southwestern front where Jin faced Sichuan. The new treaty, signed in 1165, maintained the 1142 borders. The border markets reopened with 60,000 Jin troops garrisoned on the border, and thereupon, for the next forty years, the border was peaceful.

Taken jointly, the lengthy successive reigns of the emperors Gaozong (r. 1127–62) and Xiaozong (r. 1163–90) constituted a relatively peaceful time within the empire. It was a time marked by a healthy economy and limited factional debate at court. Moreover, later historians have recognized this period of more than a half-century as the age in which Zhu Xi (1130–1200) and other intellectuals established schools, salons, and publishing ventures in which they debated and propagated new approaches to ethics and education. It was, in the terms of one influential monograph, a time when China "turned inward."[58] Peace and prosperity lasted into the early thirteenth century, when it was punctured by the rising power of the Mongols, disastrous inflation, and ineffectual or venal leadership at court. The territorial landscape of the empire was quite stable for the duration of the Song era.

Despite the optimistic reports from the 1160s, the Huainan frontier, dependent on large-scale waterworks, recovered its former prosperity and agricultural productivity only slowly. Even by the 1223 census, it had regained only a fraction of its Northern Song population. During the Xiaozong era, local official Zhong Bing (fl. 1170) reported that in Jin prefecture in southwestern Huainan, even though the battles had ceased long before, famine was still widespread, and even though harvests were plentiful, populations were still very small in many places, with some counties having a population of only forty or fifty families.[59] In Tai prefecture on the coast, which had a population of 200,000 people at the end of the Northern Song, there were still expanses of dozens of *li* that were completely depopulated. The area of cultivated land, 120,000 *qing* in the Northern Song, was only 3,000 *qing* in the early Xiaozong reign.[60] In spite of new arrangements for counties and prefectures that were supposed to support repopulation and reconstruction, in spite of land surveys and maps, and in spite of a well-defined border with regulated markets, Southern Song Huainan never fully recovered its Northern Song vitality. One factor that constrained the restoration of agricultural productivity in Huainan was the large number of troops permanently garrisoned there. They supported themselves by requisitioning farmland for state farms that took land away from local subjects and off of the tax rolls.[61] Creating, measuring, and documenting a postwar geography for the Huainan frontier did not make it prosperous.

In the wake of the 1161 battles, the spatial organization of the borderland, which had been stable for several years, was revised once again. As late as 1162, Jin troops remained in control of Chu[2] prefecture, the terminus of the Grand Canal at the Huai River. However, although they held the prefectural capital, they did not dominate all of its hinterland. One of its constituent counties, Lianshui, remained in Song hands. It was placed—provisionally—under the jurisdiction of a new prefecture, Hai. But the solution was far from optimal. The distance from Chu[2] to Hai was more than 200 *li* (seventy miles) through perilous territory, and this was a temporary fix indeed. The Huainan East circuit military (*shuaishi*), fiscal (*caoshi*), and judicial intendants (*xianshi*) reported early in 1163 that Lianshui residents had to travel much too far when they needed to conduct government business. Lianshui county was moved back to Chu[2] prefecture as soon as Chu[2] was retaken by Song troops.[62]

Lianshui had itself been a prefecture from 978 to 1072, and from 1087 to 1135. The occupation of the eastern part of Huainan by Jin forces in the early 1160s presented an opportunity for the court to scrutinize its regional geography one more time. Late in 1163, the Jiang-Huai East and West military commissioners discovered an older report from Lianshui magistrate Guo Sheng arguing that even the distance to the Chu[2] seat from Lianshui was too far for tax payers to travel. He recommended that Lianshui be made a prefecture again rather than a county of Chu[2]. This suggestion was approved, and Lianshui was made into a prefecture, a status that it thereafter maintained until the end of the dynasty.[63]

By the final decades of the twelfth century, Jin power had begun to decline precipitously. Encouraged by Jin weakness, Song military leaders in the Huai region started to violate the border regularly beginning in 1204. During this last episode of hostility between Song and Jin in the early thirteenth century, several prefectures were established in Huainan to support troop deployment. Finally, as both the Song and Jin states unraveled by the middle of the twelfth century, some counties and prefectures on the Huainan frontier fell to the Jin, to the Yuan, and to local strongmen. In these final decades, additional jurisdictions were created or reestablished along the border in an attempt to expand the state presence and bolster defense forces.

Conclusion

Throughout imperial Chinese history, frontiers were governed as collections of counties and prefectures. In Northern Song Shaanxi and Hebei, extensive bulwarks of new prefectures permitted denser troop deployment on the northern frontier. However, the war between Song and Jin created a dilemma for Song provincial administration, and for the spatial organization that it presumed. As a region of critical strategic importance, Southern Song Huainan required a high concentration of troops and officials. However, it had also been the location of an exceptionally violent war. Its demographic collapse meant that there was no way that troops and officials stationed there could be supported by local revenues and local agricultural production as Song fiscal policy required. The system addressed this fundamental contradiction only with difficulty. Other factors also constrained frontier management in twelfth-century Huainan. Information about local circumstances was confusing and often faulty, and powerful locals had vested interests in maintaining their own jurisdictions.

In the 1130s and 1140s, conditional *quan* territorial abolitions allowed counties and prefectures to be temporarily dropped from the taxation rolls. Conditional abolition permitted a county or prefecture's population and fields to recover to the point that it could support troops after a short hiatus. Certain revenue-sharing arrangements helped to facilitate this as well, by allowing counties that could still deliver tax revenue to be affiliated with the prefectures that most required their resources. In addition, a premium was placed upon empirical information gathering. Reports by prefects and magistrates governed decisions about which places to abolish and which to maintain, land surveys like *jingjie* helped to evaluate the extent of damage that the war had wrought, and maps dictated troop placements.

Although factions at court that dreamed of retaking the north remained vocal for as long as the Song dynasty persisted, and even launched campaigns of conquest, it was clear that the Huai River border signed into effect in 1142 would be a fact on the ground for the foreseeable future. The Huainan battlefields became the frontier of the empire. Lands once acclaimed for "flourishing beauty" had lost 90 percent of their population; their cities looted and their levees destroyed. In the immediate aftermath of the fighting, the court's most urgent goal was to free the region from financial burden to allow for rebuilding and repopulation. After 1142, Huainan, once known for its salt trade and its bountiful harvests, had to serve an unprecedented role as a border province. Though it had long been a key part of the empire's transportation infrastructure, its function was no longer primarily to transport grain to the north, but to afford a secure border-crossing for diplomats and traders crossing the border and efficient access by troops. The grain produced by civilians, no longer permitted to leave the province, went to the support of Huainan's massive troop deployments instead, while Huainan's formerly vaunted wealth declined as commercial land gave way to subsistence state farms whose harvests fed troops directly. In both the short term and the longer run, this required conditionally and permanently changing the spatial organization of the region. Much to the same ends especially as David Graff's foregoing chapter concerning Youzhou Lulong during the Tang dynasty as well as several of the other studies contained herein, this study of Huainan in Song times reveals that a middle-period Chinese boundary need not be limited only to being a demarcating line. On the contrary, it could be and often was an immense region that implicated and dictated the politics and administrative policies of entire provinces. Simultaneously, as it fought and negotiated for its truncated empire, the Southern Song also surveyed, mapped, and reorganized the territory of the battlefields that remained under its control. In so doing, the state created a wholly new frontier in Huainan.

Notes

1. Song China in principle had a three-tiered hierarchy of administrative units. At the lowest level were counties (*xian*). Counties were grouped into prefectures. There were four types of prefectures in Song China (civil *fu* and *zhou*, military *jun*, and industrial *jian*). I have not noted any functional differences between them and I am therefore treating them as a single category. On the Song prefectural system see Nie Chongqi, "Songdai fu, zhou, jun, jian zhi fenxi," *Yanjing xuebao* 29 (1941): 1–56. Above prefectures were provincial circuits (*lu*). All translations are mine unless otherwise noted.
2. Provincial circuits originated as inspection districts, and never became administrative units. Their functions remained largely managerial, and the work of civil and military field administration occurred within the smaller local units. The best-known work of modern scholarship on personnel administration in the Song dynasty is Umehara Kaoru, *Sōdai kanryo seido kenkyu* (Kyoto, 1985). The titles and duties of all county and prefectural officials are detailed in Tuo Tuo, *Songshi* (Beijing, 1977), 120.3972–78. Hereafter *SS*.
3. Wang Shengduo, *Liang Song caizheng shi* (Beijing, 1995), pp. 521–22.
4. In 1157, Left Gentleman for Discussion (*zuo chengyi lang*) Lu Chong detailed the receipts and expenditures for Yixing county, a wealthy district in the lower Yangzi. Tax receipts totaled 54,000 strings of cash per year. In addition to official salaries and payments to the prefectures, there were additional fixed expenses for a total of 34,000 strings. These included vehicles of state, expenses for state sacrifices, maintenance of grain reserves, shipbuilding, and materials for vehicles and utensils. There were additional fluctuating expenses that the county had to bear that could not be budgeted precisely from year to year, including visits and audiences, exchange and management of civil and military documents, and contributions to prefectural deficits. "There is not a day without these," Lu Chong complains. *SS*, 174.4216. Yixing would have had a large population, extensive commercial activity, and relatively low military expenditures, making it better off than most Song jurisdictions.
5. Wang Shengduo, *Liang Song caizheng shi*, pp. 522–23.
6. Wang Shengduo, *Liang Song caizheng shi*, pp. 529–34.
7. Ruth Mostern, "Apprehending the Realm: Territoriality and Political Power in Song China, 960–1276 CE" (Ph.D diss., University of California, Berkeley, 2003), pp. 107–18.
8. As we will see, cost and revenue-sharing arrangements were periodically agreed upon between neighboring jurisdictions, but this was painstaking and required explicit court approval of detailed written recommendations, and this did not occur often.
9. *SS*, 88.2178.
10. Christian Lamouroux, "Espace et peuplement dans la Chine des Song: La géographie du bassin de la Huai au XI^c siècle," *Études Chinoises* 9.1 (1990): 35–94.

11. Mira Mihelich, "Polders and the Politics of Land Reclamation in Southeast China during the Northern Song Dynasty" (Ph.D. diss., Cornell University, 1979), pp. 33–42.
12. Qin Guan, *Huaihai ji* (Taibei, 1983), 38.13b–14.
13. Cheng Minsheng, *Songdai diyu jingji* (Taibei, 1995), pp. 28–29.
14. Sun Yingshi, *Chuhu ji* (Taibei, 1983), 9.21.
15. Shiba Yoshinobu, *Commerce and Society in Song China*, tr. Mark Elvin (Ann Arbor, 1970), p. 50.
16. Herbert Franke, "The Jin Dynasty" in *The Cambridge History of China*, vol. 6: *Alien Regimes and Border States, 907–1368*, ed. Herbert Franke and Denis Twitchett (Cambridge, 1994), p. 231. Readers should note that Chu[1] and Chu[2] herein represent a reversal of the enumerative nomenclature found in Hope Wright, *Alphabetical List of Geographical Names in Sung China* (Albany, 1992), p. 37.
17. J. P. McDermott, "Land Tenure and Rural Control in the Liangche Region during the Southern Sung" (Ph.D. diss., University of Cambridge, 1978), p. 68.
18. McDermott, "Land Tenure and Rural Control," pp. 68–72; Wu Songdi, *Bei Song yimin yu Nan Song shehui bianqian* (Taibei, 1993), pp. 105–11.
19. Liang Fangzhong, *Zhongguo lishi hukou, tiandi, tianze tongji* (Shanghai, 1980), pp. 161–62. Liang's source is Yuan Zhen, "Songdai renkou," *Lishi yanjiu* 3 (1957): 9–46. Yuan, in turn, derived the figures from the "population (*hukou*) monograph" of *Wenxian tongkao*.
20. Although the term literally means simply "temporary" or "provisional," *quan* became a key concept in political culture by the mid-Southern Song. Conrad Schirokauer has examined the concept of *quan* in the writing of the influential thirteenth-century moral philosopher Zhu Xi. *Quan* was the term that Zhu used to describe the problem of "how to adhere to timeless values while living and acting in an imperfect and changing world," a central concern of Zhu and other Confucian thinkers. See Conrad Schirokauer, "Chu Hsi's Sense of History" in *Ordering the World: Approaches to State and Society in Sung Dynasty China*, ed. Robert P. Hymes and Conrad Schirokauer (Berkeley, 1993), p. 208. Originally a concrete noun denoting a scale or steelyard, the term *quan*, early on, came to carry a range of metaphorical senses akin to those associated with the Western "scales of justice": weighing and surveying options, dividing things righteously, exercising authority. Chen Hanbo, *Hanyu da cidian* (Shanghai, 1990), 4.1359–60. Josephine Chiu-Duke, in a recent book about policy debates after An Lushan's rebellion in the eighth century, explains that the Tang principle of *quan* represented the ability to react to crisis in a tactical fashion that was appropriate to circumstances without compromising ideals of righteousness. Josephine Chiu-Duke, *"To Rebuild the Empire": Lu Chih's Confucian Pragmatist Approach to the Mid-T'ang Predicament* (Albany, 2000). In the Northern Song, Cheng Yi typified *quan* as the application of the "standard" in a specific time and place (Schirokauer, "Chu Hsi's Sense of History," p. 210). The term does not appear to have been applied to administrative geography until Southern Song times.
21. Yao Wentian, *Guangling shilue* (1821), 1.12a–b. The author of an early Qing gazetteer for Liuhe county records the same complaint. With regard to Liuhe county, he writes, "There was no set jurisdiction [in the Shaoxing period (1131–62)]...it is not possible to record it precisely." Wang Xuan, *Liuhe xianzhi*

(1684), 1.10. An anonymous late Ming (ca.1621–28) chronicler of Huai'an prefecture complains that early Southern Song maps, then still extant, continued to list Huai'an as part of the Song Empire, even though it was under Jin control for some of that time. He admits that he does not know when it was actually recovered. *Huai'an fuzhi*, 1.12b–13.
22. Yao Wentian, *Guangling shilue*, 1.12.
23. Yao Wentian, *Guangling shilue*, 4.12b.
24. Lu Shi, *Yizhen ji* (1718), 2.2b.
25. Jin Bingzuo, *Shanyang xianzhi* (1749), 1.5b–6. Huai'an was soon occupied by Jin forces, and when it was recovered in 1131, it was a county once again. Chu itself was occupied in March 1129, and recaptured in the summer of 1130, but reestablished as a prefecture only after a delay of almost a year (Jin, *Shanyang xianzhi*, 9.19).
26. The same kinds of changes were occurring at the same time in Jiangnan, to the south of Huainan, and continued to occur there once the court moved from Yang prefecture in Huainan to Hang prefecture in Jiangnan. During the 1130s, many prefectures were raised in status, allowing for the appointment of larger staffs, higher rank officials, and higher tax quotas. In 1130, Hang prefecture was raised from *zhou* to *fu* status. Its name was changed to Lin'an. At the same time, four cantons (*du*) of Hang were moved under the direct jurisdiction of the Border Military Commission: they were removed from the territory of Hang and distributed instead among adjacent prefectures that were deemed to require an enhanced troop presence. See Xu Song, *Song huiyao jigao* (Beijing, 1957), *fangyu* [territories] section), 6.21. Hereafter *SHY:FY*. In late 1131, the Jiangnan prefecture of Yue, which then served as a base for the exiled court, was also raised from *zhou* status to the highest *fu* status. It was renamed Shaoxing, after the emperor's reign name, "in order to make manifest the joy at the personal presence of the emperor," and to acknowledge the significance of this jurisdiction as the staging ground for numerous military expeditions. The following week, the officials, literati, religious officials, and elders of the region were invited "to give thanks" for the changes (*SHY:FY*, 6.22).
27. *SHY:FY*, 6.11b.
28. Population figures from Wang Cun, *Yuanfeng jiuyu zhi* (Taibei, 1986), cited in Wright, *Alphabetical List of Geographical Names*, p. 147.
29. Private militias were widespread during the campaigns against the Jin beginning early in Gaozong's reign. Among these, Liu Gang's militia was a small one. See Huang Kuanchong, *Nan Song shidai kang Jin de yijun* (Taibei, 1988), p. 61.
30. *SHY:FY*, 6.13b. For the term *zhenfu*, see Chen, *Hanyu da cidian*, 11.1364. This was a special administrative territory established in the Song-Jin battle zones in the early Southern Song in Huainan, Jingdong West and Jinghu North. See also *SHY:FY* 6.15, wherein Zhao Li is appointed to be the administrator of the *zhenfu* constituted by Chu[1], Chu[2], Si, Cheng, and Lianshui prefectures. He was simultaneously appointed to serve as prefect of Chu[2].
31. *SHY:FY*, 6.13b.
32. Yao Wentian, *Guangling shilue*, 4.30b. The Song History lists only three abolitions in 1130s Huainan, but from the documentary record preserved in the Drafted Documents, it is evident that many more were discussed and approved, and may have taken effect briefly.
33. *SHY:FY*, 6.12.

34. *SHY:FY*, 6.11b–12.
35. *SHY:FY*, 6.12b.
36. The government agency named in the report is the Three Departments. This was a quasi-official collective reference to the Department of State Affairs (*shangshu sheng*), the Chancellery (*menxia sheng*), and the Secretariat (*zhongshu sheng*), traditionally the three topmost agencies for the central government. See Charles O. Hucker, *A Dictionary of Official Titles in Imperial China* (Stanford, 1985), p. 401.
37. *SHY:FY*, 6.9a–b.
38. *SHY:FY*, 6.9–10.
39. This was a generic title that was used to denote an official's rank (in this case 9b) and did not carry with it any functional responsibilities. See Hucker, *Dictionary of Official Titles*, p. 125.
40. *SHY:FY*, 6.14b. The Huainan West circuit military commissioner proposed an even more extensive list of territories that he believed ought to be pruned. See *SHY:FY*, 6.17.
41. *SHY:FY*, 6.13.
42. Taihu and Susong counties, along the Yangzi River in Shu prefecture, and Luotian county in mountainous western Qi prefecture, were all restored that year. *SHY:FY* 6.18a–b. In 1136, the offices that had been abolished by imperial order in 1133 were also restored. Yao Wentian, *Guangling shilue*, 4.33b.
43. *SHY:FY*, 6.12b.
44. *SHY:FY*, 6.18.
45. To cite another example, Tongshan county, in Kui prefecture (modern Sichuan), lost much of its population after a rebellion in 1137. Within months of the pacification of the rebels, 800 households had already returned. The entire prefectural population, divided among five counties, was only 46,641 households in the 1070s (*Yuanfeng jiuyu zhi* cited in Wright, *Alphabetical List of Geographical Names*, p. 150), so this implies that essentially the entire county population became refugees, but returned as soon as feasible. On *jingjie*, see *SHY: shihuo* (commodities) section, 6.36–38.
46. On border trenches, see Wang Guowei, "Jin jiehao kao," *Yanjing xuebao* 1 (1927): 1–14 and Ma Zhenglin, *Zhongguo lishi dili jianlun* (Xi'an, 1987), pp. 228–30. See also of course Peter Lorge's chapter in the present volume (chapter 3).
47. Both sides resolved to regulate trade and establish licensed frontier markets in order to rebuild the commercial sphere that had been severed by the war, see Osaki Fujio, "Sō-Kin bōeki no katazama," *Hiroshima daigaku bungakubu kiyō* 5 (1954):159–82.
48. Sun Yingshi, *Chuhu ji*, 9.21.
49. Li Chunnian makes this claim in the memorial calling for the *jingjie* land survey. See *SHY:FY* 6.36–38. The most extended scholarly discussion of it is in Yu Tanjun, "Nan Song jingjie fa de yanjiu" (Ph.D. diss., Zhongguo wenhua daxue, 1993). In addition, with the rise of the commercial printing industry and flourishing local economies in much of South China, the production of privately sponsored geographical encyclopedias for counties and prefectures (*difangzhi*) expanded rapidly. (There is a very large literature on this topic. One recent article of note is James M. Hargett, "Song Dynasty Local Gazetteers and Their Place in the History of *Difangzhi* Writing," *Harvard Journal of Asiatic Studies* 56.2 (1996): 405–42.) Circuit-level maps were still produced for military planning.
50. Yao Wentian, *Guangling shilue*, 5.10a–b.

51. *SHY:FY*, 6.13b.
52. *SHY:FY*, 6.15.
53. *SHY:FY*, 6.15–16.
54. *SHY:FY*, 6.10.
55. *SHY:FY*, 6.10.
56. He reigned as emperor but was stripped of his title posthumously because of the disastrous war along with violent and destabilizing domestic practices.
57. Tao Jingsheng, *Jin Hailing di de fa Song yu Caishi zhanyi de kaoshi* (Taibei, 1963).
58. James T. C. Liu, *China Turning Inward: Intellectual and Political Changes in the Early Twelfth Century* (Cambridge, MA, 1988).
59. Zhong Bing, *Fushan ji* (Taibei, 1983), 4.2.
60. Sun Yingshi, *Chuhu ji*, 9.22.
61. Cheng Minsheng, *Songdai diyu jingji*, p. 347.
62. *SHY:FY*, 6.12.
63. *SHY:FY*, 6.12a–b.

Glossary

Bin 濱
caoshi 漕使
Chaixu 柴墟
Cheng 澄
Cheng Minsheng 程民生
Cheng Yi 程頤
chengjie lang 承節郎
Chu[1] 滁
Chu[2] 楚
Daohua 導化
difangzhi 地方志
du 都
fangyu 方域
fu 府
Gaoyou 高郵
Gaozong 高宗
Guangji 廣濟
Guangling 廣陵
Guangnan 廣南
Guo Sheng 郭昇
Hai 海
Hailing wang 海陵王
Hang 杭
Hangzhou 杭州
Hao 豪
He 和
He Yang 河洋
Hebei 河北
hukou 戶口
Huai 淮

Huai'an 淮安
Huainan 淮南
Huainan dong 淮南東
Huainan xi 淮南西
Huaiyin 淮陰
Huaiyuan 懷遠
Huan he 渙河
jian 監
Jiankang 健康
Jiang 江
Jiangdu 江都
Jiangnan 江南
Jin 蘄 [prefecture]
Jingdong 京東
Jinghu 荊湖
jingjie 經界
juzhen 巨鎮
jun 軍
Jurchen [Nüzhen 女眞]
Kaifeng 開封
Kui 夔
Laian 來安
Li Chunnian 李春年
li 里
Lianshui 漣水
Liangzhe 兩浙
Lin'an 臨安
Liu Gang 劉綱
Liuhe 六合
Lu 盧
lu 路
Lu Chong 魯沖
Lulong 盧龍
luren 虜人
Luotian 羅田
menxia sheng 門下省
Ming 明
Nanjing 南京
Qi 蘄
qing 頃
Qing 清
Qingliu 清流
quan 權
quan zhi junzhou shi 權知軍州事
Quanjiao 全椒
Shaanxi 陝西
Shanyang 山陽
shangshu 尚書
shangshu sheng 尚書省

Shaoxing 紹興
Shen Gai 沈該
shengli 盛麗
shi 石
shi chaoting you neitu 時朝廷有內圖
shihuo 食貨
Shizong 世宗
Shou 壽
Shu 舒
shuaifu 帥府
shuaishi 帥使
Si 泗
si gui shi 思歸勢
Sichuan 四川
Song huiyao jigao 宋會要輯稿
Song Xiao 宋孝
Songshi 宋史
sudiao 速調
Susong 宿松
Sun Yingshi 孫應時
Tai 泰
Taihu 太湖
Taixing 泰興
Tang Chenye 湯陳野
tidian Huainan lianglu gongshi 提點淮南兩路公事
Tianchang 天長
Tong 通
Tongshan 通山
turen 土人
tuntian 屯田
Wenxian tongkao 文獻通考
Wucheng 吳成
Wujiang 烏江
Wuwei 無為
xian 縣
xianshi 憲使
xianwei 縣尉
Xiaozong 孝宗
Xinghua 興化
Yancheng 鹽城
Yang 揚
Yang Hang 楊杭
Yao Wentian 姚文田
Ye Huan 葉煥
Yixing 宜興
Yizhen 義真
Youzhou 幽州
Yutai 魚臺
Yuanfeng jiuyu zhi 元豐九域志
Yue 越

Zhang Zhongwu 張仲武
Zhao Fan 趙范
Zhao Li 趙立
Zhaoxin 招信
Zhen 真
zhenfu 鎮撫
zhixian 知縣
Zhong Bing 仲並
zhongshu sheng 中書省
zhou 州
Zhu Xi 朱熹
zhuanyun fushi 轉運副使
zuo chengyi lang 左承議郎

Bibliography

Anon. *Huai'an fuzhi* 淮安府志 [Huai'an Prefecture Gazetteer]. ca. 1621–8.
Chen Hanbo 陳翰伯. *Hanyu da cidian* 漢語大詞典 [Great Dictionary of the Chinese Language]. 12 vols. Shanghai: Hanyu dacidian chubanshe, 1990.
Cheng Minsheng 程民生. *Songdai diyu jingji* 宋代地域經濟 [Song Regional Economies]. Taibei: Yunlong chubanshe, 1995.
Chiu-Duke, Josephine. *"To Rebuild the Empire": Lu Chih's Confucian Pragmatist Approach to the Mid-T'ang Predicament*. Albany, NY: SUNY University Press, 2000.
Franke, Herbert. "The Jin Dynasty." In *The Cambridge History of China. Vol. 6: Alien Regimes and Border States, 907–1368*, ed. Herbert Franke and Denis Twitchett. Cambridge: Cambridge University Press, 1994.
Hargett, James M. "Song Dynasty Local Gazetteers and Their Place in the History of Difangzhi Writing," *Harvard Journal of Asiatic Studies* 56.2 (December 1996):405–42.
Huang Kuanchong 黃寬重. *Nan Song shidai kang Jin de yijun* 南宋時代抗金的義軍 ["Righteous Armies" of Jin Resistance in the Southern Song Era]. Taibei: Lianjing chubanshe, 1988.
Hucker, Charles O. *A Dictionary of Official Titles in Imperial China*. Stanford: Stanford University Press, 1985.
Jin Bingzuo 金秉柞. *Shanyang xianzhi* 山陽縣志 [Shanyang county gazetteer]. 1749.
Lamouroux, Christian. "Espace et peuplement dans la Chine des Song: La géographie du bassin de la Huai au XI^c siècle." *Études Chinoises* 9.1 (1990):35–94.
Liang Fangzhong 梁方鐘. *Zhongguo lishi hukou, tiandi, tianfu tongji* 中國歷史戶口, 田地,田賦統計 [Chinese Historical Population, Land, and Land Tax Statistics]. Shanghai: Renmin chubanshe, 1980.
Liu, James T. C. *China Turning Inward: Intellectual and Political Changes in the Early Twelfth Century*. Cambridge, MA: Harvard University Press, 1988.
Lu Shi 陸師. *Yizhen ji* 儀真志 [Yizhen gazetteer]. 1718.
Ma Zhenglin 馬正林. *Zhongguo lishi dili jianlun* 中國歷史地理簡論 [A Brief on Chinese Historical Geography]. Xi'an: Shaanxi renmin chubanshe, 1987.
McDermott, J. P. "Land Tenure and Rural Control in the Liangche Region during the Southern Sung." Ph.D. diss. Cambridge: University of Cambridge, 1978.
Mihelich, Mira. "Polders and the Politics of Land Reclamation in Southeast China during the Northern Song Dynasty." Ph.D. diss. Ithaca, NY: Cornell University, 1979.
Mostern, Ruth. "Apprehending the Realm: Territoriality and Political Power in Song China, 960–1276 CE." Ph.D diss. Berkeley: University of California, 2003.

Nie Chongqi 聶崇崎. "Songdai fu, zhou, jun, jian zhi fenxi" 宋代府州軍監分析 [An Analysis of *fu, zhou, jun,* and *jian* (Prefectures) in the Song Dynasty]. *Yanjing xuebao* 燕京學報 [Yanjing Journal] 29 (1941):1–56.

Osaki Fujio 大崎富士夫. "Sō-Kin bōeki no katazama." 宋金貿易の型態 [Types of Trade between Song and Jin] *Hiroshima daigaku bungakubu kiyō* 廣島大學文學部紀要 [Minutes of the Literature Department of Hiroshima University] 5 (1954):159–182.

Qin Guan 秦觀. *Huaihai ji* 淮海集 [Collected Works from Huaihai]. *Siku quanshu (SKQS)* 四庫全書 [Complete Books of the Four Treasuries] edition. Taibei: Taiwan shangwu yinshuguan, 1983.

Schirokauer, Conrad. "Chu Hsi's Sense of History." In *Ordering the World: Approaches to State and Society in Sung Dynasty China.*, ed. Robert P. Hymes and Conrad Schirokauer. Studies on China 16. Berkeley: University of California Press, 1993.

Shiba, Yoshinobu. *Commerce and Society in Song China.* Ann Arbor: Center for Chinese Studies, University of Michigan, 1970.

Sun Yingshi 孫應時. *Chuhu ji* 燭湖集 [Collected Works from Candle Lake]. *SKQS* 四庫全書 [Complete Books of the Four Treasuries] edn. Taibei: Shangwu yinshuguan, 1983.

Tao Jingsheng 陶晉生. *Jin Hailing di de fa Song yu Caishi zhanyi de kaoshi* 金海陵帝的伐宋與采石戰役的考實 [An Examination of Jin Emperor Hailing's Attack on Song and the Quarry Battle]. Taibei: Guoli Taiwan daxue wenxueyuan, 1963.

Tuo Tuo 脱脱. *Song*shi 宋史 [Song History]. 40 vols. Beijing: Zhonghua shuju, 1977.

Umehara Kaoru 梅原郁. *Sōdai kanryo seido kenkyū* 宋代官僚制度研究 [A Study of the System of Officialdom during the Song Dynasty]. Kyoto: Dohosha, 1985.

Wang Cun 王存. *Yuanfeng jiuyu zhi* 元豐九域志 [A Gazetteer of the Nine Provinces from the Yuanfeng Era]. 2 vols. Taibei: Huashi chubanshe, 1986.

Wang Guowei 王國維. "Jin jiehao kao" 金界壕考 [A Study of Jin Border Trenches]. *Yanjing xuebao* 燕京學報 [Yanjing Journal] 1 (1927):1–14.

Wang Shengduo 汪聖鐸. *Liang Song caizheng shi* 兩宋財政史 [The History of Government Finance in the Two Song Eras]. Beijing: Zhonghua shuju, 1995.

Wang Xuan 汪鋐. *Liuhe xianzhi* 六合縣志 [Liuhe county Gazetteer]. 1684.

Wright, Hope. *Alphabetical List of Geographical Names in Sung China.* Albany, NY: Journal of Sung-Yuan Studies, 1992.

Wu Songdi 吳松弟. *Beifang yimin yu Nan Song shehui bianqian* 北方移民與南宋社會變遷 [Northern Immigrants and Southern Song Social Change]. Taibei: Wenjing chubanshe, 1993.

Xu Song 徐松, ed. *Song huiyao jigao* 宋會要輯搞 [Drafted Documents on Song State matters]. 8 vols. Beijing: Zhonghua shuju, 1957.

Yao Wentian 姚文田. *Guangling shilue* 廣陵事略 [An Outline of Affairs in Guangling]. 1812.

Yu Tanjun 俞坦濬. "Nan Song jingjie fa de yanjiu" 南宋經界法的研究 [A Study of the *jingjie* Cadastral Survey in the Southern Song]. Ph.D. diss. Taiwan: Zhongguo wenhua daxue, 1993.

Yuan Zhen 袁震. "Songdai renkou" 宋代人口 [Song Dynasty Population]. *Lishi yanjiu* 歷史研究 [Historical Studies] 3 (1957):9–46.

Zhong Bing 仲并. *Fushan ji* 浮山集 [Collected Works from Floating Mountain]. *(SKQS)* 四庫全書 [Complete Books of the Four Treasuries] edition. Taibei: Shangwu yinshuguan, 1983.

CHAPTER 9

PEOPLE IN THE MIDDLE: UYGHURS IN THE
NORTHWEST FRONTIER ZONE

Michael C. Brose

During most of the Chinese middle period, the area to China's north and west was a contested space where several autonomous regional states and tribal peoples vied for power, and where China's influence waxed and waned with the times. In many senses, the entire northern frontier zone, from present-day western Xinjiang across the steppe to Heilongjiang, during the late Tang in the ninth century CE until the rise of the Mongol confederation in the twelfth, was a true frontier area—one that comprised a "meeting place of peoples in which geographic and cultural borders were not clearly defined" and a territory where the mixing and accommodation of peoples and cultures was the dominant motif.[1] This northern zone, demarcated from the traditional Chinese heartland by the Great Wall, is also known to historians as the Inner Asian frontier. It consists of a specific environmental and cultural climate that both the sedentary Chinese agriculturalists and the nomadic people of the steppe consider marginal, and it is a place that has seen movement across it by peoples from both sides.[2] Although the Chinese may have seen this northern frontier as suggested by Frederick Jackson Turner, an empty wilderness where expansion could occur, the inability of the area to sustain intense settled agriculture seems to have prevented China from serious colonization. Thus, the late historian of Central Asia Owen Lattimore once termed this northern frontier zone as a static frontier of exclusion, a zone that both Chinese and nomads crossed frequently, and in which their cultures met and interacted.[3]

To offer this assessment, however, is not to suggest that the northern frontier zone was never a disputed area. The western half of this northern frontier zone was especially contested throughout the Chinese middle period, even during times when large sections were incorporated into the successive Qidan Liao and Jurchen [Nüzhen] Jin dynasties. But as Ruth Mostern has already demonstrated in the case of Huainan, that contest sometimes even reached down into central-South China when the frontier moved because of war and conquest. In fact, the story of Southern Song Huainan suggests that a frontier area can be largely defined as a process, in which the commingling of two societies by virtue of war or trade necessarily involves the opening, closing, and shifting of specific borders.

Describing a frontier process means, ideally, that there is a beginning and endpoint to any frontier. In the initial stage, the locals do not perceive the intruders onto a frontier area as a threat. But, over time, the power of the newcomers increases at the expense of the indigenous society, and frontier ends when the new group establishes political control over the old, and reestablishes a bipolar world, consisting of relations between two dominant states.[4] The specific geographic setting and the groups involved determine the contours of this frontier process, and it is a specific historical process, defined by the relationships between two or more different societies. This dynamic model of the frontier zone also implies that the frontier is mobile, and may shift over time. Thus, not every part of China's northern frontier zone may have been one continuous, simultaneous frontier. But the meeting and mixing of Chinese and steppe nomadic elements along the frontier spanned the gamut of war and peace, and usually involved some aspect of trade. In fact, the centrality of trade to the northern frontier region has been well documented and is the focus of much recent scholarship.[5]

One element of the northern frontier, however, continues to elude close inspection. Most of these studies on China's northern frontier have focused on the interactions of sedentary China with its northern steppe neighbors, with relatively little attention to the peoples who may have actually inhabited the frontier zone itself. The Turnerian assumption of an empty frontier, peopled from one side or the other, seems to be implied in these studies.[6] This assumption may result from the fact that most scholars have focused their attention on the area to the *north* of traditional China, as it has become defined over time by various manifestations of the Great Wall.[7] In terms of environment, geography, and sociopolitical history, it seems that the area between traditional China and the steppe presents a fairly straightforward story of difference and encounter between these two culture areas. The same cannot be said of that part of the frontier zone farther west, in modern Xinjiang province.

From all of these perspectives, the area that the Chinese have traditionally referred to as the Western Regions (Xiyu) appears to be more complex than that part of the frontier demarcated by the Great Wall.[8] If we wish to discover the people who lived "in the middle," this is the place to do so. Thus, my focus in this chapter is on the Uyghur (Weiwuer) Kingdom situated in the Tarim Basin, to the northwest of China proper, (hereafter "Uyghuristan"). The geography and climate of the belt of land stretching from the western end of the Great Wall in Gansu (at Jiayuguan) to Lake Issuk Kul and Kashgar at the western end of the Tarim Basin provided a unique zone of habitation that was marginal beyond anything imaginable in the frontier zone farther east. The history of this region is similarly unique, one of people who truly lived "in the middle," between desert and mountains, between nomadic and sedentary societies. Uyghuristan was a kingdom that survived there for over three centuries, always as a kind of regional frontier state. This study is an attempt to describe the history of that state and people as a people "in the middle," who became a unique people and polity native to that particular frontier zone.[9]

Although it was not one of the military powerhouses of the time, Uyghuristan was nonetheless an important, albeit smaller, regional state in that area from the mid-ninth century until its absorption into the Chagadai Qanate in the late-thirteenth century. Its importance stemmed from its cultural heritage and status among neighboring tribes and states, its inherited political history as a steppe empire, and its ability to manage a diverse population of nomadic and semisedentary peoples that included Sogdian, Türk, Tibetan, Chinese, and Uyghur cultures. Uyghuristan's geographic setting also contributed to its role in the frontier process. The Tarim Basin area was a complex zone that consisted of discrete oasis areas with at least three distinct culture areas, Türko-Mongol, Tibetan, and Chinese, and was traversed by the ancient overland trade routes.

This arid zone to the northwest of China provides an ideal setting in which to examine this concept of the frontier process for it was a place where nomadic and sedentary societies intermingled for centuries. It was also an area that neighboring kingdoms strove to control for centuries; the northwest was always on China's mind, and various dynasties from the Han (206 BCE–220 CE) on struggled to maintain their dominance over the area. As we know, however, China's power over the region fluctuated greatly from dynasty to dynasty, and by the fall of the Tang, China was no longer the dominant power.

I have chosen to focus on the Uyghur Kingdom that was established there in the ninth century because its history over the next three centuries can, in many senses, be described as one long frontier process. Initially, of course, the members of the Uyghur-remnant-aristocratic elite who flooded into the area after their expulsion from their steppe empire by the Qirgiz were the outsiders, who gradually came to dominate the local Sogdian-Turkic population. At the same time, the oases that those Uyghur immigrants inhabited shaped their collective identity. By the eleventh century the Uyghurs had themselves become Tarim Basin indigenes whose kingdom controlled the area, and whose identity was shaped by their ancient imperial history and their immediate sociocultural context. They, in their turn, had then to contend with other outsiders who wished to control the area, including the Qarakhitay, a remnant of the Liao dynasty also known as the Western Liao that ruled in eastern Transoxiana from 1131 to 1213, and, finally, the Mongols. I argue that this frontier process continued until Qubilai Qan (1215–94) lost control of the Tarim Basin area in the 1280s, at which point Uyghuristan ceased to exist as a (relatively) independent entity. Owing to the kinds of primary sources at my disposal, I limit my examination of the role of these Uyghurs in this frontier to this latter stage, from just before their submission to Chinggis Qan (1167–1227) in 1209 to their removal to China proper in the 1280s.

Accompanying the notion of Uyghuristan as a regional frontier state, I am also trying to uncover the history of Uyghuristan and its aristocratic elites as people in "the middle" in the sense that they and their state inhabited a middle ground between dominant states or dominant cultures.[10] The Tarim Basin in the eleventh and twelfth centuries was certainly a type of middle ground, situated between and separated from both steppe and sown by mountain ranges and desert. In fact, the mountains and desert dominated and contextualized life in the Tarim Basin for its inhabitants; it was marginal for agriculture and herding, and the various cities that arose in the area did so in the oases scattered around the northern and southern rims of the Taklamakan Desert, drawing life from the waters that flowed from the high mountain ranges.

The Tarim Basin was also a kind of cultural middle ground, home to a heterogeneous mix of languages, religions, ethnicities, and political loyalties. That cultural diversity sprang out of the one feature that really marked the Tarim Basin as special, the fact that the most important East-West overland trade routes ran along its northern and southern fringes. Because of the presence of those trade routes, control of the Tarim Basin was always a goal of the various surrounding dynasts. China had had a military presence in the area at least as far back as the Han dynasty, but Sogdians, Tibetans, Turks, and other peoples had also held sway there at one time or other.

Beginning in the mid-ninth century, Uyghur refugees from the steppe formed a kingdom in the Tarim Basin that lasted for several centuries. Thus, they became people "in the middle," a characteristic that, I argue, stayed with them over time and that provided them with strategies and resources to survive their eventual absorption in the Mongol Empire. This chapter has two aims. First, it presents a history of the Uyghur Tarim Basin Kingdom and the elites who ruled that kingdom as an example of a people and polity "in the middle." Second, it extends my analysis of the Uyghurs as a people in the middle to their situation after their absorption into the Mongol Empire. In this section, I argue that the identity as a people in the middle continued to define the Uyghurs even as they had lost their physical homeland in the Tarim Basin.

We have already seen evidence of the agency and importance of people who truly live in the middle from two case studies of South China in this volume—Sherry Mou's work on Grand Mistress Xian and James Anderson's study of the role of Tai-speaking tribes in Sino-Viet relations. My own consideration of the Uyghurs here continues the exploration of this important theme in relation to peoples to the north of China proper. In ways quite reminiscent of earlier non-Han peoples who lived in the Baiyue region and the hilly upland areas between China and Vietnam, the Uyghuristan Uyghurs were not simply passive recipients of their geopolitical roles in the Tarim Basin. On the contrary, they actively involved themselves in determining their own roles on the frontier. Moreover, in keeping with these earlier southern precedents, the circumstances of the Uyghurs of Uyghuristan differed from that of their cousins who ended up in Gansu and China proper following their eviction from their steppe kingdom in 840 because it was only the Uyghuristan–Tarim Basin Uyghurs who maintained their independent existence for as long as they did.

I argue that Uyghuristan was a unique regional frontier kingdom whose aristocratic elites interacted with neighboring states and tribes as political and cultural advisers because of some resources at their disposal, and that they were able to retain their identity as political and cultural elites even after they were dispersed from their homeland by using those same modes or strategies as people "in the middle." The strategies and resources developed by members of the Uyghur aristocracy were vital to their state-state interactions, and we benefit from understanding how and why they worked. Those strategies and resources consisted of their ethnicity (or their place of origin), their cultural skills and achievements, and their administrative experience and prowess, all of which stemmed from their legacy as a steppe empire and their ability to administer their seminomadic, multiethnic state in East Turkestan. Ethnicity for these Tarim Basin inhabitants was inferred from their place of origin; if a man was identified as a Gaochang native (*Gaochang ren*), then the audience would know with some certainty that he was a Uyghur. As Gaochang was one of the Uyghur capital cities, association with that toponym also often implied the social status of the person. Thus, virtually all of the Uyghur elites identified in the sources as *Gaochang ren* occupied relatively high social and political office at the Uyghur court.[11]

The Uyghur tribes that first moved into the upper Tarim Basin after their eviction from the steppe possessed a valuable legacy as descendants of the powerful Türk–Uyghur steppe empire period. The A-tis clan that formed a new seat of government in the Northern Tarim Basin and Eastern Tianshan Mountain area at Gaochang and Beiting appear to have replaced the ruling Yaghlaqar clan in the 790s.[12] The remnant Uyghur aristocrats established their rule over the older Turkic and Indo-Iranian populace (Qarluqs, Basmil, remnant Sogdians, etc.) in the Tarim Basin, where they quickly emerged as the dominant regional state. As the largely nomadic Uyghurs settled into that area they also adopted many of the local features, including their writing system, their religions, and important aspects of their administrative systems (Manicheism, Buddhism, art and architecture, and a wide variety of written and spoken languages were in the area long before the 800s). For example, the old Sogdian written language that was adopted by the Uyghurs became known as the Uyghur script. Uyghur aristocratic elites who ruled the Tarim Basin State used all those elements to maintain their advantage in their own state and also in their relations with neighboring states and tribes.

Uyghur identity (whether expressed as a type of ethnic category or as place of origin) was the vehicle through which those other forms of cultural and social capital were used. To be an Uyghur elite came to mean one skilled in the arts of administration, languages, and culture. People from Gaochang and Beiting used those resources, types of cultural capital, to carve out for themselves places at the highest levels of power in the various states they contacted. That same tactic held true when they were assimilated into the newly emergent Mongol Empire in the early-thirteenth century.

Uyghur Elites in Tarim Basin Politics

The Uyghurs who inhabited the northern area of the Tarim Basin and the eastern end of the Tianshan Mountains had a long history of involvement in regional affairs from the time they established their state in the mid-ninth century. The Uyghur State in the Tarim Basin was established in the late 800s by remnants of the Uyghur royal clan and other aristocratic clans whose steppe kingdom in Northern Mongolia was conquered by the Kirgiz in 840. The Uyghur-Tarim Basin Kingdom eventually revolved around two capital cities, Beshbaliq (known as Beiting to the Chinese) and Qocho (Gaochang to the Chinese), situated in oases to the north and south of the Tianshan Mountain Range.[13]

The Uyghuristan State had ongoing formal relations with all of the neighboring states and peoples from the time of its establishment until its absorption into the Mongol Empire. Uyghur embassies were sent to the Liao and Jin courts that ruled, successively, parts of the steppe and North China, to the Five Dynasties era Later Zhou court (951–60) and to the Song court. It appears that Uyghuristan was under some sort of tributary relation to the Liao, but the details are not clear. Uyghur envoys were sent several times to the Northern and Southern Song courts, and they were even immortalized in stone spirit way statues of the Northern Song imperial tombs.[14] We are also fortunate to have the record of a Song envoy to the Uyghurs, Wang Yande (939–1006), who went to Gaochang in 981.[15]

On the whole, the Tarim Basin Uyghurs seem to have maintained their relative independence until the early-twelfth century when they came under the subjection of the Qarakhitay.[16] Their duties to the Qarakhitay appear to have been light, consisting mainly of annual tax payments, until the early 1200s, when the Qarakhitay Qan began to demand more from them. Even at that time, however, the Uyghurs were able to maintain their relative autonomy, continuing to maintain diplomatic relations with neighboring states and tribes, and sending Uyghur envoys abroad to neighboring courts as advisors and, presumably, to reinforce Uyghur cultural, if not outright political, authority in the area. This tenacity of the Uyghurs was probably also because of their status as cultural "first-among-peers" in the region. Uyghur envoys performed advisory and administrative roles as well as representing the Uyghur king, and those activities illustrate the status of the Uyghur State and its elites among rival states and tribes in the area. It is at this point, sometime after the demands from the Qarakhitay increased, that we pick up the story. I here examine the activities of the Uyghur king and two high-ranking Uyghur aristocratic elites before and leading up to the critical year 1209, as their actions and roles in state and interstate affairs illustrate the position of Uyghuristan as a prime mover in the northwest frontier zone during that period.

We shall examine four members of the Uyghur aristocracy at Gaochang who exemplify the notion of Uyghuristan as actively involved in the northwest frontier zone, members of the Uyghur royal family, two of his officials, Tatar Tongga (fl. 1190–1204) and Qara Igach Buyruk (fl. 1190–1209), and Mengsus (1206–67), an Uyghur who, while not an official in Uyghuristan, was active as an official in the frontier zone in the early days of the Mongol empire. The Uyghur kings (known by the Uyghur title *iduqut* held relatively autonomous power at Uyghuristan for decades after they submitted to the Mongols, and both Tatar and Qara Igach functioned as envoys of the Uyghur court to the Qans of neighboring nomadic and sedentary states. All four examples underscore the agency of the Uyghurs as actors in the frontier zone.

The "Yuan *Iduquts*"

The easygoing relationship between the Qarakhitay and the Uyghurs came to an end in the early-thirteenth century, when a new representative was sent to Gaochang by the Qarakhitay Qan. That man, a Buddhist monk, infuriated the Uyghurs with his demands for more tax money and his overt greed, and it was in response to his demands and arrogance that the Uyghur *iduqut* decided to throw his hand in with Chinggis. The Uyghur *iduqut* Barchuq el-Tegin (fl. 1190s–1230s) had the Qarakhitay overseer assassinated and promptly submitted to Chinggis Qan. That decisive step was an important political and military coup for Chinggis Qan, and it set the tone for the status of the Uyghur royal house within the Mongol Empire for several generations.

As stated above, the Gaochang Uyghur Kingdom was one of the most important states that submitted in the early stages of Chinggis Qan's expansion of Mongol power, and this voluntary submission resulted in substantial benefits for the Uyghur imperial family and aristocracy under their new masters. The person who benefited most immediately was, of course, the Uyghur *iduqut* Barchuq.[17] After he submitted to the Mongols by having the resident Qarakhitay overseer murdered, he was accepted as a subject. Barchuq immediately demonstrated his loyalty to the Mongols when he denied a request for sanctuary from the Mongols by the Merkid tribe. Barchuq did not have a personal interview with Chinggis Qan until two years later (1211), but when this finally occurred, Chinggis Qan was so pleased with him that he decreed that Barchuq was "to be [his] fifth son, to be bound as a brother with the emperor's sons," and gave him one of his daughters in marriage.[18] These honors indicate the importance to the Mongols of Barchuq's early, voluntary, submission; he was the only ruler of any subject state who was "adopted" as a fifth son, and he was allowed to retain his Uyghur imperial title and function as *iduqut* in Uyghuristan. Moreover, Barchuq was allowed to request that his former subjects, Uyghurs who had become scattered throughout the rapidly expanding Mongol Empire, be allowed to return to Uyghuristan.[19] Barchuq was, however, reduced in his absolute power, like all other rulers of states who submitted to the Mongols. For example, he was obliged to accompany the Mongols on military expeditions, campaigning in the west against the Naiman and the Khwarazm Shah in 1216, and again in 1225 against the Tanguts. Barchuq continued to reign as the Uyghur *iduqut* at Gaochang until his death sometime between 1229 and 1241, but his demise did not signal the end of Uyghuristan as a political entity or of the position of Barchuq's family as hereditary *iduqut*.

Barchuq had several sons who succeeded him as *iduqut* at Gaochang. The first son to succeed him after his death was Kesmez.[20] He reigned only four years, from 1242 to 1246, apparently dying prematurely of natural causes. According to Persian sources from the period, he married a daughter of Chinggis Qan who had been promised to his father, Barchuq.[21] After Kesmez died in 1246, he was replaced by another of Barchuq's sons, Salindi (or Salin Tegin) (fl. 1246–53) by the order of the widow of Ögödei Qan (1186–1248), who was then acting as Regent.

Salindi continued the tradition of independent rule at Gaochang, but he became embroiled in the disputed succession of Mongke (1209–59) as Grand Qan over the Mongol Empire, and his actions eventually cost him his life. According to Persian sources, Salindi was talked into killing all of the Muslims who were living in the Uyghur summer capital, Beiting, apparently at the behest of Guyuk's widow who was contending for power with a rival Chinggisid family, the descendants of Tolui. In 1252, Salindi assembled an army of approximately 50,000 Uyghurs and was on his way to the northern capital, Beiting, to put the plan into action when a servant who knew of the plan leaked it to a high official in Beiting who was close to Mongke Qan. Salindi, upon hearing of this breach, went in person to paper things over. Confessions from all parties were taken down, and it was then decided that the parties should travel to Mongke Qan's court in the steppe to be properly judged. After suitable torture, the *iduqut* confessed to his crime. He and his accomplices were sent back to Beiting where his own brother, Ögrünch Tegin (r. 1253–57), was forced to execute him. That occurred in 1253, and Ögrünch was then appointed to be the next *iduqut* over the Uyghurs.[22]

We know little about Ögrünch's rule at Gaochang other than the fact that he was only on the throne a short time, and after his death his son (or possibly his younger brother?) Mamuraq Tegin was appointed as the next *iduqut* of the Uyghurs at Gaochang, and he ruled in that capacity for about nine years, dying in 1265 or 1266.

The last *iduqut* who ruled at Gaochang was a great grandson of Barchuq, a certain Qochgar Tegin. He was installed as *iduqut* in 1266 and died in Gaochang in 1280 at the hands of anti-Qubilai Mongols who were waging a war over control of the region. His young son, Ne'uril Tegin, petitioned Qubilai Qan for troops to avenge his father's death but by that time Qubilai Qan had lost effective control of the region and removed the Uyghur royal family to exile in Gansu. Ne'uril Tegin was recognized as the head of the Uyghur government-in-exile from 1280, but was only installed as *iduqut* in 1308, holding that title until his death in 1318.[23]

Qubilai Qan's loss of control of Uyghuristan effectively meant the end of the autonomy of the Uyghurs to rule their homeland, but it did not spell the end of the

Uyghur administrative system. Descendants of the *iduqut* continued to inherit and hold that hereditary office in China through the 1350s. By that time the office was largely ceremonial in nature, probably maintained as a favor to the many Uyghurs who held real power as administrators in Mongol China. But these "Yuan" *iduquts* were not, however, simply resigned to powerless positions as rulers-in-exile; many also served in other high-level administrative positions in China. For example, Temür Buqa (r. 1318–29), the great-great-great grandson of Barchuq, was assigned the office of junior chief councilor in the Yuan Central Secretariat (*zhongshu zuo chengxiang*) under the Emperor Toghon Temur.[24] The last *iduqut* appointed by the Mongols was a seventh-generation descendant of Barchuq, a certain But/Bodun Sari, who was awarded the title by the last Yuan Emperor in the mid to late 1350s.

The relative autonomy of Uyghuristan and its rulers, at least during the years immediately following their absorption into the growing Mongol Empire, is noteworthy among the history of subject states. But what degree of autonomy did Uyghuristan enjoy under the Mongols? Some scholars have argued that Uyghuristan occupied a special place in the Mongol Empire, as a type of "Fifth Qanate" with all implied political and administrative autonomy. This theory is based on the fact that Chinggis Qan adopted Barchuq as a "fifth son."[25] Although Barchuq and at least some of his successors were allowed a relatively free hand in governing Uyghuristan after 1209, it is a mistake to interpret the historical record as indicating that the Mongols granted the Uyghur virtually complete autonomy at Gaochang. One reason is that we know of at least two other foreigners who were called "fifth son" by the Qan. It is true that neither of those individuals ruled over a kingdom, but the favor indicated by Chinggis Qan in granting that title did not necessarily translate into independent political rights. Moreover, once Barchuq submitted to Chinggis Qan, there was no doubt that Uyghuristan was effectively under Mongol control. And we should remember that Barchuq was not the only ruler of a submitted state who was allowed to remain in his homeland with his titles intact; this was a time-honored practice used by the Mongols as a way to delegate authority to subjects in return for their continued loyalty.

At the same time, however, we must acknowledge that the Uyghurs, at least during Barchuq's lifetime and those of his eldest sons, did enjoy a great deal of autonomy in running their own affairs in Uyghuristan. It was common practice for the Mongols to appoint overseers or agents (*darughachi*) to recently conquered areas to act as the Qan's eyes and ears on the ground, and they had wide-ranging authority over civil and military matters where they were appointed. They were often Mongols, especially in the early decades of the empire, but native elites were also sometimes appointed, especially if the state in question had submitted peacefully and showed loyalty to the Mongols.[26] At least two Uyghurs were appointed as overseers to towns in Uyghuristan.[27] But, surprisingly, there is no record of a Mongol being assigned to any of the Uyghur capital cities. This arrangement was somewhat unusual because most conquered capital cities were regularly assigned overseers. The fact that Uyghurs were assigned as overseers of their own hometowns, and the absence of foreign overseers were absent from Gaochang and Beshbaliq, indicate that the *iduqut* and his retinue of Uyghur elites enjoyed a rare level of autonomy, and Uyghuristan continued to function very much as it had before the Mongol conquest, as a de facto autonomous regional state in the Tarim Basin frontier zone.

To be sure, some of the autonomy of the Uyghurs was taken away after Salindi became involved in the succession dispute between Guyuk's widow and Mongke. Loyalty to the wrong side proved deadly, and the Uyghur *iduqut* was not the only one who got caught up in that saga. We do not really know enough about events in Uyghuristan during the *iduqut* Ogrunch's reign to determine if his predecessor's actions resulted in a decreased ability to govern independently, or if more Mongol Agents were placed in Gaochang. We do know, however, that Ögrünch's successor, Mamuraq Tegin (r. 1257–66), was obliged to accompany Mongke Qan on military campaign in China against the Song dynasty, something that his great grandfather Barchuq was also obliged to do. Mamuraq Tegin's accompaniment of Mongke Qan may indicate a decline in the Mongol Qan's trust of the Uyghur *iduquts*. In any event, a much larger dispute between branches of the Mongol royal family, that between Qubilai Qan and his Chagadai cousins, would soon overtake the Uyghurs at Gaochang and force their final expulsion from their native land.

Uyghur elites continued to occupy positions of great importance in Mongol China until the very end of the Yuan dynasty in 1368. The fact that a remnant of the Uyghur *iduqut* was maintained by the Mongol Qans in China during that time is further proof of their ongoing status as political elites, whether or not the *iduquts* themselves wielded real power. But by the time the *iduquts* were removed to China, most of the Uyghurs in China had already integrated into the power structure in China, and may no longer have needed that institution as a source of identity.

If anything, the history of Uyghuristan before and during the early years of their integration into the Mongol Empire reveals the fact that the Uyghurs were quite adept at using their political and cultural capital to maintain their status and identity as political elites even as they were subjects of a much stronger entity. Their history in the steppe and in the Tarim Basin is one not of a barbarian people but of a sophisticated, highly cultured kingdom, whose aristocracy knew how to use that legacy as a form of cultural capital to their own benefit.

Tatar Tongga

Tatar Tongga was a member of the Uyghur aristocracy who was sent as a representative of the Uyghur *iduqut* at the Naiman court sometime in the last decades of the twelfth century. The Naiman were a Turko-Mongol tribe who occupied the steppe area north of Uyghuristan and west of the Mongol confederation. They were also longstanding enemies of Chinggis Qan.[28] We know little about Uyghur-Naiman formal relations, but it does appear that there was substantial borrowing of administrative practices between the two groups, and it appears that the Naiman were literate in Chinese, and perhaps also Uyghur. Tatar was more than a simple envoy; he seems to have been assigned the fairly important duties of heading up the Naiman tax collection system. The sources imply that Tatar introduced elements of that system to the Naiman Qan, especially the use of seals and other administrative technologies with which he would have been familiar as a member of the Uyghur aristocratic elite. Tatar was in that job when Chinggis Qan defeated the Naiman in 1204.

As soon as the Naiman fell to the Mongols, Tatar grabbed the seals that were in his possession and tried to flee, but was quickly captured by an alert Mongol soldier and brought before Chinggis Qan. From the exchange between Chinggis Qan and Tatar recorded in Tatar's official biography in the History of the Yuan Dynasty (*Yuanshi*) it is clear that Chinggis Qan was well aware of the need for his emerging empire to develop an administrative system that would function on written orders and that would use all of the most advanced techniques to collect revenue from subject populations.

> Tatar Tongga was an Uyghur familiar with his native country's language and literature. The Naiman Qan Tayang honored him by appointing him as an advisor, and he was put in charge of the gold seal. When Chinggis Qan defeated the Naiman [1204], Tatar took the seals and fled but was quickly apprehended and brought before Chinggis Qan, who asked Tatar ". . .what are these seals you are carrying?" and then asked him how they were used. Tatar replied saying: "the seals are used when someone is sent out to collect taxes; in each case the person who is officiating will use it as an official stamp of approval." Chinggis Qan was pleased with this, and ordered Tatar to join the ranks of his officials. Later, whenever there was an official edict, [he] began to use the seals on them. Chinggis Qan also appointed Tatar to teach his sons his native written language.[29]

Tatar is better known for introducing the Uyghur writing system to the Mongols, whose script was used for all official Mongol court documents, than he is for his role as a Naiman tax official. This latter role, however, is an important indication of the relative cultural and administrative strength of the Uyghurs among their nomadic neighbors, and shows us the extent to which Uyghuristan was one of the principle actors in the Tarim Basin frontier zone, first to the Naiman and eventually to the emerging Mongol Empire.

Tatar was inducted into the Mongol administration in 1204, two years before Temujin was elected Grand Qan, and five years before his own people came under Mongol sway. He was one of the first Uyghurs to join the Mongols, and very likely one of Chinggis Qan's first foreign advisors. Tatar's experience as a literate advisor to the Naiman Qan, especially his command of technical aspects of administrative systems such as the proper use of official stamps and seals, seems to have been the crucial factor.

Qara Igach Buyruk

Qara Igach Buyruk was also a member of the Uyghur aristocracy who served as an envoy to at least two neighboring states, and his story reveals a good deal about Uyghur involvement in interstate relations in twelfth- and thirteenth-century Central Asia.[30] Qara Igach's first official position was as a judge (*duanshiguan*) at Sairam, a tributary of the Uyghur Kingdom located in present-day Xinjiang, between Kucha and Aksu.[31] A judge was a representative of the Uyghur king at a foreign court and had wide-ranging authority over tribute payments and state relations. Although Sairam was a small state located on the far western fringe of the area controlled by Gaochang and was not a major power in Central Asia, the fact that Uyghuristan continued tributary relations with such states into the late-twelfth century, even after they had become tributaries to the Qarakhitay, indicates the Uyghurs' continuing political power and prestige in the region. Sometime after his assignment to Sairam, the Qarakhitay Qan requested that Qara Igach be assigned to his court, to "serve as a tutor to his sons" in addition to retaining his official title and duties as judge.[32] By this time the Uyghurs had been in a tributary relationship with the Qarakhitay, and Qara Igach's official duties and titles there indicate that the Uyghurs enjoyed a good relationship with their political masters. The sources do not tell us how long he served the Qarakhitay, or the exact nature of his duties beyond acting as a tutor, but he probably advised the Qan on matters of state and society in addition to his duties as a tutor. His presence at the Qarakhitay court may also have been as a type of insurance for Uyghur fulfillment of their tribute obligations.

The Uyghur *iduqut* had the Qarakhitay overseer at Gaochang killed while Qara Igach was stationed at the Qarakhitay court as the first step in submitting to the Mongols. Qara Igach then "returned and submitted" to the Mongols along with the rest of the Uyghur court. Qara Igach's family was among those Uyghur elites who continued to rule in their homeland.

Sometime after 1209, Chinggis Qan inducted Qara Igach's son, Ödösh Inal (fl. 1220s), into his personal bodyguard. This was routine for sons of high officials from states that had submitted to or were conquered by the Mongols, and admission into the Qan's bodyguard meant that, in addition to being a type of hostage that guaranteed the continuing loyalty of the high official, his son would have access to the surest route of upward mobility in the Mongol administration, since the bodyguard was routinely used as a training ground for civil and military officials. Qara Igach, meanwhile, accompanied Chinggis Qan in his military campaigns in the western regions (against the Qarakhitay).

While he was traveling through the Beshbaliq area of Uyghuristan en route west, Chinggis Qan brought Ödösh Inal back to his homeland and assigned him to be an agent where he was put in charge of both civilian and military affairs there.[33] As a sign of his authority and power as the Qan's representative, Ödösh Inal was bestowed the highest Uyghur and Mongol titles and signs of office; he was given the Uyghur hereditary titles *dudu* and *darqan*, and the Mongol symbol of authority, the Gold Tiger Tablet (C. *jinhufu*; M. *bars terig ü altan gerege*).³⁴ In fact, this is an interesting example of the ongoing role that Uyghurs played in their own land as high officials under the Mongols. The fact that the Mongols continued to allow the use of Uyghur hereditary official titles also demonstrates the Mongols were not threatened by Uyghur ambitions, and that they probably needed to keep such institutions intact in order to retain the loyalty of the Uyghurs. Qara Igach's grandson and great-grandson also inherited those same titles and offices and ruled on behalf of the Mongols until Qubilai Qan lost control of the Gaochang Qanate in the late 1270s.³⁵

Mengsus

Our last example of an Uyghur aristocratic elite who served in an important position in the northern frontier zone is Mengsus (1206–67).³⁶ We know that his family had lived in the Uyghur capital Besbaliq for generations and that his father was the governor of his region. According to his official biography in the *Yuanshi*, Mengsus was a child prodigy in his native written language:

> By age 15 he was said to be thoroughly familiar with his country's script. Chinggis Qan heard about him and commanded him to appear before him. Upon first seeing him he was pleased and said "this young man is full of energy and will be of great use [to us]." Chinggis Qan then ordered him to go and serve Tolui [and] he was put in charge of annual taxation on Tolui's appanage at Zhending [in North China].³⁷

At some point after his summons to the Qan he was put in charge of collecting the taxes on Tolui's appanage lands in North China. Chinggis Qan granted appanage lands to all of his brothers and to other Mongol princes in North China. They were the single most important source of income for the Mongol princes, and administration of the resources and revenue derived from those areas was one of the most important positions that a person could hold in the early–Mongol Empire period. Uyghurs and other Central Asian personnel whose states and tribes had submitted to Chinggis Qan were often assigned to these positions because they possessed the requisite literary and administrative skills and experience to see to the collection of revenue on behalf of their Mongol masters. As the official in charge of taxation in Tolui's appanage, Mengsus would have had a great deal of authority over the population who resided there, and his activities would have had a big impact over the course of events in Zhending.

Mengsus eventually became a trusted advisor to Qubilai Qan and was even nominated for the office of chancellor by the Qan but declined the offer. He died in the Yuan capital Dadu in 1267, and the Yuan court later granted him several honorific posthumous titles. Mengsus's descendants continued to hold high positions at the Yuan court and the family appears to have prospered for several generations, their success having been based at least in part on their mastery of the Uyghur writing system. In fact, one son of Mengsus, a certain Asiq Temür (1249–1309), was eventually promoted to the influential Hanlin Academy (*hanlin yuan*) where he was assigned to teach the future Yuan emperor Qaishan (r. 1308–11) the Uyghur script.

Uyghurs in Mongol China

The strategies that Tarim Basin Uyghurs employed in their relations with their neighbors were based on their cultural and political resources that they monopolized and that their neighbors needed or valued. As a result, Uyghur elites moved among and were employed by the leaders of various states as advisors and tutors in their capacity as official representatives. We have seen a few notable examples of these activities above.

Adept use of resources enabled the Uyghur aristocracy to maintain their kingdom as a vital actor in the northwest frontier zone for a long period of time, even after they had become nominal subjects of the Qarakhitay and other dominant states in the region. That experience as people in the frontier zone continued to mark the Uyghurs' experience after they were subsumed into the Mongol empire, and the lessons they learned at Gaochang continued to be applied by savvy Uyghurs who were interested in maintaining their own identity and power even as they were dispersed to various parts of the Mongol Empire. This was certainly true for many members of the Uyghur aristocracy who were moved to China proper in service to the Mongols. The Uyghur diaspora continued to occupy a middle ground, but now a sociopolitical middle ground rather than a physical one. The "frontier" I argue, only shifted with their dispersal into Mongol China from a physical frontier zone to the less-tangible but no less important one that existed between the Mongol conquerors and the Chinese subjects.

I next examine two examples of Uyghur elites who migrated to China in service to the Mongols after 1209 and whose careers and stories manifest this new frontier process. The two individuals, whose descendants eventually became known by the Chinese-type surnames Xie and Lian, were both members of important families at the Uyghur court, and they and their descendants occupied places of mediation in China quite similar to their predecessors in the Tarim Basin. They retained their identity and authority even as a diaspora group in a foreign land under Mongol authority where they continued to act as people "in the middle."

The Xie Family[38]

The ancestors of the people who eventually became known in China by the surname Xie were the most important members of the Uyghur aristocracy after the *iduqut* Barchuq. A certain Kezhipuer (fl. 1100) held several honorary and functional titles at the Uyghur court in the early twelfth century that indicate his high status, including state minister (*guoxiang*), free noble (*darqan*), and elder statesman (*aday tutung*).[39] Kezhipuer was sent to the Qidan Liao court by the Uyghur *iduqut* as his representative where he continued to use these same titles. According to the sources, "the Liao king conferred [on Kezhipuer] the titles of grand preceptor (*taishi*), grand counselor-in-chief (*da chengxiang*), and he was put in charge of the granaries in the capital and other regions (*zongguan nei wai cangshi*)."[40] At least one of these was a functional title within the Liao administration, because we are also told that Kezhipuer established a system of government storehouses that provided emergency food for the poor in times of scarcity, for which the people praised him.

This is an interesting example of Uyghur actions in the northwest frontier zone. First, not only was a member of the Uyghur aristocratic elite sent to the Liao court where he retained his official Uyghur titles, but he was also assigned to an important administrative position there, and given additional titles by the Liao king. These facts indicate the high regard in which their neighbors held the Uyghurs, even the powerful Qidan Liao to their east.

Kezhipuer's descendants continued to occupy the high titles at the Uyghur court for several generations. His great-grandson, Bilge Buqa (also known as Bilge Temur) (fl. 1190s–1209), also occupied the office of state minister at the Uyghur court, under the *iduqut* Barchuq el Tegin, and claimed the same hereditary titles as his ancestors. In fact, we know little more about Bilge Buqa than we do his immediate ancestors, except for the fact that he played a key role in the Uyghurs' break with the Qarakhitay and their subsequent submission to the Mongols in 1209. Despite the little we know, the sources are unanimous on one fact about Bilge Buqa. They all portray him as the mastermind behind Barchuq's decision to kill off the Qarakhitay overseer at Gaochang. Some of the sources even portray him as leading the actual assault on that man.

Bilge's father must have died an untimely death, because he inherited his titles at the relatively young age of sixteen. It was at about this same time that the Qarakhitay sent their avaricious representative to Gaochang. After Barchuq murmured his discontent about the arrogance of the Qarakhitay agent to Bilge, he carried out his duties with considerable relish. According to the Xie family history, Bilge proposed that he could kill the agent, so that the Uyghurs would be free to switch their allegiance to the Mongols. Accordingly, Bilge led soldiers to attack the agent, and he chased him up into a building, cut off the agent's head, and threw it down to the ground.[41] This occurred in 1209.

Bilge was rewarded for his actions with the honorific style name of Bilge Quti (*Bilijiehudi*, which means "His Highness Bilge"), and he was promoted to the presumably honorary rank of *mingbieji* by the Uyghur *iduqut* Barchuq.[42] Here the chronology of events is not entirely clear. The Xie family history supplies a precise list of the honorary titles that Bilge and other family members were given as a result of his actions, and it says that "his sons and brothers served their country as great officials. . ."[43] This may mean that the assassination either occurred sometime before the *iduqut* formally submitted to Chinggis Qan, or that Bilge's elevated status applied to him and his siblings after their entry into the Mongol camp.

Sometime after Bilge committed these acts and his king submitted to the Mongols Chinggis Qan rewarded him with numerous material gifts and symbols of Mongol imperial authority. He was "given the Golden Tiger Tablet (*jinhufu*) to wear, a silver seal with an embossed lion (*shi niu yinyin*), a gold dragon chair (*jin chiyi*), a robe of gold-embroidered cloth (*jin zhisun*), the dedicated service of four Mongol military officers (*xiaowei siren*), food and drink were set out for him almost as if he were part of the [Q]an's family, and he was given [control over] the food resources of twenty-three villages and fifty thousand *liang* of silver."[44] This is an impressive list of honors, and indicates the esteem in which Chinggis Qan held Bilge.

Curiously, Bilge drops out of the Chinese sources at this point; the texts abruptly state that he became ill and died. This sudden disappearance of Bilge from the story would not be remarkable except for the fact that more details about him are provided in the contemporaneous history of the Mongols by the Persian historian Juvaini (1226–83).[45] Specifically, in addition to confirming Bilge's role as one of the chief instigators of the assassination of the Qarakhitay agent, this account includes details about Bilge that are totally absent from the Chinese sources. This account also provides additional evidence to support my contention that the Uyghurs continued to play active roles in the northern frontier zone even after they submitted to the Mongols.

Juvaini's history includes details of the activities of high-level Uyghur aristocrats who were involved in an attempt to overthrow Mongke's authority at Gaochang. For example, Juvaini reports a plot that was hatched by some Uyghur nobles to kill all the Muslims who were living in Uyghuristan. Among the Uyghurs involved was a certain Bilge Quti. In fact, it was Bilge's slave who overheard the plotters and brought it to the attention of the authorities. Juvaini makes it clear that the Uyghur king was also involved, and that this was really a plot against Mongke. The Mongols acted with characteristic swiftness in this matter. After bringing everyone involved to the court, and obtaining confessions from the *iduqut* and the other Uyghurs involved, they were all executed, including Bilge. According to Juvaini, this occurred in 1252.[46]

The Bilge Quti of Juvaini's account is certainly the same Bilge of the Chinese sources who was involved in the assassination of the Qarakhitay agent, and who submitted to the Mongols in 1209. First, the honorific title *quti* borne by the Bilge who plotted against the Muslims in Uyghuristan appears to be the same title that was conferred on Bilge Temur by the Uyghur *iduqut* after he killed the Qarakhitai agent. Furthermore, it is likely that Bilge would have remained in Uyghuristan as a loyal retainer of the Mongols after he had submitted in 1209. Chinggis Qan often retained high officials of states who had submitted to him in their home area as a means of controlling the local population. The symbols of authority and other gifts that Chinggis Qan bestowed on Bilge would also have been most useful to a representative of Mongol power stationed in Uyghuristan. We also know that Bilge's younger brother, Eren Temur (Yuelin tiemuer) (fl. 1209–50s), and Bilge's nephew, Sergius (Sajisi) (fl. 1260s), were taken into the Qan's personal guards corps as hostages, from where they eventually made their ways up into the higher levels of the Mongol civil bureaucracy. There is no mention of Bilge having been inducted into Chinggis Qan's bodyguard unit, and it appears that Bilge was instead returned to his powerful position in Uyghuristan, now as a loyal retainer of the Mongols.

Eren Temur and Sergius were the first members of this prominent Uyghur family to be removed from their homeland and serve out their careers as members of a diaspora group of Central Asian elites who became important members of the Mongol administrative system over conquered sedentary populations, in this case China. Both men continued to follow career patterns set out by their ancestors as activist political and cultural elites, but now in a new place under new masters in the growing Mongol empire. This was a pattern followed by the family members of many other important Uyghur elites in China.

Eren Temur and Sergius

Eren Temur was inducted into Chinggis Qan's personal bodyguard at the age of fifteen, and then he was made to accompany the Qan in his western military campaigns against the Khwarazm-Shah that began in 1219, and perhaps also on later campaigns against the Tanguts.[47] Sometime thereafter he was sent by Chinggis Qan to serve his younger brother Temüge Odchigin (fl. 1220–40s) as a tutor at Temüge's appanage lands in Eastern Shandong province. Eren's duties were not limited to teaching the prince's sons, but also included general oversight of those appanage lands, especially when Temüge was not in residence, and his position within this princely family ensured his rapid climb up the ranks of the Mongol civil administrative system.

Eren was eventually sent into other parts of North China as an administrator for the Mongols. Ögödei Qan assigned him to be a grand judge (*da duanshiguan*) at an unspecified location in North China, and after his participation in a successful military campaign in Henan he was assigned to that region as an agent for civil and military affairs there (*junmindu darughuachi*). As a symbol of his authority he was given the Golden Tiger Tablet, and was also provided with four women from the Qan's own harem as concubines. Eren apparently settled happily into his new life in China; he married a woman from a prominent Jurchen family who lived in Shandong, undoubtedly having met her while in Temüge's employ, and he seems to have had a successful career in Henan, his last posting of record. Eren died at age sixty-seven, and was later awarded several posthumous honorary titles by the Mongol court.

Sergius was also placed in Temüge's appanage lands in Shandong as an adviser, and his career, even more than Eren's, reveals the power that Uyghur elites carried with them into the Mongol empire and continued to wield as agents of their own identities as political elites in the northern frontier zone. The sources make clear that Sergius taught Temüge and his sons the Uyghur script, but he also seems to have been used as an advisor to the Prince. He is known for his activities in two important events that occurred while he was living in Shandong in Temüge's employ, his meddling in a succession dispute among the Mongol princes after Ögödei Qan's early death in 1241, and his participation in the campaign to suppress the Shandong local warlord Li Tan in the first years of Qubilai Qan's reign.[48]

Sergius's prescient participation in both issues resulted in a stellar career for him as an administrator for the Mongols in North China. After Güyük's election as *qaghan* in 1246, Sergius was awarded the office of magistrate over the area of Heishan in northeastern China. After the successful suppression of Li Tan's rebellion in Shandong in 1262, Sergius was appointed to the position of high military commissioner of Yidu circuit in Shandong (*Yidulu xingsheng da dudu*, in February 1263), and was also given control of Li Tan's personal property, including some five thousand *mu* of land that contained several herds of horses, forests, gardens, a water mill and a postal station. Sergius ended up being one of the most influential Uyghur elites in the early decades of the Mongol rule of North China.

Eren's son, Qara Buqa, followed a career path similar to his father and other important Uyghurs. He was also inducted into the Qan's personal bodyguard, and was eventually appointed to the post of regional transport minister and sent to South China in the 1270s, where he was killed in the line of duty in 1284. Qara Buqa's oldest son, Xie Wenzhi, followed in his father's footsteps and had a successful career as an official for the Mongols. Wenzhi also interacted with Chinese people in ways reminiscent of his ancestors' interactions with Mongols, a strategy that proved successful for his family's survival in China. He settled into a community in southeastern China, adopted a Chinese-style surname, and acted very much like a typical Chinese literatus. Wenzhi hired tutors to educate his sons in the classic Chinese tradition. This strategy paid off handsomely, for all five of his sons obtained the "presented scholar" or *jinshi* degree in the renewed civil service examinations. The sources almost universally comment on this feat, and the Xie family gained considerable fame because of it. Wenzhi's sons went on to achieve great success both in the political and in cultural realms. His third son, Xie Zhedu, was especially successful in straddling the two worlds of political and cultural elite.

I now turn to my final example of Uyghur activities as exemplifying a people "in the middle"; this is the example of another prominent Uyghur family who thrived in Mongol China, the Lian family. We do not know as much about this family's activities or status in Uyghuristan as we do about the Xie family ancestors. But I include the Lians here as an example of the shift in strategies adopted by many important Uyghur elites who worked for the Mongols in China. Coming from their long experience as people in the frontier zone who had the power and experience to shape their own destinies in that frontier zone, and as part of that specific frontier process, Uyghurs like the Xies and Lians who were moved out of

Uyghuristan into China by the Mongols adapted that history and that experience to their new setting. In China they continued to act as people in the middle, but in new ways and between new groups. Their experience in Mongol China, I argue, constituted a new kind of frontier process, no longer one determined by geopolitical state boundaries, but by ethnic and cultural boundaries.

The Lian Family[49]

The Lian family provides an interesting parallel to the Xies. Lian ancestors were also part of the Uyghur aristocracy for at least three generations before 1209. Buyruq Qaya (1197–1229), the first family member on record, must have been a younger cohort of Bilge Buqa at Gaochang since he is listed among the group of leaders who followed the Uyghur *iduqut* in submitting to Chinggis Qan. His subsequent career was also very similar to the Xie family ancestors. After being inducted into Chinggis Qan's personal bodyguard unit he accompanied the Mongol leader on at least one military campaign in Central Asia. At some point thereafter he was appointed as an overseer of Prince Tolui's wife's appanage lands and households in North China (at Zhending), and served in a number of other high offices in North China.

Like the Qara Buqa's son, Buyruq also adopted a Chinese-style surname. He chose the name Lian because it was the first character of his official title, investigation officer (*lianfang shi*) at the time of the birth of his second son, Lian Xixian, in 1231. The Lian family eventually became well-known members of the Chinese literati elite and survived in China well beyond the Mongols. Buyruq had thirteen sons, several of whom went on to distinguished careers as administrators and as literati.

His second son, Lian Xixian (1231–80), was the best known of thirteen siblings. He had a long and varied career at the Mongol court, too long to examine here. But a couple of incidents are worth looking at for what they tell us about Xixian's attitude toward Chinese culture, and his strategies as an Uyghur elite in Mongol China. First, Xixian was inducted into Qubilai's personal bodyguard at age fourteen. Xixian's early induction into this elite group ensured his political career. Just as important, it also provided Xixian with an introduction to some important Chinese scholar/officials who would have an enormous impact on the direction of his life and career. While he was stationed at Qubilai's court as a member of the royal bodyguard he was able to study with the famous Chinese literatus, Wang E (1190–1273). It was in this period that Xixian also got his nickname, "Lian Mencius" (Lian Mengzi). One day in the court Qubilai Qan noticed Lian carrying a copy of the *Mencius* (*Mengzi*), quizzed him on its contents, and was so impressed that he called him "Lian Mencius," a sobriquet that stuck with him thereafter. Lian Xixian went on to serve in several high positions under Qubilai, both in the central government and in provincial postings, and died relatively young in 1280 at age forty-nine. Xixian may have been the most politically successful of his family, but several of his siblings also had careers as important officials from the *Semuren* social status group and as cultural actors.[50] Space does not permit me to elaborate on the careers of all of these men, but a perusal of Lian family history indicates that Xixian and his siblings adapted comfortably and fully into Chinese culture. At the same time that they were becoming part of the Chinese cultural establishment, however, the Lian family also maintained their Uyghur identity and continued to perform as Uyghur political elites.

The Lian family used marriage ties to reinforce their Uyghur identity. Lian Ximin (fl. 1250s), Buyruq's eldest son, married a daughter of an important Uyghur, Guan Zhige (fl. 1270s).[51] Buyruq's second son, Xixian married twice; his first wife was a daughter of the prominent Uyghur Mengsu (discussed above). She bore him one son and three daughters (all three daughters married Chinese men). His second wife was a woman from a Jurchen family who bore him five sons. Another of Buyruq's sons, Lian Xishu (fl. 1285–92), married a daughter of yet another important Uyghur clan, the Gusulu clan (and in a further twist, a sister to Xishu's wife married Xie Zhedu). Further cementing this relationship between Uyghur clans, a great-grandson of Lian Xixian, a certain Lian Yaoyao (fl. 1340s), married a daughter of Xie Zhedu.

Another strategy employed by the Lian family (and other prominent Uyghurs like the Xies) for maintaining their Uyghur identity involved the selection and retention of Chinese-style surnames and personal names. Lian is an unusual Chinese surname and was only used by members of that particular family. Since, as we have seen, the character Lian was adopted as a surname by a member of that family because it was the first part of his father's title as a high-level civil official under the Mongols, continued use of this unique name would have acted as a constant reminder to later family members of their family's ancestry and origins as diaspora Uyghurs who came to China as Mongol subjects. It would have also reminded any literate Chinese of the new social order imposed by the Mongols. At the same time, adopting a Chinese-style surname would have made those Uyghurs appear to accommodate to Chinese culture, a move that was undoubtedly intended to smooth relations with their Chinese elite peers.

Personal name practices also reflect this dual approach. Ten of Buyruq Qaya's sons used Chinese-style personal names that began with Xi.[52] At the same time, his youngest son seems to have only used his Uyghur name, Arqun Qaya, without the Lian surname. Some family members used a Uyghur-style surname and the Lian surname, such as one of Xixian's grandsons, Lian Anianbaqa. Other Lian family member personal names also have a distinctive Uyghur flavor to them, such as Xixian's great-grandson Yaoyao, mentioned above. Similar variation in naming practices down through successive generations can also be seen in other prominent Yuan China Uyghur families such as the Xies.

Conclusion

The Uyghurs here examined were all members of the aristocratic elite at Gaochang who functioned as envoys to other states or as advisors and administrators for the

Mongols. One of the traits they all share in common is the way in which they utilized resources at their disposal in their positions. I have chosen to focus on Uyghurs who were either especially skilled in administrative techniques or who used their literacy to their advantage. Other examples of Uyghurs who were important merchants or who had particular military skills could also have been chosen to illustrate their actions in the northwest frontier zone. But the critical point would remain the same in any case, and it is that these Uyghurs from the Tarim Basin used the resources available to them to mold and shape the political and social space around them, creating a frontier process in which they had agency and that ended when they lost their autonomy.

The Uyghur State in the Tarim Basin was formed at a time of great instability in the region; Tang China was on the verge of dissolution as a unified empire and the great Uyghur Empire in the steppe had just been overrun. To the east, the Qidan people had conquered part of North China and established their own kingdom that became known as the Liao State. These regional states in the northwest frontier zone were truly states in the middle, defined by their geographic settings and the political context. Small regional states such as Uyghuristan became active agents in the frontier process by focusing on the social relations with their neighbors. For the Uyghurs this meant using the substantial cultural capital at their disposal, such as their multilinguality and cultural experience, to frame those relationships to their advantage. At the same time, hard political and geographic boundaries such as well-defined borders, deserts, and other naturally limiting phenomena tended to become less immediately relevant.

The Uyghurs, like other regional polities of both north and south, saw accommodation and the construction of alliances as the norm in state-state relations. In that world, ethnicity (or local identity) and tribal or political association were not necessarily divisive. As Sherry Mou has already shown, the actions of Grand Mistress Xian and her polity in the frontier zone south of China serves as a good example of earlier, similarly employed strategies. For the Tarim Basin Uyghurs, their resources and their identity served as the glue that bound their regional state together. Given that others clearly wanted what the Uyghurs had, resources and identity were also useful forms of capital in their relations with other states. In both cases, boundaries were porous, not absolute.

In their own kingdom, immigrant Uyghurs interacted with but also maintained their political power over groups that had lived in the Tarim Basin before their arrival in the ninth century. Once they had established their control and Uyghuristan became a player in the region, Uyghur elites maintained friendly, constructive relations with neighboring states and tribes. Those relationships revolved around the appropriate deployment of resources, and Uyghur tribal or ethnic identity was not a negative factor. Indeed, their history in the Tarim Basin is one of constant engagement with other states and tribes. Even when the Uyghurs were technically the subordinates in tributary relationships with other more powerful states, such as the Qarakhitay, they managed to assert their own agency as a state and a people in the region. They actively controlled the frontier process in that inhospitable place that was dominated by desert, mountain ranges, and the trade routes.

Even after they were subsumed into the Mongol Empire in 1209, the Uyghurs continued to assert their control of the frontier process, both in Uyghuristan and in the early decades of Mongol control of North China. We have seen that the *iduqut* was retained there until rather late in Qubilai Qan's reign, when the whole region was lost to his control. That point should be considered the terminus point of the frontier process for the northwest area. Thereafter, Uyghuristan and all points west were incorporated into the Chaghadai Qanate, and the division between the two strong imperial states dominated the region and created a bipolar world. In Barfield's terms, small regional states like Uyghuristan had no place in that environment.

But even as they lost their position as a relatively independent people in their home area in the northwest, the Uyghurs continued to act as people "in the middle." Adopting the strategy of employing their resources, their cultural capital, in their new setting as a diaspora group in Mongol China, Uyghur elites formed alliances with the two important communities that mattered most to them, the Mongols and the Chinese elite. We may therefore liken them to the people of the autonomous northern frontier province Lulong earlier described by David Graff, whose existence was always framed by relations with the northern nomads as well as with Chinese. That this strategy worked to the Uyghurs' advantage is obvious. In the political realm, Uyghurs constituted the highest, most trusted level of the group of Central Asian administrators imported into China to work for the Mongols. In the cultural realm, within two or three generations, Uyghurs had become associated with the most important Chinese literati, and had begun to establish their credentials as members of that exclusive group.

One of the key resources for those Uyghurs was their ethnicity. As I have already argued above, while "ethnicity" was not a distinct category of identity for the thirteenth-century Uyghurs in the same way that we think of it today, it was made a salient feature of their identity by constant reference to native place and by a strategic employment of personal and surnames. In the Yuan era sources, *Semuren* personnel such as the Uyghurs are always identified by a toponym; virtually all Uyghurs are identified as natives of one of the two Uyghur capital cities. Thus, their Uyghur ethnicity was a product of their natal place of origin. That identity, in turn, was powerful cultural capital for members of the Uyghur diaspora in China as the Mongols viewed the Uyghurs as people of high culture who could bring their linguistic and administrative expertise to work for the benefit of the new Mongol Empire. From the Chinese perspective, Uyghur ethnic identity undoubtedly marked them as non-Mongol, but probably also was an indicator of cultural achievement, especially over time as Uyghurs increasingly participated in Chinese cultural pursuits and became less phenotypically distinctive from the Chinese population. The key in both relationships was resource, but the vehicle for using those resources was their ethnicity.

Many Uyghurs also used Chinese- and Uyghur-style surnames and personal names to establish and reinforce their identity in the political and cultural realms. As we have seen, adoption of a Chinese-style surname was an important move for Uyghur elites because it preserved some sense of their Uyghur identity while at the same time enabling them to accommodate to Chinese cultural ways. This strategy is even more clearly revealed in the selective use by some Uyghurs of Chinese- or Uyghur-style personal names, apparently depending on context. By an adroit use of names, these Uyghurs were able to appeal simultaneously to the Mongol political elite and the Chinese cultural elite. The successful dual career tracks of many of these Uyghurs as *Semuren* officials as well as Chinese-style cultural literati demonstrate the usefulness of this strategy.

On the face of it, for the sake of retaining their own hegemony and identity, we would expect the Mongols to have been intent on separating themselves from all of their subjects, whether Central Asian or Chinese. Yet, the social history of the Mongols in China is largely one of vast cooperation, especially between the Mongols and their Central Asian brethren. It is merely that scholars have heretofore given less attention to the persuasively inclusive and universalistic claims that the Mongols employed in their dealings with the various peoples they conquered and brought into their empire than they have to Mongol methods of devastatingly effective violent coercion.

As we have seen from the examples discussed, the story of the Uyghur elites who served the Mongols in China certainly cancels the notion of hard lines and divisions between those groups. It is also clear from the Yuan sources that the Chinese at the time were less concerned with ethnic issues than they were with making their way in their own world that was ruled by foreigners. It may not have been difficult for the average Chinese to tell "conqueror" from "conquered," but it seems clear that at least some of the Chinese who counted were willing to accept foreigners into their ranks if they displayed the appropriate cultural and intellectual qualities. The record of Uyghur cultural accomplishments in China is quite clear, and people like the Xies and the Lians were highly respected by the weightiest Chinese literati of the time. Uyghur ethnicity did not stand in their way and may even have served as a convenient vehicle to enter that world.

With a foot in both Mongol and Chinese worlds, the Uyghur elites who lived and worked in China adapted a new strategy that enabled them to maintain their hold on powerful political positions while at the same time becoming part of the powerful local groups of Chinese literati. In a very real sense, then, they continued to function as people "in the middle," their specific methods only differing according to their specific context. In contrast to their ancestors, who were part of the Uyghur aristocratic elite in their own state in the Tarim Basin, these people were part of a diaspora in China. Removed from their homeland, these Uyghurs adapted their strategies of using the cultural and political resources at their disposal to their new setting in China. Now they still acted as people "in the middle," but no longer in the northern frontier zone. Now they occupied a middle ground between the

Mongol conquerors and the Chinese conquered population. They appealed to each side with different resources and different strategies, and their history in Yuan-dynasty China is one of continual migration across community boundaries. They remained active agents in determining their fate, and they initiated a new type of frontier process, no longer geographically determined. That new frontier process began with their absorption into Mongol-controlled China, and ended only when the Mongols themselves were driven out of China in 1368.

Notes

This chapter was first presented under the title "Porous Boundaries: Uyghurs and Social Change on China's Northern Frontier Zone" as a panel paper at the 2002 annual meeting of the Association for Asian Studies. I am indebted to comments and suggestions from Bob Hymes, Don Wyatt, my fellow panelists Jamie Anderson and Jon Skaff, and Naomi Standen. All translations are mine unless otherwise noted.

1. See Jeremy Adelman and Stephen Aron, "From Borderlands to Borders: Empires, Nation-States, and the Peoples in between in North American History," *American Historical Review* 104.3 (June, 1999):814–41.
2. The locus classicus of the northern frontier zone as the *Inner Asian* frontier is in Owen Lattimore, *Inner Asian Frontiers of China*, American Geographical Society Research Series 21 (New York, 1940).
3. Owen Lattimore specifically contrasted the northern frontier with China's southern frontier zone, seeing the latter as radically different because it contained an environment and climate suitable for agriculture and because the non-Chinese in that area were closer to the "Chinese matrix" than were the outer barbarians of the northern steppe. See his "The Frontier in History" in *Studies in Frontier History, Collected Papers 1928–1958* (London, 1962), pp. 469–91. Frederick Jackson Turner (1861–1932) first propounded his frontier thesis in 1893, and is the founder of the school of frontier studies in the United States. There are many problematic aspects to his original thesis, including American exceptionalism and the idea of the frontier as an empty area. Nevertheless, his act of placing the frontier at the center and viewing it as a process continues to counterbalance seeing history only from the perspective of areas of settlement. See his "The Significance of the Frontier in American History" in *The Frontier in American History* (New York, 1920; rpr. Tucson, 1986), pp. 1–38.
4. Along with Adelman and Aron, *From Borderlands to Borders*, cited above, for elaboration on the notion of the frontier as process, see also Leonard Thompson and Howard Lamar, "Comparative Frontier History" in *The Frontier in History: North America and Southern Africa Compared*, ed. Howard Lamar and Leonard Thompson (New Haven; London, 1981), pp. 3–13. Thompson further develops this thesis in his later essay "The Southern African Frontier in Comparative Perspective" in *Essays on Frontiers in World History*, ed. George Wolfskill and Stanley Palmer (College Station, 1983), pp. 101–34.
5. The centrality of trade to the relations between China and steppe nomads is the focus of two important studies, both of which also stress the northern frontier

zone as a kind of process. See Thomas J. Barfield, *The Perilous Frontier: Nomadic Empires and China* (Cambridge; Oxford, 1989). See also Sechin Jagchid and Van Jay Symons, *Peace, War, and Trade Along the Great Wall: Nomadic-Chinese Interaction through Two Millennia* (Bloomington, 1989).

6. Lattimore goes the furthest in giving the frontier zone an identity of its own. He describes the belt of marginal lands as gradually acquiring an importance of their own because they were "not fully homogeneous with either China or the steppe. . ." But even Lattimore sees the marginal frontier area as being peopled by either Chinese or steppe nomads, and the push-pull of these two groups resulting in the frontier style being both positive and negative in any given historical period. Lattimore, *Inner Asian Frontiers*, pp. 423–24.

7. The lingering Sinocentric paradigm is also reflected, I believe, in the very term "northern" frontier, which defines the frontier with respect to China, which lies to its south. Although I wish to problematize this terminology in this study, I will continue to use these terms for ease of reference. Perhaps this means that I too am still stuck in the Sinocentric worldview?

8. See Arthur Waldron, *The Great Wall: From History to Myth* (Cambridge, 1990).

9. An earlier example of a frontier society on China's northern frontier zone that exhibited characteristics similar to the Uyghurs, as people in the middle, is that of the Tabgatch. See Scott Pearce, "The Land of Tai: The Origins, Evolution and Historical Significance of a Community of the Inner Asian Frontier" in *Opuscula Altaica: Essays Presented in Honor of Henry Schwarz*, ed. Edward H. Kaplan and Donald W. Whisenhunt (Bellingham, 1994), pp. 465–98.

10. For this discourse on middle ground I have borrowed from Richard White's well known monograph *The Middle Ground: Indians, Empires, and Republics in the Great Lakes Region, 1650–1815* (Cambridge, 1991). See also Adelman and Aron, *From Borderlands to Borders*, cited above, for development of this theme.

11. In fact, ethnonym and toponym are usually conflated in the sources from the period, and there seems to be very little understanding of ethnicity apart from place of origin. Ethnicity as it is commonly understood and used by scholars is a product of the modern nation-state, and the application of this term to premodern peoples such as the Uyghurs must be understood to include location. See, for example, Dru C. Gladney, "Sedentarization, Socioecology, and State Definition: The Ethnogenesis of the Uighur" in *Rulers from the Steppe: State Formation on the Eurasian Periphery*, ed. Gary Seaman and Daniel Marks (Los Angeles, 1991), pp. 308–40. Uyghur identity in the twelfth century appears to have been grounded first and foremost in native place, from which contemporaneous people would have derived a sort of ethnic identity. Thus, in the sources I use, Uyghurs are always identified by their place of origin, as "Gaochang native" (*Gaochang ren*), etc. It was only in secondary sources, such as the Yuan legal code or descriptions by Chinese writers, that people were identified by an ethnic description as Uyghurs (*Weiwuer ren*).

12. Larry V. Clark, "Introduction to the Uyghur Civil Documents of East Turkestan (13th–14th cc.)" (Ph.D. diss., Indiana University, 1975), pp. 4–7, 33 n. 10.

13. The Uyghur ruling family seems initially to have held control over a wide swath of territory that included the Tarim Basin and east into present-day Gansu, and sometime after their flight broke up into the two states situated in the Tarim-Tianshan area and in Gansu. For studies of the history of the Uyghur capital cities see Takeo Abe, "Where Was the Capital of the West Uighurs?" *Silver*

Jubilee Volume of the Zinbun Kagaku Kenkyusyo (Kyoto, 1954), 435–50; Shimazaki Akira, "On Pei-t'ing (Bišbalïq) and K'o-han Fu-t'u-ch'êng," *Memoirs of the Research Department of the Tôyô Bunko* 32 (1974):99–117; Hilda Ecsedy, "Uighurs and Tibetans in Pei-T'ing (790–791 A.D.)," *Acta Orientalia Hungaricae* 17 (1964):83–112; and Paul Pelliot, "Kao-Tch'ang, Qoco, Houo-Tcheou et Qarä-Khodja," *Journal Asiatique* series 10, vol. 19 (1912):578–603. For the general history of the Uyghur Kingdom, see Emil Bretschneider, *Medieval Researches from Eastern Asiatic Sources*, 2 vols. (London, 1887; rpr. 1967). For Uyghur relations with Five Dynasties era China, see James R. Hamilton, *Les Ouïghours a l'Époque des Cinq Dynasties* (Paris, 1955; rpr. 1988). For Uyghurs in the Mongol period, see Thomas T. Allsen, "The Yuan Dynasty and the Uighurs of Turfan in the 13th Century" in *China among Equals: The Middle Kingdom and Its Neighbors, 10th–14th Centuries*, ed. Morris Rossabi (Berkeley, 1983), pp. 243–80; *Weiwuerzu jianshi* (Urumqi, 1991); and Li Futong, "Weiwuerren duiyu Yuanchao jianguo zhi gongxian," *Shixue lunji* 3 (1977):328–98. Li's and Allsen's works are the most comprehensive studies of Uygurs in Mongol China to date. For the cultural history of the Uyghur Kingdom, see Annemarie von Gabain, *Das Leben im uigurischen Konigreich von Qoco, 850–1250* (Wiesbaden, 1973), and Monique Maillard, "Essai sur la vie materielle dans l'oasis de Tourfan pendant le haut moyen age," *Arts Asiatique* 29 (1973):3–185. I shall use the Chinese renderings of the names of the two Uyghur capital cities, Gaochang and Beiting, rather than the Uyghur names Qocho and Beshbaliq, throughout this chapter, as my sources use those versions.

14. See Ann Paludan, "Some Foreigners in the Spirit Roads of the Northern Song Imperial Tombs," *Oriental Art* 29.4 (Winter 1983/84):377–88, and especially Figures 18–20. That these figures probably represent Uyghurs from the Tarim Basin is evident from the clothing, hair, and jewelry styles. Türks from Turfan were also listed among the foreign emissaries who visited the Northern Song court.

15. See Toghto [Tuotuo], *Songshi* (Beijing, 1976), *juan* 490 for Wang's account of his mission to the Uyghurs, translated into French in 1847 by Stanislaus Julien, "Les Oïgours. Kao-Tch'ang-hing-ki, ou Relation d'un voyage (officiel) dans le pays des Oïgours (de 981 à 983), par Wang-Yen-Té," *Journal Asiatique* 4 (1847):50–66, retranslated by Emil Bretschneider, *Medieval Researches*, 1:244.

16. See Karl A. Wittfogel and Feng Chia-sheng, *History of Chinese Society: Liao (907–1125)*, Transactions of the American Philosophical Society, New Series 46 (Philadelphia, 1946). The Gaochang Uyghurs seem to have remained relatively free of attachment to the Liao State while their kinsmen in Gansu were more closely tied to Liao. Gaochang sent only one tribute mission to Liao, in 1049.

17. For a description of Barchuq's submission to Chinggis, as well as for details concerning his descendants, see Allsen, "Yuan Dynasty and the Uighurs of Turfan"; and Luo Xianyou, "Yuandai Weiwuer yiduhu puxi yu qi diwei bianqian," *Minzu yanjiu* 2 (1997):70–80. See also Barchuq's official biography in Song Lian, *Yuanshi* (Beijing, 1976), 122.2999–3002, part of which has been translated by Bretschneider, *Medieval Researches*, 1:249–50. *Yuanshi* is hereafter designated by YS. For Barchuq's family tree see, Qian Daxin, comp., "Yuanshi shizu biao" in *Ershiwushi bubian* (Shanghai, 1937), 6:8333–34 (hereafter *ESWSBB*). For a more condensed list of all Yuan *iduquts*, see Volker Rybatzki, "Titles of Turk and Uigur Rulers in the Old Turkic Inscriptions," *Central Asiatic Journal* 44.2

(2000):253–54. See also the Uyghur stela inscription translated by Geng Shimin and James Hamilton, "L'Inscription Ouigoure de la Stele Commemorative des Iduq Qut de Qoco," *Turcica* 13 (1981):10–54; R. Rahmeti Arat, "Der Herrschertitel Iduq-qut," *Ural-Altaische Jahrbücher* 35.B (1964):150–57; and the account by the Persian historian 'Ala-ad-Din 'Ata-Malik Juvaini, *The History of the World-Conqueror*, tr. John A. Boyle (Manchester, 1958). I have consulted all of these works for the following discussion.

18. The designation as "fifth son" was honorific, and not meant as a type of literal adoption into Chinggis Qan's family. Nor was the title unique to Barchuq, as at least two other individuals who submitted to Chinggis Qan also appear to have been called "fifth son." See Allsen, "Yuan Dynasty and the Uighurs of Turfan," pp. 247–48, and 271, n. 31.

19. Allsen, "Yuan Dynasty and the Uighurs of Turfan," p. 248.

20. Kesmez is mentioned only in Juvaini's history and, thus, there is no Chinese rendering of his name.

21. Juvaini, *History of the World-Conqueror*, pp. 47–48.

22. Juvaini, *History of the World-Conqueror*, pp. 48–53. See also Allsen, "Yuan Dynasty and the Uighurs of Turfan," pp. 250–51.

23. The Chagadai Qans who wrested control of Uyghuristan away from Qubilai Qan in the 1280s also maintained a line of Uyghur *iduquts* who continued to rule at Turfan from the early-fourteenth century through at least the 1350s. For a partial reconstruction of this line, see Rybatzki, "Titles of Türk and Uigur Rulers" pp. 254–55.

24. Primary sources for Temür Buqa include Yu Ji, *Daoyuan xuegu lu*, SBCK edition, 24.6 and *YS*, 122.4–6. As an example of the ongoing interconnections and alliances maintained by important Uyghurs throughout the Mongol period in China, Temur Buqa was involved in an incident at the Yuan court that involved a descendant of Qara Igach Buyruk, a certain Shalaban. I have discussed this particular incident, as well as other examples of Uyghur alliances, in my dissertation. See Michael C. Brose, "Strategies of Survival: Uyghur Elites in Yuan and Early Ming China" (Ph.D. diss., University of Pennsylvania, 2000), especially pp. 25–27.

25. Takeo Abe was the first scholar to argue this point, in his "Where Was the Capital of the West Uighurs?" See also Barfield, *Perilous Frontier*. Allsen disagrees with the theory that Uyguristan constituted a Fifth Qanate. See his "Yuan Dynasty and the Uighurs of Turfan," pp. 249–50 [243–80], from which I have drawn information for the following discussion.

26. On the office of the *darughuachi*, see Elizabeth Endicott-West, *Mongolian Rule in China: Local Administration in the Yuan Dynasty* (Cambridge, MA, 1989) and Igor de Rachewiltz, "Personnel and Personalities in North China in the Early Mongol Period," *Journal of the Economic and Social History of the Orient* 9 (1966): 88–144.

27. Allsen, "Yuan Dynasty and the Uighurs of Turfan," p. 251.

28. Historians have long recognized the importance of Tatar Tonga to Mongol and Yuan history. In 1829, his biography was translated by J.-P. Abel Remusat, "Tha-Tha-Toung-'O," *Nouveaux Mélanges Asiatiques* 2 (1829):61–63. Igor de Rachewiltz has compiled the most up-to-date complete bibliography of primary and secondary sources that pertain to Tatar, as well as the reconstruction of his name, in his study of Türks in Yuan China. See Igor de Rachewiltz, "Turks in

China Under the Mongols" in *China among Equals*, ed. Rossabi, pp. 283–84, 298, n. 9.
29. *YS*, 124.3048.
30. Primary and secondary sources for the history of this individual and his family that I have consulted in the following discussion include biographical entries in *YS*, 124.3046–47; Tu Ji, *Mengwuer shiji* (hereafter *MWESJ*) (Jiangxi, 1934; rpr. Taibei, 1983), 45.1–3; and poems written in honor of Qara Igach's family collected by Yang Yu in his collectanea *Shanju xinhua*, *SKQS* edn. (rpr. Taibei, 1966), chs. 4, 8, 15. See also *ESWSBB*, 6:8338, for a diagram of this family tree. I have relied on de Rachewiltz, "Turks in China," p. 298, for a rendering of Qara Igach's name.
31. According to the *Xiyu diming*, Sairam (Suolimu) was the name of a lake, Heavenly Lake (Tian chi), and a district, Baicheng district (Baicheng xian) in ancient sources. See Feng Chengjun, comp., *Xiyu diming* (Taiwan, 1976), p. 62. Bretschneider identifies Sairam as a place that was "inhabited from ancient times by Turkish tribes. . .an ancient and very large city, with forty gates," which was conquered by the Mongol general Xietalahai. Bretschneider, *Medieval Researches*, 2:94–95, citing the biography of Jiatalahun in *YS*, 151. Footnotes that accompany Qara Igach's biography in the *MWESJ* state that Sairam was a tributary state of the Uyghur Kingdom. See *MWESJ*, 45.1b. See also Peter B. Golden, "Sayrām" in *The Encyclopedia of Islam*, new ed. (Leiden, 1997), 9:114–15.
32. *YS*, 124.3046 and *MWESJ*, 45.2. On the rendering of the name of the Qarakhitay king as Jirgu, see de Rachewiltz, "Turks in China," p. 298, n. 11.
33. For information on the duties and rights of an agent, see Endicott-West, *Mongolian Rule in China*.
34. On the office of *dudu*, see Charles O. Hucker, *A Dictionary of Official Titles in Imperial China* (Stanford, 1985; rpr. Taibei, 1988), p. 544. Shang Yanbin renders this same title as *tutung*. See his *Yuandai Weiwuer yanjiu* (Beijing, 1999), p. 60. On the title *darqan*, see David M. Farquhar, *The Government of China Under Mongolian Rule: A Reference Guide* (Stuttgart, 1990), pp. 29–30 and Han Rulin, "Menggu dalahan kao" in *Qionglu ji* Han Rulin (Shijiazhuang, 2000), pp. 23–53. Farquhar translates *darqan* as "Free Noble," an inherited title originally conferred for "military merit, the title gave the grantee freedom from many of the customary obligations owed to his superior." It probably had a similar meaning in the Uyghur administration. Ecsedy notes that the title *dudu* is one of the oldest examples of Chinese administrative terms borrowed by the Türks and the Uyghurs. *Dudu* meant "governor of a province, [or] leader of high rank," and many other Central Asian nomadic peoples, such as the Qidan, used the term. See Hilda Ecsedy, "Old Turkic Titles of Chinese Origin," *Acta Orientalia Hungaricae* 18 (1965): 83–91. The Gold Tiger Tablet was given to high-level officials in both the civil and military administrative organs in Yuan China to symbolize their authority. For a partial bibliography of the use of these tablets in the Mongol Empire, see Francis W. Cleaves, "Daru(a and Gerege," *Harvard Journal of Asiatic Studies* 16.1–2 (1953):256–57, n. 73 and 74. For a list of ranks of military officers awarded the Gold Tiger Tablet, see Hsiao Ch'i-ch'ing, *The Military Establishment of the Yuan Dynasty* (Cambridge, MA; London, 1978), pp. 72–3, 170–71 n. 27 and 28.
35. For a narrative of the struggle between Qubilai and Qaidu, see Michal Biran, *Qaidu and the Rise of the Independent Mongol State in Central Asia* (Surrey, UK,

1997) and Allsen, "Yuan Dynasty and the Uighurs of Turfan," pp. 253–55. Interestingly, Qara Igach Buyruk's family occupied positions of high power throughout the Mongol period in China, in ways very similar to the Xie and Lian families that are further on.

36. Several Yuan-era primary sources document the life and activities of Mengsus. See his official biography in YS, 124. See also two inscriptions written by the noted Chinese literatus Cheng Jufu (1249–1318) to honor Mengsus and his family. These are "Wudu Zhimin wang shude zhibei" and "Wudu Zhongjianwang shendaobei" in *Xuelou ji* (rpr. Taibei, 1983), 6.9a–12b and 7.4–7, respectively. Mengsus has also been the subject of one English-language study. See Herbert Franke, "A Sino-Uighur Family Portrait: Notes on a Woodcut from Turfan," *The Canada-Mongolia Review* 4.1 (1978): 33–40. A genealogy of the family of Mengsus is to be found in *ESWSBB*, 6:8335–36.

37. *YS*, 124.3059. Mengsus's biography and other details are also rephrased, with editorial notes, in *MWESJ*, 45.11–12.

38. The major biographical sources for the Xie family include the family biography written by Ouyang Xuan, "Gaochang Xieshi Jiazhuan" in *Guizhai wenji*, SBCK edn., 11.3–13. A punctuated edition of this essay is contained in Chen Gaohua, ed., *Yuandai Weiwuer-Halalu ziliao jilu* (Urumqi, 1986), pp. 75–82. See also the official biographies of Xie family members in the YS, reprinted, with editorial comments, in *MWESJ*, and numerous entries in the gazetteer for Liyang county, *Liyang xianzhi*. For an in-depth study of the Xie family, see Brose, "Strategies of Survival."

39. Kezhipuer's dates cannot be determined with any accuracy, but he appears to have flourished around 1100. The titles he was granted were all hereditary aristocratic titles conferred by the Uyghur *iduqut* on the officials of the highest level in the civil government in Uyghuristan, and many of these have ancient Türk or Chinese origins. For the rendering of *aday tutung*, see Shang, *Yuandai Weiwuer yanjiu*, p. 60. Serruys remarks on the adoption of the Chinese honorary title *taishi*, which evolved into a very powerful office in nomadic confederations as early as the Liao. The high distinction of the Grand Preceptor undoubtedly has to do with the high importance nomadic chiefs placed on literacy and the people who wielded authority in those areas. See Henry Serruys, "The Office of *Tayisi* in Mongolia in the Fifteenth Century," *Harvard Journal of Asian Studies* 37 (1977): 353–80.

40. Ouyang Xuan, "Gaochang Xieshi Jiazhuan," 11.4b.

41. Juvaini records a slightly different version: In his account, the Uyghur king ordered that his troops surround the junior supervisor in a house in Gaochang, which they then pulled down on him, killing him. Bilge is not mentioned in Juvaini's account. See Juvaini, *History of the World-Conqueror*, pp. 44–45. See also Wittfogel and Feng, *Liao*, p. 651.

42. For the reconstruction and meaning of Bilge Quti, see Juvaini, *The History of the World-Conqueror*, p. 48, n. 4. I have not been able to reconstruct a reading of the term *mingbieji*.

43. Ouyang Xuan, "Gaochang Xieshi Jiazhuan," 11.5b.

44. Ouyang Xuan, "Gaochang Xieshi Jiazhuan," 11.6. A similar list, minus a few items, is given in the official biography of Bilge's younger brother, Eren Temur. See *YS*, 124.3050. The Gold Tiger Emblem was one of the highest symbols of Mongol imperial authority and it was normally only given to imperial princes to

wear. The silver emblem and the chair, both of which were also important symbols of royal authority and prerogative, complemented that symbol. The robe, made out of expensive gold brocade, was a highly prized item in nomadic circles, and also a symbol of imperial pleasure and acceptance. For a discussion of the significance of the *zhisun* robe, see Thomas T. Allsen, *Commodity and Exchange in the Mongol Empire* (Cambridge, 1997), p. 20. The *MWESJ* rendering of this passage comments that the Uyghurs had towns, but not the higher-level administrative category of prefecture or commandery (*jun*). See *MWESJ*, 45.4. On the importance of seals in general and that of imperial insignia, *paizi*, in the Mongol world, see de Rachewiltz, "Personnel and Personalities," p. 90.

45. Juvaini's history is an important source for this period since he began work on his history in 1234, and much of it was based on what he personally witnessed in the Mongol Empire, including two trips he made to Qarakhorum. Juvaini was also privy to Mongol court documents and gossip, having spent most of his career in Persia, most notably as governor of Baghdad. Juvaini's history is also helpful for my study because he paid particular attention to the Uyghurs. His text includes accounts of the origins of the Uyghur people, the circumstances surrounding their submission to Chinggis, and later events that involved prominent Uyghurs. For commentary on the importance of Persian sources such as Juvaini's history, see David Morgan, *The Mongols* (Cambridge, MA, 1986), pp. 16–23.

46. See Chapter 6 of Juvaini's original account, pp. 48–53, which is titled "Of the Further History of the Uyghur" by the translator.

47. Sources for Eren Temur include his official biography in *YS*, 124, the Xie family history in *Guizhai Wenji*, as cited above, and a eulogy text written for Eren's famous son, Qara Buqa, by the Chinese writer Huang Jin (1277–1357), "Guangdongdao duzhuanyun yanshi zeng tuicheng shouzhong quanjie gongchen zidedafu Henan Jiangbei dengchu xingzhongshusheng youcheng shanghujun zhuifeng Gaochang jungong shi zhongmin Halapuhuagong shendaobei," *Jinhua Huang xiansheng wenji* (rpr. Shanghai, 1925), 25.1a–5b.

48. After Ögödei Qan died in 1241, his widow Töregene qatun (fl. 1242–45) took up the role of regent until a new male qaghan could be elected by a *khuriltai*. She quickly set about to get her son Güyük elected, but was met with stiff opposition from several Mongol princes. Sergius recommended to Töregene that she adopt Temüge's grandson Tachar, undoubtedly so that he would be able to continue Temüge's line. Töregene accepted his advice and Tachar was brought into Ögödei's family. See Thomas Allsen, "The Rise of the Mongolian Empire and Mongolian Rule in North China" in *The Cambridge History of China*, Vol. 6: *Alien Regimes and Border States, 907–1368*, ed. Herbert Franke and Denis Twitchett (Cambridge, 1994), pp. 382–90. Li Tan was an official in Shandong who helped secure the area for Mongol control when Möngke Qan campaigned there in the 1250s. Li, however, decided to resist Mongol control of his district when Qubilai became Qaghan in 1260, and rebelled in 1262. Sergius volunteered to help fight Li Tan, and he was quickly defeated by August of the same year. See Hok-lam Chan, "Li T'an (?–1262)" in *In the Service of the Khan: Eminent Personalities of the Early Mongol-Yüan Period (1200–1300)*, ed. Igor de Rachewiltz, Hok-lam Chan, Hsiao Ch'i-ch'ing, and Peter W. Geier (Wiesbaden, 1993), pp. 500–519.

49. The lists of primary sources that mention the prolific Lian clan are too numerous even to list here. Some of the main ones include biographies in *YS*, 125 and

126; Ke Shaomin, *Xin Yuanshi* (Tianjin, 1922), 155; and *MWESJ*, 79. See also the indices prepared by Igor de Rachewiltz and May Wang, *Repertory of Proper Names in Yüan Literary Sources* (Taibei, 1988); and Wang Deyi, Li Rongcun, and Pan Bocheng, ed., *Yuanren zhuanji ziliao suoyin* (Taibei, 1980), pp. 1247–50 and 1506–7, respectively. The Lian family tree is diagramed in *ESWSBB*, 6:8340–42. Important secondary scholarship on the Lian clan includes Ch'en Yuan's discussion scattered throughout his *Western and Central Asians in China under the Mongols*, tr. Ch'ien Hsing-hai and L. Carrington Goodrich, Monumenta Serica Monograph, 15 (Los Angeles, 1966). See also a biography of Lian Xixian by Hsiao Ch'i-ch'ing, "Lien Hsi-Hsien (1231–1280)" in *In the Service of the Khan*, ed. Igor de Rachewiltz et al., pp. 480–99 and an article by Wang Meitang, "Yuandai neiqian Weiwuerzu shijia—Lianshi jiazu kaoshu" (unpublished: Hong Kong, 1997).

50. The *Semuren* status group was one of four categories imposed on the population of China by the Mongols. The term means "people of various categories" and consisted of all personnel from Central and West Asia who had been brought into China to serve the Mongols as administrators, advisers, technicians, etc. The system of four social status groups was composed, in descending order, of Mongols, *Semuren*, Chinese (*Hanren*, which included Chinese, Jurchens, and others who lived in North China), and southerners (*Nanren*, all people from South China). For studies of the Mongol social class system see Meng Siming, *Yuandai shehui jieji zhidu* (1938; rpr. Beijing, 1980).

51. Guan Zhige was the father of the famous Uyghur poet Xiaoyunshi Qaya (also known by his Chinese name of Guan Yunshi) (1286–1324), who, in like the Xie and Lian families, adopted a Chinese-style surname, with Guan just happening to be the first syllable of Zhige's father's name. For more on Guan Yunshi and his family, see Yang Tsung-han, "Hsiao-Yün-Shih Khaya," *Monumenta Serica* 9 (1944): 92–100 and Richard John Lynn, *Kuan Yün-Shih* (Boston, 1980).

52. For a complete list of these names, from the oldest son, Lian Ximin through the tenth son, Lian Xigua, see the Lian family tree in *ESWSBB*, 6:8340–41.

Glossary

aday tutung 阿大都督
Arqun Qaya 阿魯渾海牙
Asiq Temür 阿失帖木兒
Baicheng xian 拜城縣
Barchuq el-Tegin 巴而术阿而忒的斤
Beiting 北庭
Bilge Buqa 比俚伽普華
Bilge Temur 比俚伽帖穆爾
Bilijiehudi 比俚伽忽底
But/Bodun Sari 不答失里
Buyruq Qaya 布魯海牙
Cheng Jufu 程鉅夫
Chinggis Qan 成吉思汗
da chengxiang 大丞相
da duanshiguan 大斷事官

Dadu 大都
darqan 答剌罕
darughachi 達魯花赤
duanshiguan 斷事官
dudu 都督
Gansu 甘肅
Gaochang 高昌
Gaochang ren 高昌人
Guan Yunshi 貫雲石
Guan Zhige 貫只哥
guoxiang 國相
hanlin yuan 翰林院
Han 漢
Hanren 漢人
Heilongjiang 黑龍江
Heishan 黑山
Henan 河南
iduqut 亦都護
Jiatalahun 賈塔剌渾
Jiayuguan 嘉峪關
jin chiyi 金螭椅
jin zhisun 金直孫
jinhufu 金虎符
jinshi 進士
juan 卷
jun 郡
junmindu darughuachi 軍民都達魯花赤
Jurchen [Nüzhen 女真]
Kezhipuer 克直普爾
Li Tan 李璮
Lian 廉
Lian Anianbaqa 廉阿年八哈
Lian Mengzi 廉孟子
Lian Xigua 廉希括
Lian Ximin 廉希閔
Lian Xishu 廉希恕
Lian Xixian 廉希憲
Lian Yaoyao 廉咬咬
lianfang shi 廉訪使
liang 兩
Mamuraq Tegin 馬木剌的斤
Mengsus 孟速思
Mengzi 孟子
mingbieji 明別吉
mu 畝
Nanren 南人
Ne'uril Tegin 紐林的斤
Ödösh Inal 月朵失野訥
Ögödei Qan 窩闊台汗

Ögrünch Tegin 玉古倫赤的斤
paizi 牌子
Qara Igach Buyruk 哈剌亦哈赤北魯
Qidan 契丹
Qochgar Tegin 火赤哈兒的斤
Qubilai Qan 忽必烈汗
Sajisi 撒吉思
Salin Tegin 薩侖的斤
Semuren 色目人
Shandong 山東
shi niu yinyin 獅鈕銀印
Suolimu 賽里木
Tachar 塔察兒
taishi 太師
Tatar Tongga 塔塔統阿
Temür Buqa 帖木兒補化
Temüge Odchigin 鐵木格斡赤斤
Tian chi 天池
Tianshan 天山
Töregene qatun 脱列哥那皇后
Wang E 王鶚
Wang Yande 王延德
Weiwuer 畏吾兒 [Uyghur]
Weiwuer ren 畏吾兒人 [Uyghur man/person]
Xi 希
Xiyu 西域
xiaowei siren 校尉四人
Xiaoyunshi Qaya 小雲石海涯
Xie 偰
Xie Wenzhi 偰文質
Xie Zhedu 偰哲篤
Xinjiang 新疆
Yidulu xingsheng da dudu 益都路行省大都督
Yuanshi 元史
Yuelin tiemuer 岳璘帖穆爾
Zhending 真定
zhongshu zuo chengxiang 中書左承相
zongguan nei wai cangshi 總管內外倉事

Bibliography

Abe, Takeo. "Where Was the Capital of the West Uighurs?" *Silver Jubilee Volume of the Zinbun Kagaku Kenkyusyo* [Research Institute for Humanistic Studies]. Kyoto (1954):435–50.

Adelman, Jeremy and Stephen Aron. "From Borderlands to Borders: Empires, Nation-States, and the Peoples in Between in North American History." *American Historical Review* 104.3 (June 1999):814–41.

Allsen, Thomas T. "The Yuan Dynasty and the Uighurs of Turfan in the 13th Century." In *China among Equals: The Middle Kingdom and Its Neighbors, 10th–14th Centuries*, ed. Morris Rossabi. Berkeley: University of California Press, 1983.

———. "The Rise of the Mongolian Empire and Mongolian Rule in North China." In *The Cambridge History of China*, Vol. 6: *Alien Regimes and Border States, 907–1368*, ed. Herbert Franke and Denis Twitchett. Cambridge: Cambridge University Press, 1994.

———. *Commodity and Exchange in the Mongol Empire*. Cambridge Studies in Islamic Civilization. Cambridge: Cambridge University Press, 1997.

Arat, R. Rahmeti. "Der Herrschertitel Iduq-qut." *Ural-Altaische Jahrbücher* 35.B (1964):150–57.

Barfield, Thomas J. *The Perilous Frontier: Nomadic Empires and China*. Studies in Social Discontinuity. Cambridge, MA and Oxford: Basil Blackwell, 1989.

Biran, Michal. *Qaidu and the Rise of the Independent Mongol State in Central Asia*. Surrey, UK: Curzon Press, 1997.

Bretschneider, Emil. *Medieval Researches from Eastern Asiatic Sources*. 2 vols. London: Kegan, Paul, Trench, Trübner & Co., 1887; rpr. 1967.

Brose, Michael C. "Strategies of Survival: Uyghur Elites in Yuan and Early Ming China." Ph.D. diss. Philadelphia: University of Pennsylvania, 2000.

Chen Gaohua 陈高华, ed. *Yuandai Weiwuer-Halalu ziliao jilu* 元代维吾尔 哈剌鲁资料辑录 [Compilation of Historical Materials on Yuan-dynasty Uyghurs and Qarluqs]. Urumqi: Xinjiang renmin chubanshe, 1986.

Ch'en Yuan. *Western and Central Asians in China under the Mongols*, tr. Ch'ien Hsing-hai and L. Carrington Goodrich. Monumenta Serica Monograph 15. Los Angeles: Monumenta Serica at the University of Calfornia, 1966.

Cheng Jufu 程鉅夫. "Wudu Zhiminwang shude zhibei" 武都智敏王述德之碑 [An Inscription Transmitting the Virtue of Prince Zhimin of Wudu]. In *Xuelou ji* 雪樓集 [Collection from the Snowy Hut]. Taibei: Taiwan shangwu yinshuguan, rpr. 1983.

———. "Wudu Zhongjianwang shendaobei" 武都忠簡王神道碑 [Funerary Inscription for Prince Zhongjian of Wudu]. In *Xuelou ji* 雪樓集 [Collection from the Snowy Hut].

Clark, Larry V. "Introduction to the Uyghur Civil Documents of East Turkestan (13th–14th cc.)." Ph.D. diss. Bloomington: Indiana University, 1975.

Cleaves, Francis W. "Daruγa and Gerege." *Harvard Journal of Asiatic Studies* 16.1–2 (June 1953):237–59.

de Rachewiltz, Igor. "Personnel and Personalities in North China in the Early Mongol Period." *Journal of the Economic and Social History of the Orient* 9 (1966):88–144.

———. "Turks in China Under the Mongols." In *China among Equals: The Middle Kingdom and Its Neighbors, 10th–14th Centuries*, ed. Morris Rossabi. Berkeley: University of California Press, 1983.

de Rachewiltz, Igor and May Wang. *Repertory of Proper Names in Yüan Literary Sources*. 4 vols. Taibei: Southern Materials Center, 1988.

Ecsedy, Hilda. "Uighurs and Tibetans in Pei-T'ing (790–791 A.D.)." *Acta Orientalia Hungaricae* 17 (1964):83–112.

———. "Old Turkic Titles of Chinese Origin." *Acta Orientalia Hungaricae* 18 (1965):83–91.

Endicott-West, Elizabeth. *Mongolian Rule in China: Local Administration in the Yuan Dynasty*. Harvard-Yenching Institute, 29. Cambridge, MA: Council on East Asian Studies, Harvard University Press, 1989.

Farquhar, David M. *The Government of China Under Mongolian Rule: A Reference Guide.* Münchener Ostasiatische Studien 53. Stuttgart, Germany: Franz Steiner Verlag, 1990.

Feng Chengjun 馮承鈞, comp. *Xiyu Diming* 西域地名 [Place Names in the Western Regions]. Taiwan: Huashi Press, 1976.

Franke, Herbert. "A Sino-Uighur Family Portrait: Notes on a Woodcut from Turfan." *The Canada-Mongolia Review* 4.1 (1978):33–40.

von Gabain, Annemarie. *Das Leben im uigurischen Konigreich von Qoco, 850–1250.* Wiesbaden, Germany: Otto Harrassowitz Verlag, 1973.

Geng Shimin and James Hamilton. "L'Inscription Ouigoure de la Stele Commemorative des Iduq Qut de Qoco." *Turcica* 13 (1981):10–54.

Gladney, Dru C. Gladney. "Sedentarization, Socioecology, and State Definition: The Ethnogenesis of the Uighur." In *Rulers from the Steppe: State Formation on the Eurasian Periphery,* ed. Gary Seaman and Daniel Marks. Ethnographics Monograph Series, 2. Los Angeles, CA: Ethnographics Press, 1991.

Golden, Peter B. "Sayrām." In *The Encyclopedia of Islam,* new edition. 11 vols. vol. 9:114–15. Leiden, Halland: E. J. Brill, 1997.

Hamilton, James R. *Les Ouïghours a l'Époque des Cinq Dynasties* [The Uyghurs of the Five Dynasties Period]. Paris: Institut des Hautes Études Chinoises, 1955; rpr. 1988.

Han Rulin 韓儒林. "Menggu dalahan kao" 蒙古答剌罕考 [A study of the Mongol darqan]. In *Qionglu ji* 穹廬集 [Collection from the Domed Studio], ed. Han Rulin. Ershi shiji Zhongguo shixue mingzhu 二十世紀中國史學名著 [Famous Authors of twentieth-Century Chinese Historical Studies]. Shijiazhuang: Hebei jiaoyu chubanshe, 2000.

Hok-lam Chan. "Li T'an (?–1262)." In *In the Service of the Khan: Eminent Personalities of the Early Mongol-Yüan Period (1200–1300),* ed. Igor de Rachewiltz, Hok-lam Chan, Hsiao Ch'i-ch'ing, and Peter W. Geier. Wiesbaden, Germany: Otto Harrassowitz Verlag, 1993.

Hsiao Ch'i-ch'ing. *The Military Establishment of the Yuan Dynasty.* Cambridge, MA and London: Council on East Asian Studies, Harvard University Press, 1978.

———. "Lien Hsi-Hsien (1231–1280)." In *In the Service of the Khan: Eminent Personalities of the Early Mongol-Yüan Period (1200–1300),* ed. Igor de Rachewiltz, Hok-lam Chan, Hsiao Chi'i-chïng, and Peter W. Geier. Wiesbaden, Germany: Otto Harrassowitz Verlag, 1993.

Huang Jin 黃溍. "Guangdongdao duzhuanyun yanshi zeng tuicheng shouzhong quanjie gongchen zidedafu Henan Jiangbei dengchu xingzhongshusheng youcheng shanghujun zhuifeng Gaochang jungong shi zhongmin Halapuhuagong shendaobei" 廣東道都轉運鹽使贈推誠守忠全節功臣資德大夫河南江北等處行中書省右承上護軍追封高昌郡公謚忠憨佘剌普華公神道碑 [Spirit-way eulogy of Master Qara Buqa, Commissioner for Salt Distribution for the Guangdong Region, Posthumously Honored with the Titles "Virtuous Official Who Confidently Protected His Loyalty and Was Entirely Virtuous"; "Grandee of the Fifth Class"; "Minister on the right in Henan, Jiangbei and other regions"; "Supreme Protector"; and the style name "Loyal and Sympathetic"]. *Jinhua Huang xiansheng wenji* 金華黃先生文集 [Collected Works of Master Huang of Jinhua] 25.1a–5b. rpr. Shanghai: Shangwu yinshuguan, 1925.

Hucker, Charles O. *A Dictionary of Official Titles in Imperial China.* Stanford: Stanford University Press, 1985; rpr. Taibei: Southern Materials Center, 1988.

Jagchid, Sechin and Van Jay Symons. *Peace, War, and Trade Along the Great Wall: Nomadic-Chinese Interaction through Two Millennia*. Bloomington: Indiana University Press, 1989.

Julien, Stanislaus. "Les Oïgours. Kao-Tch'ang-hing-ki, ou Relation d'un voyage (officiel) dans le pays des Oïgours (de 981 à 983), par Wang-Yen-Té." *Journal Asiatique* 4 (1847):50–66.

Juvaini, 'Ala-ad-Din 'Ata-Malik. *The History of the World-Conqueror*, tr. John Andrew Boyle. Manchester, UK: University of Manchester Press, 1958.

Ke Shaomin 柯劭忞. *Xin Yuanshi* 新元史 [New History of the Yuan Dynasty]. 60 vols. Tianjin: Tuigeng tang, 1922.

Lattimore, Owen. *Inner Asian Frontiers of China*. American Geographical Society Research Series 21. New York: American Geographical Society, 1940.

———. "The Frontier in History." In *Studies in Frontier History, Collected Papers 1928-1958*. London: Oxford University Press, 1962.

Li Futong 李符桐. "Weiwuerren duiyu Yuanchao jianguo zhi gongxian" 畏兀兒人對於元朝建國之貢獻 [Uyghurs in the Founding of the Yuan Dynasty]. *Shixue lunji* 史學論集 [Collected Discussions in the Study of history] 3 (1977): 328-98.

Liyang xianzhi 溧陽縣志 [Gazetteer for Liyang County]. Microfilm of 1498 edition.

Luo Xianyou 罗贤佑. "Yuandai Weiwuer yiduhu puxi yu qi diwei bianqian" 元代畏兀儿亦都护谱系及其地位变迁 [The Family History and Change in Status of the Yuan-Dynasty Uyghur iduqut]. *Minzu yanjiu* 民族研究 [Nationalities Research] (no. 2 1997):70–80.

Lynn, Richard John. *Kuan Yün-Shih*. Boston, MA: Twayne Publishers, 1980.

Maillard, Monique. "Essai sur la vie materielle dans l'oasis de Tourfan pendant le haut moyen age." *Arts Asiatique* 29 (1973):3–185.

Meng Siming 蒙思明. *Yuandai shehui jieji zhidu* 元代社會階級制度 [The Social Class System of Yuan-Dynasty China]. 1938; rpr. Beijing: Zhonghua shuju, 1980.

Morgan, David. *The Mongols*. Cambridge, MA: Blackwell, 1986.

Ouyang Xuan 歐陽玄 "Gaochang Xieshi Jiazhuan" 高昌偰氏家傳 [Biography of the Xie Family of Gaochang]. In *Guizhai wenji* 圭齋文集 [Collected Works of the Jade-Tablet Studio]. *Sibu congkan (SBCK)* 四部叢刊 [Collected Editions of the four Divisions] edition.

Paludan, Ann. "Some Foreigners in the Spirit Roads of the Northern Song Imperial Tombs." *Oriental Art* 29.4 (Winter 1983/84):377–88.

Pearce, Scott. "The Land of Tai: The Origins, Evolution and Historical Significance of a Community of the Inner Asian Frontier." In *Opuscula Altaica: Essays Presented in Honor of Henry Schwarz*, ed. Edward H. Kaplan and Donald W. Whisenhunt. Studies on East Asia, vol. 19. Bellingham, WA: Western Washington University, Center for East Asian Studies, 1994.

Pelliot, Paul. "Kao-Tch'ang, Qoco, Houo-Tcheou et Qarä-Khodja." *Journal Asiatique* 10.19 (1912):578–603.

Qian Daxin 錢大昕, comp. "Yuanshi shizu biao" 元史氏族表 [Table of Clans in the History of the Yuan Dynasty]. In *Ershiwushi bubian* 二十五史補編 [Supplements to the Twenty-five Dynastic Histories]. 6 vols. Shanghai: Kaiming shudian, 1937.

Remusat, J.-P. Abel. "Tha-Tha-Toung-'O." *Nouveaux Mélanges Asiatiques* 2 (1829):61–3.

Rybatzki, Volker. "Titles of Turk and Uigur Rulers in the Old Turkic Inscriptions." *Central Asiatic Journal* 44.2 (2000):205–92.
Serruys, Henry. "The Office of *Tayisi* in Mongolia in the Fifteenth Century." *Harvard Journal of Asian Studies* 37. 2 (December 1977):353–80.
Shang Yanbin 尚衍斌. *Yuandai Weiwuer yanjiu* 元代畏兀儿研 [Research on Uyghurs in the Yuan Dynasty]. Beijing: Minzu chubanshe, 1999.
Shimazaki Akira. "On Pei-t'ing (Bišbaliq) and K'o-han Fu-t'u-ch'êng." *Memoirs of the Research Department of the Tôyô Bunko* [Oriental Library] 32 (1974):99–117.
Song Lian 宋濂. *Yuanshi* 元史 [History of the Yuan Dynasty]. 1370. 15 vols. rpr. Beijing: Zhonghua shuju, 1976.
Thompson, Leonard. "The Southern African Frontier in Comparative Perspective." In *Essays on Frontiers in World History*, ed. George Wolfskill and Stanley Palmer. College Station: Texas A&M University Press, 1983.
Thompson, Leonard and Howard Lamar. "Comparative Frontier History." In *The Frontier in History: North America and Southern Africa Compared*, ed. Howard Lamar and Leonard Thompson. New Haven, CT: Yale University Press, 1981.
Toghto [Tuotuo] 脱脱. *Songshi* 宋史 [History of the Song Dynasty]. 1345. 40 vols. rpr. Beijing: Zhonghua shuju, 1976.
Tu Ji 屠寄. *Mengwuer shiji* 蒙兀兒史記 [History of the Mongols]. 8 vols. Jiangxi, 1934. rpr. Taibei: Shijie shuju, 1983.
Turner, Frederick Jackson. "The Significance of the Frontier in American History." In *The Frontier in American History*. New York: Henry Holt, 1920; rpr. Tucson: University of Arizona Press, 1986.
Waldron, Arthur. *The Great Wall of China: From History to Myth*. Cambridge: Cambridge University Press, 1990.
Wang Deyi 王德毅, Li Rongcun 李榮村, and Pan Bocheng 潘柏澄, ed. *Yuanren zhuanji ziliao suoyin* 元人傳記資料索引 [Index to Biographical Materials of Yuan Figures]. 5 vols. Taibei: Xinwenshuang chubanshe, 1980.
Wang Meitang 王梅堂. "Yuandai neiqian Weiwuerzu shijia—Lianshi jiazu kaoshu" 元代內迁维吾尔族世家廉氏家族考述 [Uyghur Families Transplanted to interior Yuan China—a study of the Lian Family]. Unpublished paper prepared for Conference on Yuan History, Hong Kong, 1997.
Weiwuerzu jianshi 维吾尔族简史 [Simplified History of the Uyghur People]. Urumqi: Xinjiang renmin chubanshe, 1991.
White, Richard. *The Middle Ground: Indians, Empires, and Republics in the Great Lakes Region, 1650–1815*. Cambridge: Cambridge University Press, 1991.
Wittfogel, Karl A. and Feng Chia-sheng. *History of Chinese Society: Liao (907–1125)*. Transactions of the American Philosophical Society, New Series 46. Philadelphia, PA: American Philosophical Society, 1946.
Yang Tsung-han. "Hsiao-Yün-Shih Khaya." *Monumenta Serica* 9 (1944):92–100.
Yang Yu 楊瑀, comp. *Shanju xinhua* 山居新話 [New Conversations from the Mountain Dweller]. *Siku quanshu* (SKQS) 四庫全書 [Complete Books of the Four Treasuries] edition. rpr. Taibei: Iwu Press, 1966.
Yu Ji 虞集, comp. *Daoyuan xuegu lu* 道園學古錄 [Record of Studying the Ancient in the Daoist garden]. *Sibu congkan* (SBCK) 四部叢刊 [Collected Editions of the four divisions] edition.

NOTES ON CONTRIBUTORS

James A. Anderson is Associate Professor in the History Department at the University of North Carolina at Greensboro (UNCG). A historian in premodern China and Vietnam, Anderson joined the UNCG faculty in 1999. A graduate of Harvard College, he holds M.A. and Ph.D. degrees from the University of Washington. From January to September 2001, he conducted research as a Visiting Fellow at the Research School of Pacific and Asian Studies in the Australian National University in Canberra, Australia. From February to August 2004, Anderson was a Luce Fellow in the John W. Kluge Center for International Studies at the Library of Congress (Washington, DC). Anderson's *The Rebel Den of Nùng Trí Cao: Loyalty and Identity along the Sino-Vietnamese Frontier* was published in 2007.

Michael C. Brose is Associate Professor of History at University of Wyoming. His most recent publications include his book, *Subjects and Masters: Uyghurs in the Mongol Empire* (Bellingham, WA: Western Washington University, Center for East Asian Studies, 2007); "Realism and Idealism in the *Yuanshi* Chapters on Foreign Relations," *Asia Major*, 3rd Series 19.1–2 (2006): 327–47; "Uyghur Technologists of Writing and Literacy in Mongol China," *T'oung Pao* 91.4–5 (2005):396–435; and "Mingchu Yunnan de Weiwu'erren jiqi Musilin houqi" [Uyghurs in Early Ming Yunnan and Their Muslim Descendants], in *Proceedings of the First International Symposium on Sayyid Ajall Omer Shams al-Din*, ed. Gao Fayuan (Kunming, China: Yunnan University Press, 2004), 396–403. Brose continues to research Uyghurs and other Central Asians in Yuan and Ming China, and has also begun a new project focused on the history and current status of the Muslim Hui community in Yunnan province.

M. A. Butler is Visiting Assistant Professor of History at Case Western Reserve University in Cleveland. She has also taught in the History Department at the State University of New York at Potsdam and, prior to her current post, was Assistant Professor of History and Humanities at Hawai'i Pacific University. Her doctoral dissertation, "Reflections of a Military Medium: Ritual and Magic in the Eleventh- and Twelfth-Century Chinese Military," is in the process of revision for publication.

David A. Graff is Associate Professor of History at Kansas State University. He received his Ph.D. in East Asian Studies from Princeton University in 1995. His research focuses on the military history of China and his publications include *A Military History of China* (with Robin Higham as coeditor; Boulder, CO: Westview Press, 2002) and *Medieval Chinese Warfare, 300–900* (New York: Routledge, 2002). Among his works in progress is a comparative study of Chinese and Byzantine military practice in the seventh century CE.

NOTES ON CONTRIBUTORS

Peter Lorge is Senior Lecturer in the Department of History at Vanderbilt University, where he teaches film as well as history. He is the author of *War, Politics and Society in Early Modern China, 900–1795* (New York: Routledge, 2005) and editor of *Warfare in China to 1600* (Aldershot, UK: Ashgate, 2005). His most recently completed book is *The Asian Military Revolution: From Gunpowder to the Bomb* (Cambridge: Cambridge University Press, 2008) and he is currently writing a history of Chinese martial arts.

Michael C. McGrath, Professor of History and East Asian Studies at Adrian College, earned his Ph.D. at Princeton University under the late James Tzu-chien [T. C.] Liu in 1982. He has contributed "Jen-tsung (r.1023–1063) and Ying-tsung (r.1063–1067)" in the *Cambridge History of China*, vol. 5 (forthcoming). He is writing a military history of the Song period. McGrath was an infantry officer between 1964 and 1969.

Ruth Mostern is Assistant Professor and member of the Founding Faculty in the School of Social Sciences, Humanities and Arts at the University of California, Merced. Beyond her involvement in her specialty of the political landscape of imperial China, Mostern's research interests include spatial history and humanities computing. Her work has either been published or is forthcoming in the journals *Shimen, International Journal of Geographic Information Science, Historical Methods, History and Computing, Central Eurasian Studies Review*, and *College and Research Libraries*. She is presently completing a book tentatively titled *Dividing the Realm in Order to Govern: The Territorial State in Song China, 960–1276 CE*.

Sherry J. Mou is Associate Professor of Chinese at DePauw University. She is the editor of *Presence and Presentation: Women in the Chinese Literati Tradition* (New York: St. Martin's, 1999) and guest editor of a special issue of *Chinese Studies in History* on "Women Warriors in China" (Winter 2001–2). Her recent book, *Gentlemen's Prescriptions for Women's Lives: A Thousand Years of Biographies of Chinese Women* (Armonk, NY: M. E. Sharpe, 2004), describes the inception and the development of the first thousand years of the writing of women's biographies in the Chinese official histories. She is currently working on a book-length study of contemporary Chinese cinema, examining the influence of the Confucian tradition upon the Fifth Generation directors, their kung-fu films, and the cinematic representation of historical events.

Don J. Wyatt is Professor and Chair of the Department of History at Middlebury College. He is coeditor of *Political Frontiers, Ethnic Boundaries, and Human Geographies in Chinese History* (with Nicola Di Cosmo; London: RoutledgeCurzon, 2003). Among his forthcoming publications is a work on the earliest confirmable contacts between Chinese and Africans, titled *The Blacks of Premodern China* (Philadelphia: University of Pennsylvania Press, 2009).

INDEX

Abaoji, 48
Abe, Takeo, 279n 25
aday tutung (elder statesman), 267
Ái, 219n 104
Allsen, Thomas, 279n 25
An Lushan Rebellion, 3, 43–4, 46–7, 49, 52, 119, 245n 20
An'er, 154
anfu (to restore; quell, pacify), 170
anfu shi (pacification intendant/military commisioner), 158
anfu si (pacification commision), 197
Annandao zhaotaoshi (Annan circuit punitive expedition officer), 208
Anyuan, 162, 163
Arqun Qaya, 272
arts: martial, 112, 130, 135; occult, 111–16, 118, 120, 125–7, 129–35
Asiq Temür, 266

Baibao, 161
Baicheng xian, 280n 31
Baiyue, 2, 12, 15–16, 31–2, 256
Bakhtin, Mikhail, 114
Ban Zhao, 13, 35nn 15, 16, 37n 64
bao (ten-household group), 128
Bảo Lạc, 213
Bảo Thắng, 213
Baoan (jun), 159, 161, 171
baojia (local defense system), 128
Baoyi, 170
Baoyuan, 161
Barchuq el-Tegin, 259–62, 266, 267, 278nn 17, 18
Barlow, Jeffrey, 194
bát ải (Eight Passes), 210
Bates, Robert, 100n 4
bazi (Eight Characters), 123
Bei Wei, 23, 157

Bei Yan, 14
Beibian yaolan (Essential Readings for Border Preparations), 163
Beishi (History of the Northern Dynasties), 12
Beiting (or Beshbaliq), 257, 258, 260, 278
Benchao huawai zhoujun tu (An Illustration of Prefectures and Commanderies Beyond the Influence of Our Dynasty), 211, 214
benji (basic annals), 218n 84
Bi Gia Dụ, 200
Bian he, 43
Bianliang, 93
Bilge Buqa (or Bilge Temur), 267, 271
Bilijiehudi (His Highness Bilge), 267
Bin, 229
Bin(zhou), 170
bingbu langzhong (Ministry of War director), 100n 5
bingbu shilang (Ministry of War vice minister), 76
Binzhou, 197
binh bộ thị lang (director of military personnel), 210
Bình, 219n 104
Bingzhou, 155, 177n 39
Bohai (also Bohai wan or Gulf of Bohai), 46, 59
Bol, Peter, 205
Bong Thánh, 199
border: identity and, 2, 8; war and, 2, 8
bushu (military commander), 159
But/Bodun Sari, 261
Buyruq Qaya, 271, 272

Cầm, 219n 104
can (participants), 161

INDEX

Cảnh, 219n 104
canzheng zaixiang (participant in determining government matters and grand councilor), 90
canzhi zhengshi (participant in determining government matters), 101n 15
Cao Cao, 133
Cao taihou (Empress Cao), 155
caoshi (fiscal intendant), 242
Certeau, Michel de, 131
Chagadai, 255, 262, 279n 23
Chaixu, 237
Chang'an, 3, 43, 44, 49, 50
Changcheng hou (duke of Changcheng), 15
Change, Book of, 121, 124
changping cang (price-regulating granaries), 163
Chanyuan, 77, 88, 102n 28
Chanyuan zhi meng (Chanyuan Accord/Covenant/Peace Agreement/Treaty): longevity of, 60, 71, 72; perception of, 87, 95, 99; significance of, 1; signing of, 180n 106; violation of, 167
Chanzhou, 167, 180n 106
Chao [prefecture], 25
Chao [surname], 118, 119
chaoting (the court), 152
chen (subject, servant), 157, 171, 175
Chen [surname], 119
Chen Baxian, 15, 23
Chen Gongyan, 52
Chen Pengnian, 89
Chen Xingtai, 55n 30
Chen Yinque, 43, 52
Chen Zhizhong, 165, 167
Cheng [Baiyue prefecture], 25
Cheng [Huainan prefecture], 235
Cheng Jufu, 281n 36
Cheng Minsheng, 230
Cheng Yi, 245n 20
Cheng Zhuo, 210
Chengde, 43, 46, 51, 54n 15
chengjie lang (gentleman for fostering temperance), 236
Chengjing furen (consort of sincerity and respect), 18

Chengping zhai, 159, 161, 165
Chengtian taihou (Dowager Empress Chengtian), 65
chi (foot) [linear measurement], 129
Chi(zhou), 168
Chinggis Qan, 255, 259–65, 268–9, 271, 279n 18
Chongning, 212
Chu[1], 231, 234, 235, 236, 245n 16, 246n 30
Chu[2], 231, 233, 234, 235, 236, 242, 245n 16, 246n 30
chujie liang (expeditionary rations), 54n 15
Chunqiu (Spring and Autumn Annals), 98
Chuntian ji (Collection of the Spring), 36n 54
Chunzhou, 26
Chuoli, 48
Co Lang, 208
cosmograph, *see shi* (cosmograph)

da chengxiang (grand counselor-in-chief), 267
da duanshiguan (grand judge), 269
Da Xia huangdi (emperor of great Xia), 157
Dadu, 265
Đại Cồ Việt, 215n 1
Đại Việt, 6
Daixingling, 154
daizhi (edict attendant), 159, 162
Daizhou, 118
dajiangjun wei youqianniu (great general and personal guardian general of the right), 203
dali shi (commissioner of grand ceremonies), 88
Daming, 76
Dan'er, 14, 30
Dangxiang (Tangut), 77, 175n 1
dao (Way), 117
Daohua, 236, 237
darqan (free noble), 265, 267, 280n 34
darughachi (overseers, agents), 261
Dazhong xiangfu, 78, 82
Defang, 67
Deshun, 153
Dezhao, 67
Dezong, 51

INDEX

di (enemy, rival), 104n 61
Di Qing, 160, 195, 198, 199
dianqian shiwei si (Palace Command), 169
Diễn, 219n 104
Điền, 219n 104
difangzhi (geographical encyclopedia), 247n 49
diguo (rival, enemy state), 99, 152
dili (geography), 216n 30
Ding Du, 163, 169, 179n 87
Ding Wei (also Ding Yaxiang), 80, 89, 101n 15
Ding(zhou), 167, 170
Dingchuan, 152, 157, 158, 170
Đinh Bộ Lĩnh, 215n 1
đô hộ phủ (protected prefectures), 205
Donghezhou, 26
dongjiang (grotto militia leader), 197
Donglan, 216n 31
Dou Yan, 116
du (canton), 246n 26
Du Yan, 166
duanshiguan (judge), 264
dubushu (regional commandant; Military Command), 155, 177n 37
duda tiju chama si (Tea and Horse Agency), 206
dudu (governor-general, commander-in-chief, provincial governor), 15, 208, 265, 280n 34
dun (hidden), 112
dunjia (Hidden Period), 111, 118
Dunjia fuying jing (Classic of the Talismanic Response of the Hidden Period), 119
Duong Cảnh Thông, 205
Dupuy, Trevor, 174
dutou (troop commandant), 197
duzhijunshi (commander-in-chief), 197

Ecsedy, Hilda, 280n 34
Eren Temur (also Yuelin tiemuer), 269, 281n 44

fa (particularized rules), 127–8, 132
fan (foreign, non-Chinese, barbarian), 165, 172
Fan Ye, 34n 3
Fan Yong, 158, 160, 161, 163, 166

Fan Zhongyan, 161–2, 164–5, 168, 170–3
Fang Fan, 218n 73
Fang Hao, 133
fangyu (territories), 246n 26
Fanyang, 44, 50
Farquhar, David, 280n 34
fashi (method), 127–8
Fei Gun, 83
feiqi (flying chessmen), 129
feiyi weici zhi fa (rules of flying positions), 129
Feng Ang, 17, 25, 26, 29, 36n 52
Feng Bao, 2, 12–15, 17, 22–3, 28–9, 31
Feng Hun, 16
Feng Pu, 15, 16, 17, 31
Feng Rong, 14, 22, 23
Feng Xuan, 16, 17
Feng Ye, 22
Feng(zhou), 166
fengmi (examinee confidentiality), 101n 7; see also *huming*
fengshan (Sacrifice to Heaven and Earth), 87, 89
Fengshan [county in Guangxi], 198, 216n 31
Fengshan [mountain in Hebei], 95
Fengshan xianzhi (A Record of Fengshan County), 198
Fengxiang, 170
Foucault, Michel, 12, 29
fu (superior civil prefecture), 228, 244n 1
Fu[1](zhou), 153, 155–6, 158–60, 166, 168–9
Fu[2](zhou), 165
Fu Bi, 159, 160, 161, 167, 169, 173
fu bushu (deputy circuit military commander), 159
Fu Xi, 102n 30
Funan, 16
Fuyan lu, 155

gan (Jiangxi emigrees), 198
Ganshi, 15
Gansu, 254, 256, 260, 277n 13, 278n 16
ganyong (bravos), 165
Ganzhou, 154
Gao Lishi, 26
Gaoan, 15

Gaochang (or Qocho), 257–62, 264, 266–8
Gaochang ren (Gaochang native), 257, 277n 11
Gaoliang, 14, 22, 31, 32
Gaoliang he, 67
Gaoyou, 231, 235, 240
Gaozhou cishi (Gaozhou regional inspector), 17
Gaozong [Song], 241, 246n 29
Gaozu [Sui], 16, 17, 26
Ge Hong, 115
Ge Huaimin, 165, 170
Gelven, Michael, 8
Geng Fu, 165
Giao Chỉ, 198, 210, 211
Giáp Đung, 199, 213
Grand Canal, 229, 231, 233, 242
Great Ditch: compared with Great Wall, 3–4, 59, 60, 62; construction of, 60–1, 64–5; fate of, 71
Great Wall, 49, 253, 254
Guan Zhige (also Guan Yunshi), 272, 283n 51
guanchashi (civil governor), 49
Guangdong, 12, 27, 198
Guangji, 237
Guangling, 233
Guangnan, 199, 200, 207, 210, 212
Guangwu, 103n 31
Guangxi, 12, 194, 196–8, 206, 207
Guangzhou zongguan (area commander-in-chief of Guangzhou), 17
Guangzhou, 15, 16, 17, 26, 35n 17
guanke (official guest), 213
Guannan, 62, 65, 70
Guanzi, 102n 30
Guizhou, 197, 201, 203, 207
guizha (cunning and deceit), 133
Guazhou, 154
Gui, 45, 46, 47
guidao (Way of deception), 132–3
Guihua, 207, 210, 213
Guilin, 207, 218n 73
guo (state), 152
Guo Kui, 208, 209
Guo Maoqian, 34n 7
Guo Sheng, 242
guojia (state), 152

guoxiang (state minister), 267
Guwan, 207, 218n 77
Guwu, 203
guxu (orphans and empties), 121

Hà Văn Thư, 193–4
Hai, 242
Hailing wang (prince of Hailing), 240
Hainan, 14, 26, 35, 213
Han [dynasty], 11, 22, 37n 64, 87, 103n 31, 256
han (Han) [ethnicity], 1, 7, 12, 14, 23, 28, 165, 283n 50
Han Qi, 160, 162–3, 164–5, 168, 170, 171, 172–3, 178n 53
Han Shizhong, 34n 9
Han Yi (also Han Zhongxian), 83
Han Yincheng, 152
Hang, 231
Hangzhou, 230
hanlin yuan (Hanlin Academy), 160, 163, 164, 207, 266
Hanren (Chinese), 283n 50
Hanyang taishou (grand protector of Hanyang), 25
Hao, 233, 234
Haoshuichuan, 152, 157, 158, 165, 166
Hartwell, Robert, 173, 178n 49
He, 237
He Chengju, 60–1, 68
He Congxu, 167, 171
He Gui, 118
"He Tao nigu jiushou" (Nine Poems in Response to Tao Yuanming), 36n 63
He Yang, 236
Hebei, 43–5, 47–9, 52, 59
Hebei san zhen (three garrisons of Hebei), 43
Hedong, 44, 48, 55n 52, 153, 155–6, 158
Heilbrun, Carolyn G., 13
Heilongjiang, 253
Heishan, 270
Helan, 156
Henan, 43, 45, 76, 269
Henghai, 51
Hengzhou, 197
Hoan, 219n 104
Hoàn, 219n 104

INDEX   297

Hoàng Trọng Khanh, 197, 202
Hoàng Xuân Hãn, 192–3
Hong(zhou), 156
Hong Mai, 90–1, 140n 39
Hou Hanshu (History of the Later Han Dynasty; History of the Latter Han), 11, 34n 3, 115
Hou Jing, 15, 24
houfei zhuan (biographies of empresses and imperial concubines), 34n 9
Howard, Michael, 100n 4
hu (barbarian; Sogdian), 52
Hua Xia, 215n 15
Huai [river], 7, 229, 230–1, 234, 238, 240–1, 242, 243
Huai(zhou), 156
Huai'an, 233, 246nn 21, 25
Huainan, 6–7, 45, 48, 51, 85, 160, 163, 179n 81
Huainan dong (Huainan East), 227
Huainan xi (Huainan West), 227
Huainanzi, 115
Huaiyin, 235
Huaiyuan, 165, 231
Huan(zhou), 153, 156
Huan he (Huan River), 229
Huang Chao, 51
Huang Di, 102n 30
"Huanghou ji" (Chronicles of the Empresses), 34n 3
huhua ("barbarianize"), 52
Hui(zhou), 156
Huige, 156
Huihe (Uyghur), 45
hukou (population), 245n 19
huming (examinee confidentiality), 101n 7; see also *fengmi*
Hunan, 77, 198, 229
Huqian jing (Tiger Seal Classic), 5, 111, 139n 24
Hurun, 201
Huanqing lu, 155, 158, 160, 165, 168, 170
Hùng Lược, 199

identity: border and, 2, 8; war and, 2, 8
iduqut (king), 259–62, 264, 266–8, 271, 274

Japan, 156, 159
Ji, 45, 46
jia (hundred-household group; tithings), 128, 197
Jia Changchao, 160
jian (industrial prefecture), 228, 244n 1
jian bangjia (to form a state), 157
jiang (commands), 162
Jiang, 242
Jiang(zhou), 168
Jiangdu, 233
Jiangnan, 160, 204, 231, 239, 246n 26
Jiangxi, 198, 207
jiangxiao (military commanders), 155, 177n 37
Jiankang, 231
jianyi dafu (grand master of remonstrance), 84
Jiatalahun, 280n 31
jiatou (tithing heads), 216n 28
Jiayuguan, 254
jiazhang (tithing chiefs), 216n 28
jiedushi [or *jiedu shi*] (military governor), 43, 49, 50, 51, 55n 30, 158, 159
jimi ("loose reins" policy), 194
Jin (fief of future Sui Yangdi), 16
Jin [prefecture], 237
jin chiyi (gold dragon chair), 268
Jin Guliang, 30, 31, 32
jin zhisun (gold-embroidered robe), 268
jinchen (close officials), 159
jing (canon), 133
Jing[1](zhou), 153, 165, 170
Jing[2](zhou), 156
Jingde, 94
Jingdong, 163, 164, 167, 246n 30
Jinghu, 246n 30
jingji (capital district), 173
jingjie (cadastre), 237
jinglue anfu shi (military pacification intendant), 163
Jinglue jun (Jinglue army), 55n 32
jinglueshi (court-appointed military commissioner), 196
Jingxi, 196, 201
Jingyou yuesui xinjing (New Canon of the Essence of Music of the Jingyou Period), 139n 29

Jingyuan lu, 158, 164, 168, 170
Jingzong, 175n 3
jinhufu (gold tiger tablet), 265
Jinming, 161, 162, 166
jinshi (presented scholar), 77, 83, 84, 160, 270
Jixian, 44
Jizhou, 48
Jones, Archer, 151
ju (pacing), 130, 142n 102
juan (book, chapter), 19, 98
Jue-si-luo, 154, 158
jun (military prefecture), 228, 244n 1
junmindu darughuachi (agent for civil and military affairs), 269
Jurchen (Jürchen, Nüzhen), 7
Juvaini, 268, 281n 41, 282nn 45, 46
juzhen (powerful jurisdictions), 229

Kaifeng, 93
Kangding, 161
Kangxi, 36n 64
Karabalghasun, 50
kehan (*khan*), 171; see also *shanyu*
Kezhipuer, 266–7, 281n 39
khaghan (Tangut "emperor"), 178n 51
Khai Hoàng, 199
Khúc Thùa Mỹ, 195
Kirghiz, 50; see also Qirgiz
Kongzi (Confucius), 92
Korea, 22, 23, 77, 85, 156
Kou Zhun, 70, 77, 80, 81, 87, 89, 102nn 17, 28
Kracke, Edward, 97
Kuan(zhou), 160–1
Kui, 247n 45
Kunlun guan (Kunlun Pass), 208

Lã Văn Lô, 193–4
Laian, 236
Lâm, 219n 104
Lạng Châu, 213
laocheng (prisoner units), 163
Lattimore, Owen, 253–4, 276n 3, 277n 6
Lê Dình Sỹ, 193
Lê Hoàn, 195, 199
Lê Mạo, 197, 202
Lê Thành Khôi, 193
Lê Van Thình, 210

Leach, Edmund, 123
Lee, Thomas H. C., 98
Lei Gong (Duke of Thunder), 119, 123–4, 137–8n 6
Lewis, Mark Edward, 5, 100n 3
li (one-third of a mile), 241
li[1] (appropriate behavior; rite, ritual), 19, 111
li[2] (pattern, principle), 135
Li [surname], 175n 3
Li [tribal minority people], 12, 17, 35n 13
Li Bo, 37n 64
Li Chunnian, 237–8, 239, 247n 49
Li Cunxu, 48, 55n 52
Li Deming, 78
Li Deyu, 50
Li Di, 81, 84
Li Fuxian, 111, 128
Li Guochang, 51–2
Li Hang, 92–6, 103n 47
Li Huaixian, 52
Li Jing, 117, 140n 36
Li Jiqian, 176n 3
Li Keju, 51–2
Li Maoxun, 52–3
Li Qianshi, 15, 23, 31
Li Quan, 117–18
Li Tan, 270, 282n 48
Li Wengui, 171
Li Wenxiong, 198, 216n 32
Li Yanshou, 12
Li Yuan'gang, 101nn 14, 15, 17
Li Yuanhao: acceptance of peace with Song, 172–5; claims to legitimacy of, 154–8; confrontations with Song, 151–4, 158–71; leadership of Xia, 5–6, 157–8
Li Zaiyi, 48, 51
Lian [surname], 266
Lian Anianbaqa, 272
Lian Xigua, 283n 52
Lian Ximin, 272, 283n 52
Lian Xishu, 272
Lian Xixian (also Lian Mengzi), 271
Lian Yaoyao, 272
lianfang shi (investigation officer), 271
liang [weight measure of about two ounces], 156, 178n 48, 268

Liang(zhou), 154
Liang Hongyu, 12, 34n 9
Liang Shi, 167, 169
Liang Taizu, 118
Liangzhe, 160, 231
Lianshui, 230, 234–5, 242
Lianzhou, 208, 213
Liao [tribal minority people], 17, 35n 38
libu gongyuan (Examination Office of the Ministry of Rites), 101n 7
"Lienü" (biographies of women), 34n 3
lienü zhuan (biographies of women), 34n 9
Liệu Thông, 202
Lijing (Classic of Rites), 87
Lin(zhou), 155, 156, 158, 166
Lin Te, 83
Lin Tianwei, 26, 27, 35n 18, 36n 59
Lin'an, 230, 238, 246n 26
ling (statute), 142n 92
Ling(zhou), 156
Lingnan, 16, 17, 31
Liu Gang, 233–4, 246n 29
Liu Gong, 195
Liu, James T. C., 79
Liu Ji, 46, 48, 50, 54n 15
Liu Liufu, 167
Liu Ping, 155, 158, 160, 161, 162, 165
Liu Rengong, 46, 49
Liu Shouguang, 55n 52
Liu Xiang, 11, 19, 36n 46
Liu Xiu, 103n 31
Liu Yi, 207
Liu Yin, 194
Liu Zong, 46, 49
Liuchao (Six Dynasties), 121
Liucheng, 52
Liuhe, 245n 21
Liupan shan, 165
liuren (Six Water Cycles), 111
Liuzhou, 197
Liyang [county in Henan], 76
Long Dự, 199
Long Fan, 218n 73
Long(zhou) [also Longzhou], 156, 198
Longcheng, 23
Longgan cheng, 165
Longjin xianzhi (A Record of Longjin County), 198, 216n 33

longtu ge (Dragon Diagram Pavilion), 159
Lu, 231, 233
lu (circuit), 155, 228, 244n 1
Lư Báo, 197, 202, 203, 216n 25
Lu Chong, 244n 4
Lu Shen, 197, 201, 202
Lu Shouqin, 159, 162
Lulong, 3, 44–50, 51–2, 54n 11, 55n 30, 63, 233, 243, 274
luren (slaves), 237
Lü Buwei, 100n 2
Lü Yijian, 81, 159, 162, 163, 167, 168
Lü Zhu, 37n 64
Lüshi chunqiu (Spring and Autumn Annals of Mister Lü), 100n 2
Lục, 219n 104
Luo Fan, 218n 73
Luotian, 247n 42
Luozhou, 14, 17, 22
Luozhou cishi (Luozhou regional inspector), 17
Lunyu (Analects), 92
Luu Ký, 202, 207, 208
Lý, 191, 215n 1
Lý Can Đức, 204, 210, 217n 62
Lý Hion, 218n 84
Lý Ko Tiên, 201, 217n 48
Lý Nhân Tông, 217n 62
Lý Nhật Tôn, 199, 200, 202, 203, 204, 215n 1
Lý Phật Mã, 199, 204, 205
Lý Thường Kiệt, 193, 194, 204, 206, 207–9

Ma Shao, 116, 117
Mai Cảnh Tiên, 217n 48
Mamuraq Tegin, 260, 262
manzei (barbarian bandits), 204
Matsui Shūichi, 44
McKnight, Brian, 126–8, 131
menxia sheng (Chancellery), 76, 247n 36
menxia shilang (vice director of the Chancellery), 93
Mengsus, 259, 265–6, 272, 281nn 36, 37
Mengxi bitan (Brush Strokes from Dream Creek), 202
Mengzi (Mencius), 97, 104n 58, 271

Mengzi yinyi (Pronunciation and Meaning in Mencius), 98
Miao [tribal minority people], 198
middle period: character of, 1–2, 5–6, 8–9; contested space and relations in, 60, 95, 104n 61, 191, 243, 253; functions of ritual in, 111; periodization of, 1
min (Fujian emigrees), 198
Ming [dynasty], 13
mingbieji, 267, 281n 42
Mingdao, 177n 36
minzu ("people of the clan"), 27
mu (one-sixth of an acre), 270
Mo, 45
Mohe, 47
Môn Châu, 209, 218n 77
Mongols, 7
mufu (private secretariat), 17
Mulan, 12, 34n 7, 37n 64
"Mulan ci" (The Ballad of Mulan), 34n 7

na ("submitting an offering"; tribute), 167
Naiman, 7, 262
nandu ("southern push"), 198–9
Nanjiao, 211
Nanjing, 231
Nankang, 16
nanping wang (king of the southern pacified region), 202
Nanren (peoples of South China), 283n 50
Nanyue, 14, 26, 35n 17
neicang ku (Palace Storehouse, Inner Palace Treasury), 156, 178n 49
neifu ("Interior Dependency"), 195–6
neitang (Inner Treasury), 82–3
Ne'uril Tegin, 260
Nghiêm, 219n 104
Ngự Long, 199
Nguy Trọng Hòa, 199
Như Nguyệt [river], 208
Nhương, 219n 104
Ningyuan, 166
Niu Sengru, 50
nüde (womanly virtue), 18
Nüzhen (Jurchen, Jürchen), *see* Jurchen
Nùng Binh, 196

Nùng Hạ Khanh, 196
Nùng Lượng, 196
Nùng Nhật Tân, 195, 201
Nùng Tông Đán, 193, 195, 201, 202
Nùng Trí Cao (Nong Zhigao): insurgency of, 6, 191–4, 201; negotiations with Song after defeat of, 191–2, 200, 209–14; perceived treachery of, 201–5; suppression of, 195, 198
Nùng Trí Hội, 196, 202, 203–4, 207, 210
Nùng Trí Xuân, 210

Okada Koji, 212
Ouyang He, 15–16
Ouyang Xiu, 36n 52, 171, 177n 22, 216n 30
Ödösh Inal, 264
Ögödei Qan, 260, 269, 270, 282n 48
Ögrünch Tegin, 260
Ôn, 219n 104

paizi (imperial insignia), 282n 44
Pang Ji, 157, 168, 170, 171
Pang Xun, 51
Pei Ju, 17
Pelley, Patricia, 192
Phan Huy Lê, 193
Phong, 219n 104
Phúc Lộc, 219n 104
Ping, 45, 46, 47, 48
ping Yue zhonglang jiang (leader of court gentlemen who quelled the Yue), 16
Pingjiang, 77
Pinglu, 44

Qara Igach Buyruk, 259, 264, 279n 24, 281n 35
Qarakhitai, 7
Qi, 247n 42
qi[1] (irregular), 123
qi[2] (vital universal essence, vapors, breath), 123, 124, 129, 131
Qianlong, 207, 218n 77
Qiang [tribal minority people], 165, 172, 175; *see also* Tibetans
qiangjie (fixed border), 210
qianxia (zone commanders), 155

INDEX 301

Qianzhou, 207
Qiao guo furen (consort of state Qiao), 12, 17
Qiao guo gong (duke of the state of Qiao), 17
Qidan (Khitan), 3, 7
qihao (signal banner), 197
qimen dunjia (Irregular Opening/Hidden Period), 5, 115, 120–1, 122–3, 137–8n 6
Qin [dynasty], 75
Qin Gui, 4, 89, 103n 38
Qin Liangyu, 12, 34n 9
Qinfeng, 158, 168, 170
qing (15 acres), 241
Qing [dynasty], 27
Qing(zhou) [also Qingzhou], 153, 155, 156, 165, 168, 170
Qingdushan, 48
Qingjian, 171
Qingli, 117, 169
Qingliu, 236
Qingtang, 154
Qinzhou, 208, 211, 213
Qirgiz, 255; see also Kirghiz
Qiu Ying, 19
Qochgar Tegin, 260
quan (conditional), 232
quan zhi junzhou shi (acting prefect), 236
Quanjiao, 236
Quang Lang, 209
Qubilai Qan, 255, 260, 262, 265, 270–1, 274, 279n 23
qumiyuan (Bureau of Military Affairs), 203
Quyté Lý, 208
Quảng Nguyên, 209–10, 211, 213, 219n 104

Rachewiltz, Igor de, 279n 28
Rao(zhou), 168
Ren Fu, 161, 165
Ren Zhongshi, 173
Renshou, 18, 25, 31
Renzong: engagement in ritual practices of, 115, 117, 139n 29; as opponent of Xia, 151, 152–4, 155, 157, 158–9, 160–75; rapprochement with southern leaders of, 196, 197, 200

rituals: diversity of aims of, 5, 87–9, 157, 199; military applications of, 111–15, 117–20, 125–30, 132–7
Rongan, 197
Rongzhai suibi wuji (Jottings of Rongzhai in Five Collections; Essays and Notes from Hong Mai's Brush in Five Collections), 90
Rongzhou, 197
ruzhong (delivery system), 156
Ruan Yuan, 35n 12, 215n 15

Saimen, 162, 163
Sajisi (or Sergius), 269–70, 282n 48
Salin Tegin, 260
St Augustine, 100n 1
Sanbai, 156
sancai (Three Potentials; Heaven, man, Earth), 123, 126, 127, 135
Sanchuankou, 152
Sang Daomou, 118
Sang Yi, 165
sanshi (Three Cosmographies), 111
sanshi guan (Office of the Three Cosmographies), 119
sansi (Finance Commission), 158
sansi shi (finance commissioner), 162
Sawyer, Ralph, 133
Schipper, Kristofer, 114, 121
Semuren (people of various categories), 271, 274, 275, 283n 50
Sha (fierce god, malignant spirit), 124
Shaanxi, 102n 22, 152
Shaanxi dubushu jian jinglue anfu shi (Shaanxi imperial infantry and cavalry and military pacification intendant), 163
Shatuo [Türk subgroup], 48, 51, 73n 4
Shazhou, 154
Shandong, 76
Shangshu (Book of History), 215n 15
shangshu (minister; administrator), 234
shangshu sheng (Department of State Affairs), 247n 36
shangshu you puye (right vice director of the Department of State Affairs), 93
Shangsi, 218n 77
Shanxi, 44
Shanyang, 233, 246n 25

302 INDEX

shanyu (khan), 171; see also kehan
Shao Bowen, 92, 94–5, 96, 103n 44
Shao Liangzuo, 171
Shao Yong, 103n 44
Shaoxing, 245n 21, 246n 26
sheji (gods of soil and grain), 152
Shen Gai, 240
Shen Kuo (or Shen Kua), 140n 39, 202, 216n 26
Shen Nong, 102n 30
Shen Qi, 207
Shenwu milue (Confidential Synopsis of Effective Military Strategy), 156
Shenzong, 173, 202, 206–7
Sheng(zhou), 156
sheng bing (bearers of arms), 47
shengli (flourishing beauty), 230
shengshi (departmental examination), 97
Shengshui yantan lu (Record of Banquet Conversations along the Sheng River), 78
shi (cosmograph): description of, 111–12; military applications of, 111–15, 117–20, 125–30, 132–7; as implement of power, 113–15, 117, 123, 124–5, 127, 129, 131–3, 134–6; rituals associated with, 111; transgression of boundaries through, 113–15, 120, 123, 125, 127, 132, 134, 135–7
shi (picul), 240
shi chaoting you neitu (internal-use maps from the court), 239
Shi Fan, 218n 73
Shi Jingtang, 73n 4
Shi Kang, 118
shi niu yinyin (embossed-lion silver seal), 268
Shi Yuansun, 161
Shi Yuanzhong, 55n 48
shihuo (commodities), 247n 45
shilang (vice director), 91
Shiliu zhou (Sixteen Prefectures), 60–1, 63, 66–8, 72, 73n 4, 211
Shilong taishou (governor of Shilong), 16
Shilong tai furen (grand consort of Shilong), 16
Shisan jing (Thirteen Classics), 98
Shiwei, 47, 48, 50

Shizong, 241
Shou [prefecture], 229, 231
shouzhuo (defense detachments), 49
shu (post), 49
shu (number; regularity; emblem), 113–14, 116, 123, 124, 135
Shu, 235, 237, 247n 42
shumiyuan (Bureau of Military Affairs), 159
shuaifu (commandery prefectures), 233
shuaishi (circuit military), 242
Shun'anzhou (*Shun'an zhou*) ["Pacified Prefecture"], 193, 196, 203, 209, 213
Shunzhou, 211
Si, 233, 234
Sichuan, 158
Siku shumu (Four Treasuries catalogue), 119
Sima Guang, 81–2, 83, 93–6, 205
Sima Qian, 28–9, 37n 64
Siming, 218n 77
Sishu (Four Books), 98
Sivin, Nathan, 125
siwei (Four Secondary Cables), 121
Sixteen Prefectures, see Shiliu zhou
Smith, Paul, 206
Son, 219n 104
Song huiyao jigao (Drafted Documents on Song State Matters), 233
Song Qi, 159
Song Shou, 155, 162
Song Taizu, 66, 73n 6, 128
Song Xiao, 236
Songkang jun furen (commandery consort of Songkang), 16
Songkang yi (Songkang district enfeoffment), 17
Songlun (Deliberations on the Song), 89
Songshi (History of the Song Dynasty; Song History; Official History of the Song), 34n 9, 78, 118, 195, 229
Stallybrass, Peter, 114
Su(zhou), 154
Su Jiaqing, 129
Su Jian, 208
Su Shen, 160
Su Shi, 30, 33, 36n 63

INDEX

Su Yijian, 77
sudiao (rapid surveys), 239
Susang, 210
Susong, 237, 247n 42
Sui(zhou), 156
Suishu (History of the Sui Dynasty), 12
Sun Fu, 171
Sun Shi, 98
Sun Yingshi, 230
Sunzi bingfa ([Sunzi's] Art of War), 132–3
Suolimu (Sairam), 280n 31
Swann, Nancy, 13

tabu (or taboo), 114, 116, 134, 155
Tachar, 282n 48
Tai, 235, 236–7, 241
Taibo yinjing (Secret Classic of Venus, Planet of War), 5, 111, 139n 24
Taihang shan, 43
Taihu, 237, 247n 42
Taiping, 207, 213
Taiping huanyu ji (Record of the Empire's Borders and Dimensions during the Taiping Period), 216n 29
Taiping zaixiang (grand councilor of great peace), 77
taishi (grand preceptor), 267, 281n 39
taishou (grand protector), 14
Taixing, 233, 236–7
Taiyuan, 177n 39
Taizong, 60–1, 64–9, 72, 76, 100n 5, 117, 128, 173
Tan, 45, 46, 47
Tanzhou, 48
Tang Chenye, 236
Tangguchang (Tangut), 77
Tao Bi, 208, 209, 211
Tao, Jing-shen, 1
Tao Qian, 37n64
Tao Shiyu, 37n 65
Tarim Basin, 7, 195, 254–8, 262–6, 273, 275, 277n 13, 278n 14
Tatar Tongga, 259, 262, 263
tattooing, 133, 170, 199, 213
Temo, 196, 213
Temür Buqa, 261, 279n 24
Temüge Odchigin, 269
thái bảo (grand guardian), 205

thái úy (defender-in-chief), 204
Thần Điện, 199
Thăng Long, 191, 193, 199, 200–3, 206, 208, 209, 213
Thiên Đức, 218n 77
Tian chi, 280n 31
Tian Yue, 46
Tianchang, 239–40
Tianjin, 51
Tianshan, 257, 258, 277n 13
tianxia (all-under-Heaven), 152, 175
Tianxiong jun, 167
Tibetans, 43, 51, 175, 256; *see also* Qiang
tidian Huainan lianglu gongshi (superintendent for public affairs for the two Huainan circuits), 237
tieqi (Iron Cavalry), 156
tiliang anfu shi (investigating pacification intendant), 164
Tingmei, 67
Tô Mậu Châu, 209
Tong [prefecture], 230, 231
tong Shaanxi dubushu jian jingluehanfu yuanbian zhaotao shi (Shaanxi military pacification cointendant and regional commandant), 165
tong zhi liyiyuan (Ritual Academy codirector), 159
Tongshan, 247n 45
Tongzhi (Comprehensive Treatise), 119
tongzhong shumen xiaping zhangshi (concurrent Secretariat-Chancellery manager of governmental affairs), 200
Töregene qatun, 282n 48
Trần Trọng Kim, 193
Truòng, 219n 104
Trương Hát, 209
tù (outlaws), 205
Tư Lang Châu, 209
tuding (local chieftain), 201
Tuhuzhen he, 47
turen (locals), 234
tuntian (state farm), 228
Tuoba, 157
Türks, 50, 52, 140n 36, 256, 278n 14, 279n 28

Turner, Frederick Jackson, 253, 254, 276n 3
Turner, Victor, 114, 133
Twitchett, Denis, 43

Uyghurs, 3, 7
Uyghuristan, 254

Vạn Tiệp, 199
Việt Sử Lược (A Survey of the History of Việt), 205
Việt, 204
Vũ An, 219n 104
Vũ Thbng, 199

waiyi (outer barbarians), 203
Waldron, Arthur, 59
Wanli, 36n 43
Wang Anshi, 6, 163, 191, 205–11
Wang Che, 76
Wang Chengzong, 54n 15
Wang Dan: as advocate of peace, 4, 96–9; background of, 75–8; Li Hang and, 91–6; Zhenzong and, 79–80, 86–7; reputation of, 89–91; strategies of, 78–91
Wang Daokun, 19, 21, 22, 23, 24–5, 29
Wang Deyong, 159
Wang E, 271
Wang Fu, 140n 39
Wang Fuzhi, 89–91
Wang Gui, 165
Wang Han, 195, 196
Wang Heshang, 169
Wang Hsiu-huei, 114, 121
Wang Junyu (or Wang Qi), 82
Wang Pizhi, 78
Wang Pu, 116
Wang Qinruo, 87–9
Wang Shouzhong, 163
Wang Su, 101n 14
Wang Tong, 102–3n 30
Wang Xiangzhi, 198
Wang Yan [Tang era], 76
Wang Yan [Song era], 170
Wang Yande, 258
Wang Yaochen, 164, 173
Wang Yiyong, 162
Wang You, 76
Wang Yu, 19, 36n 43
Wang Zeng, 81
Wang Zhongxuan, 16–17, 24
Waqiao guan (Waqiao Pass), 167
war: border and, 2, 8; identity and, 2, 8; "just," 75–6, 98–9, 100n 1
wansheng (Ever Victorious), 166
Wei Guang, 16
Wei[1](zhou), 153, 157, 164, 165, 168, 170
Wei[2](zhou), 156
Wei-Bo, 43, 46, 51
Weigong, 78, 80
Weiming Shanyu, 157
weiwei si (Court of Imperial Regalia), 142n 96
Weiwuer (Uyghur), 254
Weiwuer ren (Uyghur man/person), 277n 11
wen (civil or cultured), 96
wen shi bufen ("history and literature are inseparable"), 28
Wen Zhongzi, 102–3n 30
Wenjing, 92, 93, 94
Wenmen dong (Wenmen Grotto), 201
Wenshan, 196
Wenxian tongkao (General Investigation on Important Writings; Comprehensive Investigations into the Literary Inheritance), 119, 233
Wenzhen, 83
Wenzheng, 82, 90, 93, 94
White, Allon, 114
wu (martial), 135
Wu Han, 13, 26, 27–8, 29
wu xingfan (Five Clans), 207, 218n 73
Wu Ying, 165
Wucheng, 235
Wude, 26
Wuhuaishi, 102n 30
Wujiang, 237
Wujing zongyao (Comprehensive Military Essentials), 5, 111, 139n 24
wuku (Imperial Martial Warehouse), 128, 142n 96
Wushuang pu (Catalogue of the Unparalleled), 31, 32, 36–7n 64

INDEX

"*Wushuang pu* xu" ("Preface to Catalogue of the Unparalleled"), 30, 37n 65
Wuwei, 231, 235
Wuyang, 207
wuzong jiangjun (loyal warrior), 196
wuzu (son of Blue Heaven), 157, 178n 51

Xi [tribal minority people], 3
Xia(zhou), 161
Xia Shouyun, 159, 163
Xia Song, 102n 21, 158, 160, 163, 165
xian (county), 228
Xian furen (also Consort or Grand Mistress Xian): biographies of, 13–23; as commander, 23–4; legacy of, 2–3, 28–33
xiang (Hunan emigrees), 198
Xiang Minzhong, 84, 85
xiangjun (provincial troops), 159
Xiangzhou, 197, 213
xianlang fangzheng (decree examination), 160
Xianping, 94
xianshi (judicial intendant), 242
xianwei (district defender), 236
xianzhi (prescience), 94, 103n 47
Xianzong, 51
Xiao Bo, 15
Xiao Gu, 196, 203–4
Xiao Temo, 167
xiaowei siren (four Mongol military officers), 268
Xiaoyunshi Qaya (also Guan Yunshi), 283n 51
xiaozhang (guard commander), 216n 28
Xiaozong, 241
Xie [surname], 266
Xie Wenzhi, 270
Xie Zhedu, 270, 272
Xifan, 156, 171
Xin, 76
Xindu hou (duke of Xindu), 16
xinfa (New Policies), 191, 206, 212
Xinhui, 22
Xinjiang, 253
Xing(zhou), 156
xingbu langzhong (Ministry of Justice), 207
Xinghua, 235

Xingqing fu, 156
Xingtai, 95
Xingzong, 166, 167, 168
Xiong Ben, 210
Xishan, 95
Xiyu (Western Regions), 254
Xu Deng, 16
Xu Dong, 119, 139n 24
Xu Fu, 117
Xu Huaide, 159
Xu Ji, 117
xuanfu (pacification intendant), 173
xuanfu shi (pacification commissioner), 166
Xuanzong, 26
xunjian (military inspector), 200

Y̌ Lan, 204
ya Xi Qidan liangfan shi (Xi- and Qidan-controlling commissioner), 49
Yaghlaqar, 257
Yan[1](zhou), 153, 157, 160–2, 164, 166, 168, 170, 171
Yan[2](zhou), 156
Yan Di, 102n 30
Yancheng, 234–5
Yang [prefecture], 229, 230, 231, 233, 235, 236–7, 239, 240, 246n 26
Yang Baocai, 199, 200
Yang Hang, 240
Yang jia jiang (Yang [family] women generals), 12
Yang Jie, 160
Yang Su, 25, 26, 36n 52
Yang Weide, 119
Yang Zhicheng, 50
Yangchuan, 83
Yangchun junshou (Yangchun grand protector), 15
Yangdi, 16
Yangzhou, 83
Yao Wentian, 236
Ye Huan, 236–7
Ye Qingchen, 160
Yeli Wangrong, 170
yibing ("righteous armaments"; "just arms"), 75, 100n 2
Yidulu xingsheng da dudu (Shandong Yidu circuit high military commissioner), 270

Yijing, see *Change, Book of*
Yin(zhou), 161
yin/yang, 121, 135
Ying[1], 45
Ying[2], 45, 46
yingtian (military colony), 163
Yingzhou, 47, 52
Yingzong (b. Zhao Shu), 200, 201, 202, 216n 25
yitong sansi ("unequaled in honor"), 16
Yixing, 244n 4
yiyong ("righteous brave"), 168
yizhan ("just war"), 98
Yizhen, 233
Yizhou, 197
yong (brave and courageous), 98
Yongping, 210, 213, 218n 77
Yongxing, 165, 166, 170
Yongzhou, 200, 201, 202, 207, 208, 209, 211, 213
You[1](zhou), 156
You[2](zhou), 166, 167
You[3](zhou), 167
you qianniu weijiangjun (personal guardian general of the right), 196
Youbeiping, 48
Youzhou, 3, 43–53
Yu, 129, 130
Yu Jing, 199–200
Yuan(zhou), 153, 156
yuanbian zhaotao shi (border zone bandit suppression commissioner), 163
Yuanhao, see Li Yuanhao
Yuanshi (History of the Yuan Dynasty), 263, 265
Yudi jisheng (A Record of This Region's Merits), 198
yue (Guangdong emigrees), 198
Yue, 12
Yue Fei, 14, 37n 64
Yue guo gong (duke of the state of Yue), 26
Yue Shi, 198
yuefu ("music-bureau"), 30
Yuqing gong (Jade-pure Palace), 80
Yuqing zhaoying gong (Jade-pure Palace of the Luminous Response), 101–2n 15
Yutai, 239–40

Yuwen Cuizhong, 128
Yuyang, 48

zangjing (Buddhist canon), 155
Ze-Lu, 51
zeng (gift-giving), 167
Zeng Gongliang, 176n 18, 179n 87
Zhang Fan, 218n 73
Zhang Fangping, 169, 179n 94
Zhang Gongsu, 52
Zhang Guogang, 43
Zhang Hongjing, 51
Zhang Jiang, 55n 30
Zhang Kang, 166
Zhang Lei, 80
Zhang Liang, 37n 64
Zhang Quhua, 102n 23
Zhang Shide, 84–5, 102n 23
Zhang Shixun, 81, 163
Zhang Shoujie, 208
Zhang shui (Zhang River), 45
Zhang Tian, 203
Zhang Yunshen, 48, 51
Zhang Zhaoda, 16
Zhang Zhongwu [Tang era], 48, 49, 50–1
Zhang Zhongwu [Song era], 236
Zhangjia bao, 165
Zhao [surname], 151
Zhao Deming, 78
Zhao Di, 208
Zhao Ding, 198, 216n 72
Zhao E., 37n 64
Zhao Fan, 239
Zhao Li, 246n 30
Zhao Na, 17
Zhao Xu, 202
Zhao Yanyi, 117
Zhao Yuanhao, see Li Yuanhao
Zhaocheng di, 22, 23
zhaotao shi (bandit suppression commissioner), 170
Zhaoxin, 233–4
Zhaozong, 117
Zhe Jimin, 166
zhen (garrison), 43, 49
Zhen [prefecture], 231, 233
Zhending, 265, 271
Zhending fu, 167

INDEX

zhenfu (special administrative district), 234
Zheng Jian, 170
Zheng Qiao, 119
zhengdao (the upright Way), 135
zhengming (rectification of names), 131
Zhengsu fang (Methods of Distinguishing the Orthodox from the Heterodox), 218n 75
Zhenrong, 153, 156, 165
Zhenwu, 50
Zhenzong: border concerns of, 61, 65, 66, 68; gullibility of, 88–90; mentality of, 69–70; reputation of, 4, 78, 79, 82, 85–7, 101n 13
Zhenzong shilu (Veritable Records of Zhenzong), 86
zhi jianyuan (Remonstrance Bureau), 169
zhi shiguan (Institute of History auxiliary), 160
Zhidai, 26, 27
Zhide, 16
zhigong ju (examination administrator), 77
zhijie (principle and integrity), 19
zhijunshi (aboriginal commander), 197
zhixian (acting county magistrate), 233
Zhiyu, 26
Zhong Bing, 241
Zhong Shiheng, 160–1, 169, 172
Zhong Shixiong, 36n 41
zhongshu (Secretariat-Chancellery), 82
zhongshu menxia sheng (Secretariat), 162
zhongshu sheng (Secretariat), 80
zhongshu shilang (Secretariat vice director), 93
zhongshu zuo chengxiang (Secretariat junior chief councilor [under Yuan]), 261

zhongxiao zhi bao ("reward of loyalty and filiality"), 29
zhongyuan (Central Plain), 198
zhou (civil prefecture), 228, 244n 1
Zhou Dunyi, 127
Zhou Shizong, 62, 65, 73n 5
Zhou Taizu, 117
Zhou Weide, 155
Zhu Ci, 51
Zhu Kerong, 46, 51, 54n 11
Zhu Tao, 46, 51, 53, 54n 12
Zhu Xi, 241, 245n 20
Zhu Xicai, 49
zhuanyun fushi (vice fiscal commissioner), 240
zhuanyunshi (or *zhuanyun shi*) (fiscal intendant, fiscal commissioner), 153–4, 196
Zhuge Liang, 37n 64, 112
Zhuo, 45
zizheng dian (Aid-in-Governance Hall academician), 165
Zong'ge, 154
zongguan (area commander-in-chief), 16
zongguan nei wai cangshi (supervisor for granaries in the capital and other regions), 267
zongmiao (clan ancestral temple), 152
zuo chengyi lang (left gentleman for discussion), 244n 4
zuo qianniu weijiangjun (left personal guardian general), 196
zuo shiyi (reminder of the left), 76
Zuoyou jiang (Left and Right Rivers), 197

GPSR Compliance
The European Union's (EU) General Product Safety Regulation (GPSR) is a set of rules that requires consumer products to be safe and our obligations to ensure this.

If you have any concerns about our products, you can contact us on

ProductSafety@springernature.com

In case Publisher is established outside the EU, the EU authorized representative is:

Springer Nature Customer Service Center GmbH
Europaplatz 3
69115 Heidelberg, Germany

www.ingramcontent.com/pod-product-compliance
Lightning Source LLC
LaVergne TN
LVHW011800060526
838200LV00053B/3638